WEAVING A LEGACY

The White-Inyo Mountains near Independence, 1996. Flanking the eastern side of Owens Valley, the White-Inyo Mountains rise from 4,000 feet in elevation to over 14,000 feet. This range gets fewer than twelve inches of precipitation a year. Little grows on the dry, windswept slopes except ancient bristlecone pine trees, many of which are more than 2,000 years old.

WEAVING A LEGACY

INDIAN BASKETS & THE PEOPLE OF OWENS VALLEY, CALIFORNIA

Sharon E. Dean

Peggy S. Ratcheson

Judith W. Finger

Ellen F. Daus

with Craig D. Bates

THE UNIVERSITY OF UTAH PRESS
Salt Lake City

DEDICATED TO OUR FRIEND AND COLLEAGUE
ELLEN F. DAUS
1941–2000

 The Defiance House Man colophon is a registered trademark
of the University of Utah Press. It is based upon a four-foot-tall,
Ancient Puebloan pictograph (late PIII) near Glen Canyon, Utah.

Library of Congress Cataloging-in-Publication Data

Weaving a legacy : Indian baskets and the people of Owens Valley, California /
Sharon E. Dean . . . [et al.].
    p.   cm.
    Includes bibliographical references and index.
    ISBN 0-87480-807-3 (cloth : alk. paper) — ISBN 0-87480-808-1 (pbk. :
alk. paper)
    1. Paiute baskets — California — Owens Valley.   2. Shoshoni baskets —
California — Owens Valley.   3. Willow baskets — California — Owens Valley.
4. Willow weaving — California — Owens Valley.   5. Owens Valley (Calif.) —
Social life and customs.   I. Dean, Sharon E., 1959–
    E99.P2W43   2004
    746.41'2'089974574079487 — dc22   2004014907

09 08 07 06 05 04
5 4 3 2 1

CONTENTS

FOREWORD

Jessie C. Durant (Ku–Za–Te–Ka–A)

Handwoven baskets are an integral part of our Paiute tradition. The baskets represent the relationship between our lives as a people and Mother Earth, who sustains our culture. They signify what we did to survive in our environment, how we used the plants around us, and how much time we spent gathering and carefully preparing our basket materials.

In our family, basket making played a major role, and baskets were used for a wide variety of purposes. Our *mu–ah,* Grandmother Nellie Charlie, taught my sister and me basket making at an early age. In the late 1940s I made a small basket and beaded it part way. I still have this unfinished beaded basket, and like my life, it is a work in progress.

In 1956 sister Rosie and I went with our two *mu–ahs,* Grandmother Nellie and her sister, Tina Charlie, to visit the old mining town of Bodie. At one time, many Indians lived there. They lived on the west side of town in small cabins. That trip brought back many memories of a bygone era to my grandmothers. Two original cabins remained. One belonged to Katie Toms, a distant relation. I remember seeing Katie Toms's basket-making materials of willow tied in coils and still hanging on the walls of her cabin.

I have all of Grandmother Nellie's utility baskets, and when I occasionally use them, it seems to me as if part of my *mu–ah* is with me even now. I get a sense that the past is still here in the present.

ACKNOWLEDGMENTS

The pleasure of fieldwork has belonged to the authors, but the hard work of producing this book has been a collaborative effort on the part of many. First and foremost, we thank the residents of Owens Valley who graciously shared their life stories and their homes with us during our many visits. Jim Kelley and Enid Ashworth opened the door to the community for us. Weavers Jessie Durant, Richard Stewart, Gretchen Hess, and Shirley Slee, along with Paiute elder Clara Rambeau, spent inordinate amounts of time familiarizing us with the process of basket weaving and the use of baskets in everyday activities. Other Owens Valley weavers who gave liberally of their time for this project were Ellen Pueblo, Charlotte Bacoch, Lillian Andreas, Janet Stone, Bernardine Summers, Alta Rogers, and Sandra Jefferson Yonge. Eleanor Bethel, Ruth Brown, Pearl Budke, and Phyllis Hunter educated us about traditional Paiute culture. Chris Plakos, at the Owens Valley office of the Los Angeles Department of Water and Power, assisted us in obtaining up-to-date information on the Los Angeles aqueduct system. Ray "Fish" Milovich, Willis Smith, and Winona Roach, along with Ernest Kinney and Jan Kinney, provided local color and a host of recollections about earlier days in the valley. Peggy Zimmerman, Bob Schaefer, Vernon Miller, Roseanne Kelley, Dorothy Stewart, John MacQueen, and Donald MacQueen were especially helpful in furnishing information about their families' basket collections.

We also express our appreciation to the many individuals who provided invaluable research assistance and archival materials. We are particularly indebted to Craig Bates, curator of ethnology at the Yosemite Museum, Yosemite National Park, who added much of the information that makes this book rich in detail. Kay Fowler, professor of anthropology at the University of Nevada, Reno, provided guidance and direction and helped bring this book to fruition. Bill Michael and Beth Sennett Walker Porter of the Eastern California Museum of Inyo County, Independence, graciously opened their museum resources for research and study. Barbara Moss and Howard Holland of the Laws Museum in Bishop and Kathleen O'Connor of the Federal Records Center in San Bruno, California, provided timely assistance in retrieving hard-to-find historical information. Bruce Bernstein of the National Museum of the American Indian, Washington, D.C.; Suzanne Griset of the Arizona State Museum, Tucson; Sherrie Smith-Ferri of the Grace Hudson Museum and Sun House, Ukiah, California; independent researcher John Kania; and basket collector Eva Slater all kindly shared their knowledge about baskets and basket collecting. Additionally, we thank anthropologist Nancy Peterson Walter of Mammoth Lakes, who has worked with the Owens Valley Paiute people for nearly thirty years, and Robert Palazzo, who has researched the town of Darwin, California.

We are indebted to Blair Davenport of the Death Valley National Monument; Kim Walters, Bryn Potter, and Duane King of the Southwest Museum of the American Indian, Autry National Center, in Pasadena; John Cahoon of the Seaver Center for Western Research at the Natural History Museum of Los Angeles County; Chris Coleman of the Natural History Museum of Los Angeles County; Paul Soifer of the Bancroft Archival Group in Los Angeles; Pete Garra of the Los Angeles Department of Water and Power; Jack von Euw of the Bancroft Library at the University of California, Berkeley; Winifred Glover and Pat McLean of the Ulster Museum, Belfast, Ireland; Susan Haskell of the Peabody Museum of Archaeology and Ethnology in Cambridge, Massachusetts; William Maher of the University of Illinois at Urbana-Champaign; Elva Younkin of the Maturango Museum in Ridgecrest, California; and Jennifer Watts, Kate McGuinn, and Bill Frank of the Huntington Library in San Marino, California, for their assistance in providing archival materials and photographs.

In addition, we are grateful to the following museum staff members who granted us access to their basket collections: Ellen Howard of the Paiute-Shoshone Cultural Center in Bishop, California; Lisa Deitz at the University of California, Davis; Leslie Freund of the Phoebe Apperson Hearst Museum, University of California, Berkeley; Betty Smart, Billie Elliston, and Sandy Taugher of the State Museum Resource Center of the California Department of Parks and Recreation in Sacramento; Isabel Neri of the Field Museum, Chicago; Elisa Aguilar, Janice Klein, and Diane Gutenkauf, formerly of the Field Museum; and Diane Curry of the Oakland Museum, Oakland, California. We would also like to recognize Bruce Frumker and Greg Petusky for their excellent photography, as well as Esther Bockhoff, Tom Block, and Gwen Jensen for their assistance.

Lastly, we thank our family members Michael Daus, Jim Daus, Caryn Daus Flanagan, Bob Ratcheson, Abby Ratcheson, Andrew Finger, David Finger, Jon Finger, David Dean, and Matthew Dean for their steadfast support and encouragement.

1. GATHERING THE WILLOW

Paiute Life in Owens Valley
Prior to the Time of Contact

Owens Valley, California, is an area of intense beauty and dramatic contrasts (Plate 1). About ten thousand years ago, at the end of the last ice age in North America, the valley held an inland sea (Hill 1975:145–147). As the area's moist, cool environment gradually turned dry and hot, the sea dried to a lake with seasonal salt marshes along a residual river. Owens Lake, named (like the valley) after nineteenth-century explorer Richard Owens, was located at the southeastern end of the valley and was fed by the Owens River. When first described in 1859, the lake was approximately nineteen miles long and four to eight miles wide, and the river averaged fifty feet wide and fifteen feet deep (Wilke and Lawton 1976: 24–25). Today the river is half to a quarter its former size, and the lake, for all practical purposes, is dried up.

Native peoples lived in Owens Valley long before they saw horses or heard the thunder of rifles, and before explorers, miners, and settlers changed the landscape forever (Figure 1.1). Although scholars suggest that human occupation of this region may date back 7,500 to 10,000 years, the people known today as Owens Valley Paiutes first became identifiable archaeologically at around A.D. 600 to 1000 (Burton and Farrell 1996:173; Campbell 1974; Elston 1986:148; Liljeblad and Fowler 1986: 412).[1] Paiute legends affirm a long residency in the area and tell how the people were created long, long ago in Round Valley, just north of Owens Valley (Steward 1936a:365–368). By the time of contact with non-Indians, these early residents, who called themselves *nü'ma* or *nümü,* meaning "The People" (Steward 1933: 235, 1936a:355), likely numbered some two thousand individuals (Lawton et al. 1976:15, 28–29). They spoke Owens Valley Paiute, a Mono language in the Numic branch of the Uto-Aztecan language family of the Great Basin (Liljeblad and Fowler 1986:412).

The homeland of the Owens Valley Paiutes is on the western edge of the Great Basin (Figure 1.2). Owens Valley itself is more than eighty miles long and four to ten miles wide. It lies at about 4,000 feet above sea level between the towering peaks of the Sierra Nevada to the west and the White and Inyo mountains to the east. To the south the region abuts the Mojave Desert. Rocky outcroppings, exposed bedrock, warm springs, and fingerlike projections of old lava flows run through the valley. Despite sparse rainfall (four to six inches per year), Owens Valley is host to a surprising variety of flora and fauna. The huge mass of the Sierra Nevada catches most of the moisture coming off the Pacific Ocean and receives snow every winter. When the weather warms, the snow melts and icy streams pour down the narrow canyons above Owens Valley and spill out along alluvial fans to the valley floor, its river, and its lake.

The Owens Valley Paiutes shared the southern section of their valley with small groups of Panamint Shoshone people who had seasonal camps to the east and south of Owens Lake and one sparsely populated village at its south end. The Panamint settlements marked the southwest boundary of the Western Shoshone culture (Figure 1.3) (Grosscup 1977:118; Merriam n.d.b; Thomas et al. 1986:264). These camp sites, located in less fertile portions of Owens Valley than the areas occupied by the neighboring Paiutes, had specific purposes. The Panamint Shoshones collected brine fly

Figure 1.1. Rock Art in Owens Valley, date unknown. Indian peoples left evidence of their existence in the form of rock art. Chipped into exposures of volcanic rock, these petroglyphs are often found in conjunction with evidence of hunting activities.

family. Both groups practiced diverse and adaptive harvest patterns; they consumed many of the same foods and produced similar shelters and utilitarian baskets. Certain types of baskets differed markedly between the two groups, however, as did other aspects of social and material culture. For example, the Panamint Shoshones had extremely limited opportunities to develop irrigation, but the Paiute areas of Owens Valley afforded some potential for irrigation, which the Paiutes developed to an extent (Liljeblad and Fowler 1986:414–415; Steward 1933:235–236; Thomas et al. 1986:278).

Our knowledge of ancient Paiute life in Owens Valley is derived from archaeological evidence, journals of early explorers, ethnographic fieldwork after 1900, personal recollections of valley residents, oral histories from the Paiute people, and observations of Paiute traditions practiced during the twentieth century. Archaeology yields many pieces of information: ancient storage and fire pits provide clues about food resources and methods of preparation, and identifiable food residues on remnants of cooking vessels help determine their specific uses. Raw and manufactured materials not associated with the indigenous resources of Owens Valley shed light on trade patterns.[2] It is through a combination of such sources that the everyday life of the Owens Valley Paiutes just before the arrival of non-Indians can be reconstructed.

EVERYDAY LIFE OF "THE PEOPLE"

The Owens Valley region has a variety of environments, and the Paiute people exploited them all. The concentrations of piñon pine in the White and Inyo mountains were important sources of pine nuts, and the lower slopes of these ranges supported a variety of Great Basin flora and fauna (see Appendix I). Pandora moth larvae, a delicacy, were harvested in Jeffrey pine forests to the west and north, where mule deer were also found. In the southern end of Owens Valley, Mojave Desert species were available.

Most cultures of the vast, dry Great Basin moved continually in small groups in search

larvae on the east shore of Owens Lake, fished in the lake's tributaries, and harvested piñon pine nuts near springs in the mountains (Grosscup 1977:118; Lawton et al. 1976:42; Liljeblad and Fowler 1986:418). Their social and political organization was more fluid than that of the Owens Valley Paiutes, reflecting the higher mobility required by the unpredictable and widely dispersed resources of their Mojave Desert home (Thomas et al. 1986:278).

The Owens Valley Paiutes and Panamint Shoshones lived in overlapping geographic areas but spoke different languages within the Numic branch of the Uto-Aztecan language

of intermittent and often meager subsistence resources, but the Owens Valley Paiutes, occupants of an area rich in plants and animals and containing permanent sources of water, lived in small, semipermanent camps (Figure 1.4). The sizes of these camps, always situated on a creek or other reliable water source, varied greatly, from perhaps twenty to as many as two hundred individuals.[3] These villages were composed of ever expanding and contracting clusters of related families. Families came and left at will, traveling to gather seeds, pine nuts, and other plant foods as they ripened. During the winter people generally lived away from the river in the piñon pine—juniper belt near the new pine nut crop (Busby et al. 1979:ix; Lawton et al. 1976:15; Liljeblad and Fowler 1986:413–414, 427; Steward 1933:238–239).

Nuclear families were mostly self-sufficient groups, but some enterprises required cooperation among families or villages within defined ranges. For these ventures, organized leadership was required. A headman, *poginabi* (from *pogi-* or *poki-*, "to announce, to give orders"),[4] directed irrigation activities and rabbit, antelope, and deer drives; conducted festivals, dances, and ceremonies; and kept people informed about upcoming events. Occasionally, a headman might choose a more skilled man to lead certain activities. The position of headman was usually inherited, subject to the approval of the group, but a nonrelative could be selected and approved by a meeting of men and women (Liljeblad and Fowler 1986:428; Steward 1933:304).

The Owens Valley Paiutes were apparently the only group in the Great Basin to carry out a form of irrigation. The practice was widespread in Owens Valley and well developed by the time of contact with non-Indians, when the Paiutes had irrigated nearly all the arable land in the valley. By building dams and digging ditches, the Paiutes diverted water from streams to low-lying moist areas, increasing the natural yield of noncultivated food crops, in particular yellow nutgrass *(tüpüsi'),* wild hyacinth (blue dick), and *nā'hāvīta* (spike rush), whose bulbs were eaten. Some of the ditches were more

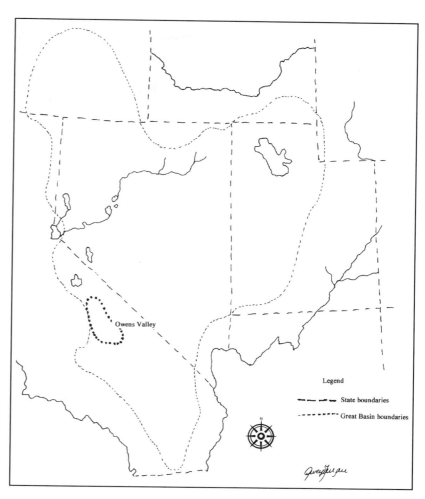

Figure 1.2. The Great Basin. The Great Basin, spanning six western states, is a mixture of mountains, plateaus, river drainages, and high-elevation meadows. Characterized by a semiarid climate, the region is a "sinkhole," meaning that none of its surface water flows outside its boundaries.

than two or three miles in length. Although all men might participate in constructing and maintaining the dams and ditches, a publicly elected irrigator, *tuvaijuu*, directed and participated in the building and day-to-day management of the system. Beyond the swampy areas that were intentionally irrigated, a variety of seed plants, including rice grass and wild rye, benefited from the unintentional runoff from irrigated areas. The use of these irrigated lowlands was extensive, and it is likely that they provided the primary plant foods for the Owens Valley Paiutes in precontact times (Doyle 1983:158; Earl 1976:63; Lawton et al. 1976; Liljeblad and Fowler 1986:417; Steward 1933:247).[5]

Plant foods were an important part of the diet of the Owens Valley Paiutes. The women gathered more than forty food plants for their nuts, berries, roots, bulbs, or seeds

Figure 1.3. Locations of Selected Tribal Groups in the Great Basin and Central California. The boundaries of the many tribal groups inhabiting these areas are somewhat arbitrary because of such factors as seasonal mobility and trade.

(see Appendix I). At certain times of the year, as these different plant foods ripened, the Paiutes temporarily left their villages near the valley floor to take advantage of familiar harvests beyond their daily reach. Insects were another food source, and families sometimes traveled north to the forests of the Mono Lake basin to harvest the larvae of the Pandora moth, *piagui*. The larvae of the brine fly, called *kachavi* at Mono Lake and *inara* or *picwada* at Owens Lake, were gathered and processed into a highly valued food for local consumption or trade (Aldrich 1921; Doyle 1983:157; Earl 1976:61; Liljeblad and Fowler 1986:418–419; Muir 1894:80–81; Steward 1933:242–246; Sutton 1988:33–39, 45–49).

Men hunted a variety of waterfowl and game. Small rodents were caught in traps. Rabbits were killed by bow and arrow or in communal drives, the latter held in the fall in conjunction with a festival in which hundreds of rabbits were caught in a large net. Larger

mammals were hunted with finely crafted bows, backed with deer sinew for strength, and arrows tipped with neatly flaked obsidian points. Deer and mountain sheep were hunted singly or in communal drives. In the latter case, experienced hunters concealed themselves, often in rock enclosures on mountain summits, while others frightened the sheep toward them. Similar tactics were used in hunting pronghorn in the lower elevations. Deer, shot with bow and arrow or caught in complex multi-plied rope snares of native hemp fiber, were relatively plentiful and provided not only meat but also hides for clothing and sinew for sewing, backing bows, and fletching arrows. The Owens Valley Paiutes avoided hunting grizzly bears, which were feared for their strength and ferocity. Grizzlies were also credited with supernatural powers and thought to resemble humans too closely to hunt. Few fish were endemic to Owens Valley; native suckers were killed with a fish spear, and the smaller pupfish were caught in large quantities with fish poison in dammed streams (Liljeblad and Fowler 1986:418–419; Osborne and Riddell 1978; Steward 1933: 252–255; 1934:431, 433–434, 436).

Although they collected most of their food, medicinal plants, and other materials locally, the Owens Valley Paiutes also established patterns of commerce with their neighbors, in spite of linguistic differences, trading salt, sinew-backed bows, piñon pine nuts, and other items for shell beads, fine Yokuts baskets, and additional goods not found in their own territory. Occasionally, men of neighboring districts agreed to the reciprocal use of resources for hunting and fishing. The frequent traveling involved in this trans-Sierran commerce often resulted in the intermarriage of Owens Valley Paiutes with their western neighbors. Sierra Nevada passes, such as Mammoth, Piute, Taboose, Kearsarge, and Cottonwood, facilitated these trips and were part of a well-established trail system. Such trips were not confined to summer, for sometimes Paiute men traveled over the mountains in winter, wearing snowshoes. These travels took them northwest to the territory of the Sierra Miwoks; westward

Figure 1.4. A Portion of Tom Bell's Camp near Big Pine, ca. 1915. Left to right: Unknown, Ollie Kane, Hank Baker *(on horse),* Tom Bell, Gladys Harry, George Collins, Teha Bell, Mary Bell *(both seated),* Jeff Yandell *(on horse).* Almost all work—cooking, basket making, and so forth—was done outside during good weather. The sunshade, under which the Paiute women in the photograph are sitting, was made of willow branches. In the foreground the people have piled sagebrush into a semi-circular windbreak.

to the Western Monos (Monache), with whom they were linguistically related; and southwest to the Tubatulabals, Kawaiisus, and Yokuts on the mountain slopes and in the western foothills of the Sierra. Owens Valley Paiute men sometimes wintered on the west side of the Sierra Nevada, staying in Western Mono or Yosemite-area Miwok villages. At least one source (Barrett and Gifford 1933:251, 256) credits the Paiutes with occasionally traveling to the coast to obtain shells. Those Yokuts men who were professional traders traveled both to the coast and to Owens Valley, moving artifacts and raw materials across California (Arkush 1993:621–623; Barrett and Gifford 1933:251, 255–256; Davis 1974:20–22; Earl 1976:147; Gayton 1948:56; Latta 1949:64; Liljeblad and Fowler 1986:412–415; Spier 1978:426–427; Steward 1933:257–258; 1934:431, 437).[6]

Although they spent much of their time hunting, gathering, and producing the baskets, houses, and other material objects important in their lives, the Owens Valley Paiutes had a rich oral tradition and many leisure-time activities.

Most if not all games were accompanied by the wagering of strings of shell beads, rabbit skin blankets, baskets, and other kinds of personal property (Figure 1.5). "Double ball," a favorite field sports game played by women, involved tossing a pair of connected balls with three-foot-long sticks.[7] Men played a hoop-and-pole game on a specially prepared field some fifty feet in length.[8] The hand game so widespread among Great Basin and California tribes was perhaps the most popular gambling game. Two teams played against each other, two players concealing four small cylindrical sections of polished bone in their hands while singing songs composed especially for the game. Two of the bones were wrapped around their centers with dark material. People bet on which hand held unmarked bone, and score was kept with ten sticks.[9] Popular, too, was the woman's stick dice game, played with eight split cane pieces ten or more inches in length, with the interior, concave side painted red (Busby et al. 1979:174; Steward 1933:285–287, 1934:433, 1941:302–306).

Figure 1.5. Panamint Shoshone People Gambling, ca. 1920. Gambling, with old-time guessing games or card games introduced by non-Indians, was and is a favorite pastime among most of the native people of eastern California. Spectators and players alike bet on the outcome of games. In former times they bet strings of shell beads, baskets, blankets, and other items of value, but by the twentieth century, money was most commonly wagered.

Stories provided explanations for the world as well as entertainment for both adults and children. Paiute myths were generally direct narratives in which characters engaged in extensive dialogue, not unlike in Western novels. Myths were numerous and covered a vast array of subjects, such as creation, the origin of fire, and the exploits of mythological beings. Many stories were considered quite humorous, and sometimes songs were used to introduce characters in these stories. Regardless of content, these renderings served not only to entertain but also to demonstrate the skill of the narrator. Individual storytellers narrated myths differently, and some individuals were recognized as exceptional storytellers. Paiute legends were supposed to be told only during prescribed seasons. Summer was not ideal because it was the season for food gathering. Rather, the proper time to tell stories commenced "after the snakes had disappeared" in late fall or in "winter when the animals hibernate" and continued throughout the long winter evenings (Earl 1976:107, 1980; Steward 1933: 323, 1936a).

Supernatural power came from many sources in the natural world and was usually obtained in a vision or dream. Some men became successful hunters through the power of a bullet hawk or eagle; after dreaming of an eagle or eagle feathers, men might become faster travelers or women faster at gathering plant foods. Other people might obtain similar powers from bears, rattlesnakes, or other animal spirits. Shamans, or doctors, were men or women who had obtained potent supernatural power through dreams or visions. They cured people troubled with bad dreams or those whose bad thoughts or bad deeds caused them to be ill. Shamans sometimes exercised indirect influence on a community in a clandestine manner. By acting as a witch and making people ill by supernatural means, the shaman could make a leader dependent on his services, in this manner exercising an influence on local affairs (Liljeblad and Fowler 1986:428–429; Steward 1933:308–316, 1934:425–426, 428).

Paiute ceremonies were of several types; the two largest were held in the autumn. The annual fall mourning ceremony, commemorating those who had died in the preceding year, included the burning of property that had belonged to the deceased along with offerings from the deceased's family. With a ritual face washing, mourners were released from their mandatory year of mourning. Held during the same season were celebrations surrounding the annual rabbit drives and harvests of seeds and piñon pine nuts. Headmen sent runners to

Figure 1.6. Owens Valley Paiute People Dancing, 1932. Men wore ceremonial garb and body paint as they reenacted a traditional communal celebration for the San Fernando Mission Fiesta in 1932 (Harrington 1932). Importing materials from Owens Valley, they created a Paiute village environment, including the willow fence and tule-thatched house seen here. The dancers wear skirts made from strings into which duck down was twisted, and three of them wear headpieces of magpie tail feathers.

invite Paiute people from surrounding areas, and Western Mono people from across the Sierra sometimes attended as well. Dances, gambling, feasting, and orations by headmen characterized these gatherings (Figure 1.6). More private rituals included the puberty ceremony for girls, which ensured their future good health, dedicated them to an industrious life, and prepared them for childbirth. A less formalized ceremony was held for boys when they killed their first deer, to ensure that they would be successful hunters (Steward 1933:293–294, 320–323).

Marriage had its own set of rules. A traceable blood relationship between potential partners was taboo. Spouses came not only from other Owens Valley Paiute families but also from Panamint Shoshones, Western Monos, Southern Miwoks, and other Paiute groups to the north or east. Polygyny sometimes occurred, but only a few men were wealthy enough to have two wives. Families exchanged presents over several weeks or months before the actual marriage day, when the newlyweds spent the night together. In rare cases, a man did not marry a woman; some of these men were transvestites, *tuyayap*, who dressed like females and assumed a female role, including making baskets (Driver 1937:90; Fowler and Dawson 1986:732; Roscoe 1998:239; Steward 1933:238, 294–296; 1941:253, 312).

Baskets were an integral part of everyday life among the Owens Valley Paiutes and figured prominently in some ancient legends.[10] Made primarily of willow shoots, baskets were woven according to prescribed techniques and in a multitude of shapes, each designed to serve a specific need: to carry infants (Figure 1.7), to prepare and gather foods, to carry loads, to store food and other items, and to be given as special gifts. Basket weaving was the responsibility of women, who began to learn the skill in early childhood. By the time a woman was in her teens, she was a competent weaver.

For an average-sized, open-twined winnowing basket, a competent weaver likely spent about four hours cutting, splitting, and/or scraping willow shoots to make the two hundred split sewing strands and two hundred willow rods needed. Then she worked another seven hours with her moistened materials to weave her basket. Tightly woven coiled baskets took much longer; a bowl-shaped basket, of a

Figure 1.7. Paiute Girl in Her Cradle Basket, ca. 1910. The sunshade of this cradle basket was decorated with a pattern of connecting diamonds, indicating the baby was female. Slanted lines would have indicated a male.

Figure 1.8. Owens Valley Paiute Basket Cap. Weaver unknown, ca. 1900. The basket cap, shown here upsidedown to view the interior, was twined with split, peeled willow and split willow with the inner bark adhering. The rust-colored inner bark was used to produce a pattern, the reverse of which showed on the inside as the weaver manipulated the weft strands. The rust-colored pattern was overpainted in its entirety on the exterior and in only a few spots on the interior. Most of the cap was diagonally or twill-twined. The start and the finishing row, however, were produced in three-strand twining.

size that would hold a gallon of water, might require one hundred to two hundred hours of weaving time.[11]

Owens Valley Paiute weavers produced many undecorated twined utilitarian baskets, but they sometimes wove designs on closely twined baskets. The primary design material was "sunburned" or "winter-peeled" willow, split willow whose brown inner bark was still in place. A half twist to the dark weft thread pro-

duced a pattern on the outside of the work with its reverse on the inside. Gathering or burden baskets sometimes had two or three bands of linear design at the top. Geometric designs woven on these baskets, and on women's caps (Figure 1.8), were generally painted over with a stain to make the pattern even darker.

Unlike other Paiute groups to the north, the Owens Valley Paiute people made pottery vessels for boiling foods (Figure 1.9). Thus they had no need to produce the tightly coiled cooking baskets so common among their northern neighbors and among the Western Mono and Yokuts peoples to the west. The presence of a ceramic tradition indicates that the Owens Valley Paiutes enjoyed a relatively settled lifestyle, since pottery was more cumbersome than baskets for migratory people to carry. This pottery was sometimes exchanged with the Panamint Shoshones for salt from Saline Valley (Burton and Farrell 1996:155).

A great deal of confusion exists regarding the classification and dating of brownware pottery from the Great Basin in general and from Owens Valley in particular (Griset 1986: 119; Pippin 1986:15; Prince 1986:3). Archaeological estimates regarding the beginnings of pottery among the Owens Valley Paiutes range from A.D. 800 (Eerkins et al. 1999:280) to 1300 (Madsen 1986:214) to the mid–1600s (Liljeblad and Fowler 1986:421). Some scholars agree, however, that the concentrated use of pottery in everyday life began between A.D. 1350 and 1400 (Eerkins et al. 1999:283; Suzanne Griset, personal communication 2000).[12] In the mid to late 1800s the growing availability of metal containers and cooking vessels, which were generally lighter and stronger, replaced native pottery, resulting in the demise of pottery making among the Owens Valley Paiutes (Arkush 1995:35; Baldwin 1950: 50; Jelmer Eerkins, personal communication 2000; Suzanne Griset, personal communication 2000; Liljeblad and Fowler 1986:421; Prince 1986:3).

Steward observed two Owens Valley Paiute women making pottery in 1927–30 (1933:267), so it is evident that the knowledge of pottery making survived among at least some native women into the 1930s.[13] Lack of archaeological data supporting the continuation of the relict industry may reflect the fact that relatively few sites from the 1870–1940 era have been excavated by archaeologists. In addition, pottery may have always been the work of relatively few women (Steward 1933:267).

In Owens Valley, pottery, like basketry, was made by women. They dug clay from the riverbed and size-sorted the dried, ground fine powder using a winnowing basket to remove impurities (Arkush 1995:29; Steward 1933:266). This powder was mixed with the boiled sap of desert mallow and then shaped into long coils. From a rounded base, spirals were coiled upward to shape the pot and then the sides were scraped smooth. After sun drying, the pot was coated again with the mallow sap and pit-fired under a cover of sage and willow bark. The finished pottery, smoky black or brown, is known by archaeologists as Owens Valley brownware. Vessel forms of this simple, unglazed pottery generally had flat or rounded bases and straight or flared sides (Liljeblad and Fowler 1986:421; Steward 1933:240). Sometimes they were decorated around the rim with thumbnail incisions (Steward 1933:268).

Despite the semipermanent nature of their villages, the lives of the Owens Valley Paiutes were governed largely by the changing of the seasons. People always arose before daybreak and generally ate two meals a day, but the days were filled with activities that depended on the time of year as different plant foods ripened or special insect foods were gathered. Thus, through an annual round of activities, repeated year after year, the Owens Valley Paiutes used the region to support themselves admirably.

THE ANNUAL ROUND

Taawano: *Spring*

Taawano began when the dark, cold days began to lengthen and warm. Birds started to sing, ground squirrels awoke, and the first small green leaves appeared. Heavy mountain snows began to melt. Waterfalls and noisy streams

Figure 1.9. Owens Valley Brownware Pot. Maker and date unknown. This brownware pot is representative of the pottery the Owens Valley Paiutes and their southern neighbors made and used for over a thousand years (ca. A.D. 800–1900). Pottery made by the Owens Valley Paiutes was coiled, thinned by scraping, smoothed or wiped, and pit-fired. It was unglazed, and its color ranged from a mottled brown to black. Paiute women used these pots to cook acorn mush as well as mush made from other roots or seeds. Sheriff Merrill Howard of Independence found this pot in a cave ca. 1970 and donated it to the Eastern California Museum.

started pouring down steep slopes into the valley, through thickets of buckberry bushes and stands of cottonwood trees, flooding marshes along the braided river of the valley.

Taawano marked the time when those Paiutes who had wintered in the mountains moved back to their camps in the valley below.[14] Sometimes they carried fire in the form of smoldering embers carefully wrapped in juniper bark. Women filled large, conical, twined baskets with cooking tools and their few personal belongings and with any stores of piñon pine nuts that had not been eaten during the winter. These burden or gathering baskets were called *kuddutssi, kuwhamma, or kavvonno,* depending on whether they were large, medium, or small (Figure 1.10). They were strengthened at the rim with a heavy wooden rod sewn in place. Often the base was repaired or reinforced by the addition of a patch of tanned deerskin. These baskets were carried by women using a tumpline that passed around the basket and over the forehead (Figure 1.11). Women laced their babies into cradle baskets, *hupph,* for the journey. Men transported their belongings in buckskin bundles slung by a strap over one shoulder; they carried their bows in their left hand and a quiver of arrows over the left shoulder.

Arriving back in the valley, the Paiutes repaired and rebuilt their homes in the villages. They used flat stones, brush, and poles to strengthen the windbreaks, *suhunovi.* They uncovered their caches of baskets, tools, and surplus stores of seeds and bulbs that had not

Figure 1.10. Panamint Shoshone Burden Basket. Weaver, Mamie Joaquin Button (?), ca. 1950. Open, plain-twined weaving characterized the bodies of burden baskets. This one has a reinforcing rod mounted inside. This Panamint Shoshone basket, likely made by the noted weaver Mamie Button, is similar to Owens Valley Paiute examples. The use of redbud, obtained in trade from west of the Sierra crest, is an innovative touch. Button lived near Bishop in the 1950s and 1960s and likely obtained the split redbud from Paiute neighbors.

been needed while the people were wintering in the mountains. Arising early in the morning, men went hunting and women began to gather plant foods as they ripened. People had plenty of leisure time to spend in gambling, smoking, and talking.

The search began for available food when the plants were just beginning to grow. Girls accompanied their mothers, who carried twined gathering baskets to marshy areas near the river to collect greens and wild onions. Men and older sons hunted. They fished the river and its feeder streams, using bone hooks or cane spears with two bone points, or drove fish into sloughs and trapped them in nets. Sometimes they would stupefy the fish by using false Solomon's seal, *tügwü'va,* which was mashed and placed in the water. Other times they dragged open-twined burden baskets through the water and scooped up fish or fastened the baskets below dams to catch the fish that came over with the water flow (Steward 1933:250–252).

As the desert days grew warmer and the nights less cold, grasses and flowers began to respond. Willows sent out new shoots. Tules in the marshes climbed skyward. The yellow nut-grass, *tüpüsi',* grew in wet areas near the river. To increase the harvest of this dietary staple, the Owens Valley Paiutes irrigated the land where it naturally occurred. Channeled by small dams and canals, the water encouraged the *tüpüsi',*

with its coconut-flavored tubers, to spread into the expanded wetland area and grow quickly. Irrigation also increased the yield of wild hyacinth, *nā'hāvīta* (spike rush), and other incidental root and seed crops. The women harvested the roots after the dams were destroyed in the fall (Lawton et al. 1976:19; Liljeblad and Fowler 1986:417).

Thuzzuwano: *Early Summer*

Thuzzuwano began when the weather turned hot. The narrow window of availability for edible plants, each of whose proximity to camp and time of ripeness differed, required careful planning to maximize the harvest. Flexibility was necessary to cope with the vagaries of weather and unpredictable competition from birds and animals (Bettinger 1991:473).

During *thuzzuwano* Paiute men continued to hunt. They made cane spears, flaked new obsidian points for their arrows, and made bows and arrows. In the sagebrush of the valley, Paiute boys hunted rabbits. Using sticks, they flushed the animals from their holes and brushy shelters, causing the rabbits to hop away frantically and often to run in circles. The boys would begin to give chase, wait for them to return, and then kill them with rocks. Hunters also rigged snares or deadfall traps to catch rabbits and squirrels (C. Fowler 1986:91; Steward 1933:239; Richard Stewart, personal communication 1997).

Tthuzzutuvvihinggh: *Midsummer*

A relentless sun moved slowly across a hazy, light blue sky. Snow disappeared from all but the highest mountain peaks, permitting easy travel to the west side of the Sierra Nevada and the resumption of trans-Sierran trade. In preparation for the long trek across the mountains, men assembled dried tobacco, obsidian blanks and points, salt, mineral paints, clay pipes, rabbit skin blankets, and some of the women's baskets to trade. The men hoped to return with acorns, elderberries, manzanita berries, and shell beads. In addition, they wanted to obtain coils of split redbud shoots and black-dyed bracken fern roots, prized by the women for incorporating into the weave and decoration of their baskets (Davis 1974: 20–22).

Acorns were found only in four small areas in Owens Valley. With such a small local supply, most acorns were obtained in trade from west of the Sierra crest. The nuts received in trade were already cracked and had their outer shells and peanut-like skin removed. The Paiute women pounded them with stone pestles on flat exposures of bedrock. Daughters watched their mothers pound the nutmeats to flour and winnow the flour with close-twined winnowing tray baskets. Leaching removed the fine flour's natural bitterness. A basin was carefully prepared in clean sand near a watercourse, and the pounded and sifted flour was placed in it. Water was poured over the flour and allowed to percolate through it into the sand. After many applications of water the bitterness was gone. The leached dough was carefully removed from the basin and any adhering sand washed from it. Then, using brownware pottery bowls made specially for cooking acorn mush, the women mixed the flour with water and boiled it into a thick, nutritious mush. Most Owens Valley Paiute people preferred acorn mush to any other kind (Busby et al. 1979:164; C. Fowler 1986: 67; Liljeblad and Fowler 1986:416; Steward 1933:246).

Tthuzzutuvvihinggh was also the time to collect and dry the larvae of the brine fly (*Hydrophyrus hians*). The Owens Valley Paiutes called the larvae *inara* or *picwada* and gathered them from the shores of the saline Owens Lake in the southern end of the valley.[15] In August the winds drove the insects ashore, leaving a band of larvae along the lakeshore some two or more feet in width and an inch or more in depth. The larvae were gathered by the women and dried in baskets in the sun. The dried larvae were stored for winter foods and traded widely to surrounding tribes. Women often dried hundreds of bushels of this food yearly (Liljeblad and Fowler 1986:418; Steward 1933:256; Sutton 1988:44–48; Wilke and Lawton 1976:48).

Every other year, families left their valley to collect *piagui,* the edible larvae of the Pandora

Figure 1.11. Maggie Ross with Baskets, ca. 1910. A tumpline over this woman's head supports a twined, conical burden basket. A woven water canteen, made watertight with piñon pine pitch, lies at her feet along with a winnowing basket.

moth (*Coloradia pandora*). Although the larvae could usually be collected biennially, the moth population peaked every twenty to thirty years, providing a bountiful harvest of this important source of fat and protein. The larvae were found only in the Jeffrey pine forests that lay to the north on the ridges that separated the Owens Valley and Mono Lake basins. Around the bases of the pines the people dug trenches to trap the descending larvae as they left the trees over about a three-week period to pupate in the ground.[16] The gatherers collected the larvae in open-twined, pouch-shaped *piagui* baskets made especially for this harvest (Figure 1.12). The women roasted the larvae in fire-heated sand pits for a short time, tossed them in winnowing baskets to remove the sand and dirt, and then washed them. The larvae were then boiled and eaten immediately or made

Figure 1.12. Owens Valley Paiute *Piagui* Gathering Basket. Weaver unknown, ca. 1900. Pouch-shaped, open-twined baskets were used specifically for collecting *piagui,* the larvae of the Pandora moth, during midsummer. Only the Owens Valley Paiutes and their Mono Lake Paiute neighbors produced this type of basket.

into stew with other meats and plants. Surplus *piagui* were dried in the shade for a few days to two weeks and then stored in a cool, elevated location in pole and bark sheds or in pits. The dried larvae would keep for several months under such conditions (Aldrich 1921; Doyle 1983:157; Earl 1976:61; C. Fowler 1986:91; Fowler and Walter 1985:157–160; Liljeblad and Fowler 1986:419; Merriam 1955:122; Sutton 1988:33–38).

As the first of the seed-bearing plants began to ripen, the women and girls spent time gathering rice grass, sunflower, and other grass

Figure 1.13. Owens Valley Paiute Seed Beater. Weaver unknown, ca. 1940. The willow warps of this seed beater's open, plain-twined body are gathered into a handle and twined together. This basket, which shows no signs of use, was likely made as a model of the type of basket used to beat grass seeds into a burden basket.

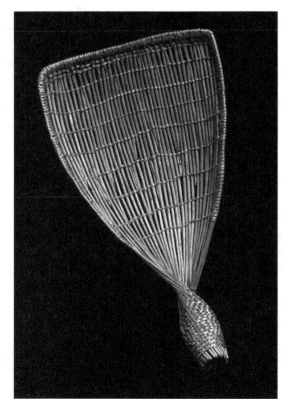

seeds. Working purposefully in slow-moving groups, the gatherers used seed beaters, *tana'ku,* which were spoon-shaped baskets with handles, to thresh the wild grasses and loosen ripe seeds, knocking the seeds into close-twined burden baskets held in the other hand (Figure 1.13). The gatherers took the seeds home in these burden baskets. To begin processing the seeds, they put them into shallow, fan-shaped, closely twill-twined winnowing baskets called *tuwaa* (Figure 1.14) (Fowler and Liljeblad 1986:441).

Experienced women showed the girls how to separate the chaff from the seeds by placing handfuls of seeds in more tightly twined winnowing baskets and tossing the seeds rhythmically and gently into the air (Figure 1.15). Loosened chaff blew off in the wind while the seeds fell back into the baskets. Seeds were sometimes roasted with coals and were then ground into flour with manos and metates. The flour was sometimes eaten dry but more commonly, Paiute women mixed the flour with water to make mush, which might be thick or thin. If the mush was cooked, it was placed in deep pottery vessels, *winabi',* which were put directly into the coals and the mush boiled until it thickened.[17] Occasionally, women prepared a thick dough from flour and water that was shaped into small loaves and cooked slowly in the ashes of the fire (Bettinger 1991:468; Driver 1937: 65; Jessie Durant, personal communication 1999; Powers 1975:29; Steward 1933:239–240).

Yuuwano: *Autumn*

Yuuwano was the season for the Owens Valley Paiutes' annual migration eastward out of the valley and up into the forests of the White and Inyo mountains, where the piñon pines grew. But before that, the harvesting of the seed-bearing plants, begun in the last days of summer, had to be finished.

Also in this season *tüpüsi'* tubers in the irrigated fields were ready for harvest. In preparation, dams were dismantled to allow the water to return to the original streambeds. Women used their digging sticks to excavate the tubers, and the people often ate some tubers raw. Others they dried and stored, then roasted and ground into flour, from which they made mush.

Communal rabbit drives were directed by the district headmen. Several nets, each three feet high and fifty feet long, were placed end to end in an arc. Some men hid behind this net while others drove the rabbits into it. The rabbits were clubbed or shot as they approached the net and were clubbed as they became entangled. Sometimes hundreds of rabbits were taken in such a drive. After the last night of a successful drive the people celebrated with a feast and special songs performed by paid singers (Steward 1933:253–254).

With the completion of the rabbit drive, men prepared rabbit skins for weaving the blankets that their families used year-round. With obsidian blades, they cut skins into long thin strips, using continuous circular motions to make a strip about ten feet long. Several skin strips were linked together and doubled. One end was attached to a tree, and a string tied a stick to the other end. The stick was rolled on the thigh, twisting the rabbit skin into a fur rope, which was stretched and dried. Then, on upright, vertical wooden frames, the skins of fifty to seventy-five rabbits were used to weave a blanket. Men usually did the weaving, although they were sometimes assisted by the women (Steward 1933:269). Besides offering protection from the winter cold, these coverings provided soft beds for adults and children (Figure 1.16) (Steward 1933:269–270; Wheat 1967: 75–77).

The people watched the piñon pine groves in the mountains to judge the harvest. If the harvest was poor, the families stayed at the valley villages for the winter, substituting the seeds gathered in the late summer and fall for the pine nuts. If it was a good year, families journeyed to the mountains, leaving behind their summer shelters. They cached the tools that they used only in their summer camps, knowing that others who passed by would respect their property. Grandfathers and grandmothers, fathers and mothers, sons and daughters all snaked their way through the

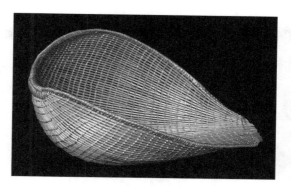

Figure 1.14. Panamint Shoshone Winnowing Basket. Weaver, Mamie Joaquin Button, ca. 1930. This finely made winnowing tray is similar to those made by the Owens Valley Paiutes. Used to separate the meats of the piñon nuts from bits of their shells, this winnower was made of willow with carefully spaced rows of plain twining.

Figure 1.15. Mary Lent Winnowing Piñon Pine Nuts, ca. 1910. Women used open-twined winnowing baskets in a rhythmic tossing motion to separate nuts and seeds from shells and chaff. Mary Lent (Nav-a-do-ne) (ca. 1865–1918), was born near Mono Lake. Mary married Harlen Jennings Lent, a non-Indian, in 1885 at the town of Laws, near Bishop. She died during the influenza epidemic of 1918. Photographer Andrew A. Forbes titled this image "The Winnower" and sold prints of the image to travelers through Owens Valley.

sagebrush and straw-colored grasses. They traveled across gullies and up hillsides to the places in the mountains, two thousand or more feet above the valley floor, where the piñon trees grew. They camped as close as possible to a winter water supply and began preparing for the long, cold season that lay ahead. If the pine nut harvest proved sufficient, they would remain in these mountain camps all winter. If not, they would travel back down to their camps in the valley (Figure 1.17) (Michael 1993:11).

For their winter homes in the mountains, men used juniper and piñon pine poles to build a communal assembly lodge and shelters called *waghonis* for their families (Bettinger 1991:465; Steward 1933:263, 1941:233). Women built

Figure 1.16. Mary Bell *(left)* and Teha Bell at Home near Big Pine, ca. 1902. Teha, an elderly Owens Valley Paiute woman, wears a blanket woven of twisted rabbit skin strips. Both Teha and her daughter, Mary, wear finely made basketry caps. A burden basket is behind them, inside of which is a coiled basket bowl, probably of Owens Valley Paiute manufacture.

Figure 1.17. Owens Valley Paiute Home, ca. 1916. Shelters of the Owens Valley Paiutes varied with season and location. Pictured here is a *toni*, the tule-thatched winter home used in the valley. Well insulated with bundles of tule, they were twelve to twenty feet in diameter and had a central smoke hole.

small structures to use for storage and cooking. Children collected firewood and carried water in canteens, *kuduosa,* that were tightly twill-twined of willow and made watertight by coating the exterior with red earth and boiled pine pitch (Figure 1.18).

While camp was being established, the complex process of the pine nut harvest began (Figure 1.19). Men and older boys repaired the long "hooks" left from previous years or cut tall willows into long sticks and attached hooks, inverted forked saplings, to the ends. These tools were used to pull the green cones, full of nutritious seeds, out of the tops of the piñon pines.[18] Women filled large, conical burden baskets with the cones that fell to the ground and took them back to camp. To prevent sticking to everything they touched, they coated their hands with pine pitch and then rubbed them in dirt. At the end of the day, they peeled

off these "gloves" (Jessie Durant, personal communication 1999).

Sometimes the women left the collected cones in the sun to dry and open. Other times they hurried the drying process by nesting the cones in hot coals. After enough time and heat they pulled the opened cones from the fire and shook out the nuts. The nut-removal step would be eliminated later in the season, when the cones still remaining on the trees would open spontaneously and drop their nuts to the ground. Though it was easy to collect the nuts from the ground, it was more efficient to gather entire, full cones.

To get at the edible meats, the women tossed the nuts with hot coals in openwork, plain-twined parching baskets until a popping noise indicated that the shells were cracking open (Liljeblad and Fowler 1986:22). Next the women removed the soft, creamy-white nut-meats and parched them again. After brushing or blowing off the ashes, they dried the meats. Once prepared, these pine nuts were either eaten as they were or ground to flour that would be mixed with water to make a kind of piñon mush *(ikevah).*

A family of four could harvest about twelve hundred pounds of piñon nuts, enough to last them until the following *taawano* (Thomas et al. 1986:266). The Paiutes protected unused pinecones from depredation by storing them on sunny slopes in pits lined with rocks and covered with pine needles, pine boughs, and stones. Nuts removed from the cones were kept in similar pits that were lined with grass (Steward 1933:242).

As the piñon harvest drew to a close, men focused on hunting in anticipation of the long, cold season ahead. Women sometimes made short trips back to the valley to gather willows from their favorite stands to start preparing basket materials. The days grew shorter, the nights colder.

Too'wanno: *Winter*

Food and warmth were the primary concerns during *too'wanno.* During the pine nut harvest, gathering firewood had been children's work.

Now everyone helped fill the large, open, plain-twined burden baskets with firewood.

During *too'wanno* the men made snow-shoes with bent wood frames and crosspieces of rawhide-wrapped cordage. To supplement the daily meal of piñon mush, they roamed through the snow in search of game.

This was the season when women turned to basket making. The handsome utilitarian baskets that were such integral parts of their lives needed repair and replacement. Now there was time for mothers to work closely with their daughters, passing along Paiute weaving traditions from generation to generation (Figure 1.20).

In the midst of the coldest, darkest days of winter the Owens Valley Paiutes entertained themselves as they had done for generations. They gambled, but most evenings they told stories. Paiute elders passed along to succeeding generations the myths and legends of their culture that were important for the young people to learn, to understand, and to remember. Grandfathers told stories to their grandsons, grandmothers to their granddaughters — stories about the origins of the people and about the magic of the animals, the spirits, and the land.

Figure 1.18. Panamint Shoshone Water Jar. Weaver unknown, ca. 1910. Water bottles were diagonally, or twill-, twined, then coated with piñon pine pitch and red earth to make them watertight. The narrow neck helped prevent evaporation and spillage and made pouring easier. The pointed base could be inserted into the sand and also made it easier to carry the water jar against the body or in a burden basket. Cordage tied through the two lug handles facilitated carrying. Panamint Shoshone and Owens Valley Paiute water jug baskets are similar.

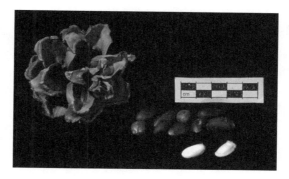

Figure 1.19. Piñon Pine Cone, Nuts, and Shelled Nut Meats. The nut meat of the piñon pine provided a protein-rich food source.

Figure 1.20. Panamint Shoshone Woman Teaching a Young Girl to Weave, ca. 1930. The photographer entitled this image "Basket making is taught down through the generations," and it was marketed as a postcard. The woman, who remains unidentified, is apparently showing the young girl how to use an awl to make a stitch in the unfinished coiled basket. Strands of split willow shoots lie on the older woman's thigh, and a finished coiled basket and a Hills Brothers Coffee can, possibly used to hold water to soak the basket materials, are at her feet.

2. SPLITTING THE WILLOW

The Effects of Non-Indian Exploration and Settlement on Paiute Life

Life in Owens Valley was not static during the estimated ten thousand years of human occupation. Subsistence during the Pre-Archaic period (approximately 8000–6000 B.C.) was probably based on big game hunting, use of smaller animals, and consumption of certain marsh plants (Elston 1986:137). Little else is known about this era because of the paucity of archaeological material (Arkush 1995:3; Elston 1986:138). Evidence from the Early Archaic period (approximately 5000–2000 B.C.) suggests the establishment of more permanent settlements and trans-Sierran trade (Arkush 1995:3; Elston 1986:141).

Archaeological evidence in the Middle Archaic period suggests that climatic changes and population increases changed subsistence practices sometime between 2000 B.C. and A.D. 500 (Bettinger 1976:91; Elston 1986:145). As the climate became warmer and drier, increasing numbers of people migrated from southeastern California into the region, and the exploitation of plants and animals shifted and broadened (Bettinger 1991:484–485). Changes in the relative importance of plants from wet and dry areas affected the location of villages and the distances over which large animals were pursued. Intensive piñon pine nut collecting, one of the mainstays of Paiute subsistence at the time of contact with non-Indians, likely began around A.D. 600, at about the same time that large game hunting decreased (Bettinger 1977, 1982; Curry 1971).

Access to items of Euro-American material culture preceded the arrival of non-Indians in Owens Valley. For instance, the glass beads that replaced shell beads as an important trade item among Indian people in the Sierra Nevada region were apparently acquired by the Paiute people of the nearby Mono Basin via trans-Sierran trade during the last quarter of the eighteenth century. Although the Owens Valley Paiutes likely knew of horses by the end of the eighteenth century, even in the mid-nineteenth century there were few horses among them.[1] Trade with neighboring groups during the first half of the nineteenth century must have brought not only goods but information about the arrival of the Spanish, the mission system, epidemics, and the horse raiding activities of the Yokuts and Miwok peoples (Arkush 1993, 1995:36; Burton and Farrell 1996).[2]

EARLY ADVENTURERS

It may never be known which group of non-Indians was the first to enter Owens Valley.[3] Perhaps the earliest known non-Indian traveler to the region was Peter Skene Ogden, an agent of the Hudson's Bay Company based in the Pacific Northwest. Seeking opportunities for fur trapping, in 1829–30 Ogden traveled from the Columbia River to the Colorado River, crossing more than a thousand miles of what was, to non-Indians, unexplored wilderness. Although geographic descriptions in his journals are brief, it appears that he passed through Owens Valley. Whatever contact he may have had with native people was ephemeral at most (Cline 1963:136–127; Phillips 1977:32–33).

Joseph Reddeford Walker was the next non-Indian to lead expeditions through Owens Valley.[4] Walker crossed the valley for the first time in 1834 while returning from a beaver-trapping foray to California commissioned by U.S. Army captain Benjamin Bonneville. Zenas Leonard, a member of Walker's party, recorded

that as they passed through Owens Valley, "we occasionally found the traces of Indians, but as yet, we have not been able to gain an audience with any of them, as they flee to the mountain as soon as we approach" (Ewers 1959:125). Walker led or accompanied other expeditions through the area in 1843, 1845, and 1846 (Ewers 1959:123–124; Fletcher 1987:13–14; Lawton et al. 1976:21).

In 1843, as a guide for the J. B. Childs emigrant party, Walker passed through Owens Valley, exiting by way of Walker Pass. In 1845, on John C. Frémont's third exploratory expedition, he and Theodore Talbot reached the Owens River on December 16 and gave it its present name. On the 1846 trip Walker, having left Frémont's party, retraced the route in leaving California. All these trips by non-Indians during the 1840s were fleeting and likely involved little physical impact on the environment or cultural exchange with the Paiutes (Farquhar 1965:53–61; Phillips 1977:42–48).[5]

During the next decade officials in the new state of California became interested in surveying its eastern border. In 1855, under contract with the U.S. government for the state of California, A. W. von Schmidt surveyed the area from Mono Lake to Owens Lake. Von Schmidt sketched the earliest maps of this area and made some observations about the Owens Valley Paiutes during the early contact period (Fletcher 1987:27). He was also the first to document native irrigation in the Owens Valley region, from Rock Creek south to Independence Creek (Chalfant 1933:21; Lawton et al. 1976).

For both Round and Owens valleys, von Schmidt noted, "soil 1st rate, fine grass, and mostly irrigated by the Indians." On Pine Creek in Round Valley he commented more extensively: "I found many Indians in this fractional township, who live in the deep mountain ravines, and come down here for grass to eat, also to dig roots called by them 'sabouse,' which forms their principal article of food" (von Schmidt in Lawton et al. 1976:23). About Indian people in Owens Valley in general he said: "This valley contains about 1000 Indians

of the Mono tribe, and they are a fine looking set of men. They live principally on pine nuts, fish and hares, which are very plenty" (quoted in Chalfant 1922:72). Only once does von Schmidt comment, "Laid off today to fight Indians" (quoted in Chalfant 1922:73). Otherwise, it appears that the surveying party and the local Paiute people had little trouble with each other.

Of all the early adventurers who explored the eastern Sierra prior to permanent non-Indian settlement, probably Captain John W. Davidson gave the most favorable picture of Owens Valley. Davidson was sent to the Owens Valley region in July 1859 by Lt. Col. Benjamin L. Beale, commander of Fort Tejon, in pursuit of alleged Paiute horse thieves. Discovering no horses in the valley, Davidson returned to Fort Tejon.[6] Traveling in summer, Davidson found the climate "delightful" and the grass, water, and timber abundant. "Nature," he said, "has been lavish of her stores" (Chalfant 1922:79; Wilke and Lawton 1976:18–20, 24–27).

Davidson's experience with the Owens Valley Paiutes was peaceful. The Indians ran from his group at first, but after he was able to meet with them and explain why he had come, they felt comfortable enough to return to their homes (Wilke and Lawton 1976:20). This meeting presented Davidson with an opportunity to observe Owens Valley Paiute people firsthand, and he recorded the earliest detailed descriptions of them (Lawton et al. 1976:30).

Davidson estimated the Indian population in the valley to be twelve hundred (Wilke and Lawton 1976:29).[7] He reported on the Paiutes' habitation, subsistence practices, physical appearance, weaponry, religious beliefs, character, and morals (Wilke and Lawton 1976:19, 29–31). He noted their summer shelters made of tree boughs, their use of irrigation, their practice of catching pupfish in sieve-like baskets, and their reliance on brine fly larvae, seeds, and tubers for food. He found the Paiutes generally to be honest and trustworthy, "of fine stature, the women good-looking, and the men robust," and called them "an interesting, peaceful, industrious people . . . not wanting

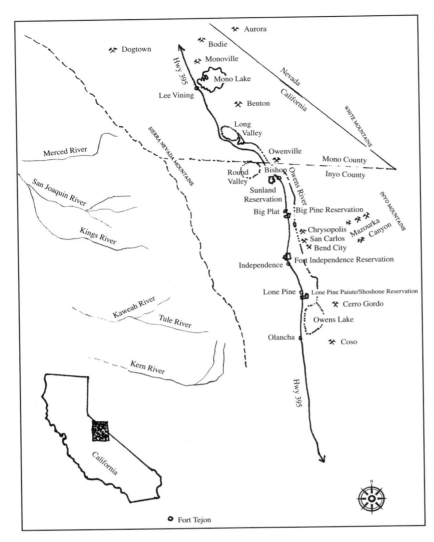

Figure 2.1. Place Names in Owens Valley. This map shows contemporary towns and Indian reservations, as well as historic mining camps.

PROSPECTORS AND MINERS

At the time Davidson was passing through Owens Valley, mining operations were starting to develop to the north. The discovery by non-Indians of valuable minerals north of Mono Lake brought miners from across the crest of the Sierra Nevada. In 1857 Dogtown, the first mining camp along the eastern slopes, was established approximately ten miles north of Mono Lake, just west of present-day Highway 395 (Busby et al. 1979:45; DeDecker 1993:5, 15; Fletcher 1987:30). By 1859 the discovery of abundant gold deposits about six miles southeast in Mono Gulch attracted more miners to the region. Eventually, this camp became the town of Monoville, with a population of two to three thousand. Additional strikes followed in 1859–60 at Bodie, Benton, and Aurora (Figures 2.2 and 2.3) (Busby et al. 1979:45; Cain 1961:4–5; Chalfant 1928:39–40, 1933: 127; Chappell 1947:236–237; DeDecker 1993: 15–16).

These strikes in northern Mono County were followed by mining activity to the south in Owens Valley. In 1859 mining operations were reported in the southeastern part of what is today Inyo County. At about the same time a party named Hill prospected near the present-day towns of Lone Pine and Independence. Serious mining activity in the Owens Valley region did not begin until March 1860, however, when the party of Dr. Darwin French discovered the mineral-bearing ledges of Coso, which lay approximately twelve miles southeast of Owens Lake, just outside Owens Valley. Additional claims were staked at the same time in Mazourka Canyon, about fifteen miles north of Owens Lake, and near present-day Independence. Four months after the initial discovery of gold, silver, and other ores, the riches of the Coso mines had lured three hundred to five hundred prospectors to the Owens Valley area (Figure 2.4) (Chalfant 1933:128–130). Mining brought visibility to the lands immediately east of the Sierra and produced the first steady

in intelligence" (Wilke and Lawton 1976:19, 30, 31). By the time Davidson left Owens Valley, he regretted not having more time to explore the country and learn the history and customs of its people (Wilke and Lawton 1976: 19, 20, 29–31).

Recorded oral history among the Owens Valley Paiutes generally does not appear to go back as far as these first non-Indian forays into the region but dwells on later events. Edna Piper, an Owens Valley basket weaver who died in 1996 at age eighty-five, remembered one account that may refer to these early non-Indian visitors. Piper recalled her great-aunt's impression of the first white people to come into the valley: "Their tracks were so big I got all flustered" (Edna Piper, personal communication 1995). Just which group of non-Indians

Figure 2.2. Bodie, California, ca. 1910. Noted for its violence, drinking, gambling, opium dens, and bordellos, the mining town of Bodie, north of Owens Valley, boomed between 1877 and 1888. During its heyday the town had more than ten thousand residents and its mines yielded $35 million in gold and silver.

transportation link between Owens Valley and the outside, non-Indian world.

SEEDS OF CONFLICT

By 1861 conflict between the influx of non-Indians and the resident Paiute people had begun. The first non-Indian settlers had arrived in Owens Valley by then (Busby et al. 1979:48–49); just two years later, cattlemen from Nevada and California, who drove huge herds of cattle and were looking for new grazing grounds, built permanent settlements to the north in what is today Mono County (Chalfant 1922:88–90; Maule 1938:10). Ranches, farms, and stores were established, and produce from Owens Valley was sold to miners to the north and south of Owens Valley. The cattlemen kept their stock in fields that were under irrigation and cultivation by the Paiutes, but when the Paiutes complained, they were ignored (Cragen 1975:4–5).

The introduction of ranching and farming to Owens Valley wreaked havoc on the native

Figure 2.3. Bodie, California, a Ghost Town, 1998. Most of the Bodie mines closed by the late 1880s, and the town's population fell to a few hundred. Mining returned briefly at the turn of the century with the introduction of the cyanide gold-leaching process, but the town never regained its vitality. A fire in 1932 destroyed much of the residential section, and the only school closed in 1940. The state of California acquired the town in 1962 and made it a state historic park two years later.

Figure 2.4. Reward Mine, ca. 1900. This typical mine was located south of Independence near Bend City. Mules pulled carts loaded with ore out of the tunnels. Although the work was dangerous, the rewards were potentially great.

ecosystem as well as on the Paiutes' traditional hunting and gathering activities. Woodcutting affected the piñon pine nut harvest. Timber cutting in the Jeffrey pine forests no doubt diminished the Pandora moth populations (Figure 2.5). Grazing of sheep and cattle greatly reduced native bunchgrasses, trampled the foraging areas of indigenous animals, and polluted accessible springs (DeDecker 1988:13). Cattle grazing also reduced the availability of the seeds and roots that were staples of the Paiute diet (DeDecker 1988:9). Farmers diverted water from the Paiutes' irrigation ditches to their own fields. In addition, settlers killed off much of the available wild game and slaughtered waterfowl on Owens Lake (DeDecker 1988:13). In short, the lifestyle of non-Indians was incompatible with the way of life of the Owens Valley Paiutes.

Conflict came to a head during the particularly harsh winter of 1861–62. To prevent starvation exacerbated by the loss of their traditional subsistence resources, the Paiutes turned to the cattle herds of the ranchers for food (Chalfant 1922:98, 1933:148). After showing initial restraint, a herder, Al Thompson,

shot a Paiute man; the Paiutes retaliated by killing "Yank" Crossen. The situation was volatile, and the Paiutes and ranchers tried to resolve their differences peacefully by signing a treaty in January 1862, agreeing "to let what is past be buried in oblivion" (Chalfant 1922: 99–100). Nonetheless, fighting began in earnest within a month. Battles took place in Owens Valley, and fifteen settlers barricaded themselves in the stone Putnam's Store at the site of today's town of Independence. The Paiutes were soon in control of Owens Valley and apparently had joined forces under several leaders, including Captain George, from southern Owens Valley, and Joaquin Jim, a Yokuts man from west of the Sierra Nevada.[8]

The U.S. Army was called, and on April 4, 1862, troops of the California Volunteers arrived at Putnam's Store. In the East the army was fighting the Civil War, and thus it was the California Volunteers, Second California Cavalry, that came to Owens Valley. The troops, led by Lt. Col. George S. Evans, traveled through Owens Valley and engaged the Paiutes. Evans estimated that some eight hundred to one thousand Indian men had more than one hundred

Figure 2.5. Sawmill in the Pines, ca. 1910. Sawmills flourished to turn raw timber into lumber for construction. The cutting of timber, primarily Jeffrey pine, likely reduced Paiute gathering areas, especially those forests that were home to the Pandora moth, whose larvae were prized. The exact location of this mill, in the Owens Valley or Mono Basin region, is unknown.

guns, and that they had killed nine white men and dried the meat of over one thousand head of cattle. By May the Paiutes were still in complete control of the region, with Captain George and Joaquin Jim the principal leaders. On July 4 the California Volunteers founded Camp Independence at a site that is now part of the Fort Independence Reservation. Fighting continued, although shortly after the establishment of the fort a truce was reached through a meeting between Lt. Col. Evans and Captain George. A treaty was negotiated with Indian agent Wasson of the Nevada District. Paiute people promised to turn in property taken from non-Indians, to surrender their guns and horses, and to provide some of the leaders and their families, including Captain George, as hostages to guarantee the truce (Cragen 1975:4–10, 23–29; DeDecker 1993:10).

The truce was a difficult one, and friction was quick to develop. Non-Indian men would sometimes lasso or otherwise capture Indian women and, as Evans wrote, "satisfy their vicious lusts by having carnal connection with such women." Evans responded by issuing an order that he would arrest and punish any men who molested or interfered with Indian women in the valley. John P. H. Wentworth, Indian subagent for the Southern District of California,

proposed to make Owens Valley an Indian reservation. Non-Indians were strongly opposed to this idea; the lush agricultural lands and nearby mineral deposits made the valley far too desirable to set aside for Indians, and the proposal was abandoned (Cragen 1975:30–33; Michael 1993:59).

The situation was complicated by additional problems that plagued the military, including difficulties with transportation of supplies to the fort. The lack of supplies left the soldiers destitute, and seemingly forgotten, while the rest of the United States was involved in the Civil War. The Indians were also ignored, and after complying with the terms demanded of them in the treaty, they waited for food, clothing, and other items that never arrived (Cragen 1975:30–33; Michael 1993:59).

By September 1862 the situation was becoming desperate, and Evans feared another outbreak of hostilities. Although Indian Agent Wentworth distributed blankets, clothing, and provisions and set up a reservation, the Indian people drifted away from the fort. Repeated promises from the Indian Service were seldom kept. Some ranchers drove Indians away from their lands; others employed Paiute laborers and then sometimes refused to pay them. Additional stockmen continued to move into Owens

Valley. Three mills were in operation in the Coso district to the southeast, and prospectors were scouring the nearby mountains. Skirmishes occurred occasionally, and Indians under Joaquin Jim sometimes launched attacks. By January 1863 hostilities resumed in full (Cragen 1975:47–48).

Open warfare prevailed throughout the valley in early 1863, and both Indians and non-Indians were killed. In March a group of soldiers and citizens killed between 35 and 41 Indians at Owens Lake. Other battles ensued, and the unrest kept non-Indians from settling and developing Owens Valley as they desired.[9] Under Capt. Moses A. McLaughlin a "scorched earth" campaign was launched, and soldiers burned whatever food caches they could find, imprisoned or shot many of the Indians, and raped the women; unlike Col. Evans, the new military leaders offered no protection to the Paiutes. Although the local Indian people, aided by Indians from Tejon, Tehachapi, and elsewhere, fought hard to protect their way of life, they eventually were subdued by the California Volunteers and white settlers (Busby et al. 1979:56; Chalfant 1933:187; Cragen 1975:33–34, 49–59; Davis et al. 1897:23).

RELOCATION

With the cessation of hostilities in the summer of 1863, Indian people began to come in groups to surrender at Camp Independence. With the number of individuals reaching over nine hundred, food supplies became inadequate. The military was ill equipped to handle the large number of starving Paiutes and Shoshones now under its jurisdiction. The army was anxious to rid itself of the problem, and Col. R. C. Drum, assistant adjutant general of California, promoted the relocation of the Indians to San Sebastian, a reservation 250 miles to the southwest of Owens Valley near Fort Tejon. On July 11, 1863, more than nine hundred Indian men, women, and children prisoners were forcibly marched from Camp Independence to the San Sebastian Reservation (Cragen 1975:57–61; Liljeblad and Fowler 1986:430; Michael 1993:81).[10]

Besides the resident Paiutes and Shoshones, the Indian population removed from Owens Valley included people from the western slope of the southern Sierra, such as Yokuts and perhaps Kawaiisu and Tubatulabal peoples (Chalfant 1933:123–124, 190; Hudson 1904a: 25). J. M. Hutchings, who had been prospecting in the Owens Valley region, apparently saw the Indian people being marched out of the valley. His description of the event was published in the July 31, 1863, edition of the *Daily Alta California*: "Some squaws were fortunate enough to get to ride in wagons with the children and other valuables, consisting of baskets, old clothing, etc., and looked as pleased as children over their first ride in a carriage. The men and remaining women trudged on afoot and looked, generally, pretty serious" (Chalfant 1933:194).

Along the way to Fort Tejon the Indian captives began to evade their guards and desert the caravan; others were killed or died. By the time the group reached Fort Tejon, nearly one hundred people had died or escaped during the march. As a young girl on this trip, Jennie Cashbaugh witnessed a soldier stab her grandmother through the heart.[11] She and her family eventually escaped along the removal route: "We traveled for days. . . . At last nature played its part and opened a way for us, we crawled close together in the brush taking care that the two soldiers who were looking for us would not find us. I saw them coming near, just 50 feet away. I felt chills run through me, death was to claim us . . . the soldiers turned away, took another route, and we knew we were safe" (cited in Michael 1993:83).

The soldiers, according to native elder Hank Hunter, made numerous additional threats to shoot the Indians and occasionally carried through: "In one instance an old lady being tired and thirsty seeing a small spring of water along the way stepped out of the caravan towards the spring [and] was shot in the back by one of the soldier guards. No burial or anything to the dead woman. She was left there for the coyotes and the buzzards" (Hulse 1935:5).

The reservation at Fort Tejon was ill-equipped to deal with the influx of Indian people. Apparently, the Indians from Owens Valley were almost completely ignored, and nearly all the able-bodied Paiutes were able to escape during the next few months. By January 1864 the remaining 380 Paiute people, primarily older men and women and small children, were in a state of starvation. Capt. John Schmidt, the new commander at Fort Tejon, arranged the transfer of the remaining Indians to the Tule River Farm (eventually the Tule River Reservation). The Farm, some distance to the northeast of Fort Tejon, had been established in connection with the Tejon Reservation and was already the home of more than three hundred Yokuts Indian people. There the land was cultivated and the Indian agent in charge assisted the Indian people with farming. At Fort Tejon and Tule River the Owens Valley Paiutes were interned with not only Yokuts but also Chumash, Tubatulabal, and other California and Nevada Indians (Cragen 1975:69–70; Davis et al. 1897:733–734; Hudson 1904a:25; James 1903c:6; U.S. Department of the Interior 1860:9, 29–30).

RETURN TO THE VALLEY

Most of the displaced Paiutes eventually drifted back to Owens Valley; few stayed at the reservations for more than a year. When they returned, the valley was a changed place. One observer in 1864 reported tens of thousands of cattle there (Farquhar 1930:535). The increased cattle grazing in the valley continued to alter the traditional subsistence patterns of the Paiutes. During July 1864 it was rumored that Joaquin Jim would lead the Paiutes in an uprising (Farquhar 1930:537). In late November several white miners were attacked, and a group of eight or ten Indian men killed a miner and a woman and child. In retaliation, a group of citizen volunteers formed a posse and slaughtered forty-one Indian men, women, and children as they slept in their camp on the shore of Owens Lake (Chalfant 1922:177–187; Cragen 1975:71–75; Farquhar 1930:538–540).

Indian people feared for their lives, and many moved away from Owens Valley. Indians who stayed in the region were apparently protected to some degree by soldiers from Camp Independence. Keeping the peace was difficult, as some non-Indians wanted the Indian people exterminated, and some blamed any plundering on the Indians, even if committed by non-Indians. Indian people in the area were so devastated by recent events that it is unlikely they could have mounted an uprising. By 1866 Owens Valley was generally peaceful, and non-Indians came in numbers to settle. The presence of soldiers at Camp Independence provided a sense of security for the non-Indian citizenry (Cragen 1975:76–88).

In 1870 some of the local Paiutes, apparently in concert with Indians from the Bakersfield area, likely Yokuts and their neighbors, began to steal cattle and extort money and food from whites. Some Indians left their jobs at ranches and were seen riding in large groups, giving rise to a rumor that they were preparing for war. Non-Indians in the region became worried, and troops from Camp Independence were sent into Round Valley, their mere presence effectively quelling the supposed uprising. The Indian wars in Owens Valley were over, with an estimated death toll of sixty non-Indians and at least two hundred fifty Indians (Chalfant 1922:189–191; Cragen 1975:89–90).

WAGE LABOR

Farming and ranching brought an aspect of permanence to Anglo settlement of the area. Towns arose, and modern amenities arrived. Inyo County was formed on March 22, 1866. Between 1867 and 1869 the number of cultivated acres grew from two thousand to five thousand. As the area developed, there was no longer a need for a military presence, and Camp Independence was abandoned in 1877. The valley's first newspaper, the *Inyo Independent,* started in the town of Independence in 1870. That decade also brought the first telegraph to Owens Valley, along with a rudimentary large-scale irrigation system that proved strategic in the region's subsequent agricultural development. By 1886 Bishop Creek, a town of six hundred, boasted two Baptist churches, three hotels, and a school (Chalfant 1933: 245–246, 329–330; Cragen 1975:76–86, 127, 161–165).

Paiutes living in Owens Valley had to integrate themselves into the local economy controlled by non-Indians. With their land usurped and lifeways disrupted, they participated in the local wage market. As early as the 1860s, after the cessation of Indian-white hostilities, Paiute men found employment on local farms and ranches, where they worked as irrigators, laborers, range riders, and herders (Ford 1930:5). The Paiutes cleared land, made fences, sowed, reaped, and threshed (Dale 1949:81), working as farmhands not only during the harvest but year-round.[12] The men were also hired as road builders, mechanics, and miners, and the women found jobs as cooks, laundresses, and other kinds of household employees (Figure 2.6).

Although sometimes paid less than their white counterparts, the Paiute men were considered hard workers and an asset to the operation of a ranch (Dale 1949:81). One rancher characterized his Paiute employee as "a good worker . . . an honest man and a faithful friend" (Earl 1976:147). Over the years, the Paiute people developed a symbiotic relationship with their non-Indian neighbors. Some ranch owners treated the local Indian people well, advancing them credit or giving them food in times of need (Earl 1976:147; Jones 1992:5).

Paiute wage labor became indispensable to the local community. By 1873, according to the *Inyo Independent,* it was "of essential importance in the public economy," supplying "a want in that direction no other can do as well." In regard to agriculture, for example, a local resident observed: "Without [the Indians'] assistance, the farm work of the valley (which comprises barley, wheat, oats, corn, and vegetables to supply the mines of Silver Peak, Belmont, and Cerro Gordo and for home consumption) would cease" (Dale 1949:81).

Paiute involvement in the local wage-labor market contributed to the growth of the Owens Valley economy, and employment in the white community provided the Paiutes a source of income that enabled them to survive. Paiute people dressed in Western clothing and ate a diet that incorporated both native and introduced foods. Pots and pans replaced some baskets and pottery, scarves and bandanas replaced basketry caps, and firearms began to replace bows and arrows (Figures 2.7, 2.8) (Liljeblad and Fowler 1986:430; Uhlmeyer 1991a; Walton 1992:24).

Small settlements were established near places of employment, sometimes near towns. Mountaineer Clarence King described a Paiute village near Lone Pine in the fall of 1866:

> A little further on we passed an Indian ranchero where several willow wickyups were built upon the bank of a cold brook. Half naked children played about here and there, a few old squaws bustled at household work; but nearly all lay outstretched, dozing. A sort of tattered brilliancy characterized the place.

Figure 2.6. Paiute Laundress, ca. 1910. By the time this photograph of an unidentified Paiute woman doing laundry was taken, Paiute women had been doing laundry for non-Indians for more than forty years.

Gay, high-colored squalor reigned. There seemed hardly more lack of thrift or sense of decorum than in the American ranches yet somehow the latter send a stab of horror through one, while this quaint indolence and picturesque neglect seem aptly contrived to set off the Indian genius for loafing, and leave you with a sort of aesthetic satisfaction, rather than the sorrow their half development should properly evoke. (King 1872: 273–274)

The Owens Valley Paiutes sometimes forged close friendships with non-Indian residents of the valley in the late nineteenth century. One non-Indian with strong ties to the local Indian people was John Shepard, a farmer who lived at George's Creek, now known as Manzanar. Shepard eventually owned more than two thousand acres and employed Paiute people from the large village just west of his ranch. Paiute men worked at ranch chores and irrigation, and the women performed domestic tasks and winnowed grain. Local Paiute people often went to Shepard for advice, and he apparently treated them well. When he died in 1908, the Paiute people asked and were granted permission to perform a funeral ceremony for him. Held at the Masonic Hall in Independence, the funeral was attended by more than four hundred Paiutes. The ceremonies included dancing around the coffin, songs and wailing, and the casting of pine nuts and other foods over the coffin. The request of Paiute people to perform such a ceremony for a non-Indian, and the permission granted to allow them to do so, suggest a close relationship and mutual respect at odds with the earlier relations between Indians and whites in Owens Valley (Burton and Wehrey 1996:129; Earl 1976:100–104, 151).

The Earls, who settled some eight miles north of John Shepard in the 1860s, also formed a close friendship with the Indians who worked on or lived on or near their ranch. Paiute men and occasionally young boys performed farming and ranching chores, and at least one young Paiute woman was employed as a household servant. Some of the local Indian people adopted *Earl* as their surname, and at least one of the

Figure 2.7. A Paiute Village, ca. 1912. The native lifestyle of the Owens Valley Paiute people had been changed significantly by the time this photograph was taken. More than sixty years of contact with non-Indians had resulted in the adoption of Western dress, metal pots and pans, and other objects of material culture seen in this photograph. The traditional tule-thatched home has a door made of commercial lumber. Although these dwellings were still in use at this time, they too would become a thing of the past by the mid-twentieth century.

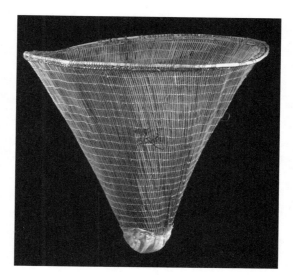

Figure 2.8. Owens Valley Paiute Burden Basket. Weaver unknown, ca. 1900. Repairs that would formerly have been done with brain-tanned hide or rawhide were replaced by cloth. Cloth was readily available in Owens Valley and, although not as durable as hide, was easy to use. This basket, identical to others collected from Owens Valley Paiute people, was given to Anna Kelley by A. C. Dean, who purportedly found it in a cave on the east side of Saline Valley, in Panamint Shoshone territory. Nonetheless, the basket has all the hallmarks of Owens Valley Paiute, rather than Panamint Shoshone, construction.

Earls' children, Guy Chaffee Earl, learned to speak Owens Valley Paiute fluently (Bernasconi 1988:85; Earl 1976:147–155, 1980:48).

Although the non-Indians used a good portion of the land and resources in Owens Valley, the valley was still the Paiutes' homeland. Even while making accommodations to the new social order, the Paiutes were able to retain parts of their native culture. They depended on food bought from earned wages but where possible still used their traditional food resources. Hunting, pine-nut gathering, seed gathering, basketry, traditional healing, and many other aspects of their traditional culture were maintained through the late nineteenth century and into the first third of the twentieth century. Even though they worked as wage laborers in the homes of non-Indians, the Paiutes maintained their own households and communities separate from those of non-Indians (Hurtado 1982:253–258; Michael 1993:136–139; Steward 1933:237–238).

In 1873 the Bureau of Indian Affairs (BIA) officially established the Tule River Reservation at the site of the Tule River Farm, which had been connected to the Fort Tejon Reservation operations. The objective of the federal government was to relocate all the Indian people from the region onto one reservation. The original intent was for Tule River to be home not only for native peoples from the west side of the southern Sierra Nevada but also for those living to the east of the Sierra crest, including Owens Valley. The number of Indian people in the valley at this time was sizable; the 1870 census had counted 1,150. Owens Valley Paiutes objected strenuously to this proposal and made it known that they would fight to stay in their traditional homeland. Non-Indian residents, some of whom had fought against the Paiutes in the early 1860s, came to their defense and opposed their removal to Tule River. The Paiutes were an important workforce in the valley, and their labor was essential to the profitable operation of local farms and ranches. In the end, the opposition of Owens Valley Paiute people and local white residents prevailed, and the Paiutes were able to stay in Owens Valley (Busby et al. 1979:57; Crum 2001:19; Ewan 2000:113; Sauder 1994:63).[13]

GROWTH AND ASSIMILATION

Not all Paiutes were completely dependent on wage labor. During the 1870s at least five Owens Valley Paiute people acquired legal title to 160-acre homesteads. In the 1890s the Bureau of Indian Affairs helped several other Paiutes to obtain public-domain land allotments in the valley. Others filed for homesteads through 1923. Thus by the early 1900s

fifty-two Paiute people had land allotments of 80 or 160 acres, which they farmed or leased to white ranchers (Crum 2001:19; Walter 1986: 165–168).

Through the 1890s, mining and the slow, steady growth of ranching and agriculture continued to define Owens Valley. Insufficient transportation still hindered the expansion of markets for beef, grain, and farm produce. Significantly, the federal government began to increase its presence in the affairs of the valley. In 1893 the government established the Sierra Forest Reserve, covering approximately four million acres of forest, which later became known as the Inyo and Toiyabe national forests (Busby et al. 1979:73; Inyo County Board of Supervisors 1966:7). Though not immediately of much notice in Owens Valley, in the twentieth century the National Forest Service would be an important presence in the region. Too, governmental designation of land use in Owens Valley represented a precedent with far-reaching consequences for the valley's later development.

In 1890 the BIA opened an off-reservation boarding school near Carson City, Nevada, a school that some Owens Valley Paiute children would attend (see Chapter 5). Indian day schools were also established in Owens Valley. The first was apparently opened in 1896 at Bishop by the National Indian Association in conjunction with the federal government (Taber 1911:63). Soon after, the federal government established Indian public schools in Big Pine and Independence and later at Lone Pine (Jones 1897:12; Liljeblad and Fowler 1986:430; Taber 1911:63).[14]

Christian missionaries also directed their activities toward the Owens Valley Paiutes in the early 1900s. For example, in 1908 the Northern California Indian Association, in cooperation with the American Sunday School Union of the Pacific Coast, sent a young student missionary to work among the Paiutes. In 1910 the Presbyterian Board of Missions sent Rev. W. N. Price to take over the missionary work, and he and his family lived near one of the Indian settlements. Price preached regularly at Bishop, Big Pine, Independence, and Round Valley, and Rev. W. B. Noble organized an Indian church in the valley (Taber 1911: 63–65). These proselytizing efforts were yet another of the many pressures of assimilation felt by the Owens Valley Paiutes in this period.

By 1910 the situation of Indian people in Owens Valley was often seen as quite bleak by outsiders. In 1911 a sympathetic observer recorded:

> The Indians . . . , one thousand or more within the limits of Inyo County, [live] in little settlements of from twenty-five to four hundred, wherever work and a bit of land may be found. The old semi-nomadic life, with its freedom and abundant food supply, has been more and more circumscribed as the white men have taken up the arable land and drawn off the water of the river. To be sure, some Indians have secured allotments, mostly, however, without water rights. Little board houses have to a great extent taken the place of the brush wickiups, and harvest time brings an opportunity each year, for work and good wages. But, side by side with these material gains, have come the white man's whiskey and the white man's immorality, which, added to the Indians' native vice of gambling, have produced a condition worse, morally, than when the white man entered the valley, fifty years ago. (Taber 1911:63)

By the end of the nineteenth century Owens Valley was the home of a thousand or more Indian people, who lived in settlements spread throughout the valley (Steward 1933: 237). They had survived a period of terrible upheaval and bloody warfare but made the best of their situation by adapting their lifestyle to accommodate the ever-increasing number of non-Indians who now ruled their homeland. Although many worked at wage labor for non-Indians, they still spoke their native language, Paiute women made baskets, and they harvested many native foods. Keeping what they chose to of old Paiute culture, they adopted many new practices and objects from non-Indians and made a new way of life for themselves and their children. These adaptations were only the har-

bingers of more drastic changes that were forthcoming in the twentieth century.

At the beginning of the twentieth century, except for the few Paiute people with homesteads, Indians in Owens Valley were without lands and needed property on which they could live permanently. To this end, the federal government established several Indian reservations in Owens Valley. Separate federal grants in 1902 and 1912 allocated a total of 69,000 acres of Owens Valley land for Indian home sites near Bishop, Big Pine, Lone Pine, and the original Camp Independence. The allocation of these lands to the Paiutes gave the people a place to live on a permanent basis. Much of the land was relatively worthless for agriculture, but ownership included valuable water rights (Liljeblad and Fowler 1986:430; Walton 1992:208–209).

THE LOS ANGELES AQUEDUCT

In the post-settlement period water was already a topic of concern in Owens Valley. Some farmers and ranchers took over the Paiute irrigation ditches directly; others began their own projects. By 1906 nineteen irrigation canals existed in Owens Valley along with numerous artesian wells (Blunt 1906, cited in Busby et al. 1979:75; Smith 1978:191–192). As the population increased, conflict over water was inevitable. The water issue came to a head when the city of Los Angeles, with support from the federal government, began to usurp water resources from the Owens Valley area, eventually constructing the Los Angeles Aqueduct. The aqueduct project changed life for both whites and Indians in Owens Valley.

At the beginning of the twentieth century Los Angeles was booming. Its population rose rapidly, from 4,500 in 1868, to over 100,000 in 1900, to nearly 320,000 in 1910, and to more than 1.2 million by 1930 (Figure 2.9). The steady influx of people required ever-increasing amounts of raw materials, food, fuel, and water (Busby et al. 1979:78; Nadeau 1997:10; Simon 1994:72). Because three deserts and an ocean surrounded Los Angeles, supplying the city with an adequate supply of water was a major

Selected Measures of Los Angeles and Inyo County Development
1870 – 1930

	1870	1880	1890	1900	1910	1920	1930
Population Los Angeles				102,479	319,198	576,673	1,238,048
Population Inyo County	1,956	2,928	3,544	4,377	6,974	7,031	6,600
No. of Farms, Inyo County		242	249	424	438	521	218
Acres of Farmland, Inyo County		50,487	68,256	141,059	110,142	140,029	94,567
% Owner-Occupied Farms, Inyo County			91	85	76	82	80	40

Sources: Ninth, Tenth, Eleventh, Twelfth, Thirteenth, Fourteenth, and Fifteenth U.S. Census of Population and U.S. Census of Agriculture.

Figure 2.9. Selected Measures of Los Angeles and Inyo County Development, 1870–1930. The soaring population of Los Angeles in the first third of the 1900s led to the building of the Los Angeles Aqueduct. As the amount of farmland owned by Los Angeles increased, the percentage of owner-occupied farms decreased dramatically.

problem. The Los Angeles Basin, which constituted 6 percent of California's habitable land, possessed only 0.06 percent of the state's natural streamflow (McWilliams 1973:183).

Members of the Los Angeles Water Commission began to look elsewhere for supplemental water and settled on Owens Valley, some 250 miles away. In 1904 the city of Los Angeles sent representatives to the valley to purchase the water options, lands, and rights-of-way needed for an aqueduct. Although the city's agents did nothing patently illegal in acquiring these lands, they were careful not to reveal that they were working for the city of Los Angeles until 1905, when the plans were made public. The annulment of a preexisting federal plan for a large-scale irrigation project in Owens Valley, along with the transfer of public lands needed for the right-of-way to Los Angeles, ensured that the project would be completed. In 1907 the voters of Los Angeles approved bond issues to fund the aqueduct project. Construction began later that year and ended in 1913, making it possible to move most of the water in Owens Valley to Los Angeles (Figures 2.10 and 2.11) (Burton and Wehrey 1996:133; *Inyo Register* 1905:1; LADWP 1988; Plakos 1999:1; Reisner 1987:65).[15]

Los Angeles continued acquiring private land and water rights into the 1920s. Owens Valley residents could not agree on whether the

aqueduct would be beneficial or detrimental to their community. Some saw the project as a moneymaking opportunity and willingly sold their properties for the price offered, others held out for higher offers, and a few refused to sell at any price. These differences of opinion created an air of distrust and suspicion among valley residents (Ostrom 1953:130).

In the first part of the 1920s many Owens Valley residents grew apprehensive as Los Angeles began planning an extension of the aqueduct into the Mono Basin. By that time Los Angeles had acquired nearly 90 percent of the ranching and farming land in Owens Valley, including lands belonging to nineteen Indians. As a result, Owens Valley Paiutes lost their own lands as well as their jobs on what had been farms and ranches of non-Indians in the valley. As the city of Los Angeles began purchasing land in the northern half of Owens Valley, some valley residents rebelled openly. Between 1924 and 1931 eleven violent attacks on the aqueduct system occurred, the most famous of which was the dynamiting of the aqueduct just below the Alabama Gates spillway on May 21, 1924 (Busby et al. 1979:82; Liljeblad and Fowler 1986:430–431; Nadeau 1997:94; Walton 1992:173–174).[16]

The Mono Basin extension of the aqueduct, started in 1934 and completed six years later, did not evoke the same kind of opposition (Busby et al. 1979:84–85).[17] It drew water from the streams on the eastern slopes of the Sierras that drained into Mono Lake and diverted it into a new reservoir at Grant Lake.

At the same time Los Angeles completed the Mono Basin addition, it initiated a program to pump groundwater from Owens Valley (Figure 2.12). As a result of these two actions, the levels of both Mono Lake and the Owens Valley water table decreased drastically (Figure 2.13). Opposition by both Indian and non-Indian residents to water usurpation by the city of Los Angeles rose once again as the Owens Valley environment noticeably degraded over a very short time.[18] The construction of the Los Angeles aqueduct dramatically altered both the physical and social landscape of Owens Valley.

Before the aqueduct the valley was green, full of orchards and grain (Etcharren 1977:65). Afterward the orchards disappeared, and hunting and fishing were severely reduced. Although no studies are available to document the specific impacts on deer, waterfowl, and fish, local residents claim that hunting and fishing were "ruined" (Plate 2) (Buckmelter 1998:42; Raymond Milovich, personal communication 1998).

IMPACT OF THE AQUEDUCT

The Los Angeles aqueduct produced a precipitous population decline, a major shift in land use, and a transformation of employment opportunities in Owens Valley. Between 1900 and 1920 the population of Inyo County rose over 60 percent, but it declined nearly 21 percent during the following decade. In the midst of the Great Depression the Los Angeles Department of Water and Power (LADWP) advocated a policy of mass emigration from the valley for residents who sold their properties to the city. In support of this policy Los Angeles also tried to control growth in Owens Valley and protect its watershed from water-demanding activities by limiting the availability of economic opportunities (Walton 1992:200).

By 1933 the city of Los Angeles owned 85 percent of all town property in the valley and 95 percent of all water-bearing parcels (Sauder 1994:147). Instead of having private ownership of their commercial properties, merchants had to rent buildings for their businesses. The leases were always short-term, sometimes for only a year or two. The uncertainty of lease renewal and a reduced sense of proprietorship discouraged both local merchants and outside investors from expanding or starting new businesses (Kahrl 1976:114; Ostrom 1953:127).

By this time the city of Los Angeles had also purchased 95 percent of all farmland in the valley. The number of farms and the quantity of farmland acreage dropped between 1900 and 1930, and the percentage of owner-occupied farms was cut almost in half. Los Angeles leased a small portion of its agricultural acreage back to farmers and ranchers but impeded their

Figure 2.10. Los Angeles Construction Area near Alabama Hills, ca. 1910. The first portion of the aqueduct was 223 miles long, took five years to build, had 52 tunnels and a capacity of 485 cubic feet per second (cfs), and cost approximately $23 million. The second portion, which started with the Haiwee Reservoir south of Lone Pine, was 137 miles long, took five years to build, had a capacity of 290 cfs, and cost approximately $89 million (Plakos 1999:1).

Figure 2.11. Dedicating the Opening of the Aqueduct Gates into the San Fernando Valley, 1913. The dedication of the "Cascades" on November 5, 1913, drew thirty thousand celebrants, to whom the San Fernando Valley Chamber of Commerce distributed bottles of Owens River water (LADWP 1988:36).

ability to succeed by making sure the city's water needs were met before theirs. The decline in the viability of agriculture affected the livelihood of all those in the valley. With less water available for irrigation, many non-Indian farm owners turned to other occupations. The Paiutes, many of whom had found a niche in the wage-labor market as agricultural

Figure 2.12. Well for Drilling Groundwater, ca. 1915. After tapping all the available water from the Owens River, the LADWP began pumping groundwater to supply the aqueduct. This well may have been the first one drilled by Los Angeles.

two hundred miles northeast of Owens Valley. In the end, neither of his suggestions was followed, as the Owens Valley Paiutes wished to stay in their traditional homeland (Crum 2001:19–20).

Having acquired most of the farmland and town property in Owens Valley by the 1930s, Los Angeles began to develop strategies for managing its assets. Civic planners wanted to "maximize the water supply available for its own use and minimize unfavorable publicity that would hamper its image and operations" (Walton 1992:200). One recommendation was to revitalize Owens Valley agriculture with an eye to conserving water. The establishment of stock-raising and dairy industries was encouraged along with the development of the "playground features" of the valley (Figure 2.14) (Dykstra 1929; Packard 1925).

As fishing, hunting, camping, and skiing gained economic importance in the valley and surrounding region, more jobs became available in enterprises designed to serve the influx of tourists. The film industry bolstered the economy when Hollywood studios used the Alabama Hills, between Lone Pine and Independence, as the shooting location for hundreds of westerns (Walton 1992:213). These new opportunities helped alleviate the local economic depression that began in the 1920s and lasted through the 1930s. The local Indian population, however, was largely excluded from these jobs, partly because they lacked the necessary training. Just as non-Indian settlement had altered the Paiutes' access to their subsistence base fifty years before, the acquisition of land by Los Angeles reduced by more than half the amount of land available for the wage-labor activities on which the Owens Valley Indians and non-Indians had come to depend. In 1930, for example, only four Owens Valley Indians worked for the city of Los Angeles, even though the LADWP was a ready source of employment for non-Indians during this time period. This was a drastic change from the nineteenth century, when Indian people had formed a major workforce in the valley. These conditions, combined with the Great Depression, were

workers, became unemployed (Busby et al. 1979:83; Walton 1992:205–208).

As early as 1926–27 the situation was apparently so desperate that it drew the attention of BIA superintendent Ray Parrett of the Walker River Reservation, whose jurisdiction included Owens Valley. Parrett suggested that some younger Owens Valley Paiutes might move and settle in the San Joaquin Valley, to find employment where some of the white ranchers formerly of Owens Valley had settled. He also suggested that Owens Valley Paiute people move to the Walker River Reservation, approximately

devastating for Indian people (Walton 1992: 207–208).

From 1910 onward, Paiute women still found work in domestic service, but overall the employment situation for Indians was bleak. Whereas an estimated 83 percent of the adult Indian population was employed in 1880, by 1930 only 35 percent of Indian households had one or more persons employed full- or part-time (Uhlmeyer 1991a; Walton 1992:207–208).

The Indians became increasingly frustrated with their inability to find work and took assertive stands when possible. In 1932, when a committee of the U.S. Senate began investigating the conditions of Indian people across the country, the residents of the Fort Independence Reservation prepared a statement for the committee: "We, the Indians of Independence Fort, Calif., Inyo County, say once we Indians had our ways and had own food and meat and we owned this valley — Owens Valley. When the white people come they took away everything from us and learned us how to work, and we worked for them. Now they took the work from us, we are without work now. We want work to be given to us, we the Owens Valley Indians, right in Owens Valley" (U.S. Senate Committee on Indian Affairs 1934:15199).

The unemployment situation prompted Parker Hall, farm agent for the Bishop Subagency of the Office of Indian Affairs, to voice his concern in 1936. In a letter to Alida C. Bowler, superintendent of the Carson Indian Agency, he wrote: "The unemployment situation here at Bishop, especially in the Sunland District, has been of great concern for the past several weeks. I have contacted all known sources and have found their main work to be on highways, which is progressing slowly. It will be necessary to put a number on W.P.A. relief until work opens up" (Hall 1936).

Along with the problem of unemployment, the living conditions of the Paiutes came under scrutiny. The LADWP, desirous of lands on which Indian people lived, needed a plan of action to obtain those lands. Thus in 1930 the LADWP conducted an investigation into the living conditions of Owens Valley Indian people

Figure 2.13. Owens Lake, ca. 1907. Ancient earthquakes in the Owens Valley created Owens Lake, a basin with no outlet. The saline water was popular for its cleansing and healing properties, and it was viable for waterfowl. Paiutes used to catch ducks that were too young to fly at the mouth of the lake, but as the lake dried up, that food source disappeared.

(Ford 1930). It also made suggestions for relocating Indians so that the city of Los Angeles could acquire the lands where they currently lived. The investigation's report noted that Owens Valley Indians were

> camping or squatting in widely scattered places, some along the streams, or on the old ranches, or near the valley towns or at isolated points. In very few instances are the Indians living under what could be termed favorable conditions. Nearly all of them use immense quantities of water from the streams for irrigation. None have the advantage of good sanitary sewerage disposal. Some are living in dugouts or crudely constructed shacks that are detrimental to their health and a disgrace to American ideals. (Ford 1930:10)

THE LAND EXCHANGE

Noting that "the Indian problem," which included the Paiute ownership of lands that the city of Los Angeles wanted to acquire, would not go away by itself, the report suggested seeking a "permanent solution" that would "improve" the Paiutes' living conditions and "stabilize their future" so that "they will have something to look forward to" (Ford 1930). The report recommended relocating the Paiutes to new tracts of land in Bishop and Big Pine, adjusting the boundaries of the Fort

Figure 2.14. Fishing in Owens Valley, ca. 1988. Besides water fluctuations related to the aqueduct, livestock grazing and the use of streams for public recreation resulted in declining fish populations, wildlife habitat, and water quality in Owens Valley. Toward the end of the twentieth century, stream enhancement programs improved recreational fishing in the valley. By the 1980s the opening day of the fishing season on the river and its reservoirs attracted more than seventeen thousand anglers (LADWP 1988:56). The 1992 plan for modifying fencing and grazing practices in the Crowley Lake tributary area, the stocking of the river with rainbow trout, and the 1994 enactment of special regulations for fishing may have made the lower Owens River one of California's premier tailwater fisheries (LADWP 1998).

Independence Reservation, and designing appropriate homes for the Indians based on their average family size in 1930. Also, though nineteen Indian landholders had sold land to the city of Los Angeles during the 1910s and 1920s, there were still remaining private Indian lands that would have to be purchased by the city. The report suggested that these Indian people lease lands owned by the city (Ford 1930:11, 20–21; Walter 1986:179–184).

A second version of the report, with updated statistical data on deaths, births, and the like, was compiled in 1932 (Ford et al. 1932). The City of Los Angeles issued several more reports over the next few years as it continued in its efforts to force a land exchange. The federal government finally formulated the Owens Valley Land Exchange of 1937, which called for the Paiutes (represented by the Department of the Interior) to trade 2,914 acres of their previously allotted land to Los Angeles for 1,392 acres of land owned by the LADWP. The land exchange created four U.S. government home sites to which the Paiutes were to be relocated.[19] As with the earlier land allotment, the new Paiute reservations were to be located near Bishop, Big Pine, the original site of Camp Independence, and the Manzanar area (that is, Lone Pine). Suspicious of the intentions of the

Los Angeles city officials, the Paiutes at Camp Independence withdrew from the agreement before it was completed.[20] The plan was implemented, however, for the remaining three home sites, and the exchange was carried out (Figure 2.15). The agreement also called for the city of Los Angeles to purchase all the remaining privately owned Indian lands in the valley; the Indians relocated by this measure were to lease acreage and accompanying water rights from Los Angeles (Crum 2001:20; Walter 1986:188–228; Walton 1992:20, 209).

This new relocation project occurred without incident, although communication by the federal government and the LADWP with the Owens Valley Paiutes and local non-Indians was minimal (Vernon Miller, personal communication 1998; Walter 1986:332). The home sites at the new locations incorporated what well-meaning non-Indian designers considered the needs of the Paiute community. Each home-site area had a special building for community gatherings, gender-specific quarters for single or aged Indians, water and sewage services, electricity, and landscaping (Ford 1930:21). Because the Paiutes were not involved in planning their reservations, however, they did not always use the amenities as intended. Many of them considered their existing way of life to be quite satisfactory, and some never occupied their new dwellings (Figure 2.16) (Clara Rambeau, personal communication 1998).

As a fiduciary with respect to the trust property of Indians, the U.S. government had the legal obligation "to provide economic and social programs necessary to raise the standard of living and social well-being of the Indian people to a level comparable to the non-Indian society" (Hall 1979:2). In an attempt to comply, the government provided to the head of each Indian household in the valley a tract of land in one of the new home-site areas. The tracts were originally intended, as noted by the city of Los Angeles in its report, to be sufficient for subsistence needs and "some means of earning an income" (Ford 1930:24). Subsistence needs were not always easy to fulfill, however, and the policy of distributing land only to individual household heads failed to consider future increases in family size. Furthermore, since the household tracts of land were small, and no land or water was allotted to the home-site area as a whole, development of any community-based enterprise was difficult.

At the time of the completion of the land exchange, reservations comprised over one thousand acres of land in Owens Valley: the Big Pine Reservation at 279 acres, the Bishop Reservation at 875 acres, the Fort Independence Reservation at 356 acres, and the Lone Pine Reservation at 237 acres. The relocation to these reservations necessitated another round of selective adaptations on the part of the Owens Valley Paiutes. No longer able to make independent decisions within their family units, the Paiutes had to learn to accept centralized leadership, a concept that ran counter to their traditional culture. Their inexperience in this regard sometimes hindered the progress of community endeavors.[21]

Other changes were taking place by the 1930s, when many Indian children attended public schools in towns such as Independence. Travel by horseback was rapidly diminishing, and some Indians had automobiles. No one, at least on the reservations, used the old-style homes covered with tules or other materials,[22] and most Indians lived in small frame houses. A few, like John Symmes at Fort Independence, had small gardens and sometimes planted a few acres with alfalfa, and some kept milk cows and raised chickens or turkeys. The Indian people of Owens Valley had by this time adopted much of the material culture of the non-Indians (U.S. Senate Committee on Indian Affairs 1934:15198–15202).

During the remainder of the twentieth century the Owens Valley Paiutes adapted to the social and economic conditions imposed by non-Indian settlement and control of the region. Wage labor replaced hunting and gathering, and both males and females were employed in a variety of professions and occupations. Although some families still practiced parts of the traditional culture, most aban-

Figure 2.15. Barbecue Celebrating the Land Exchange, 1939. Daisy Williams, carrying a plate of food, joins her friends in celebrating the now-controversial land exchange. Daisy, born in 1893 in Bishop, was the daughter of Dick Birchin and Jennie Shaw; she married Casuse Williams, a Paiute man who was born in Mono County. This photograph was originally attributed to Andrew A. Forbes, but Forbes died in 1921, eighteen years before this photograph was taken.

doned the seasonal round of gathering and collecting. Some still gathered piñon nuts or processed *piagui*, but these foods came to be supplements to the largely Western diet. Some fished or hunted deer, although their equipment was identical to that used by non-Indians. The service of Owens Valley Paiutes in the armed forces during World War II brought the knowledge of a wider world to Owens Valley on their return home (Walter 1986:128–130).

During the 1970s and 1980s new homes and tribal buildings were constructed on the reservations, such as the Paiute-Shoshone Cultural Center and Museum, the Tu-Tu Up-ee a Novie Child Care Center, and an Elders Building on the Bishop Reservation. Each of the four reservations continued to be governed by elected councils and was represented in the Owens Valley Paiute–Shoshone Band of Indians, which administered federal, state, and private grant funds and programs for the valley as a whole. The 1980 census recorded 1,568 Native Americans in Inyo County, in a total county population of 17,895. The Native Americans, 8.76 percent of the population, held 6.4 percent of the jobs in Inyo County (Busby et al. 1979:180–182; Liljeblad and Fowler 1986:431; Walter 1986:90–130).

At the end of the twentieth century many of the Owens Valley Paiutes continued to live on the four reservations in Inyo County. Only a small percentage of the people, most over sixty years of age, were fluent in the Owens Valley Paiute language. The Bishop tribe sponsored

Figure 2.16. Clara Rambeau, 1998. Clara Rambeau never inhabited the new house in Big Pine that was built for her by the BIA. Until her death in 2001, Rambeau preferred to live in her small home in the old Paiute settlement just outside of town.

pow-wows that featured pan-Indian dancing, a handgame tournament, and food booths. After more than a century of tumultuous change the Owens Valley Paiutes still sustained some of their ancient traditions, including the weaving of baskets, a marker of cultural identity and a source of pride.

3. WEAVING THE WILLOW

Basketry of the Owens Valley Paiutes

Baskets were essential to the everyday existence of the Owens Valley Paiutes before the arrival of Euro-Americans in the mid-nineteenth century. Baskets provided lightweight, dependable containers for nearly every use: for storage and transport, to gather and process seed foods, to cradle infants and carry water. Some were designed for specific functions, such as the specially shaped baskets made exclusively by the Owens Valley and Mono Lake Paiutes to gather the edible Pandora moth larvae (Bates and Lee 1990:66–68; Merriam 1955:122). Coiled "treasure baskets" used to hold shell-bead money were a highly valued, nonutilitarian form of basketry and were often given away at annual mourning ceremonies. Baskets were also burned at these ceremonies, and a person's baskets were burned on his or her death (Austin 1903:237; Fowler and Dawson 1986:714; Hartman n.d.).[1]

Over thousands of years women developed an entire repertoire of baskets whose design, shape, and materials were based on function. Baskets often displayed a simple, inherent beauty derived from their shape or specific weaving technique, and some were ornamented with patterns in a contrasting color. Although both coiled and twined baskets were found in traditional Owens Valley Paiute basketry, twining was the dominant technique (Fowler and Dawson 1986:710; Hartman n.d.).

Twined baskets were manufactured in the Great Basin as early as 8000 B.C. (Adovasio 1974:114) and continue to be made, on a very limited basis, in the twenty-first century. Over the centuries, traditions and rules for basket weaving were developed and handed down.

Creation of these extraordinary baskets was, with few exceptions, the work of women.[2] Traditionally, all women made baskets, learning from their mothers, grandmothers, or other female family members (Steward 1933:274).

Little is known about the features of prehistoric baskets in Owens Valley. The study of historic collections, however, reveals that each tribal group had its own signature repertoire of basket types, designs, shapes, and materials. Variations in weaving techniques, details of construction, and patterns also differentiated one group's baskets from those of another. For example, the Owens Valley Paiutes made coiled baskets with a leftward direction of coiling and generally used one-color and relatively simple geometric patterns. The neighboring Panamint Shoshones coiled to the right and commonly used complex, two-color geometric patterns. Because historic baskets are tangible evidence of a community's resources, skills, trading activities, and traditions, we treat them here as symbols of a group's cultural identity.

BASKET MATERIALS

The Owens Valley Paiutes made baskets primarily from locally available willow, as well as a few other materials, such as bracken fern root, bulrush root, and yucca root, that were obtained in trade and occasionally used for patterns. Each woman had her favorite gathering areas from which she cut willow shoots year after year. A weaver chose first-year shoots for their strength and straightness. Harvesting these shoots led to vigorous new growth from the favored rootstock the following year (C. Fowler 1986:94). She cut the shoots after the leaves fell

in autumn and before new leaf buds appeared in spring. After cutting the usable material, the weaver cut down or burned the remaining willow bushes in order to ensure a supply of usable shoots in the following year.[3] Shortly after gathering, she sorted the raw material by shoot diameter.

To prepare the willow for weaving, the weaver left some of the stems whole, scraping off the coarse outer and soft inner barks, to use as warps or foundation rods. She gathered scraped rods of the same diameter into bundles and tied them with cordage or, later, strips of cloth. The weaver split other willow shoots into three equal strips: after dividing the tip into three equal sections, she held one section in her teeth and used her hands to pull the other two sections. She then split these three pieces again to remove the inner, pithy section. Using an obsidian knife, she scraped the split strands to remove knots or nodes (Steward 1933:270) and then dried them for a minimum of a few days. The weaver then pulled the dry strands over a finger to remove the bark to make the white or buff sewing strands. For patterns, some strands were peeled off the outer bark immediately after splitting, leaving the inner bark, which was not easily removed. This willow was left out in the sun, allowing the pale green color to turn a strong reddish brown, sometimes called "sunburned willow." This willow design material was thus reddish brown on the convex, unsplit side and white or buff-colored on the split, inner side. Strands of either type of split willow were gathered into bundles, wound into a coil, and tied with cordage or strips of rags (Bibby 1996:67; Steward 1933:270; Wheat 1967:92–95). These materials were kept in the home until used. Properly stored, prepared willow sewing strands and rods would keep indefinitely. When ready to weave, the weaver soaked the materials in water to make them flexible enough to use. The split strands were then trimmed to an even width and thickness. Warp rods were carefully matched for equal diameter in twined baskets, and in coiled baskets, rods were scraped to make them of even diameter for their entire length.

BASKETRY TECHNIQUES

In twined basketry the weft strands were the moving or active elements, given a half twist as the weaver pulled them between and around the stiff, stationary, or passive elements, known as the warp rods. The wefts moved in a horizontal direction around the vertical warps. The weaver, unless left-handed, usually worked on a twined basket from left to right. She used her right hand to pull the wefts and her left hand to make more space between the rods so the wefts could pass between them more easily. As a result of crossing and twisting the wefts in a specific fashion, stitches slanted either up to the right or down to the right. The direction of the slant was determined by tribal tradition and served as a diagnostic feature of each group's twined basketry. Owens Valley Paiute twined basketry, like that of most Great Basin peoples, was characterized by an up-to-the-right slant.

Variation in the spacing between the weft rows determined whether the weave was "open" (with warps exposed) or "closed" (with warps concealed). The appearance and the texture of the basket was influenced by the width of the weft and by the number of rods enclosed by the wefts, as well as by how they were enclosed.

In plain (or simple) twining, the number of warps enclosed by the wefts could vary, but they were treated as a single unit throughout the weaving process (Figure 3.1). In each succeeding row the same number of warps was enclosed at the same interval. Usually, single warps were enclosed by the wefts, although on occasion the warps might be paired. In diagonal (or twill) twining, two rods were enclosed in each twist of twining. The wrapping of warps shifted one rod over in each succeeding row, resulting in a staggered or diagonal appearance on the surface of the basket (Figure 3.2).

In three-strand twining, three weft strands were each individually woven in front of four rods and then behind two. Since the strands began at different points along any given row, a raised and slanted finish was produced (Figure 3.3). This type of twining, which strengthened otherwise weak areas of the basket, was used less frequently than plain or diagonal twining techniques.

Traditional Owens Valley Paiute containers such as caps, burden baskets, bowls, and *piagui* gathering baskets used radial-warp starts. To begin, the weaver laid out the warps like the spokes in a wheel and twined the weft strands in a continuous circular direction. Traditional food-processing utensils such as winnowing trays, parching trays, and seed beaters used parallel-warp starts. To begin these baskets, the weaver twined the rods together to form a narrow end, adding more warps during the twining to fan out the basket to form the desired shape.

CAPS

Basketry caps, *tsōpå"nū* or *op'*, were important possessions for all Owens Valley Paiute women.[4] Men did not wear them (Steward 1933:275). These caps were finely woven in tight diagonal twining (Plate 3). In weaving a cap, a weaver displayed her finest ability and artistry. As one writer remarked on the identical style of women's caps found among the neighboring Panamint Shoshones, "Decoration may be quite elaborate . . . as with the *chapeaus* of all cultures" (Kirk 1952:80).

Owens Valley Paiute caps were semispherical and large enough to cover the entire head. Larger than the women's basketry caps made in far northern California, they allowed women to tuck their hair underneath. Caps covered and protected heads from the elements and from piñon pine pitch while people gathered pine nuts. They also provided a cushion when tumplines, attached to burden baskets, were used to carry loads on the back (Figure 3.4) (Steward 1933:241, 258).

There are a large number of documented examples of Owens Valley Paiute caps, disproportionate to the rather small number of documented Owens Valley Paiute baskets. For example, the Rose Black Collection at the Eastern California Museum in Independence has some thirty caps made by Owens Valley Paiute weavers, including Mattie Horton and Mary Yandell. Similarly, ethnographers col-

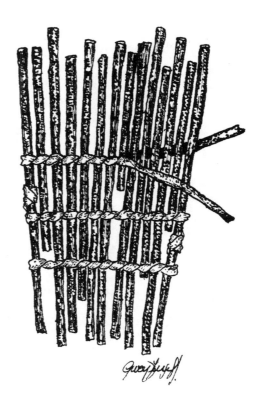

Figure 3.1. Plain Twining. Plain twining, used in most open-twined baskets, has stitches that slant up to the right.

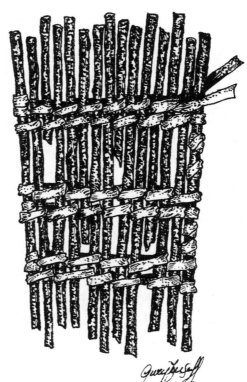

Figure 3.2. Diagonal Twining. In this technique the staggered stitches in successive rows give the surface of a basket an interesting appearance.

lecting in Owens Valley in the early twentieth century, such as John Hudson, C. Hart Merriam, and C. P. Wilcomb, all included caps in their collections. Occasionally, collectors would

Figure 3.3. Three-Strand Twining. The use of multiple wefts makes this technique the strongest form of twining.

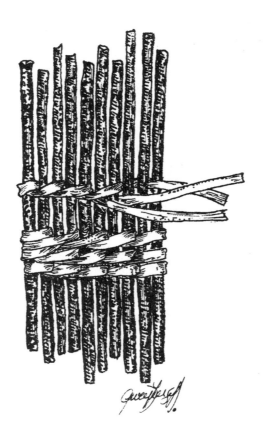

Figure 3.4. Martha Horton Demonstrating the Use of a Tumpline, ca. 1916. Martha Horton wears a traditional twined cap and carries a water jar with a tumpline balanced across her head. Many of the Paiute baskets in this photograph are part of the Eastern California Museum collection.

purchase the cap directly from the woman who was wearing it (Merriam 1901:10d, 1955:121).

The warps of the caps were scraped willow shoots, and the wefts were strands of split, peeled willow. After the initial crossing of warp rods, the start of the cap was usually woven with numerous rows of three-strand twining that helped reinforce its shape. Another row of three-strand twining was often added after the termination of the diagonal twining and just before the weaver clipped off the warp rods flush at the rim. This row of weaving created a subtle raised effect at the rim of the cap. Many caps had a loop of native cordage, or later a strip of cloth, at the start (at the top of the cap), apparently for grasping (Figure 3.5) (Fowler and Dawson 1986:712; Merriam 1955:121).

Owens Valley Paiute caps typically exhibited design elements that appeared in two and sometimes three bands. The third band tended to be narrower than the other two and consisted of one or two rows of twining. The widest band was always closest to the rim. The design element usually repeated itself in the two bands, although the number of elements varied with the circumference of the band.

The design elements were usually executed in winter-peeled, "sunburned" willow weft, a popular design material in many kinds of twined baskets made by the Owens Valley Paiutes. The weaving technique used is known as weft reversal. The weaver could twist the weft as it was twined to the outside, where the reddish colored side would be seen. Or when she turned the strand to show its white, inner side on the outer surface of the basket, the reddish colored side would be seen on the inside of the basket. This twisting resulted in a reversal of the design, with the opposite or negative of the design appearing on the inside of the basket (Figure 3.6).

After weaving was completed, the design on the cap was usually "painted" to add contrast and intensify its color. The painting was done with a mixture of chewed willow roots and water or a mixture of iron oxide and ephedra juice.[5] In either case, the concoction created

38   WEAVING A LEGACY

an indelible dye that immediately turned the reddish brown inner bark a bluish black or brownish black. Paint was carefully applied to the winter-peeled willow weft with a small, soft stick (Hudson n.d.:338, 1904a:33; Merriam n.d.a:506, 507; Steward 1933:70).

The patterns used by the Owens Valley Paiutes were traditional Numic designs,[6] patterns that were common to most of the Great Basin peoples. In addition to bands of vertical or horizontal zigzags (Sargent 1908b), common design elements included triangles (Figure 3.7), diamonds (Figure 3.8), crossed lines (Figure 3.9), a serrate (notched-edge) design angled off of slanted lines (Figure 3.10), and combinations of these elements (Figure 3.11). These patterns, arranged in horizontal bands, were usually enclosed by a solid border line at top and bottom.

These same patterns were also found on twined caps used by the Panamint Shoshones, making these caps virtually indistinguishable from those of the Owens Valley Paiutes and their provenance, therefore, difficult to determine (Figure 3.12a and b). The Panamint Shoshones are well documented as using these twined caps in their daily lives (Coville 1892: 357; Fowler and Dawson 1986:718; Kirk 1952: 80; Merriam n.d.a.:591, 592a, 592b), although they also used a coiled basketry cap (Fowler and Dawson 1986:707, 719; Kroeber 1925:591; Merriam 1955:124).[7] Ethnographer J. W. Hudson remarked on the Panamint Shoshone use of two styles of caps: "The coil and the lighter shuset (diagonally twined) ware with willow bark border. The latter is imported from the north" (1904a:33). From this comment, it is likely that at least in the early 1900s, many if not all Panamint Shoshone twined caps were made by Owens Valley Paiute weavers and imported for use by Panamint Shoshone women.[8]

Similar to the Owens Valley Paiute women's caps were the twined baskets that Northern Paiutes used as caps or bowls for eating or drinking (Fowler and Dawson 1986: 710). The Northern Paiute baskets differ in

Figure 3.5. Owens Valley Paiute Cap. Weaver unknown, ca. 1910. The loop, raised rim, and "black snake" design were typical elements in Owens Valley caps.

Figure 3.6. Weft Reversal Technique. The winter-peeled willow design on the cap's exterior is replaced with a lighter-colored willow on the inside. The outside band of twining does not appear on the interior, creating a design effect similar to that of the Northern Paiute cap shown in Figure 3.13.

that their design bands are not enclosed by a solid border line at the top and bottom and they are more rounded in form (Figure 3.13) (Lawrence E. Dawson, personal communication 1975; Moser 1986:24, no. 43).[9] In addition, the typical Northern Paiute cap has a most distinctive start. To begin, the weaver twined three pairs of warp rods with six or seven rows of plain twining. Then she crossed another set of warp rods over the first and secured the sets with six or seven rows of three-strand twining (Finger 2003a:68). By contrast, in the typical Owens Valley Paiute cap the weaver wrapped the initial rod crossings with strands of willow so that the beginning construction was not clearly visible (Finger 2003a:65).

Figure 3.7. Owens Valley Paiute Cap. Weaver, Mattie Sullivan, ca. 1910. Rows of triangles form the design. The grasping loop, here of brain-tanned deerskin, can be seen at the top of the cap.

Figure 3.8. Owens Valley Paiute Cap. Weaver unknown, ca. 1900. Two bands of stacked diamonds decorate this cap. Rows of three-strand twining were added to the start of the cap for extra strength.

Figure 3.9. Owens Valley Paiute Cap. Weaver, Mary Horton, ca. 1910. The crossed-line design that gives a net-like appearance results from weft reversal of the stacked-diamond design.

Changes in the lifestyle of the Owens Valley Paiutes, and their eventual wholesale adoption of non-Indian dress, diminished the need for basketry caps.[10] As early as 1908 Carroll S. Hartman wrote from Owens Valley: "Even caps are scarce — only the older women have any" (Hartman 1908:8). In 1918 collector Minnie C. Randolph wrote to her customer H. Shumway Lee about the difficulty of obtaining Paiute caps at that time: "The Paiute caps are not worn these days so are not made. It is years

since one has been offered . . . [although] several old weavers . . . have promised faithfully to make one" (1918).[11]

BURDEN BASKETS

Among the Owens Valley Paiutes, carrying or burden baskets, *cudu'si* or *wā'nü*, were conical shaped. The twined weave of the basket could be either open or closed, in plain or diagonal twining. The type of twining and the spacing of the rows of twining were dictated by the items to be carried in the basket. The weaver always worked from left to right (unless he or she was left-handed), warps held in an upright position, with the work surface on the exterior or convex surface.

A basket of very open, plain-twined construction with no decoration was often used to carry such items as wood and unopened piñon pinecones, as well as to transport more personal items such as blankets, clothing, or even smaller baskets. The start on some of these baskets, as well as the last row of twining at the basket's terminus, was often produced in three-strand twining. The warp rods were sturdy, scraped willow shoots, and the weft strands were split and peeled willow. At the termination of the basket the warp rods were bent, usually to the left, to form a bundle. This bundle of bent rods was then lashed together, incorporating the final row of twining, making a bundle selvedge. A thicker willow rod was then attached to the top of the bundle by coiling to add increased stability to the rim. These open-twined burden baskets were very sturdy, lightweight, easy to weave, and compared with close-twined examples, not very time-consuming to make (Figure 3.14).

The tip of a conical basket was somewhat rounded and sometimes covered with brain-tanned or untanned deerskin (or canvas, denim, or commercial leather from old boots during the postcontact period) for increased protection or repair. The Panamint Shoshones, as well as the Mono Lake Paiutes and Northern Paiutes, made similar, if not identical, baskets (Bates and Lee 1990:64; Fowler

1992:134; Fowler and Dawson 1986:710; Merriam 1902, 1955).

The Owens Valley Paiutes also used these open-twined burden baskets as fish traps. Unlike some other Paiute groups, the Owens Valley Paiutes apparently did not make fish-trap baskets per se. Openwork burden baskets were used as fish traps either by dragging them through the water or by fastening them below dams, where they trapped the fish coming over with the water (Steward 1933:25).

Other burden baskets were produced in twill or diagonal twining technique with a fineness of weave that ranged from medium to very fine and with rows of twining that ranged from slightly spaced to closely twined. The gradation of the weave was determined by the items to be carried. Closely twined baskets, *kob-un,* were used to gather grass seeds whereas more open-twined baskets likely held berries, fruits, nuts, and bulbs (Steward 1933:239, 272). The rims on these baskets were finished in the same way as those on the plain-twined burden baskets. These more finely twined burden baskets collected from Owens Valley Paiutes are identical in every respect to finely twined burden baskets collected from the Panamint Shoshones (see, for example, Figure 1.9).[12]

The more finely woven baskets required more time on the part of the weaver to produce, both for the gathering and preparing of materials and for the actual weaving. These burden baskets often exhibited one or more design bands within the upper quarter of the basket. Made from winter-peeled willow, design bands were virtually always enclosed within two solid lines. These designs were usually painted in the same fashion as on women's caps. In addition to the design bands, a band of simple checked pattern was often placed just below the rim finish, using the weft reversal technique in plain twining over paired or grouped warps (Figure 3.15). In conjunction with a twined seed beater, these baskets were used for gathering grass seeds.

On occasion, the bodies of close-twined burden baskets had one or more additional

Figure 3.10. Owens Valley Paiute Cap. Weaver unknown, ca. 1910. A common Numic pattern, the serrate or notched-edge design angled off of slanted lines, is used on this cap.

Figure 3.11. Owens Valley Paiute Cap. Weaver unknown, ca. 1910. The fancy pattern in the two bands combines horizontal zigzags with diamonds. A single row of winter-peeled willow at the top separates three-strand twining from diagonal twining.

design bands, produced in diagonal twining, as was the bulk of the basket. The design element within the succeeding bands was often a repetition of the original element, but sometimes it differed. Typically, on close-diagonal-twined baskets subtle textural variations appeared on the surface, resulting from the alternation of three-strand twining at the start, diagonal twining on the body, and plain twining over grouped warps just below the rim finish.

Most of the larger Owens Valley Paiute burden baskets were constructed for use with a tumpline. The basket rested against a woman's back, and the tumpline passed over her forehead to help balance the weight of the basket and to leave her hands free. A twined cap protected her head (see Figure 3.4). The tumpline, or strap, was made from buckskin and was attached to the basket well below the rim (Steward 1933:272). The place of tumpline

Figure 3.12. Two Panamint Shoshone and Owens Valley Paiute Caps: *(a)* Panamint Shoshone Cap. Weaver unknown, 1902. *(b)* Owens Valley Paiute Cap. Weaver unknown, 1909. The design and ferro-oxide staining on these two caps is remarkably similar, even though documentation shows them to be from two distinct locations.

Figure 3.13. Northern Paiute Cap, possibly Pyramid Lake. Weaver unknown, ca. 1910. The diamond design, also common among the Owens Valley Paiute, reverses on the exterior to a unique geometric pattern. This design, which was not enclosed to form a band, blurred when stained with a mixture of iron and ephedra. Two rows of three-strand twining finish the cap. The caps of the Northern Paiutes are generally not as large as those of the Owens Valley Paiutes.

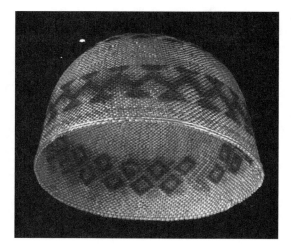

attachment varied, but usually it was somewhere in the upper quarter to third of the basket, closer to the rim rather than halfway down. The supports for this attachment were usually lashed in two places to the interior of the basket. Most often the interior attachment supports were made from a single, wider, short willow shoot. Occasionally, there were two short bundles of thinner willow shoots.

WINNOWING AND PARCHING TRAYS

When an Owens Valley Paiute woman processed and prepared food for herself and her family, she used several types of fan-shaped trays, called *tuma* or *pătsā'*, for winnowing, parching, and sifting. As with burden and gathering baskets, these twined trays exhibited open, intermediate, and closed weave. The shape and technology used in making the basket, as well as any ornamentation, was determined by the basket's intended function (Figure 3.16).

Although designed for different purposes, these various trays exhibited many similar technical traits. They were all woven from the small end, with the weaving progressing from left to right. When the right margin was reached, the tray was flipped over and the weaving again progressed from left to right. As the basket grew, more warp rods were added to increase its width. At the end of the weaving the warp rods were bent toward the middle of the last row of twining and then lashed with split willow into a bundle that included this last row of twining. All trays were fitted with a reinforcing willow rod attached around the perimeter for added strength. The warp rods, made of scraped willow shoots, usually protruded a short distance beyond this rim stick at the narrow, or beginning, end of the tray. Split and peeled willow strands were the usual weft material; winter-peeled willow weft was most often used for design elements, occasionally stained as on caps and burden baskets. Rarely, dyed bracken fern root or split redbud was used for the design weft strands.

To use a large, open-twined basket for winnowing piñon pine nuts, a woman held it in both hands and tossed the nuts into the air with a firm flick of her wrists. Air currents blew the lighter chaff away and left the remainder in the tray. These openwork trays had an additional single reinforcing rod that was lashed parallel to the rows of twining to the exterior, convex surface of the tray one-third to midway down from the wider end, usually at the widest point of the basket. The rod extended on each side slightly beyond the rim rod (Figure 3.17).

42 WEAVING A LEGACY

Some women preferred to hold the tray at this juncture of the rim and the exterior support rod when using it for winnowing or parching. Parching nuts was another use for this type of tray. Hot coals tossed in the tray with nuts cooked them evenly without burning.

Similar to the openwork winnowing or parching tray was a large tray with an even more open weave that was used as a strainer for larger foodstuffs. Food roots were placed in the tray to be washed and drained. Other diagonal-twined trays with medium-close spacing were used to sift acorn flour, to winnow grass seeds, or to strain foods.

Owens Valley Paiute close-twined trays were made in two shapes. A rounded, somewhat scoop-shaped tray was used most often as a sifter (Figure 3.18); a flatter, fan-shaped tray was used to catch ground meal as it came off the metate or grinding slab. Tightly woven trays were also used to winnow the flour produced from ground seeds or pounded acorns.

These closely and finely twined trays required more skill and work time, were often decorated, and were highly valued. The body of the basket was produced in diagonal twining. Complex design elements usually appeared in the upper quarter to upper third of the tray and were enclosed by a single horizontal line on the top and bottom of the pattern that gave the effect of a design band. Patterns within the bands were zigzag lines or other designs used on caps and burden baskets, produced in weft reversal technique. Between the design band and the warp selvedge were often several rows of plain twining over paired warps, producing a checked pattern (Figures 3.19 and 3.20).

SEED BEATERS

Seed beaters or flails, *tānāku*, were constructed of plain, open twining. The weaver began by trimming the butt ends of the warp rods and bending them over another rod, holding them neatly in place with a row of twining immediately above the other rod. Constructed on parallel warps of scraped willow shoots, the wefts were split, peeled willow shoots. The basket was woven in the same manner as a winnowing

Figure 3.14. Owens Valley Paiute Conical Burden Basket. Weaver, Mary Jim Harry, 1927. Used to carry such items as wood and pine cones, this burden basket has a tumpline that helped distribute the weight of the load.

Figure 3.15. Owens Valley Paiute Conical Seed Gathering Basket. Weaver, Mary Jim Harry, 1927. Conical in shape, diagonally twined burden baskets were used primarily to gather and transport seeds. This basket, reinforced at the tip with canvas, exhibits typical Owens Valley designs.

tray, except that at the end the warp rods were brought together to form the handle. A reinforcing rod, attached by coiling, went completely around the body of the beater, passing across the basket where the handle joined the main part of the basket.

Owens Valley Paiute seed beaters were commonly of two shapes. The first, which resembled those of the Washoes (Fowler and Dawson 1986:712) and Southern Sierra Miwoks,

Figure 3.16. Owens Valley Paiute Parching/Winnowing Tray. Weaver unknown, ca. 1915. This open-twined tray was made with scraped-willow warp rods that protrude at the narrow end of the tray. The weft material is peeled and split willow strands. A willow rod reinforces the perimeter. The darkened area in the middle shows the basket's use for parching.

Figure 3.17. Owens Valley Paiute Parching/Winnowing Tray, detail. Weaver unknown, ca. 1915. A reinforcing rod lashed horizontally across the tray extends beyond the supporting rim rod and marks the place where the tray should be held. This auxiliary rod is a unique feature of Owens Valley Paiute trays.

Figure 3.18. Owens Valley Paiute Sifter or Scoop. Weaver unknown, ca. 1901. The selvedge at the wide end of this scoop-shaped sifter is a transverse bundle of the folded-over warp rod ends. The bundle was sewn with split willow, and a rim stick was then sewn to the bundle.

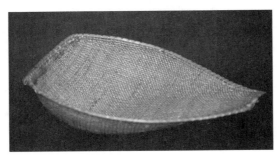

Figure 3.19. Owens Valley Paiute Winnowing/Sifting Tray. Weaver unknown, ca. 1901. The unique shape of this style of tray was well suited to meal sifting. Here the typical design band of horizontal zigzags appears below the checked band at the wide end of the basket.

possessed a short handle and was almost circular (Figure 3.21). The other, more typical type was longer and squared off at the end (Figure 3.22). It featured a tubular handle finished with diagonal twining (Fowler and Dawson 1986: 712). Women used beaters to dislodge seeds from plants, beating the ripe seed–bearing heads and directing the seeds into a closely woven burden basket held in the other hand. Seed beaters saw hard use, were brittle, and wore out relatively quickly. More important, the demise of native grasslands in Owens Valley, the subsequent obsolescence of seed beaters, and their lack of appeal as collectibles likely account for the relative rarity of these baskets.

WATER BOTTLES

The Owens Valley Paiute people used close-twined, bottle-shaped baskets, *kadu o'sa,* coated with piñon pine pitch to carry water. They used them both in their valley homes and on their gathering excursions to the upper elevations of the White Mountains and other nearby regions. Because other Paiute groups and the Panamint Shoshones had similar water bottles, it is difficult to differentiate among them. It may be that only reliable documentation can ascribe a particular tribal affiliation to a given specimen.

Water bottles were woven in close diagonal twining. Sections of the basket that required additional strength, such as the base, were often produced in three–strand twining, and rows of three–strand twining might also be included at the shoulder or near the neck. The use of three–strand twining at the start was identical to its use on burden baskets, women's caps, and twined bowls. This variation in weaving also provided a decorative variation in the texture of the basket. Although some water jars had flat bases, it seems that most traditionally began with a cone–shaped base that widened out to form a rounded shoulder and then tapered back in to form a narrow neck (Plate 4). Like the Northern Paiutes, after contact some Owens Valley Paiute weavers copied the shapes of the jugs and canteens used by Euro-Americans (Polanich 1994:129; Wheat 1967:25).

The pointed base and broad shoulder of a water basket ensured that it remained relatively upright when placed on the ground, preventing the contents from spilling. The broad middle part of the bottle acted as a fulcrum that allowed the mouth to let the water flow out and then immediately tipped the jug back to its former position. This design was convenient for filling other receptacles and for enabling a person to drink while reclining on the ground (Merriam 1901:n.p.). The unique shape also allowed the water jar to be carried securely inside a burden basket, with the pointed tip of the jar fitting into the pointed end of the burden basket. It also fit nicely against one's back for ease in carrying. Occasionally, water baskets were made with a flattened rather than pointed bottom.[13] Both shapes of water jugs were furnished with two short handles, of either native dogbane cordage or coarser horsehair cordage. The handles were woven into one side of the basket at or just above the shoulder. These loop handles allowed for easy attachment of a tumpline or rope to carry the basket on one's back or hang it from a tree or, later, the horn of a saddle.

Waterproofing a basket began by spreading ground and sifted red earth pigment over the exterior. Then piñon pitch, melted to a thin consistency, was poured into the basket and shaken with hot pebbles or small pieces of rock. The basket was turned with sticks or rolled back and forth on pine needles to help spread the pitch evenly on the inside. As the pitch leaked through the tightly woven basket, it sealed the weaving and made the basket watertight. The pitch drippings were then spread over the red ochre on the outside of the basket. Additional pitch was spread outside to produce an even finish (Hulse 1935:37, 207; Steward 1933:273).[14]

Basketry containers of this type were also made without a piñon pitch coating. These baskets were used to store grass seeds.

CRADLE BASKETS

Cradle baskets, *hūp*, offered convenience to mothers and security to babies. Several cradle styles were made, and in early times tanned

Figure 3.20. Exterior of Winnowing/Sifting Tray, 1901. Note the textural designs, produced by the alternation of the rounded side of the split willow strands on every other row, alternating with the split or flat face on the intervening rows. The result is a slight difference in color and sheen.

Figure 3.21. Owens Valley Paiute Seed Beater. Weaver unknown, ca. 1910. Seed beaters were used to dislodge seeds from a plant directly into a close-twined burden basket. Subjected to rough usage during this process, few seed beaters survive in museum collections. The parallel warp construction is typical of most seed beaters in the Great Basin and eastern California.

Figure 3.22. Owens Valley Paiute Seed Beater. Weaver, Mary Westerville, 1927. The paddle-shaped seed beater, constructed on parallel warps, was the most common form.

deerskin strips or native dogbane cordage loops were made along each side of the back of the cradle, and another strip of hide or length of cordage passed through them, securing the snugly wrapped infant in the cradle. After contact, strips of commercial cloth or commercial leather usually replaced the native materials. A wider strap attached to the backside of the cradle served as a tumpline. It passed across a mother's forehead, allowing her to carry the cradle basket on her back and have her hands free.

The Owens Valley Paiutes made few preparations for a baby before its birth. Once the baby was born, it was wrapped in rabbit skins or other soft material. The child was then kept in an old basket or was secured with buckskin onto an improvised cradle basket made by cutting a seed beater down to the proper size (Hartman n.d.; Nicholson n.d.a; Steward 1933:290; Wheat 1967:98).[15]

Traditionally, once the mother was up to the task, she was expected to start and finish a regular cradle basket in one day. If she was unable to carry out this responsibility, the privilege of making the cradle basket fell to a relative; her husband's sister or either of the child's grandmothers are usually cited as the preferred relatives for this task. After the baby was safely moved to its new cradle basket, the temporary cradle was taken away and hidden so that it would not be used again for any purpose. Sometimes another cradle was made for the child if it outgrew its first cradle before it could walk. Around 1900 the cradle baskets used by a child were always taken and hidden or "thrown away" and never burned or used for another child (Hartman n.d.; Nicholson n.d.a; Steward 1933:273, 290).

Around 1900 the Owens Valley Paiutes made three styles of cradles. All consisted of two pieces: a flat back and a sunshade. The cradle backs were different in each style, but the sunshade was always the same. This sunshade or hood was woven separately and attached to the back of the cradle. The weaver began the hood by binding seven to eleven willow rods, each about a quarter of an inch in diameter, to a number of finer, smaller, scraped willow shoots. The fine shoots made up the sunshade, and the larger rods held the shade in position above the baby's head. The binding that held these two planes of rods together was usually done with strips of commercial fabric, yarn, or string and could be used to produce distinctive patterns across the hood. Connecting patterns, such as zigzag lines and connecting diamonds, identified female babies. Designs

that did not connect, especially spaced parallel diagonal lines, often arranged in groups of three, identified males. After this pattern was completed, the fine rods were held together with spaced, paired rows of diagonal twining using split willow shoots.

On the first type of cradle the flat back was woven in spaced rows of plain or diagonal twining with willow warps and wefts. The warp rods were usually more than a quarter of an inch in diameter at the base. The basket had at least two short, half-inch-diameter rods that were lashed horizontally across the reverse of the cradle back. These stabilized the cradle back and kept it from twisting or breaking. Animal or bird skins, and later small quilts or commercial blankets, padded the twined back (Figure 3.23).[16] These cradles were identical to those used by the Mono Lake Paiutes.

The second type of cradle basket was the bound-weave variety, which was constructed in a double-warp style with the back made up of two layers. The term bound-weave referred to the fact that the two layers of warps — one arranged horizontally and the other vertically — were bound together with single weft elements. Horizontal willow rods comprised the exterior layer. The interior layer, on which the infant was laid, had vertical rods. The ends of these vertical rods were twined together and extended beyond the horizontal rods. The two layers were lashed together with dyed sinew or cordage and, later, yarn, rag strips, or commercial string.[17] This binding resulted in specific geometric patterns; as on hoods, connecting diamonds were for girls, and diagonal lines were for boys (Figure 3.24). These bound-weave cradle backs are very similar to prehistoric examples found at Anasazi and Fremont culture sites in Colorado, Utah, and New Mexico that likely date to A.D. 500–1200. It is possible that the Anasazi brought this cradle style into southern Nevada during their western expansion and the resident Paiute people began to imitate the style (Bates and Lee 1990:197–198 n. 27; Lawrence E. Dawson, personal communication 1974, 1979; Steward 1933:273).

After contact, but perhaps not until early in the twentieth century, a third type of cradle basket that was covered with buckskin was introduced to Owens Valley (Figure 3.25). Its origins are attributed to Northern Shoshone–Bannock people, from whom the Northern Paiutes copied the style. In turn, it was imitated by the Mono Lake Paiutes and Owens Valley Paiutes (Fowler and Dawson 1986:449). To make this cradle, a weaver used two chokecherry shoots, a half-inch or more in diameter, bending and lashing them together at the sides to form an ovoid frame. Next she attached horizontal braces to the frame for support. A mattress made of willow warps and wefts with spaced rows of plain twining, nearly identical to the simple plain-twined cradle back, was tied to the braces, and a cover was made of brain-tanned, and usually smoked, deerskin. After centering the cradle frame on the hide, the weaver folded and trimmed the hide and sewed it around the top edge and in the center of the upper portion of the cradle. The lower portion was furnished on each side with deerskin loops for lacing. The cradle was usually ornamented with strips of fringe on either side of these lacings and across the back of the cradle near the top. Often the cover was decorated with geometric or floral beaded patterns. Finally, a twined hood with gender-identifying designs, exactly like those used on the other cradles, was attached.[18] These cradles, often highly decorated with beaded patterns, were considered extra fancy by the Owens Valley Paiutes, who may have begun to use them in the second decade of the twentieth century.

PIAGUI BASKETS

The *piagui* basket, *gūnū,* was a radial-warp container used to gather and hold the larvae of the Pandora moth, *piagui.* This basket was made identically by the Owens Valley and Mono Lake Paiutes. Scraped willow shoots were used for the rods, and peeled, split-willow strands for the wefts. These baskets were usually woven in widely spaced rows of plain twining, although occasionally diagonal twining was used. The spaced rows of open-

work allowed for air circulation and kept the larvae alive until they could be processed. Typically, these baskets were rounded at the base with numerous rows of three-strand twining used for the start, as in most other radial-warp baskets. The rim finish was identical to that described for burden baskets, although frequently a reinforcing rim stick was not sewn to the bound bundle of warp rods. The basket tapered slightly at the top to form a narrower neck to prevent the escape of the larvae (Figure 3.26). When not used in harvesting *piagui,* collecting baskets found use as containers to hold all manner of objects and were often suspended within the home or from trees nearby (Bates and Lee 1990:68; Fowler and

Figure 3.23. Anna Garrison and Her Daughter Sadie, 1916. The two-piece, flat-back cradle basket shown here was woven with spaced rows of plain twining. The zigzag design on the shade indicates that the cradle basket was intended for a baby girl. The child in the cradle, Sadie, died when she was about two years old. She was survived by Anna and Henry Garrison's other children, Howard, Andrew, Lloyd, Della, and Sally.

Figure 3.24. Owens Valley Paiute Model Cradle Basket. Weaver, Mary Jim Harry, 1927. With the edges bound with black cloth, this bound-weave cradle basket is constructed with both horizontal and vertical rods. Slanted lines on the shade indicate a baby boy.

Dawson 1986:714; Merriam 1955:122; Steward 1933:256).[19]

Pandora moth larvae, perhaps the second largest food crop (after pine nuts) of the Owens Valley Paiutes, were rich in fat and protein. Preserved larvae were boiled with water, seasoned to taste, and eaten like meat. They were also used extensively for trade (Fowler and Dawson 1986:419; Hulse 1935:153; Liljeblad and Fowler 1986:410).

BOILING OR MUSH BOWLS

Unlike the Mono Lake Paiutes and the Western Monos, who made great use of twined mush bowls, the Owens Valley Paiutes relied mostly on pottery containers for cooking mush and soup (Liljeblad and Fowler 1986:421; Fowler and Dawson 1986:712).[20] Nonetheless, a few documented examples of Owens Valley Paiute baskets, much like the twined cooking baskets of their neighbors, exist in museum collections. Called *pot-en*, at least by the Paiute people in

Independence (Merriam n.d.b), extant specimens are identical to Mono Lake Paiute examples: three–strand twining at the start, diagonal twining in the basket's body, narrow design bands of sunburned willow, and a rim selvedge identical to that on burden baskets.[21] Whether these baskets were produced locally or were imported from the Mono Lake Paiutes to the north is uncertain.

SUGAR AND BERRY HARVESTERS

Owens Valley Paiutes wove a specific type of basket, *pă–să–vi–tci',* used for harvesting berries and storing "sugar" from native cane (Hudson 1904a:40).[22] Produced with whole tule stalks, the basket was made with spaced rows of diagonal twining on parallel warps rather than with the radial warps that typified other container baskets. The start of this type of basket was also unique, occurring at the wide end instead of at the narrow end as in other parallel-warp baskets. The tules used to make the basket were likely partly dried until they were flexible and resilient, and the basket then made immediately. It is also possible that the basket was made from dried, winter tules that had been soaked in water to make them flexible (Figure 3.27).[23]

Across the Great Basin and areas of California where it was common, tule was used in ancient times to make a variety of items, including duck decoys, sandals, houses, clothing, and baskets.[24] By historic times, Paiute people were producing few tule baskets. It is likely that this type of sugar and berry harvester, represented today by only one extant specimen (Figure 3.27), is a survivor of the once widespread style of quickly made, disposable baskets of tule (Fowler 1990, 1992:118–121).[25]

COILED BASKETRY

Although there is no archaeological evidence to date the earliest existence of coiled basketry, it likely first appeared in California between 2000 and 1500 B.C. (Dawson 1975) and thus is a much newer textile form than twining. Coiling may have been developed by individual groups of people in different locations at about the same time. It is thought to have spread outward from people who lived in interior desert regions (Adovasio 1974:125). Unlike the twining tradition, which was already well grounded with an entire body of rules for technology and use, the newer coiled baskets had no established rule structure. Weavers were therefore much more innovative with this form.

To produce a coiled basket, Owens Valley Paiute weavers wrapped a pliant sewing strand around a foundation that spiraled in an upward direction and usually was made of three scraped, unsplit willow rods. The primary sewing strands were split willow shoots, prepared as described previously for twined baskets. Unlike the foundation rods in twined baskets, the foundation rods in coiled baskets had to be of exactly the same diameter from one end to the other and thus were carefully scraped and sized prior to weaving. Originally, weavers used obsidian flakes for this task but sometime before the 1930s switched to steel knives or pieces of glass (Steward 1933:270).

The coiling process used only a single specialized tool, an awl, *wi'nivep*. It traditionally was made of a cactus needle from the Inyo Mountains, with a knob handle made of the glue-like lac from the creosote bush. This tool was replaced, in postcontact times, by a metal awl. Weavers used awls to make holes in the top rod of the lower foundation bundle, enabling the sewing strand to pass through and bind coils together tightly. Each stitch went through the top rod of the bundle in the coil below to anchor the coils together. The stitches in successive coiling rows in the baskets of the Owens Valley Paiutes did not interlock (Figure 3.28) (Steward 1933:270–271).

Typically, Owens Valley Paiute baskets coiled to the left. This meant that the ends of the foundation materials extended to the weaver's left and that each successive stitch was placed to the left of the one before it. The work surface, that is, the surface from which the weaver inserted the sewing strand, was usually the exterior side. As one looked at the work surface, the sewing stitches appeared to slant upward to the right.

Bishop Harvest Festival Indian Baby Show. 1916.   Forbes 2340

Figure 3.25. Bishop Harvest Festival Indian Baby Show, 1916. The unidentified baby boy in the buckskin-covered cradle basket in the lower center of the picture won a prize in the Baby Show at the Bishop Harvest Festival in 1916.

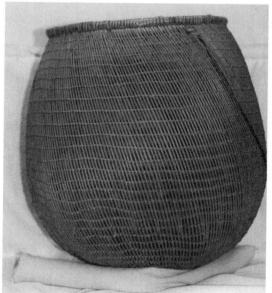

Figure 3.26. Owens Valley Paiute *Piagui* Gathering Basket. Weaver, Hattie Jones, ca. 1910. Hattie Jones won the Best Collection of Baskets prize at the 1916 Bishop Harvest Festival. Many of her baskets are included in the MacQueen Collection at the Los Angeles County Museum of Natural History. This type of basket was used to gather and transport the larvae of the Pandora moth, *piagui*.

Owens Valley Paiute weavers used a variety of materials to create designs on their coiled basketry. Bracken fern root was probably obtained in trade from the western side of the

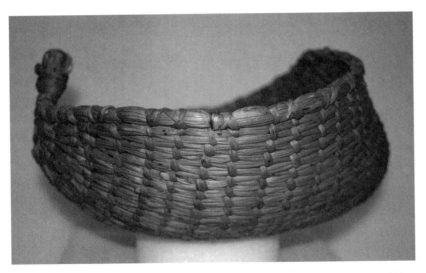

Figure 3.27. Owens Valley Paiute Berry and Sugar Harvesting Basket. Weaver unknown, 1904. This basket was constructed entirely with whole, unsplit tule stems using diagonal twining. It likely represents a type of quickly made and disposable basket that was little produced after metal containers, cloth bags, and tin cans became available.

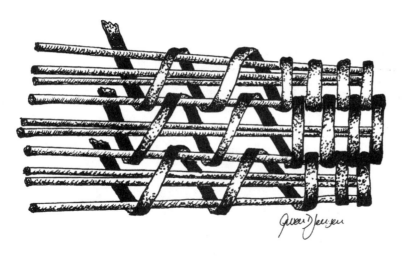

Figure 3.28. Three-Rod Coiling. This rendering shows the noninterlocked stitching technique that was traditionally found in Owens Valley coiled baskets.

artistic" (Hudson 1904a:56) but was used rarely in Owens Valley Paiute baskets. The roots turned jet black when soaked in water in a rusty tin can, much as bracken fern root was stained. Some weavers at Lone Pine used mud to turn the roots black (Esteves 1983).

From the Panamint Shoshones, Owens Valley Paiute weavers obtained the long seed-pods of devil's claw, which provided a natural black thread. The devil's claw had itself been introduced to the Panamint Shoshones by Hungry Bill, a Panamint Shoshone who had visited Fort Mohave, Arizona, where he saw the Indian people using the material in their baskets. He brought home some seeds and planted them in Johnson Canyon.[26] Panamint Shoshone weavers found the material to their liking, and it became a common design material in their coiled baskets. Even though this plant was occasionally cultivated in small amounts in Owens Valley, it was not used often in Owens Valley Paiute coiled baskets, although its popularity may have increased between 1930 and 1960. It was during that period that Panamint Shoshone weavers moved to Owens Valley and women such as Sarah Hunter and Mamie Joaquin Button cultivated devil's claw in their gardens on Rawson Creek, south of Bishop (Armstrong 1992:26; Nabhan 1987:146–148; Smith and Simpson n.d.:46; Raymond Stone, personal communication 1975).

Joshua tree root, also called yucca, and split redbud shoots, acquired by trade, provided a red color for coiled basketry patterns. The dark red strands of split redbud came primarily from Western Mono and Yokuts peoples in Kings and Madera Counties on the western side of the Sierras. The yucca, which ranged from orange to a deep red, was imported from the Death Valley and Mojave Desert regions (Hudson 1904a:55).

The use of split redbud shoots and bracken fern root became more prevalent in Owens Valley after 1910. The opening of Tioga Pass to automobile traffic in 1915 and the increased use of the U.S. mail enabled people and basket materials to travel more easily across the Sierra Nevada.[27] In addition, both the display

Sierras. The root was boiled with ashes to produce a dead-black color (Hudson 1904a:56). It is likely that Owens Valley weavers used other means to darken the root as well, such as soaking it for several days in a mixture of water and decaying vegetable material, rusty metal, acorn flour, or other materials. These dyeing methods were the ones preferred by their Mono Lake Paiute and Western Mono neighbors, who used the bracken fern root extensively (Bates and Lee 1990:61, 63). Bulrush root, sometimes referred to locally as *tule,* was found sparingly in the canyons. It yielded a brownish black that was "smooth and quite

of "imported" baskets at the Bishop Harvest Days and the relocation of some Yosemite–Mono Lake weavers to Owens Valley helped foster familiarity with non-indigenous materials.[28]

THE DIFFUSION OF COILING TRADITIONS TO THE OWENS VALLEY PAIUTES

In order to understand how the Western Mono, Southern Sierra Miwok, and Yokuts peoples from the western slope of the Sierra influenced basket making in the eastern Sierra, one needs to understand the relationship between the Western Monos and the Owens Valley Paiutes. The Owens Valley Paiutes (and the Mono Lake Paiutes) were — and sometimes continue to be — called Eastern Monos. The Western Monos descended from the Eastern Monos, who migrated in three separate waves across the Sierra Nevada during the last five hundred years. It has been suggested that the Owens Valley Paiutes learned coiling from the Western Monos, who in turn had learned it from their Yokuts neighbors (Polanich 1994, 1995).

Certainly, the basketry of the Western Mono and Yokuts peoples had many traits in common. The foundations were composed of a grass bundle, the sewing strands were sedge root, and the design materials were bracken fern root and redbud. Both types of baskets exhibited noninterlocking stitches. The Yokuts coiled in a rightward direction. The Western Monos, however, coiled in either a rightward or a leftward direction. The leftward coil direction was the only direction used by their Miwok neighbors to the northwest and by the Mono Lake Paiutes and Washoes to the north (Bates 1982:5–6; Bates and Lee 1990:52, 63; Polanich 1994).

Owens Valley Paiute people may have learned coiling from the Western Monos; certainly, the baskets from each group are made in noninterlocking stitching. However, Owens Valley Paiute coiled basketry is often impossible to differentiate from Mono Lake Paiute coiled basketry, which is very similar to Washoe and Sierra Miwok coiled basketry. Curiously,

Mono Lake coiled basketry is produced either in interlocking or noninterlocking stitch. The Mono Lake Paiutes had long-established trading patterns with the Central and Southern Sierra Miwoks and may have borrowed some of their basket-making techniques (Bates and Lee 1990:23; Steward 1933:257). The interaction between Mono Lake and Owens Valley Paiutes suggests that the flow of ideas and materials up and down the corridor of eastern California influenced the basketry of all these Paiute peoples. In the final analysis, it is uncertain where and from whom the Owens Valley Paiutes first learned to make coiled baskets. To be sure, it appears that their coiled basketry was influenced by the Western Monos and Mono Lake Paiutes and likely by other groups. By the beginning of the twentieth century their coiled ware was, in technology and materials, much like that of their Mono Lake Paiute neighbors.

Coiled basketry did not play as important a role for the Owens Valley Paiutes as it did among neighboring tribes, both before and after contact. The late arrival (likely after A.D. 1500) of coiled basketry, the long tradition of twined forms, and the common usage of pottery may help explain the overall lack of standardized coiled basketry forms among the Owens Valley Paiutes. Another reason for the paucity of coiled baskets may have been that the darker design materials, which might be thought to evoke a weaver's creativity, had to be imported. Winter-peeled willow, Owens Valley's most common design material, was difficult to work with in coiled basketry (Hudson 1904a:62). In addition, the Owens Valley Paiutes did not use coiled baskets for boiling (Driver 1937:65, 78; Hudson 1904a:53; Steward 1933:242, 246). Finally, the Owens Valley Paiutes seem to have obtained many coiled baskets in trade from neighboring groups, especially the Western Monos and Yokuts (Gayton 1948:56, 258–259). Perhaps this ready source of coiled baskets, and the preponderance of twined basket forms and pottery, made the manufacture of coiled baskets largely unnecessary.

TYPES OF COILED BASKETRY

Few definitive statements can be made about traditional Owens Valley Paiute coiled baskets because there are not many well-documented examples in museum collections. It is possible that, as already mentioned, the Owens Valley Paiutes made very few coiled baskets and that their manufacture increased as a market for baskets developed among Euro-Americans. Even with the advent of the curio trade during the late nineteenth and early twentieth centuries (see Chapter 4), it seems that collectors were not particularly eager to acquire Owens Valley Paiute coiled baskets, perhaps because these baskets were not laden with designs and the workmanship was sometimes considered inferior to that of weavers in other groups, such as the Washoes and Panamint Shoshones (Hartman 1908:8; Steward 1933:270).

The Owens Valley Paiutes used small coiled baskets with a flat base and truncated cone shape for preparing pine nut soup. This soup was a staple food, often prepared and eaten cold though sometimes boiled in a clay pot. Similarly, acorn mush was usually boiled in clay pots, thus eliminating the need for the cooking baskets used by neighboring tribes. Most coiled cooking bowls found in Owens Valley appear to have been made by weavers of other tribes (Figure 3.29) (Steward 1933: 242, 246).

Mixing bowls, ă'pӑ, were about eight inches in diameter and shaped like a half-sphere with a flat bottom; occasionally, they were slightly oval in shape. Weavers Sarah Hill and Mary Yandell were known to have made this kind of basket, and it was this type that was most commonly made for sale to non-Indian

collectors in the early twentieth century (Figure 3.30). Like other coiled baskets, these small baskets were made from willow on a three-rod foundation. They coiled in a leftward direction and had stitches appearing to lean upward to the right. Their designs were simple geometric forms such as zigzags, diamonds, rectangles, and triangles. Usually, these designs were worked in bracken fern root and redbud, although sometimes devil's claw was used. Except for the use of devil's claw, bulrush, and yucca, the baskets made by Owens Valley Paiute women are nearly identical to those made by the Mono Lake Paiutes, Northern Paiutes, and Washoes. Thus sometimes baskets made by women in these four groups are virtually indistinguishable.

The Owens Valley Paiutes are also reported to have made, or at least used, large, flat, coiled sifting trays, sa'ku (Figure 3.31) (Driver 1937: 78; Steward 1933:271).[29] Trays collected from the Owens Valley Paiutes are identical in every way, including a rightward coil direction, to trays collected from the Panamint Shoshones.[30] It is likely that the trays collected from the Owens Valley Paiutes were obtained in trade.

The Owens Valley Paiutes also wove coiled bottleneck-form gift or treasure baskets, pŏ'nŏ. These baskets were used to hold shell-bead money, finely made belts and collars of glass seed beads, especially valued arrow points, and other items of great personal importance (Doyle 1934:162). Sometimes filled with food for the dead and used as mortuary jars, this type of basket, whose prototype was likely the diagonal-twined water jar (Hudson 1904a: 34), resembled the bottleneck baskets of the Yokuts and Western Monos, although it differed in having a narrower base and neck with rounded shoulders (Figure 3.32) (Hudson 1904a:n.p.; Merriam n.d.a:497). There are few extant examples, possibly because they were very rarely made by the time non-Indians were collecting baskets (Fowler and Dawson 1986:714; Hudson 1904a:62). Those that exist today were collected from the southern end of the valley around Olancha and Lone Pine (Hudson 1904a:34). The majority of these

Figure 3.29. Western Mono Cooking Basket. Weaver unknown, ca. 1901. C. Hart Merriam purchased this basket from an elderly Paiute woman at her camp a few miles west of Bishop. She identified it as a "ceremonial cooking basket" and told him it came from the other side of the mountains. It is a typical Western Mono basket in materials, construction, and pattern.

baskets appear to be of Panamint Shoshone manufacture, based on a rightward coil direction, rim ticking, material selection, and a characteristic banding that encloses the body of the design.[31]

For years, such similarities among coiled baskets made by the Yokuts, Western Mono, Tubatulabal, Kawaiisu, Owens Valley Paiute, and Panamint Shoshone peoples have frustrated collectors and scholars. Some of these baskets, which seem to exhibit the attributes of two or more groups, may be evidence of *border blur,* a term that describes the sharing of ethnographic traits by people living in tribal border areas. Such cultural diffusion of basket traits resulted from trade, intermarriage, cultural borrowing, and geographic mobility. This mobility increased in the twentieth century with access to modern means of transportation and travel for wage labor, facilitating an increase in the blending and sharing of certain practices, including facets of basketry. To further complicate the issue, early collectors often assigned attributions based on place of collection (Figure 3.33).

Coiled, spaced-stitch, single-rod baskets, produced in noninterlocking stitching, which are found in collections made ca. 1900 and later, were made by Owens Valley Paiute women and are often indistinguishable from those made by Mono Lake Paiutes and Washoes.[32] Always produced with split willow shoots on a single-rod foundation of scraped willow, these baskets took less time to produce than close-stitched, single-rod ones. The baskets have a distinctive appearance due to the use of noninterlocking stitching. When evenly spaced, the stitches of succeeding rows stack up in vertical rib-like elements, with a section of exposed foundation rods producing a "gap" between the stitches.[33] Horizontal bands of pattern were made with bracken fern root or redbud (Figure 3.34). Vertical lines could be produced by alternating several stitches of design material with the lighter willow sewing strands. In Owens Valley, weavers such as Sally Jackson and Emma Harry wove baskets in this style.[34] Other variations in pattern involved using the

Figure 3.30. Owens Valley Paiute Coiled Basket. Weaver unknown, ca. 1920. This basket is typical of those made by Owens Valley Paiute women for sale to non-Indians. The stepped pattern was used by many Owens Valley Paiute weavers, including Mary Yandell (see Figure 3.79).

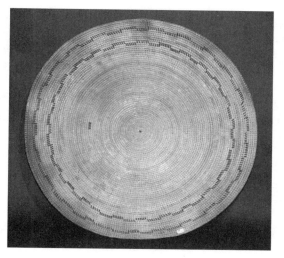

Figure 3.31. Owens Valley Paiute (?) Circular Sifting Tray. Weaver unknown, ca. 1909. Merriam obtained this winnowing tray during one of his field trips to Owens Valley. The tray is identical to Panamint Shoshone ones, including the use of a rightward coil direction. Thus it may have been obtained in trade, although Merriam attributed it to an Owens Valley Paiute weaver.

Figure 3.32. Owens Valley Paiute (?) Bottleneck Basket. Weaver unknown, ca. 1904. Although this basket with a step design was identified by Hudson as Paiute, its provenance is questionable. Unlike other Paiute baskets, it uncharacteristically coils to the right and has ticking on the rim, both hallmarks of Panamint Shoshone basketry.

design material to produce squares, stepped rectangles, and other motifs.

A second style of spaced-stitch, coiled basket was produced in noninterlocking stitching with split-willow sewing strands, on a three-rod foundation, usually in an open bowl form. These baskets were always very neatly made and usually used willow rods one-eighth inch or more in diameter with sewing strands

Figure 3.33. Owens Valley Paiute Unfinished (?) Bowl. Weaver unknown, ca. 1902. Although purchased in Independence and identified as Petonaguat (Monache Paiute), this basket has many Panamint characteristics. Devil's claw and bulrush root were materials commonly used together by Panamint weavers. The flicker quills were another Panamint feature. Merriam's comments in his field notes that the basket was unfinished because "it needs a black ring and 2 or 3 light coils to complete the top" referred to the Panamint style of enclosing a basket's pattern at top and bottom with dark rings and then adding several rows of coiling. The basket is also woven in a rightward coil direction, typical of the Panamint Shoshones and not the Owens Valley Paiutes.

Figure 3.34. Owens Valley Paiute Spaced-Stitched Basket. Weaver unknown, ca. 1900. A variety of horizontal patterns were typically made on space-stitched baskets using bracken fern root or redbud.

Figure 3.35. Owens Valley Paiute Spaced-Stitched Three-Rod Basket. Weaver, Emma Westerville Harry, ca. 1930. The weaving of a lid for a basket was a post-contact feature, popular in the first few decades of the twentieth century. The traditional step design is repeated twice on the basket.

of similar width. Designs on these baskets, commonly produced with both bracken fern root and redbud, were extremely varied. Baskets of this type, made in very large sizes, were referred to as "laundry baskets" based on their use by both Paiute and non-Indian families. Smaller, globular ones, a foot in diameter or less, were used as general receptacles by Paiutes and also found favor among non-Indian collectors. Occasionally, these baskets were made with lids (Figure 3.35).

Perhaps the most noted maker of this three-rod, gap-stitched large basket was the Mono Lake Paiute weaver Nellie Charlie, who lived with her sister, Tina Charlie, in Owens Valley for part of her life. Besides making baskets of this type for the non-Indian market, Nellie made them for her children and grandchildren (Figure 3.36). She created a variety of forms, including straight-sided baskets for holding knitting materials; a large, straight-walled bassinet; and mats for use under hot dishes on dining tables. Nellie Charlie's output of these baskets may have exceeded that of any other weaver. Certainly, the most extant, documented examples are from this remarkably prolific and artistic woman. Tina Charlie also made space-stitched coiled baskets, as did relatives Carrie Bethel and Minnie Mike, who lived north of Owens Valley near Lee Vining. These women produced baskets in this style through the 1960s.

MADE-FOR-SALE BASKETS

At the same time that the use of baskets declined at the end of the nineteenth century because of the availability of metal containers and other changes in the lives of the Owens Valley Paiutes, the interest and demand for Indian baskets among Euro-American collectors soared. Throughout the western United States baskets were traded or sold to obtain non-Indian products, which were increasingly part of native households (Bernstein 1985:5). As baskets were bartered for goods and services, weavers quickly learned what materials, forms, and designs appealed to non-Indian people. Laundry, sewing, and small gift baskets became commonplace in local non-Indian homes. Some collectors amassed a hundred or more baskets. The making of baskets was a business for Indian women, and thus the role of baskets in native society changed. Women enjoyed weaving baskets, and the products of their labor had become valuable and marketable commodities. Author Mary Austin, when living in Independence, described the situation succinctly, writing about an Owens Valley Paiute woman: "Seyavi made baskets for love and sold them for money, in a generation that preferred iron pots for utility" (Austin 1903:236).

By the early 1900s the manufacture of baskets for sale to non-Indians increased, and weavers sold baskets to visiting tourists, Indian artifact dealers, and basket collectors. Because non-Indian collectors generally preferred coiled baskets with fancy patterns to plainer, utilitarian baskets, these fancier baskets brought more in exchange or by purchase. To make their baskets more saleable to non-Indian buyers, Owens Valley weavers sometimes borrowed materials and designs from neighboring groups, especially those on the west side of the Sierras, or created new patterns or copied motifs from other sources (Figure 3.37). Owens Valley weavers saw how popular Panamint Shoshone baskets were with collectors and sometimes copied them. Except for coil direction (Panamint Shoshone baskets coil to the right whereas Owens Valley Paiute baskets coil to the left), such copies made by Owens Valley Paiutes are nearly indistinguishable from baskets made by Panamint Shoshones (Plate 5).

These baskets became known as "made-for-sale" baskets. New patterns entered the repertoire, including naturalistic animals, plants, and human motifs, as well as the duplication of embroidery and needlework patterns weavers saw in catalogs or instruction books (Figure 3.38).[35] Weavers Sally and Susie Jackson Jim, for example, used new-style floral patterns in their baskets, likely ultimately derived from these sources (Figures 3.39 and 3.40). The selection of basket shapes expanded to include lidded baskets, teacups and teapots, and baskets with pedestal bases. Ironically, as tourists looked for traditional Indian baskets, they encouraged the production of these nontraditional forms, which sold well. As a result, baskets were transformed from utilitarian objects into not only commodities but also art objects with no function. In time, non-Indian buyers sometimes showed preference for the artistry of some weavers over others (Bates and Lee 1988, 1990:73–89; Bernstein 1985; John Kania, personal communication 1999).

Woven beadwork, produced with glass seed beads, spread into eastern California in

Figure 3.36. Mono Lake Paiute Space-Stitched Three-Rod Basket. Weaver, Nellie Charlie, ca. 1950. Still in use today by Charlie's descendants, this basket was shellacked to protect it. This coating darkened the basket. Charlie made many baskets of this type for her relatives to use about their homes.

Figure 3.37. Mono Lake Paiute Flared Bowl. Weaver, Annie Poole McBride, ca. 1915. McBride's basket is a Paiute copy of the Western Mono baskets that were highly prized trade items among the Paiutes and were readily saleable to non-Indians. The interruption of the horizontal bands with vertical bands, which Merriam (1966–67:109) called a "bipolar pattern layout," is a typical feature of Western Mono basketry.

Figure 3.38. Owens Valley Paiute Lidded Basket. Weaver, Mary Gorman, ca. 1910. With realistic figures, words, lid, and small form, this bowl has all the typical features of a made-for-sale basket. It is identical in workmanship and patterns to a basket made by Joe Eugley, also collected by Rose Black and in the Eastern California Museum.

the late nineteenth century (Bates and Lee 1990:79), introducing a new set of patterns.[36] Eight-pointed stars and serrated diamonds were among the most popular of these new motifs, which were often incorporated into baskets made for sale. Weavers in the Mono

Figure 3.39. Mono Lake Paiute Coiled Basket. Weaver, Susie Jackson Jim, ca. 1915. Susie Jackson Jim was born in Mono County, but by the time this basket was made she lived near Bishop. Each flower has two sets of leaves, whose graceful curves contrast with the central straight stem. A regular triangle forms the head of the flower. The design on this basket is repeated eight times, with the only variation appearing in the base of the flower. Susie Jackson must have developed this new style from patterns she had seen in print.

Lake area first made baskets with beaded coverings in about 1908, and neighboring tribes soon adopted this form (Bates and Lee 1990: 80–81; 1993). By the 1920s the new type had reached Owens Valley, where Sally and Susie Jackson Jim excelled in making large, bottleneck, beaded baskets (Plate 6).

In California the greatest demand for made-for-sale baskets in the first half of the twentieth century was largely in the areas most frequented by tourists: Death Valley, Lake Tahoe, Pasadena, and Yosemite Valley. Since Owens Valley was not, at that time, a primary tourist destination, there were few venues for exhibiting and selling made-for-sale baskets there. Weavers began selling their wares to the few collectors who sought out baskets locally, and they participated in such community fairs as the Bishop Harvest Festival. Some may have attended the more highly publicized Indian Field Days in Yosemite Valley.

The Indian Field Days took place each summer from 1916 to 1926 and again in 1929.

Figure 3.40. Mono Lake Paiute Coiled Basket. Weaver, Sally Jackson Jim, ca. 1915. Sally Jackson Jim, like her sister Susie Jackson Jim, was a weaver of coiled baskets with creative patterns. On this basket two triangular shapes broaden and meet in the middle to form a flower. The fleur-de-lis motif was an old decorative feature in European arts but would have been an innovative design among Native Americans. The alternating design appears to represent some type of plant.

Part of the gathering's purpose was to help local Indian people maintain their traditional handicrafts as a vital part of their lives (Bates and Lee 1990:91). There were rodeo events, baby contests, basketry competitions, and beadwork displays, and cash prizes were awarded. Some of the most exciting and innovative baskets of the 1920s, produced by talented artists of Mono Lake Paiute or Miwok–Mono Lake Paiute ancestry, were displayed at the Field Days.

Weavers of neighboring tribes, including the Owens Valley Paiutes, were likely influenced by the success of those weavers. Whether at the Indian Field Days or at the homes of certain of these weavers when they lived in or near Owens Valley, Owens Valley women were exposed to finely woven coiled baskets with new design motifs and materials. In order to appeal to the tastes of tourists and collectors who visited Yosemite National Park, Owens Valley Paiute weavers emulated these highly decorative baskets. As more made-for-sale baskets entered the marketplace, collectors in turn were attracted to an increasing variety of baskets.

There is no clear documentation to substantiate the active participation of Owens Valley Paiute weavers at the Indian Field Days. However, some Mono Lake Paiute women who lived in Owens Valley attended these celebrations. For example, Captain and Susie Sam, parents of well-known Indian Field Days participant Leanna Tom, sometimes lived in Round Valley during the winters (Ford 1930:276). Leanna Tom also participated in the Bishop Harvest Days in 1916 (Bates and Lee 1990:88, 89, 179). Famous Yosemite Miwok/Mono Lake Paiute weaver Lucy Telles also lived in Round Valley occasionally (Telles 1915). What impact these weavers had on other Owens Valley weavers is unknown.[37]

Although Owens Valley was geographically convenient to such popular tourist areas as Yosemite, Death Valley, and Lake Tahoe, the valley itself was not a major tourist destination during the first half of the twentieth century. Nonetheless, local activities were developed which served to foster appreciation of the

Figure 3.41. Indian Band at the Bishop Harvest Festival, 1913. Bands and floats highlighted the parade down the Main Street of Bishop during the Harvest Festival. The inclusion of an Indian band in the parade demonstrated the extent to which the Indian population had accepted certain aspects of Western culture.

region's indigenous population (Figure 3.41). One such celebration was the annual Bishop Harvest Festival, sponsored by the community of Bishop starting in 1885 and continuing through the 1920s, except for the war years. The Board of Directors of the Harvest Festival Association called for "the hearty co-operation and assistance of the people of the valley who 'do things' and 'grow things'" (Bishop Harvest Festival 1916). Nine categories of competitions were listed under the Indian Department, including athletics, domestic science and art, basketry, and a baby show (Figures 3.42 and 3.43). Cash prizes were given in all contests. A complete list of the winners appeared in the local newspaper, the *Inyo Register*. In 1916, for example, the *Register* reported that weaver Hattie Jones won that year's prize of three dollars for best basket collection.[38]

A careful examination of photographs from the 1916 Bishop Harvest Days reveals that most of the baskets for sale at the event were made by women from groups other than the Owens Valley Paiutes (Figure 3.44) (Bates and Lee 1990:88–89).[39] Like Yosemite's Indian Field Days, these festivals provided opportunities for cultural interaction between weavers of diverse backgrounds and motivated talented weavers to produce baskets of extremely high quality.

Figure 3.42. Harvest Festival Premium List, Bishop, 1916. The Harvest Festival was held in Bishop on an almost annual basis from the early 1900s through the 1920s. Animals, farm products, crafts, and Indian babies were all judged, and cash prizes were awarded.

HARVEST FESTIVAL 1916

INDIAN DEPARTMENT

W. O. SMITH, Superintendent

Athletics

Archery contest, bow and arrow	$3.00
Foot races, three events, each	2.00
Day school relay race, for trophy.	

Live Stock

Best draft team	$3.00
Best draft colt under one year old	2.00
Best saddle horse owned and broken by an Indian	2.00
Best brood mare, draft breed	2.00

Domestic Science and Art

Best hemmed handkerchief, by Indian woman	$1.00
Best hemmed handkerchief by Indian school girl	1.00
Best buttonhole work, six buttonholes	1.00
Best home made apron	1.00
Best home made dress, by Indian woman	1.00
Best home made dress by Indian school girl	1.00
Best corset cover	1.00
Best article of bead work	2.00
Best loaf of bread made by Indian woman	1.00
Best loaf of bread made by Indian school girl	1.00
Best dozen cookies	1.00
Best cake	1.00
Best display of canned fruit	2.00
Best glass of jelly	1.00
Largest display of canned goods, all kinds	3.00
Best pie, apple	1.00
Best pie, pumpkin	1.00

Hand Craft and Manual Training

Best day school exhibit (collective)	Silk banner
Best hair lariat	$2.00
Best wood carving	2.00
Best leather carving	2.00
Best article made by Indian pupil, wood or metal	2.00

Some weavers of this generation, in fact, achieved heights of craftsmanship and artistry with their baskets that have never been matched.

In 1935 the Committee on Arts and Crafts of the Carson Indian Agency (whose jurisdiction included most of Owens Valley) founded an arts and crafts organization that offered

Figure 3.43. Harry Brown, Healthiest Baby Under One Year, Bishop Harvest Festival Indian Baby Show, 1916. The Baby Contest was a popular and much photographed event at the Bishop Harvest Festival. The photographer, Andrew A. Forbes, identified the baby as Harry Brown in his records but failed to identify the mother. A Harry Brown born in 1916 can't be located in BIA records, although there are other Brown children in two families born around the same time. Conversations with Paiute people have not resulted in any solution to the confusion, which is a good example of the difficulty of identification of Paiute people in historic photographs from Owens Valley.

bers: the Washoes, Paiutes, and Shoshones. Wa-Pai-Shone Trading Post No. 1, a prototype for collectives to follow, was established at the Stewart Indian School near Carson City, Nevada, in December 1935 and was sponsored and operated by the twelfth-grade students (Figure 3.45) (Bowler 1936:2; Dorothy Stanley, personal communication 1980).

The cooperative had six objectives: (1) to revive and perpetuate an interest in the distinctive crafts of the Washoe, Paiute, and Shoshone people; (2) to increase the production of saleable articles that evidenced good workmanship, first-class materials, and "true . . . Indian feeling in color and design"; (3) to set standards; (4) to purchase materials cooperatively so that uniformly high-grade materials would be used; (5) to establish cooperative marketing centers and stabilize prices at a reasonable level; and (6) to enable "any Indian with a genuine aptitude for craft work" to supplement "the very low family income derived from other economic resources" (Bowler 1936:2–3).

Standards were to be set by means of adopting and copyrighting a trademark that would be permitted only on objects that measured up in terms of workmanship, materials, color, and design. As the superintendent of the

Indian people of the Great Basin the chance to cooperate in selling their goods through trading posts. This organization, whose primary goal was to increase craft production and develop effective marketing strategies, was called the Wa-Pai-Shone Craftsmen Cooperative after the three groups of Indians that would be mem-

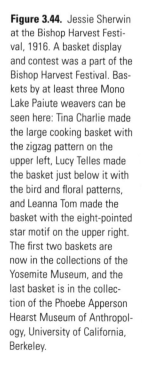

Figure 3.44. Jessie Sherwin at the Bishop Harvest Festival, 1916. A basket display and contest was a part of the Bishop Harvest Festival. Baskets by at least three Mono Lake Paiute weavers can be seen here: Tina Charlie made the large cooking basket with the zigzag pattern on the upper left, Lucy Telles made the basket just below it with the bird and floral patterns, and Leanna Tom made the basket with the eight-pointed star motif on the upper right. The first two baskets are now in the collections of the Yosemite Museum, and the last basket is in the collection of the Phoebe Apperson Hearst Museum of Anthropology, University of California, Berkeley.

Carson Indian Agency explained to her staff members:

> Indian craftsmen in this region have been making and selling quite atrocious articles in a mistaken effort to imitate white men's ways. No one seems to have tried to show them that they have, by this deterioration, tended to destroy the market for their own wares. We do not have in mind any visionary and slavish adherence to the production of articles made by these Indian people in the olden days. Some of those articles, artistically attractive and decorative, will be marketable, and their production will be encouraged. But what we want to help these craftsmen do is to utilize their distinctive skills, their own inherited patterns, their feeling for certain color combinations, in making articles that will be useful as well as decorative in this modern world. (Bowler 1936:2)

The Arts and Crafts Committee proposed Owens Valley as one of four locations where "small, picturesque, reliable Indian-owned-and-operated trading posts should do well" (Bowler 1936:3). Other potential locations were Reno, which had a consistently large transient population; Las Vegas, where tourists swarmed to visit Boulder Dam and Lake Mead; and Lake Tahoe, where throngs of tourists came during the summer vacation season. Owens Valley was considered an attractive site: its recreational assets were beginning to be developed, and it was becoming a popular hunting, fishing, and summer resort area with a relatively long season, from May 1 (when trout season opened) to October 15 (when deer season closed) (Bowler 1936:3). Over the next six years the committee's plan was implemented. Trading posts were established in Owens Valley at Bishop and Lone Pine; at Pyramid Lake, north of Reno; and at Death Valley (Kerr 1936). Wa-Pai-Shone Trading Post No. 4, in Bishop, opened on June 26, 1940.

Wa-Pai-Shone's success in developing and expanding a market for the products of Indian art and craftsmanship is difficult to measure. The craft cooperative's reputation

Figure 3.45. Wa-Pai-Shone Trading Post, Stewart Indian School, Stewart, Nevada, 1939. Irene McCauley (Northern Miwok), Dorothy (Amora) Stanley (Northern Miwok), and store manager Mary Kensington examine the display of baskets for sale at the Wa-Pai-Shone Trading Post. A large basket by Mono Lake Paiute weaver Tina Charlie is on the floor, lower left. The bulk of the baskets appear to be of Washoe and Paiute manufacture.

was apparently far-reaching enough that some of its craftspeople were asked to participate as demonstrators at the Indian market that was part of the 1939 Golden Gate International Exposition in San Francisco (Bowler 1939). During World War II, however, the collective's arts and crafts work was "curtailed," and by 1942 the organization no longer tried "to force the building up of trade" at the posts in Death Valley, Lake Tahoe, and the Bishop area. Nevertheless, that summer the original trading post at Carson Indian School did more business than any summer since the store had been in operation (Carson Agency 1942).

The Wa-Pai-Shone program was significant in that it represented a widespread effort by Indians and non-Indians to support basket making as a viable cottage industry. Although well meaning, the efforts of the Wa-Pai-Shone program were unsuccessful in perpetuating basketry among the Indian people. It appears that few if any younger women learned to weave during the years of the program.

At the same time that the Wa-Pai-Shone trading posts were operating, a few privately owned stores were selling baskets and other American Indian objects in the Mono Lake–Owens Valley area. One such store was Navajo Johnson's Trading Post, which first operated in the 1930s at Casa Diablo Hot Springs and later relocated to Mammoth (Reed 1982:106, 108, 123). Other stores farther north included the Tioga Lodge, just north of Lee Vining at Mono Lake, and the general store operated by the Cain family in Bridgeport. Baskets offered for sale at these locales were generally made by local Mono Lake Paiute people, but other baskets from the Bishop area, or baskets from Mono Lake weavers such as Nellie and Tina Charlie, who were living in Bishop, made their way to the Cain family's store. Baskets continued to be sold at the store through the early 1960s. By the end of the 1960s, though baskets still decorated the store, they were no longer for sale, for there were not enough weavers to ensure a steady supply. With the deaths of experienced weavers, basket making in Owens Valley became increasingly uncommon. The continuing acculturation of Indian people to a Western lifestyle and the attendant replacement of baskets by commercial products in everyday life were major factors in the demise of basketry in Owens Valley.

By the late 1970s virtually the only baskets to be seen for sale were older baskets in a few antique stores in Bishop and in the Bridgeport area. These baskets had been in the possession of local native and non-Indian families, who had sold them as a ready source of cash. As the twentieth century came to a close, it was increasingly difficult to find baskets for sale anywhere in Owens Valley or along Highway 395 to the north.

The attention paid to basket making from the 1890s to about 1940 by non-Indian collectors helped usher in a series of stylistic changes in weaving in Owens Valley and the surrounding areas. In the first twenty years these innovations included a reduction in the size of some baskets made for sale, the use of more complex designs (often obtained from printed materials, beadwork, or created by the weavers themselves), and a shift in emphasis from twined baskets to coiled ones. All these changes were linked to the manufacture of baskets for sale to non-Indians, as baskets changed from utilitarian objects to an art form created for non-Indians.

Many of the Paiute and Panamint Shoshone weavers in Owens Valley represented in this book lived during this transition from primarily native to primarily non-Indian ways. Indeed, most of the weavers for whom we have information made baskets both for their own use and for sale to non-Indians. Information regarding the actual number of weavers is often scant. For example, the 1910 census, which enumerated Indians engaged in selected occupations, reported a total of forty-six Paiute basket makers among all the tribes of the Great Basin (U.S. Department of Commerce, Bureau of the Census 1915:273–274). Research, recent interviews, and oral histories, however, prove this number is inaccurate; there were many more weavers in the Great Basin in 1910 (see Appendix II). Although suspicion of census takers may have routinely resulted in the underreporting of the Indian population in general (Jessie Durant, personal communication 1998), many known basket makers are listed in the 1910 census but were not enumerated as basket makers. The census count of basket weavers probably reflected only those women who reported their weaving efforts as their "occupations." It does not list as basket weavers those who considered weaving to be simply part of their everyday lives or something to do in addition to their jobs as cooks, housekeepers, laundresses, and homemakers. Many collectors never recorded the names of the women who made the baskets they purchased, and thus the majority of extant baskets are not accompanied by the names of their makers.

Some of the weavers for whom we have information, such as Emma Wright, born in Big

Pine, California, in 1882,[40] lived permanently in Owens Valley. Others, such as Mary Charlie, were more commonly associated with other regions of eastern California and lived in the valley only intermittently. Still others relocated to Owens Valley from the Mono Basin or Panamint Shoshone country. Reliable information about these people is often difficult to locate. For example, their recorded birth dates are usually mere approximations; most Indian people did not track ages carefully in the nineteenth century, and estimates were often provided by census takers or made up on the spot to accommodate compilers of official records. Too, although death records are usually available, some deaths of Indian people in the southern Owens Valley and adjacent areas went unrecorded, even in the 1930s (Richard Stewart, personal communication 2001). The following biographies rely on the available information and may well be inaccurate in certain areas.

Paiute and Panamint Shoshone people often moved some distance for employment and other reasons, especially in the period between 1900 and 1950. Thus many of the biographies presented here are of Mono Lake Paiute and Panamint Shoshone people who moved to Owens Valley. Family trees among these people are often extremely complex, and some of the weavers were closely related to one another. These population movements, and the close proximity in Owens Valley of weavers from different locations, likely influenced the basketry patterns, shapes, and materials selected by these women.

THE TRANSITIONAL GENERATION OF WEAVERS LIVING IN OWENS VALLEY

Mamie (Joaquin) Button (ca. 1904–1969)

Mamie Button, the child of Panamint Tom and Sallie Panamint, was a Panamint Shoshone woman born in Saline Valley.[41] She was known as Mamie Thompson as a young girl and was the younger half-sister of weaver Sarah Hunter. Much of Mamie's young adulthood was spent in the Saline Valley area. A small-boned, thin

woman with fine features as an adult, Mamie stood about five feet, four inches in height. Mamie married three times. She had one child with her first husband, whose name was not recorded. Her second husband was Tom Joaquin, and they had four children: Wynona (a.k.a. Winona), Lizzie, Bonnie, and Clifford.[42] Sometime between 1939 and 1942 Mamie married Bill Button, also born in Saline Valley.[43] They had one child, Dorothy.

By 1942 the Buttons, along with other Panamint Shoshone people, moved to Lone Pine, at the southern end of Owens Valley. Job opportunities were scarce, especially during the depression, and it is likely that they, like other Panamint Shoshones, had traveled to find work. By the early 1960s they had moved to a site on Rawson Creek just north of the Wilkerson Ranch and six miles south of Bishop.

Button gathered basket materials and wove baskets throughout her life. On occasion she enjoyed gathering basket materials with her sister, Sarah Hunter. Sometimes Mamie's daughter, Dorothy, accompanied her mother on these gathering expeditions. Typically, a full day was devoted to gathering whatever material was in season. Although Button changed residences over the years, she occasionally gathered willow for her baskets in the Alabama Hills. When gathering Joshua tree root, she usually sought a tree that had been uprooted rather than try to dig out the roots from the soil. A favored place for digging bulrush root was along the Owens Lake bed on the side near Keeler. Button preferred to weave in the shade, following the practice of most other weavers, who maintained that weaving in the sun dried out the materials too quickly, possibly causing sewing strands and completed stitches to break during the weaving process.

Like most Panamint Shoshone women, Button made both coiled and twined baskets. Her twined baskets are worth noting for their elegant shape and adherence to traditional Panamint Shoshone forms (Figure 3.46). She produced cradle baskets, seed beaters, winnowers, water jars, and burden baskets, likely both for use and for sale to non-Indians.

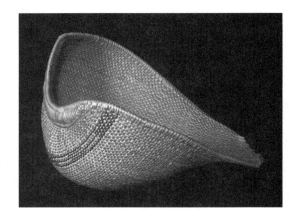

Figure 3.46. Panamint Shoshone Winnowing or Sifting Tray. Weaver, Mamie Joaquin Button, 1943. With split-peeled willow wefts, scraped-willow rod warps, up-to-the-right stitches, and an extremely deep bowl shape in its upper half, this diagonally twined sifter is typically Panamint Shoshone, although it resembles the sifters of the Owens Valley and Mono Lake Paiutes. The single row of three-strand twining below the bundle selvedge and the willow reinforcing rod lashed around the basket's perimeter are construction features common in both Panamint and Paiute sifters. The split red-bud in the basket was obtained in trade.

Button is best remembered for her fancy coiled baskets (Figure 3.47). The similarity between her designs, shapes, and materials and those of Sarah Hunter made the differentiation of their baskets difficult if not impossible. In the late 1930s both sisters made large oval baskets ornamented with patterns of realistic animal and plant forms and sometimes tapering slightly inward at the rim. Favorite motifs were birds, bighorn sheep, chuckwallas, and Joshua trees. Button's rendering of the bighorn sheep usually showed the sheep's head in profile, with the horns over the sheep's back. On other baskets, she portrayed the sheep's head in frontal view so that one horn went to the right and the other to left.[44]

Like Button, Sarah Hunter used complex geometric patterns, including serrated diamond motifs (Michael 1985:21). One slight difference in the baskets made by the two sisters is that Button's baskets sometimes have sides that turn abruptly upward from the basket's base whereas Hunter's curve up more gently from the bottom.

Button regularly used bulrush root as the black design material in her baskets, as was common for almost all Panamint Shoshone weavers in the 1910–30 era. Devil's claw, also used for black pattern material, was the only basket material planted and grown in gardens by the Panamint Shoshones. Between 1910 and 1930 Panamint Shoshone people traveled frequently, for employment and other reasons, and thus did not plant and maintain gardens regularly. As a result, bulrush root became the most common dark-colored basket material among these weavers (Bernstein 1985:9–11). After Button's move to Owens Valley in the 1940s and her permanent residence there, she and her sister grew devil's claw in their gardens. Thus in her later baskets Button made regular use of devil's claw, in addition to bulrush and Joshua tree root.

Mamie Joaquin Button was one of five Paiute and Panamint Shoshone weavers who demonstrated basketry at the Indian Arts and Crafts Board exhibition at the Golden Gate International Exposition at Treasure Island, near San Francisco, in 1939.[45] This trip, which she later described to her children, was her first to a large city. Little is known of her demonstrations at the fair, but some of her baskets were sold through the store that was a part of the Indian exhibition (Figure 3.48).

Occasionally, non-Indians came to visit Mamie and her sister Sarah at their homes on Rawson Creek to purchase baskets or ask questions about basketry. Mamie and Sarah did not read or speak much English so their "menfolk" were enlisted as interpreters.

When Mamie lived on Rawson Creek, she liked to attend the local church as well as sweat lodge ceremonies held in the area. Toward the end of her life Mamie became a diabetic and began losing her eyesight. As her sight deteriorated, her weaving became less fine; eventually, she stopped weaving because she was not happy with the quality of the baskets she was making.

Figure 3.47. Panamint Shoshone Basket. Weaver, Mamie Joaquin Button, ca. 1940. Coiled in a rightward direction on a foundation of three willow rods, this rigid, straight-sided basket depicts bighorn sheep and chuckwallas.

Mamie Button died on November 17, 1969, in Lone Pine and was buried at the Darwin Cemetery. Dorothy Button remembered her mother as a patient worker who enjoyed the weaving process, always including a piece of her soul in her extraordinary baskets.

Mary Button Charlie (1906–ca. 1950s)

Mary Button Charlie was born in Death Valley, California, on September 13, 1906.[46] Her parents, Panamint Shoshone, were Joe Button (whose father was from Telescope Peak and whose mother was from Surveyor's Wells) and Mary Button, who was also known as Maggie (whose father was Paw-ho and whose mother was How-vi-o-nee). After Joe Button's death Mary's mother married his brother George, also known as Skidoo George.

Mary's first husband was Hank Patterson, a Panamint Shoshone born in 1902.[47] They had one daughter, Josephine, born December 15, 1923. In 1928 Josephine was living with her father in Death Valley on the grounds of Scotty's Castle,[48] where he worked as a laborer. By this time Hank and Mary had separated, and Hank had married Margaret Boland, with whom he would have eleven children.[49]

Mary's second husband was Halley W. Charlie, a Panamint Shoshone born September 14, 1886, in Ash Meadows, Nevada. His parents were Ash Meadows Charlie and Mary Charlie, both Shoshone Indians from Nevada. Halley Charlie lived in Nye County, Nevada, until about 1920, when he moved to Inyo County, California. He worked as a laborer and was employed periodically at Scotty's Castle from 1926 to 1931. Mary and Halley Charlie spent the winters near Furnace Creek in Death Valley and often came into Owens Valley and stayed near Lone Pine in the summer to escape Death Valley's intense heat. Mary and Halley had two sons: Edison, born in 1925, and Billy, born in 1928. Halley Charlie died in Inyo County on February 15, 1972.

Mary Charlie and her family are representative of the close interrelationships among many of the Panamint Shoshone weavers. The well-known Panamint Shoshone weaver Laura

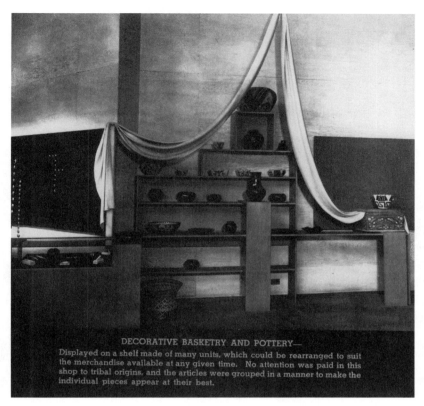

DECORATIVE BASKETRY AND POTTERY—
Displayed on a shelf made of many units, which could be rearranged to suit the merchandise available at any given time. No attention was paid in this shop to tribal origins, and the articles were grouped in a manner to make the individual pieces appear at their best.

Figure 3.48. Indian Arts and Crafts Board Display and Sales Area, Golden Gate International Exposition, 1939. The baskets made by Paiute and Shoshone weavers sit on the top three shelves in the Indian Arts and Crafts room. The basket on the top shelf is by Lucy Telles, a Miwok–Mono Lake Paiute weaver from Yosemite; the small one on the left of the second shelf appears to have been made by Mamie Joaquin Button.

(also known as Lola) Shaw, born in 1887, was Mary's sister.[50] The mother of Mary's first husband, Hank Patterson, was Minnie Patterson, who later married Robert Thompson, the brother of famed Panamint Shoshone weavers Sarah Hunter and Mamie Joaquin Button.[51] Hank Patterson's second wife was Margaret Boland, the sister of Johnnie Boland, who was married to the Panamint Shoshone weaver Dolly Boland. Dolly was the daughter of Hank's stepfather, Old Man Doc, and his second wife. When two families were already connected through marriage, often a sister or brother of one spouse married a brother or sister of his or her sibling's spouse, or two sisters might marry two brothers (Steward 1936b:562). Obviously, the family ties of Panamint Shoshone weavers are complex.[52]

Mary Charlie and her sister, Laura Shaw, lived at the Indian camp at Scotty's Castle during the castle's construction. Other Panamint Shoshone weavers living there at the time included Mabel Billson and Minnie Thompson, the latter the mother of Mary's first husband. No doubt the women spent time together while their husbands were working on the castle and were familiar with one another's basketry.[53]

In 1942 and 1943 collector Anna Kelley purchased four baskets that she identified as the work of Mary Charlie. Three of the baskets were woven in 1935 and one in 1938. Vertical designs are woven from either dyed bulrush root or Baltic juncus (Figure 3.49). On two of the baskets the vertical pattern is of stacked triangles. On the other two the pattern is a variation on the old-style "rattlesnake" design. Other patterns include realistic chuckwalla lizards. In form, the baskets include high-shouldered shapes, a lidded basket, and an open bowl. The patterns are not as intricate as those on many Panamint Shoshone baskets, but the quality of work is very good and the shouldered form that Mary seems to have favored lends a simple elegance to her work.

A search of public records failed to locate a death certificate or obituary for Mary Charlie. A member of her extended family remembered that she died in the 1950s and was buried, near her husband and sons, in the Mt. Whitney Cemetery in Lone Pine, California.

Nellie Charlie (ca. 1867–1965)

Nellie Charlie was born in the summer of 1867 near the present-day town of Lee Vining, not far from the shore of Mono Lake.[54] Her father was Pete Jim, Na-ha, a headman of the Mono Lake Paiutes, and her mother was Patsy Jim, Hi-do-nee.[55] When she was a young woman, Nellie's Paiute name was Pooseuna, also some-

times spelled *Buseeuna* or *Be-se-una* (Figure 3.50). By the time she was an older woman in the 1920s and 1930s, her relatives all called her *Mooah*, the Mono Lake Paiute word for maternal grandmother.

Both Nellie and her sister Tina, Wetoní, were married to Young Charlie, Chdué, a Miwok man from Yosemite who had moved to the Mono Lake area as a young man.[56] Young Charlie may have descended from a family of Miwok hereditary leaders, as he was sometimes referred to as a chief. In the early 1900s through the 1920s he and his wives made their home on the ranch he had acquired as an allotment through the Indian Allotment Act on lower Rush Creek, on the southwest side of Mono Lake. The property included several small frame residences, fenced pastures for the horses Young Charlie raised, and fields of potatoes, carrots, and onions; around one hundred acres were under irrigation. In the 1930s, after the Rush Creek property was purchased by the Los Angeles County Department of Water and Power, the Charlies moved upstream and lived in the flatlands just north of Rush Creek and Bloody Canyon. In 1927 Nellie divorced Young Charlie, although she continued to live in a building near her sister and Young Charlie both at lower Rush Creek and later when they moved uphill. Nellie and Young Charlie had six children: Mabel, Mildred, Henry, Daisy, Lula (Púúnéé), and Mae.

Sometime around 1910 the Charlies had lived at Mono Mills, a lumber camp on the southern side of Mono Lake. Young Charlie worked at Mono Mills, and some of the Charlie daughters cooked for the workers at the camp and worked as maids. It was there, too, that daughters Lula and Mildred met the Swiss brothers August (Gus) and William Hess, whom they married. Nellie and Young Charlie were initially opposed to their daughters marrying non-Paiutes but eventually came to accept the marriages and felt that their daughters had chosen good husbands.

Although the Charlies lived in frame homes, often worked and did business with non-Indians, and ate many introduced foods, they

Figure 3.49. Panamint Shoshone Lidded Basket. Weaver, Mary Button Charlie, ca. 1938. This basket coils to the right and exhibits a vertical design reminiscent of traditional rattlesnake patterns. Mary Button Charlie favored the use of flare-sided forms with a shoulder. The inclusion of a lid was common on many baskets that were made for sale.

still maintained their Paiute culture. Nellie used rabbit-skin blankets into the 1930s, prepared many traditional foods, and observed traditional Paiute practices surrounding death or birth. Charlie wove baskets throughout her life and taught her daughters, and a few of her granddaughters, how to weave both coiled and twined baskets.

Charlie was an expert and prolific weaver who made both traditional and new-style baskets. As early as 1903 she was making fine, three-rod coiled baskets with new patterns for sale to non-Indians. By 1916 she and her sister Tina entered baskets in the Bishop Harvest Days festival. During the 1920s she was a regular participant in the basketry contests at the Indian Field Days in Yosemite Valley and the June Lake Field Days. Charlie developed fancy, new-style patterns and made fine, three-rod coiled baskets woven with sedge root and decorated with complex patterns worked in redbud and bracken fern root. She was apparently one of the major producers of large "laundry baskets," spaced-stitched, three-rod baskets woven with split willow shoots, two feet or more in diameter and ornamented with bold patterns in red and black (Figure 3.51). Charlie also made beaded baskets and developed several design styles unlike those used by other Paiute women. She sometimes used patterns more frequently found on coiled three-rod baskets and also made at least two baskets with bold zigzag patterns unlike those found on other beaded baskets.

In addition to innovating in her patterns on fancy coiled and beaded baskets, Charlie appears to have been one of the few weavers who used patriotic motifs, such as the Union shield and American eagle, on her baskets. She also created a new pattern, consisting of a rectangle with small triangles appended near each corner. Her family commented that this looked like an "Indian H," and her daughters Lula and Mildred, who were married to the Hess brothers, were particularly pleased with the pattern as a sort of Paiute monogram. Charlie, who did not speak English, read, or write, was amused by her daughters' recogni-

tion of the design as the first letter of their surname. She also made new basketry forms for use by her children, grandchildren, and non-Indian buyers. A baby bassinet, fruit bowls, hot pads, a basket to contain knitting needles and yarns, and coasters were among the new forms she devised.

Although little is known of the weaving careers of Charlie's daughters, at least Daisy Mallory and Lula Hess were expert weavers. Judging from a few documented baskets made by these daughters before 1920, they specialized in making relatively small coiled baskets with extremely complex patterns, both geometric and realistic. After Lula married Gus Hess,

Figure 3.50. Nellie Charlie, in a Brush Sunshade next to Her Home on Rush Creek, near Mono Lake, 1903. Most commonly associated with Mono Lake and Yosemite Valley, Nellie Charlie was one of the most prolific and talented Mono Lake Paiute basket weavers of the twentieth century. Her baskets were noted for their tight and even stitches, precisely executed patterns, and high quality.

Figure 3.51. Mono Lake Paiute Basket. Weaver, Nellie Charlie, ca. 1940. Nellie Charlie made this basket for her granddaughter, Elma Blaver, to use as a laundry basket. It is sturdily made on a three-rod foundation of stout willow rods, and Blaver used it for her laundry for nearly forty years, just as her grandmother had intended.

Figure 3.52. Nellie Charlie at Her Home in Bishop, ca. 1950. Nellie Charlie sits in her home, weaving a strongly patterned single-rod basket. An enamelware container on the table holds water for keeping her weaving materials wet, and the handle of her awl is visible on the right side of the basket.

Nellie Charlie continued to weave through most of her later years, although an arthritic condition in her fingers made it difficult. At the time of her death a winnowing tray was left unfinished because of the arthritis. Nellie Charlie died on July 21, 1965, at the Northern Inyo Hospital. She was buried at the Lee Vining Cemetery, on a bluff above the northwest shore of Mono Lake.

Joe Eugley (ca. 1848–1921)

Joe Eugley was born in the Owens Valley Paiute camp called Tres Pinos (Three Pines) in the late 1840s (Graulich 1987:120). He was recognized early on as a berdache, that is, an individual who adopts one or more behaviors, occupations, or social roles of the opposite sex (Roscoe 1987:82).[57] In assuming the lifestyle usually assigned to females in Paiute society, Joe wore women's clothing and did women's work, including making baskets. He was sometimes called "Squaw Man Joe," "Squaw Buck Joe," or "Mahala Joe"; *Mahala*, likely bestowed by non-Indians, is an Anglo-American bastardization of the Spanish *mujer,* "woman" or "wife."[58]

Male berdaches in Native American societies were acknowledged and integrated members of their communities (Roscoe 1998:11). Indeed, Joe Eugley sometimes officiated as headman for the annual spring dance ceremony and was reported to be "greatly respected and feared by the Paiutes although he lives like a woman and does a woman's work and wears a dress" (Hartman n.d.:2). In Owens Valley the non-Indian community also accepted Eugley, albeit as a curiosity. One elderly resident recalled, "The people of Big Pine took him for granted. He was an oddity, but just another Indian" (Uhlmeyer 1991b:45).

Paiute tribal elder Louis Stewart told his grandson Richard Stewart what he remembered about Eugley. The following account, from the elder Mr. Stewart's memories, provides us with a Paiute view of Eugley, in contrast to that recorded by non-Indians. In the late nineteenth and early twentieth centuries it was common

she apparently never wove again. Daisy continued to weave throughout her life.

By the 1940s Nellie spent the winters with her daughter Daisy Mallory at Daisy's home in Bishop. The winters were often severe at Mono Lake, and the move to Bishop was a welcome change from the snow and cold in Mono County. By the 1950s Charlie lived on the Bishop Reservation with her granddaughter Jessie Durant, Daisy Mallory's daughter (Figure 3.52). Her sister Tina Charlie joined her there (Figure 3.53). They lived in a small cabin together and wove baskets every day (Figures 3.54 and 3.55).

to clothe both male and female Paiute children in dresses; Joe Eugley never outgrew his desire to dress like a girl and wore female clothes all the time. When he was told that men should wear pants, he did so, donning a pair of pants under his dress. Eugley generally wore pants, a dress, and boots called brogans, a type of large, lace-up work boot. Eugley was about six feet tall and very strong. He didn't like to have his photograph taken, and with his imposing height and strength, it is likely that very few ever attempted to do so. Eugley could make baskets "as good as any woman," and he was well known among both Paiutes and non-Indians for his fine baskets. Eugley was not the only man who dressed like a woman and did woman's work. Another Paiute, nicknamed "Queen Dick," lived in Bishop (Richard Stewart, personal communication 2001).

Echoing Stewart's memories of Joe Eugley are the comments of Carroll S. Hartman, a business associate of collector Grace Nicholson:

> A man of fine build, of more than normal strength, and a born leader of men. He believes himself the reincarnation of Te-li-lup, a legendary squaw man. In this, Joe, who is now about fifty years old, is thoroughly consistent. He wears woman's clothes, has never married, does woman's work, even going out washing by the day among the whites, does the ironing and is a good cook. Because Joe will not go hunting or participate in the men's games some say that he is a coward, but they never more than whisper this condemnation as all know of his great strength and fear Joe accordingly. (Hartman n.d.:n.p.)

Whites were eager to hire Eugley for his domestic skills and to do odd jobs, but they could not believe that his alternative social status was a conscious choice. Instead, they created stories attributing it to being a punishment imposed during his teen years for being weak, cowardly, and not living up to tribal standards of masculinity. According to author Mary Austin, who wrote about "Mahala Joe" in her 1910 book of short stories, *The Basket*

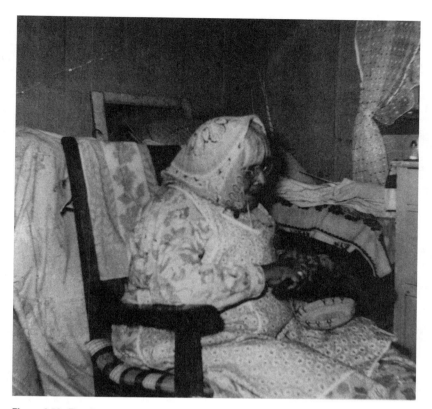

Figure 3.53. Tina Charlie Weaving at Her Home in Bishop, ca. 1950. Charlie has almost reached the halfway point on the basket in Figure 3.55. She is carefully trimming her materials so they will match in width and thickness. The three-rod foundation of the basket can barely be seen projecting beneath her hands toward her left.

Figure 3.54. Nellie and Tina Charlie's Home in Bishop, California, 1998. Nellie and Tina Charlie lived with their relative, Jessie Durant, during the 1950s on land allotted to the Mallory family during the 1939 land exchange.

Figure 3.55. Mono Lake Paiute Basket. Weaver, Tina Charlie, ca. 1950. This three-rod basket is a good example of the more finely stitched baskets woven by Tina and Nellie Charlie. Baskets of this type were prized by family members and also found a ready sale among non-Indians. See Figure 3.53, which shows Tina Charlie weaving this basket. The rim is overstitched in such a manner as to resemble a three-strand braid, a treatment that is uncommon on Paiute baskets.

Woman, Joe's castigation resulted from his refusal to fight against a white family whose son was his "sworn brother" (Austin 1999: 93–113).[59] This story must have been widespread in the non-Indian community, for Owens Valley physician and basket collector Dr. Helen M. Doyle recorded a nearly identical version (1934:162–163). Because ethnographic research specifically rejects the concept of cowardice among the Owens Valley Paiutes (Steward 1934:431), however, it is clear that Joe Eugley's preference for the female gender role was unrelated to this explanation. It appears that the stories Austin and Doyle related were one way non-Indians explained the Paiute acceptance of homosexuality, an acceptance foreign to non-Indian Americans.

Like young women in the community, Eugley probably learned to weave baskets from female family members at a young age. He no doubt first learned to weave traditional utilitarian baskets, but the only two baskets by him that survive today are later fancy coiled baskets, likely made for sale to non-Indians. These baskets were probably made between 1910 and his death in 1921 (Figure 3.56).[60]

These three-rod coiled baskets are finely woven, with neatly and evenly trimmed sewing strands and foundation rods. The baskets resemble those made for sale by the Panamint Shoshones. They differ primarily in being made with a leftward coil direction, like most Paiute baskets. It is likely that Eugley imitated the highly saleable imagery and fine stitching of

Panamint Shoshone basketry while using Owens Valley Paiute coiling techniques. Indeed, Eugley's imagery and use of English words as part of the design is nearly identical to the work of Owens Valley Paiute weaver Mary Gorman (see Figure 3.38). Like Eugley, Gorman used Paiute techniques but imitated Panamint Shoshone imagery and fine stitching.[61]

Rose Black, a well-known collector of Owens Valley baskets, interpreted the animals and arrows as expressions of Eugley's desire to be a great hunter (Eastern California Museum 1962:6). These designs, in fact, represented an entirely new style created by Panamint Shoshone weavers to appeal to the non-Indian market and had no basis in traditional Owens Valley Indian culture. The idea that the designs symbolized Eugley's wish to be a hunter, like the fanciful story of his choice of a female lifestyle, was a product of Anglo-American mythologizing rather than Paiute culture.

Mamie Gregory (1867–1951)

Born near Darwin, Panamint Shoshone weaver Mamie Gregory was the daughter of Chin-be and his wife, Wis-se-you, who was known to non-Indian residents of the area as Old Veiga or Vaiga.[62] Both of Mamie's parents had also been born near Darwin. Mamie married George Gregory, a Panamint Shoshone her senior by nearly ten years. Mamie's sister, Mary, married George Gregory's brother, Charlie Wrinkle. The brothers' different surnames came from the locally common practice in which Indian men adopted the surnames of non-Indians, who often were their employers. Gregory may have taken his name from teamster Joseph C. Gregory, who lived in Round Valley (Irwin 1980:iii). Both Mamie and Mary became well-known weavers of fancy baskets (Irwin 1980:iii; Slater 2000:37–48).

In the latter part of the nineteenth century Mamie and her husband, George, lived near Coso Hot Springs (Figure 3.57).[63] During the day Mamie walked five miles to the town of Darwin to clean houses and do laundry for white residents there; she earned one dollar a day plus her meals (Mecham 1978:2). In the evenings at her home she would weave storage and cooking baskets.

At this time she made her coiled baskets in traditional Panamint Shoshone style, using a variety of geometric patterns, including a step pattern, long traditional with the Panamint Shoshones,[64] as well as the Kawaiisu, Tubatulabal, and Yokuts peoples (Slater 1985a:60, 2000:37–39). Other baskets had vertical patterns, long popular among the same groups (Irwin 1980:iv). Gregory's traditional Panamint Shoshone coiled baskets, adhering to the traditional aesthetic conventions of the Panamint Shoshones, are nearly impossible to differentiate from the work of other weavers of her generation.[65] She apparently continued to make these traditional style Panamint Shoshone baskets through most of her life.[66]

Sometime in the early 1900s, possibly when Gregory and her husband moved closer to Darwin, her basket weaving style changed. With inexpensive tin containers readily available for purchase at the local general store, her need to make traditional baskets diminished just as the demand for fancy baskets for collectors increased. Gregory focused eventually on small gift baskets for barter or for sale, and she became well known for her butterfly designs, though she also frequently used squirrel motifs (Slater 2000:39). At the same time, she continued to produce baskets of traditional form and pattern, as well as smaller baskets with geometric patterns (Figure 3.58).[67] Collector Anna Kelley called Mamie's baskets "the work of a fine artist" (Kelley 1956).

Mamie and George were prosperous in comparison with other Panamint Shoshone people of their generation in the 1920s. In 1929 they lived on government land but valued their home at $200, their furniture at $100, and their horses, wagon, and harness at $125. George worked as a laborer. Unlike most other Panamint Shoshones, George Gregory could sign his own name. Although born into households that must have practiced primarily aboriginal lifestyles, George and Mamie adapted to the changing times, taking elements of both Panamint Shoshone culture

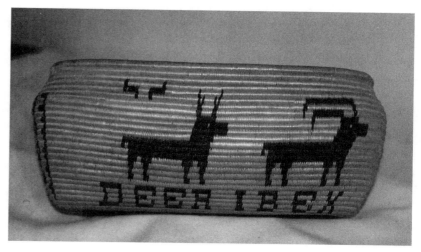

Figure 3.56. Owens Valley Paiute Oval Basket. Weaver, Joe Eugley, ca. 1910. The oblong shape, realistic figures, and words indicate that this basket was made for sale. The animal figures are nearly identical to those used by Panamint Shoshone weavers during the same time period. This basket is extremely similar in stitching and pattern to a basket made by another Owens Valley Paiute weaver, Mary Gorman (see Figure 3.38).

and Anglo culture and blending them into a new way of life.

In the summer of 1951 Mamie Gregory traveled from her home near Darwin and arrived in Owens Valley near Keough Hot Springs. She had been there for only two hours when she died, on July 26. She was buried at the Darwin Cemetery on July 29, 1951.

Figure 3.57. Mamie Gregory and Family, 1932. *Left to right:* Mamie Gregory, unknown, Addie Hanson (granddaughter), unknown. C. Hart Merriam made multiple fieldwork trips to the Owens Valley from 1902 through the 1930s. On one such trip he visited with Mamie Gregory and her family.

Figure 3.58. Panamint Shoshone Fancy Baskets. *Left:* Weaver, Mamie Gregory, ca. 1930. Rightward coil direction and rim ticking are typical Panamint Shoshone features. The realistic squirrel and perched-bird figures were popular patterns on baskets made for sale to non-Indians. The stitches, neat and even, number 26–28 per inch. The collector identified this basket as having been made by Mamie Gregory. *Right:* Weaver, possibly Mamie Gregory, ca. 1930. The oval shape and the variety of the three-dimensional representational figures indicate that this basket was made for sale to non-Indians. Dyed bulrush root and devil's claw form the squirrel and other designs, with highlights in yellow juncus. The collector purchased this basket from Emma Wright, an Owens Valley Paiute woman. However, its construction and design are consistent with other baskets attributed to Mamie Gregory.

Isabel Hanson (ca. 1880–1964)

Born in Warm Springs, Nevada, on what the Carson Indian Agency called "Indian Ranch" (Gelvin 1947:1),[68] Isabel Hanson was the daughter of Maggie (Tu-du-dle-te-hi-vi) and George Hanson (Apunzawhato). Maggie's father was Panamint Tom, the headman or chief of a small group of central and southern Death Valley Shoshone people who lived in the area known as Hungry Bill's Ranch. Seventeen relatives of Panamint Tom lived there, and the group was also known as the Tom Billson family (Sennett-Graham 1989:30, 31). After Panamint Tom's death (around 1904–5) George Hanson assumed his father-in-law's role and became known as Panamint George or Indian George (Mecham 1978:2).

George witnessed the arrival of both the forty-niners in Death Valley and the earliest non-Indian immigrants in the Panamint Valley (Potashin 1992:17). He did some prospecting around Panamint City (Potashin 1992:16) and later farmed his land, growing melons, alfalfa, and other crops near the mouth of Hall Canyon before 1900. He also herded goats (Irwin 1980:xi). Anthropologist Julian Steward gathered information concerning Death Valley and the Shoshones of the northern end of Panamint Valley from George Hanson in the 1930s (n.d.; 1941:213). In 1935 Steward collected several baskets made by Mabel, George's niece, for the Peabody Museum of Harvard University, including an open-twined sifter and two circular coiled winnowing or parching trays.

Isabel Hanson and her brothers Mike Hanson and Bill Johnson grew up in a family that practiced elements of both traditional Panamint Shoshone life and non-Indian life. It was in this environment that Hanson learned to weave at a young age in the traditional Panamint Shoshone style (Figure 3.59).[69] Hanson's weaving style evolved over the years to accommodate the wishes of non-Indian buyers, but she also continued to fashion traditional utilitarian baskets. Elizabeth Mecham, a former resident of Owens Valley, recalled that Hanson not only made fine baskets for sale but also wove storage baskets for use around the camp (Mecham 1978:1). Isabel made basketry water jars that were "better than a canteen" for keeping water cool in the desert heat (Potashin 1992:93).

Hanson worked on her baskets almost every day, even when she was doing her other work. Dugan Hanson, Isabel's nephew, recalled her sitting and weaving baskets while she herded goats (Potashin 1992:91, 94). Hanson used the typical Panamint Shoshone materials — willow, devil's claw, dyed bulrush root, and Joshua tree root — to create coiled baskets on a foundation of three willow rods. Some of her earlier storage baskets were quite large with strong vertical design bands that often incorporated the rattlesnake design (Slater 2000:35). On other baskets she used a horizontal variation of this same design to encircle the piece. Still using the traditional designs and materials, she sometimes made newer-style baskets with lids. On occasion Hanson went to Trona to sell her baskets.

Although Isabel Hanson used her maiden name throughout her life, and many have assumed that she never married, she was married for a short time to John Hunter before his marriage to Sarah Thompson.[70] John and Isabel's daughter, Molly, was born September 12, 1903. Molly used her mother's maiden name as her own surname and lived with her mother. Isabel and Molly raised Angora goats, which they had obtained from the proprietors of Darwin's general store. The sale of the goats' wool provided a good income for the Hansons.

Although at one time they were reported to have had a thousand head of goats, by the time Molly died in 1938 the herd had dwindled. Isabel continued to care for the goats and sold them sometime between 1942 and 1947. She then went to Darwin to live with her niece, Addie Hanson, who also made baskets (Plate 7). Addie was the daughter of Isabel's brother, Mike, and his wife, Annie Gregory (daughter of George and Mamie Gregory). Isabel continued to make small coiled baskets for sale for the rest of her life (Figure 3.60) (Mecham 1978:1). She died on June 3, 1964, at the Northern Inyo Hospital in Bishop and was buried four days later at the Darwin Cemetery.

Mary Harry (ca. 1845[1850?]–1942)

Mary Jim Harry was born in Hamil Valley at a place called Tepo'siinatü.[71] Her parents were McFee Jim (Tsee-qu-egy) and Se-how-u-nik-e, both from Mono County. Mary's father worked at times on the McFee Ranch, in Nevada just across the state line from Mono County, California, where they often lived. During Mary's childhood she and her family lived in several locations, including Tepo'siinatü, where they had a grass-thatched house, and Bishop, where her grandparents also lived.

Mary was a young girl when her maternal grandfather died, falling from a cliff in the White Mountains while hunting eagles. Saddened by his death, Mary's parents moved their family to Tu:na'va, the Geroux Ranch in Fish Lake Valley, northeast of Bishop, which became their winter home for many years. Her first knowledge of non-Indians occurred at age six, when she heard a report that her people fled to the hills in fright at the sight of two white men passing through the country with their pack animals.

When she was sixteen or seventeen, Mary met her future husband, Captain Harry, at a pine-nut-gathering dance festival near Pigeon Springs. Captain Harry, identified in various records as either a Paiute or Panamint Shoshone, was a widower. Traditionally, a young married couple lived for some time with the wife's family, but since Harry was thirty years

Figure 3.59. Panamint Shoshone Basket. Weaver, Isabel Hanson, 1939. One of Hanson's favorite design elements was a stylized rattlesnake, a pattern also commonly found in the basketry of the Kawaiisu, Tubatulabal, and Yokuts peoples. This basket was woven on a foundation of three willow rods, and its rightward coil direction, materials, and rim ticking are typical Panamint Shoshone features.

Figure 3.60. Isabel Hanson, 1963. In this photograph Hanson has nearly completed a basket with a pattern similar to that in Figure 3.59. Note that the rim ticking on this basket has been completed in two places, under Hanson's left hand and in the right middle. This ticking is used in the finishing row of the basket.

old and had already proved he was an adequate provider, they moved to Oasis, a small camp at the southern end of Fish Lake Valley. They lived there for three years and had three children, a daughter named Wino'hekuwa' and two sons. Later in life the older son, Robert, married Paiute weaver Emma Westerville.

The family next moved to Deep Springs, where they lived largely by hunting and gathering in the traditional Paiute way. When the Deep Springs Ranch was founded, Harry worked there from time to time. After her husband died in about 1919, Mary burned their camp and all his possessions. She then moved to Big Pine, where she spent the rest of her life with her daughter's family at the Big Pine Indian Reservation.

In the early 1930s Mary Harry was one of anthropologist Julian Steward's primary consultants during his work in the Great Basin. Probably as a result, many of her baskets appear in his classic 1933 monograph, *Ethnography of the Owens Valley Paiute* (Figure 3.61). Mary Harry was an expert weaver of Paiute twined utilitarian baskets; her burden baskets, winnowers, and women's caps are among the finest extant examples.

Mary Harry died on February 6, 1942, in Big Pine, where she was buried.

Sarah Hunter (1883–1967)

Sarah Hunter, a Panamint Shoshone weaver, spent most of her life in Hunter Canyon, in Saline Valley near Darwin.[72] Her parents were Panamint Tom and Guadalupe Thompson. As a girl, Sarah went by the name Sarah Thompson (Figure 3.62). Sarah married John Hunter, a Panamint Shoshone man born about 1885 whose father had taken the name of Hunter from William Lyle Hunter, an early non-Indian settler who had befriended the Panamint Shoshones.[73] Sarah and John Hunter had two sons, Joaquin and Kinney. Around 1937 they adopted Phillip, the child of a relative, whom they reared as their son (Figure 3.63).[74]

Although their primary home was in Hunter Canyon, the Hunters moved about considerably, living in Death Valley, Darwin, Owens Valley, and — in 1929 — in Salida in California's San Joaquin Valley. Job opportunities were scarce, especially during the depression, and it is likely that they, like other Panamint Shoshone people, traveled to where work might be found. While anthropologist Steward was doing fieldwork in Owens Valley in the early 1930s, he spent some time with the Hunters at their camp in the Saline Valley. John served as a consultant for Steward on several occasions and made models of various Panamint Shoshone games that Steward collected for the Peabody Museum (Steward 1941:213, 345).[75]

After the death of his father, Tom Hunter, John became head of his family and the owner of the 80-acre parcel of the 160-acre Saline Valley Indian Ranch that had been deeded to Tom Hunter as a homestead land grant. William Lyle Hunter had assisted Tom Hunter in filing the legal forms for this property in 1892 and had assisted the Caesar family in filing for the other 80-acre parcel of the Saline Valley Indian Ranch. As early as 1893 the ranch was planted in alfalfa, melons, squash, corn, barley, beans, and wheat, and it had a small vineyard and peach orchard. The Borax Company, whose operation was less than a mile away, purchased some of these products and paid the Indians a small royalty for the use of their water (Moyer 1996:35; Nelson 1893).

During the 1930s Johnny Hunter made enough money with the ranch operations that he purchased an automobile. It was a long,

Figure 3.61. Owens Valley Paiute Cap. Weaver, Mary Jim Harry, ca. 1927. Mary Jim Harry learned to weave in the traditional Owens Valley Paiute style. This cap has two bands of stacked diamonds with a three-strand twined start and a loop for gripping at the top. It is an excellent example of the finest twined basket style produced by Owens Valley Paiute women.

Figure 3.62. Sarah Hunter Weaving, ca. 1928. Sitting outside a traditional Panamint Shoshone thatched home, Sarah Hunter works on a small basket with a cactus design. At her feet are a large winnower and two small coiled baskets. A bundle of scraped willow rods, used for the foundation of the basket, is leaning against the home. Also leaning against the home is a coiled sifting tray basket.

open type known as a town car. Johnny didn't drive, so he employed a chauffeur who would drive him and eight or so other Panamint Shoshone people back and forth on the only road in Saline Valley.

By 1943 the Hunters no longer had their car, although they continued to farm and to keep horses and other livestock. They were the sole residents of the Indian Valley Ranch, and their closest neighbors lived near a talc mine some four or five miles away. In the summer months they sometimes lived in a shelter made by using the shade of a fig tree whose limbs spread out into a circle about thirty-five feet in diameter. The branches were propped up in places for support. The home was divided into a sleeping area with a wooden platform and mattress and a kitchen area with pots, pans, and the usual Euro-American cooking implements.

Sarah spent much of her time weaving baskets, often working in the shaded kitchen area of their living space. Like other weavers of her generation, Sarah used a tin can lid with holes punched in it to size the sewing strands for her baskets. The sale of her baskets contributed greatly to the income of the Hunter

family (Figure 3.64). Most likely, she depended on a trader to take her baskets out of the valley to sell for her and then bring back the money. She also supplied materials, especially willow, for other weavers, including Dolly Boland.

Hunter, like her half-sister Mamie Joaquin Button, was a premier weaver of fine, complexly patterned coiled baskets with realistic designs. Her three-rod, made-for-sale baskets replicated the flora and fauna of the region, frequently depicting chuckwalla lizards, birds, cacti, and bighorn sheep. Occasionally, she experimented with small floral forms and turtles. Her coiled baskets have an average stitch count of fifteen to seventeen stitches per horizontal inch. Although she made many small baskets, some of her baskets were large, ranging from twelve to twenty-three inches in diameter (Plate 8).[76] Hunter wove with all the materials used by her Panamint Shoshone contemporaries, including willow, bulrush root, devil's claw, juncus, and flicker quill.

Even though the basketry produced by Hunter and Button is very similar, one can discern small differences. For example, Hunter's rendering of the bighorn sheep, with downward-pointing horns, was sometimes

Figure 3.63. Johnny and Phillip Hunter, ca. 1937. Johnny Hunter holds Phillip, whom he and his wife, Sarah, adopted. Phillip's cradle is a variation on an old Panamint Shoshone style, made by binding crosspieces to a bent shoot frame. The cradle's hood is further decorated with pendants of glass beads and highly valued tubular shell beads from California's coast. The tab on a pull string of a small commercial tobacco sack hangs from Johnny's breast pocket.

Figure 3.64. Panamint Shoshone Basket. Weaver, Sarah Hunter, 1943. This oval coiled basket was bought directly from Hunter at her home in Saline Valley's Hunter Canyon. It is one of relatively few documented baskets known for certain to have been woven for sale during World War II. The oval shape was a favorite form used by Hunter.

identical to that made by her sister. Yet on other baskets Hunter made the tips of the sheep's horns curve around and point forward. Also, Hunter's baskets generally curve up rather

gently from the bottom whereas Button's oval baskets tend to have sides with an abrupt turn upward from the basket's base.

Like many other weavers in Saline Valley, in later life Hunter left her family home. In the early 1940s Col. A. E. Montieth bought the Hunter Canyon Mill Site and took the water that formerly flowed into the Hunter's property. Although the Hunters legally owned the bulk of the water by virtue of the California state water rights grandfather clause, Montieth was of the opinion that Indian people had no right to the water. The Hunters attempted to have a non-Indian friend intervene for them but could not obtain restitution. On January 26, 1952, Phillip Hunter, age fifteen, and his friend Irving Miller, age thirteen, took guns and confronted the caretaker of the Montieth property, Johnny Chavez. The outcome of the confrontation left Chavez dead; he was shot and wounded by Hunter and sought refuge in his cabin, to which the boys set fire. Phillip and Irving were arrested, tried, and convicted, and both served brief jail sentences. After this incident the remaining Indians in the area left Saline Valley.

Around 1950 Sarah's husband, Johnny Hunter, died. Perhaps as a result of his death and the outcome of the battle over the Hunters' water rights, Sarah went to live with her sister, Mamie Button, and her family in Lone Pine. In the early 1960s Sarah and the Buttons, along with other Panamint Shoshone people, moved to a site on Rawson Creek, just north of the Wilkerson Ranch and six miles south of Bishop, where they lived next door to each other. They cultivated devil's claw for its jet-black pods, used for the black designs in their baskets, and continued to weave baskets for sale. Certainly, their close proximity must have continued to influence the similarity of their weaving styles. In addition to devil's claw, Sarah used the yellow and yellow-brown juncus from Saline Valley as design materials. During this time she frequently wove geometric patterns on her baskets and sometimes made baskets with lids.

In 1967 Sarah Hunter became seriously ill. She died at the Northern Inyo Hospital on April 4 of that year and was buried four days later at the Darwin Cemetery. The Saline Valley Indian Ranch that was once her home, a lush garden in the desert, is now a dry and deserted flat, with only the dried remains of the ponds and the dead stump of the huge fig tree marking the site.

Susie Jackson Jim (1865–1935) and Sally Jackson Jim (1875–1946)

Susie Jackson (Oh-ha-ue-we) was born at Mammoth, California, and her sister, Sally (No-eu-buk), was born in Benton (Figure 3.65).[77] They and their sister, Mattie Jackson McBride, were the children of Mary Ann (Tu-ga-gu-an) and John Jackson (Bow-wu-net), who were both born in Mono County. Mary Ann's father, the sisters' maternal grandfather, was known as Captain or O-hot-chu-not and likely was a leader. Eventually, the sisters and their family ended up in the Owens Valley area. It is possible that their moves around Mono County followed the boom and bust cycle of the mining camps, as evidenced by each sister's being born in a different camp. Their eventual move to Owens Valley likely had a similar impetus, for as the mines ceased operation in Mono County, Indian people went elsewhere to seek employment. Indian settlements were often located on the fringes of mining towns, where the residents found employment and were able to secure supplies.[78]

Susie and Sally Jackson both married Dobie Jim, a Paiute from Adobe Meadows (about thirty miles north of Bishop) who was born in 1866.[79] The three of them lived in Bishop for much of their adult lives. Sally Jackson and Dobie Jim had one son, Dick Tom, who was born in Mono County. Susie had one daughter, Minnie (Betoit) Williams, by a non-Indian whose name is not recorded. Susie and Dobie Jim had one child, Nellie Jim Shaw. Bureau of Indian Affairs records show that Susie was divorced from Dobie Jim and was living with

Figure 3.65. Sally Jackson Jim and Josie Tom *(in cradle)*, 1916. Here Sally Jackson Jim holds her granddaughter, Josie Tom, who was born on February 12, 1916. Josie was the daughter of Sally Jackson Jim's son, Dick Tom, and his first wife, Eina. The cradle basket has a variation of the connecting zigzag pattern used for girls. The photograph was taken by Bishop photographer Andrew A. Forbes on the occasion of the 1916 Bishop Harvest Days, when Josie Tom won the award for "prettiest Indian baby under one year."

her daughter, Minnie Williams, by 1930. At that time Mary Ann Jackson, Sally and Susie's mother, was living with Sally and Dobie Jim at what was called Love Camp north of Bishop, on property owned by the city of Los Angeles. Dobie Jim was unable to work, but Sally Jim worked as a domestic for Jim Butler in Bishop.

The Jackson sisters were talented artisans whose three-rod baskets were finely woven and very similar in technique and appearance. They used bold and distinctive designs reminiscent of the style that nearby Yosemite and Mono Lake weavers were incorporating into their fancy made-for-sale baskets during the same period (see Figures 3.39, 3.40). Like other Mono Lake Paiute women, Sally and Susie wove their baskets on a three-rod willow foundation with a leftward coiling direction and exterior work surface. They favored a globular shape, and even their more flare-sided fancy baskets had a slightly inward-curving rim. Sewing strands were split willow shoots, and the design materials were black-dyed bracken

Figure 3.66. Mono Lake Paiute Gap-Stitched Basket. Weaver, Sally Jackson Jim, ca. 1920. Evenly spaced, non-interlocking stitches create the typical vertical, rib-like effect on this gap-stitched basket. Four horizontal rows with triangles in bracken fern root form the design.

Figure 3.67. Mono Lake Paiute Beaded Basket. Weaver, Sally or Susie Jackson Jim, or Mattie Jackson McBride, ca. 1930. Carefully executed floral patterns are mixed with both geometric motifs and realistic butterflies in this basket. The Jackson sisters excelled in producing these unique beaded baskets, based on the bottleneck basket form of the Western Mono, Yokuts, and Panamint Shoshone peoples.

Figure 3.68. Mono Lake Paiute Beaded Basket. Weaver, Sally or Susie Jackson Jim, or Mattie Jackson McBride, ca. 1930. Some of the beaded bottleneck baskets made by the Jackson sisters had designs that were fanciful and irregular. On this basket floral patterns, birds, and butterflies are interspersed with motifs taken from a deck of cards. The side of the basket shown in this view exhibits a yellow spade, two small birds, and geometric patterns.

fern root and redbud. When both design materials were used in the same basket, the bracken fern root often outlined the body of the design, which itself was done in redbud.

Sally and Susie Jackson used geometric designs on their baskets such as eight-pointed stars and diamonds, but they also favored interpretations of more realistic elements, including trees, birds, and flowers (Plate 9). One of their floral patterns is reminiscent of the fleur-de-lis motif from European arts.

They also made gap-stitched, three-rod coiled baskets (Figure 3.66). The three Jackson sisters — Sally, Susie, and Mattie — are the only three Paiute residents of Owens Valley known by name who made baskets that mimicked the shouldered bottleneck baskets of the neighboring Yokuts, Kawaiisu, Western Mono, and Panamint Shoshone peoples. These baskets were produced in gap-stitched, three-rod coiling and were usually covered with a network of glass seed beads (Figures 3.67 and 3.68; see also Plate 6). The sisters excelled in producing this style of beaded baskets, using only the time-consuming single-bead technique rather than the faster multiple-bead method.[80]

The designs the Jackson sisters used on these beaded bottleneck baskets were varied and often differed considerably from other Paiute beadwork motifs. Baskets attributed to them exhibit realistic floral and bird forms, butterflies, designs from playing cards (clubs, diamonds, spades, and hearts), and unique interpretations of geometric forms found in other Paiute beaded baskets. Their beaded baskets are among the finest produced by Paiute women. Susie and Sally's sister, Mattie Jackson McBride, also made beaded bottleneck baskets in this style.[81]

Examples of Susie and Sally Jackson's fine three-rod coiled baskets are at the Phoebe Apperson Hearst Museum of Anthropology, University of California at Berkeley. They were donated by Horatio Shumway Lee, who acquired them either himself while visiting Bishop or possibly through the efforts of collector Minnie Randolph.[82] Susie and Sally continued weaving throughout their lives. They enjoyed weaving together during the summer, when they would sit in the shade and visit while they worked (Figure 3.69). In addition to making baskets for sale to non-Indians, they made utilitarian baskets for use by themselves and their family, especially those used to process pine nuts.

Susie Jackson Jim died on December 16, 1935. Eleven years later, on December 28,

1946, Sally Jackson Jim died at her home on the Bishop Indian Reservation. She was buried at the Bishop Indian Cemetery on the following day.

Daisy Mallory (1890–1957)

Daisy Young Charlie Cluette Mallory was the daughter of the well-known Mono Lake Paiute weaver Nellie Charlie and her husband, Young Charlie.[83] Daisy was a distinguished weaver who carried forward the weaving traditions of her mother and her maternal grandmother, Patsy Jim, both of whom were recognized for their traditional utilitarian basketry and their fancy, three-rod baskets made for sale to non-Indians (Figure 3.70).

Daisy was born in Mono County not far from Mono Lake. Around 1900 she began attending school in the little red schoolhouse that was located on the Farrington Ranch, about five miles south of the site of today's town of Lee Vining. It was there that she learned to speak English. As was typical in traditional Paiute families, when she was a young woman her parents arranged for her marriage to Ed Cluette, a Paiute man. Daisy liked school and continued to attend after she became pregnant with her first child, Rosie. Knowing how to write, Daisy recorded the birth dates of her first two daughters, Rosie and Jessie, on the inside lid of a small trunk. To record the date of a child's birth was not a Paiute tradition; Mallory was perhaps the first in her family to keep written records (Figure 3.71).

Ed Cluette died when Jessie was still a baby.[84] After his death Daisy went to Mono Mills, located on the south shore of Mono Lake, where she cooked for the men with her sister, Lula. There she and her sister, her mother, and other women probably exchanged ideas about new basket patterns and styles. It is likely that she obtained glass seed beads from mill superintendent E. W. Billeb, enabling her to make bead-covered baskets like those of her mother. During this period Daisy made many small coiled baskets and was a proficient and innovative weaver (Plate 10). In addition to finely

Figure 3.69. Sally Jackson Jim at the Land Exchange Barbecue, 1939. Sally Jackson Jim is shown here socializing in 1939 with her friends, Daisy Williams *(left)* and Rosie Piper *(center)*.

crafted beaded baskets, Daisy made several baskets featuring eagle or butterfly motifs. It was also while at Mono Mills that Daisy learned to knit and crochet, skills she would continue to practice throughout her life.

Around 1917 Daisy and her daughters moved to Bishop, where Daisy found employment in the homes of local non-Indian families. The MacQueen family (see Chapter 4) was most likely the first Bishop household for which she worked. During the summers Daisy accompanied the family to their cabin at Mammoth, where she continued to work for them. In Bishop Dr. MacQueen settled Daisy and her family in a small cabin on East Line Street so she could have her own home. Because of her employment Daisy could have only one of her small daughters with her at any given time, so the other daughter would stay with Daisy's mother, Nellie Charlie. Daisy's daughter Jessie Durant remembers that Daisy would rise early in the morning to wash their clothes by hand before leaving for work. After cleaning and housekeeping for non-Indian families, Daisy would return home and prepare willow and other materials for weaving her baskets. Despite the long hours Mallory worked, she was "a good woman, patient with her family

Figure 3.70. Daisy Young Charlie Cluette Mallory, 1917. Daisy Mallory, the daughter of Nellie Charlie, is pictured in front of a store in Mono Mills, California, with an assortment of baskets. The basket at top center and the basket at top row right are both beaded baskets. The first was acquired by Mono County collector Ella Cain, who claimed it was one of the first beaded baskets ever made. The larger beaded basket to the right is nearly identical to others made by Mallory's mother, Nellie Charlie.

Figure 3.71. Daisy Young Charlie Cluette Mallory with Her Daughters, Rosie and Jessie, June 1913. By the time Jessie was born in 1913, the Cluettes were temporarily living in Yerrington, Nevada.

and very kind to others," according to Jessie. This characterization of Mallory is echoed by her nieces, all of whom recall that Daisy was consistently kind and cheerful.

In addition to the MacQueens, the Doyle family employed Daisy Mallory in their home. Helen MacKnight Doyle was an early settler, author, and physician, as well as the first woman to practice Western medicine in Inyo County.[85] Guy P. Doyle, her husband, was also a physician. The Doyles were prominent residents of Bishop and enthusiastic participants in civic affairs. Mallory also worked for the Garrigues family, which owned the Piñon Bookstore in Bishop, as well as the Art Hess family.[86] Jessie Durant believes that her mother gave or sold most of her baskets to her employers. These baskets remained largely in local collections rather than being dispersed by dealers to collectors and museums around the country.[87]

Around 1920 Daisy met a Paiute man, Jack Mallory, on one of his trips to Bishop to shop or visit friends. Jack lived in Round Valley, where he had been born in 1896. He was the son of Dick and Lottie Mallory. Jack and Daisy were married, and Daisy and her children moved to Round Valley to live at Jack's home. Their first daughter, Francis, was born in Round Valley in March 1921. Jack and Daisy would have six children together: Francis, Joe, Carl, Dick, Mary, and Ellen.

Although Jack Mallory had his own property in Round Valley, he also worked at various farms, ranches, and orchards, as well as at a flour mill in Round Valley. While they lived in Round Valley, Daisy took in laundry and ironing for local non-Indians and washed clothes in a big kettle on a fire outside. The Mallorys had a garden and kept some cows and chickens. They continued to live on their property in Round Valley until 1939, when they moved to the Bishop Reservation.

Daisy, along with her sister Lula, was weaving fine baskets as early as 1912. In that year they each sold several pieces to Bridgeport collector Ella Cain.[88] Cain and her husband ran a dry-goods and grocery store in Bridgeport,

California, and collected baskets from the Mono Lake Paiute people who frequented the store during the winter months; it was one of the few stores to be found in the region north of Bishop. Daisy Mallory and her mother, Nellie Charlie, knew the Cains "very well" (Jessie Durant, personal communication 2001). Among the documented fancy baskets in the Cain collection are baskets by Daisy Mallory and her sister Lula Hess, and by their aunt, Tina Charlie. Some of the baskets the sisters sold to Cain are among the finest produced by Mono Lake Paiute women. Daisy used a variety of realistic bird and butterfly motifs, as well as complex geometric forms in unique combinations.

Daisy Mallory was an industrious woman who continued to knit and crochet as well as weave baskets throughout her life. She was still working on a miniature burden basket when she died in 1957.

Annie Poole McBride (1874–1944)

Annie Poole McBride was born in Mono County in 1874 but lived most of her life in Inyo County (Sargent n.d.).[89] Her mother, Jennie Poole, was born in Benton, and her father, Doctor Charlie, was born at Hot Creek, southeast of Mammoth.

By 1900 Annie had married Arthur McBride, a Paiute man with whom she had at least one son, Jim.[90] Arthur died in 1902, and Annie moved to Bishop, where both she and her mother were living in 1930. An outstanding basket weaver, McBride nonetheless described her occupation in a 1930 census as "laundress."

As a basket weaver, McBride was recognized for her creativity and versatility. Her baskets were characterized by the use of uniform, neat stitches and complex, vertical designs and often had a unique short-necked shouldered form (Plate 11 and Figure 3.72). McBride usually used split willow shoots for the principal sewing strands, although occasionally she used sedge root, a material from the west side of the Sierra Nevada. Bracken fern root and redbud were the materials of choice for the black and

Figure 3.72. Mono Lake Paiute Bottleneck Basket. Weaver, Annie Poole McBride, ca. 1906. Similar to the basket in Plate 11 in form and design, this basket has sewing strands of sedge root, a material from the western side of the Sierras that gives the background a mottled look. The distinctive rim ticking is sedge and bracken fern root.

red colors in her designs. McBride's baskets were made with a leftward coiling direction on a foundation of three willow rods and sometimes displayed a distinctive rim finish. Using the diagonal rim finish popular with other Mono Lake women of her generation, McBride enhanced this combination by executing the finish with alternating stitches of bracken fern and willow, or bracken fern, willow, and redbud.[91] McBride made a number of baskets with a high rounded shoulder and small neck.[92] Although similar to traditional twined vessels of the Panamint Shoshones, as a form produced in coiling it was a style that seems to have been distinctly her own.[93]

McBride's baskets were appreciated by collectors during her lifetime. In 1908 Carroll S. Hartman, business associate of Indian art collector and dealer Grace Nicholson, wrote to Nicholson about a basket he purchased made by "Annie Pool."[94] He also refers to the work of a Mary Pool of Hot Creek,[95] another fine weaver, saying: "Annie Pool [sic] can exceed her work, so Mary has quit and Annie makes about one basket a year. The beautiful round bottles her work — and to my mind she puts shade on [famous Washoe weaver] Dotsolalees [sic] work. She gets $40 to 50.00 each for her baskets — Has only made six and this is her last one" (Hartman 1908:6–7).

Annie McBride was living near Bishop when she was diagnosed with cancer of the thyroid in late October 1944; she died on December 28. Family and friends buried her two days later at the Indian Sunland Cemetery near Bishop.

Figure 3.73. Emma Earl Symmes, ca. 1930. Shown with her employer's children, Charles and Betty Haines, Symmes did domestic work to earn a living.

Emma Earl Symmes (1850–?)

Emma Symmes was born at or near Fort Independence in September 1850.[96] The name of her Paiute father, who died when she was a small girl, was not recorded, but her mother was Minnie Robinson, also a Paiute. Both her parents were from Fort Independence. Emma was six when soldiers drove the Owens Valley Paiutes, including her family, south to Fort Tejon. Her people escaped and went into the hills when the group stopped to rest at Little Lake.

Emma married George Symmes, a Paiute man.[97] Little is known about their life together, except that they lived in Independence and Emma did housekeeping for the Haines family (Figure 3.73). George died in 1923. Their son, John, was active in Indian politics and testified before Congress in 1932 against the Los Angeles Aqueduct (Figure 3.74) (U.S. Senate Committee on Indian Affairs 1934:15198–15202). He was a close friend of collector

Anna Kelley and shared his knowledge of Paiute traditions and basketry with her. He made several non-basket items for her collection of Native American artifacts. John also demonstrated Paiute skills to non-Indians and taught both Paiutes and non-Indian people about Paiute culture and language in informal classes held at Ida Mae Cooney's house in Fort Independence (Bernasconi 1988:103).

Emma Symmes wove traditional utilitarian baskets, one of which she offered to Anna Kelley, who was director of welfare in Inyo County during World War II, as a thank-you gift (Figure 3.75). Kelley insisted on purchasing it, however, because she did not feel right accepting a gift that took so much time and care to make (Jim Kelley, personal communication 1998).

Minnie Williams (1896–1981)

Minnie Williams was born on August 25, 1896, the daughter of Susie Jackson and a non-Indian man whose name is not recorded.[98] She was known as Minnie Betoit in her youth and married Louis Williams, a Paiute man. She and Louis had four children: Eleanor, Wilfred, Velma, and Evelyn. In 1928 she and Louis were divorced. BIA records show that Minnie's mother, Susie, was divorced from her husband, Dobie Jim, in 1930 and was living with Minnie and her family at that time.

In addition to taking care of her family, Minnie did housework for local families and sometimes worked at the Town House Motel in Bishop. She practiced many aspects of traditional Paiute culture and annually gathered and processed piñon pine nuts during the fall harvest season (Figure 3.76). According to her daughter, Eleanor Bethel, Minnie found great pleasure and satisfaction in her weaving and always seemed to be working on a basket of some type. She excelled in making winnowing trays but made many other types of baskets as well (Figure 3.77). Although Williams sold some of her baskets, she kept many of them for her family to use and later to treasure. Williams also liked to do beadwork and made belts, neckpieces, and hatbands. She also created beaded baskets, often incorporating her favorite butterfly design.

An easygoing and gracious lady, Williams was always willing to help anyone in need. She was also happy to share her weaving and beading expertise with those who wanted to learn. Contemporary weaver Sandra Jefferson Yonge credits Williams with teaching her how to split willow shoots properly into thirds to make the sewing strands for baskets. Minnie Williams died on September 9, 1981.

Mary Harkness Yandell (1871–?)

Mary Yandell, Se-as-do-ne, was born in August 1871 at or near Bishop. Her mother's name was not recorded, although both her mother and her father, Tom Harkness, were Paiute people from Inyo County. Yandell made both twined and coiled baskets, and examples of both purportedly obtained from her are represented in the collection of the Eastern California Museum. If the twined basketry cap in the museum's collection was made by Yandell, and not obtained by her from another weaver, Yandell must have been one of the premier weavers of this particular type of twined basket in Owens Valley (Figure 3.78). Careful comparison of this cap with other caps would seem to indicate that the same weaver made many of these caps now in museum collections.[99]

Yandell's coiled basketry style is uncertain, as some of the baskets identified as her work appear to be made by different women; one is a Mono Lake Paiute basket of sedge and bracken fern roots, and another is a Panamint Shoshone basket.[100] Two other coiled baskets, however, appear to be by the same hand and may well actually be her work.

Both these coiled baskets are made on a three-rod willow foundation and are in a leftward coil direction with an outside work face and noninterlocking stitching. They are sewn with split willow shoots and use black devil's claw as the design material. In shape, both baskets are truncated cones (Figure 3.79).[101]

Attempts to locate additional information about Yandell's life and her baskets have proved unsuccessful.

Figure 3.74. Johnny Symmes, 1962. Symmes was a friend and schoolmate of collector Anna Kelley. Over a period of several years he shared with her many parts of his Indian heritage, including legends and the use of such objects as smoking reeds, brushes, and baskets.

Figure 3.75. Owens Valley Paiute Open-Twined Winnowing Basket. Weaver, Emma Earl Symmes, ca. 1934. Used by Anna Kelley in the 1960s to winnow pine nuts with the weaver's grandchildren, this basket is woven in plain, open twining with turns of twining that slant up to the right. It is typical of winnowing baskets made and used by the Owens Valley Paiutes.

Figure 3.76. Minnie Betoit Williams Winnowing Piñon Pine Nuts, ca. 1970. Minnie Betoit Williams uses a much-repaired winnowing basket to winnow piñon pine nuts.

Figure 3.77. Mono Lake Paiute Winnowing Basket. Weaver, Minnie Betoit Williams, ca. 1962. This winnowing tray was purchased from Minnie Betoit Williams at the Tri-County Fair in Bishop in 1962. Made entirely of willow, it is an excellent example of an unused Owens Valley Paiute–style winnowing tray.

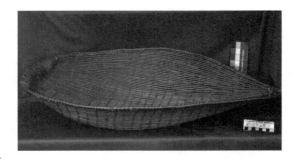

Figure 3.78. Owens Valley Paiute Cap. Weaver, Mary Harkness Yandell, ca. 1905. The two horizontal bands with zigzag designs and the loop at the top are common features of traditional Owens Valley Paiute caps.

Figure 3.79. Owens Valley Paiute Flared Bowl. Weaver, Mary Harkness Yandell, ca. 1905. Woven with split-willow shoots on a three-rod foundation, this flare-sided basket has an ascending design reminiscent of an older style of Panamint Shoshone stepped pattern. However, the coil direction is consistent with that of Owens Valley Paiute basketry.

4. TREASURING THE WILLOW

A History of Basket Collecting
in Owens Valley

Fair token, deftly wrought by savage art,
The craft of dusky fingers trained to twine
The supple willow, shaped in patterned line,
Enweaving strand by strand the dearest part
Of storied lore wild nature can impart
To breast that ever worship at her shrine,
What handiwork is more sincere than thine,

Or bears the impress of a truer heart?
I hear the mother crooning soft and low
Beside her sleeping child, while fingers fly
To shape thee, basket; weaving to and fro
The strands of love to live perpetually,
Embodied in thy form. What art can show
A higher claim to immortality?

— Charles A. Keeler, 1894[1]

Before the 1876 Centennial Exhibition in Philadelphia, the collecting of material culture lay largely in the domain of explorers, traders, missionaries, and military men. These people routinely gathered artifacts as souvenirs of their travels or as curios to sell. Sometimes they displayed them at giant expositions such as the one in Philadelphia.[2] Documentation of such objects was usually sparse, at best, and most of the artifacts remained in the homes of private collectors. By the mid-nineteenth century, as international exhibitions became popular, collecting was beginning to be formalized as an activity of museums. Museums started sponsoring acquisition trips, and documenting where and when artifacts were collected became accepted practice. This change occurred within the context of three trends that emerged concurrently in the United States: the development of the Arts and Crafts movement, the growth of the curio trade, and the rise of academic anthropology.

THE ARTS AND CRAFTS MOVEMENT

The industrial revolution, which began in the mid-eighteenth century, resulted in dramatic changes in production, transportation, and communication. The shift from hand labor to mechanization reduced prices through easier duplication and faster production. While creating economic growth and spurring advances in science and technology, industrial progress also spawned poor working conditions, business monopolies, and city slums.

One response to the results of such "progress" was the Arts and Crafts movement. The movement began in England in the late 1800s and spread across the Atlantic Ocean, reaching its peak of popularity in the United States between 1890 and 1910. One of its goals was to produce unique objects that provided pleasure to both the makers and the consumers. Indian baskets represented the antithesis of mass-produced items. They were made by hand from natural materials and were one of a kind. They required an investment of time, an internal inspiration, and a piece of the maker's soul.

THE CURIO TRADE

The curio trade was a commercial phenomenon that focused on the sale of "inter-ethnic commodities" (Cohodas 1997:4) to tourists, collectors, and dealers whose cultural backgrounds differed from those of the producers. Generally intended for display, curios were marketed as fragments of exotic foreign cultures that were in danger of vanishing. Curios of nature — such as unusual stones or snake skins — were sold,

but it was Indian artifacts that were most popular. Indian baskets were one of the most sought-after types of curio objects as they were lightweight, unbreakable, and aesthetically pleasing.

The curio trade, especially including Indian artifacts, grew into a large business in the United States between the late 1880s and 1930. As the public became more aware of the American West, tourists began to flow to that part of the country. Americans learned about the West from many sources. When Theodore Roosevelt was president (1901–9), for example, he set aside millions of acres as national parks and national forests. These areas, many of which lay west of the Mississippi, contained natural wonders, and Americans flocked to visit them.

Photography also helped shape popular perceptions of the American West. Itinerant photographer Andrew Forbes, for example, chronicled the early towns of Owens Valley, surrounding mountain scenery, and Indian encampments. His later images also documented the building of the Los Angeles Aqueduct.

A more far-reaching source of information about the West was the literary world. Writers such as Mary Austin, Horace Greeley, Mark Twain, and Zane Grey painted the West as exciting, exotic, and untamed, as a place for daring adventurers and a cure for wanderlust. As Twain explained,

> I coveted . . . particularly and especially the long, strange journey [my brother] was going to make, and the curious new world he was going to explore. He was going to travel! I never had been away from home and that word "travel" had a seductive charm for me. Pretty soon he would be hundreds and hundreds of miles away on the great plains and deserts, and among the mountains of the Far West, and would see buffaloes and Indians, and prairie dogs, and antelopes and have all kinds of adventures, and maybe get hanged. (1993:1–2)

Another source of information was the advertising done by railroad companies,[3]

steamship lines, camera companies, and other tourist-related industries. Magazines such as *National Geographic,* as well as calendars, posters, and brochures, printed catchy slogans: "Santa Fe All the Way" (James 1903a:inside back cover), "Through Apacheland to California," "Across the First Page of American History," and "The grandeur comes home with you — in pictures on Kodak film" (O'Barr 1994:50, 51, 34–35). Souvenir stores, such as those owned by the Fred Harvey Company, piggybacked onto this kind of advertising to promote themselves (Plate 12).[4] They used photographic images of rugged landscapes, snow-covered mountains, and native peoples to entice travelers to visit the West.

This general interest in the West helped focus attention on the region's Indian tribes. The fascination with Indian people evident in advertising was also manifest in such early international expositions as the 1893 World's Fair in Chicago and the 1904 World's Fair in St. Louis. At these events representatives from various tribes often wore native clothing, displayed and demonstrated their skills, and sometimes performed dances. For many, these exhibitions were a chance to see firsthand how Indians had once lived. Interest in Indian cultures and western locations such as the Grand Canyon and Yosemite National Park was furthered by the widespread use of picture postcards, many of which featured Indian people posed in traditional clothing, often in western landscapes.

All these venues helped romanticize a way of life that was no longer intact. As in the case of the Owens Valley Paiutes, contact with Euro-Americans had already started to change traditional Indian culture. The selling of the West, however, engendered a mystique that Indians had some kind of special, innate knowledge about the universe and were "near to Nature" (Curtis 1907, quoted in McCluhan 1972:xii). It left a stereotype in its wake that still exists today in American popular culture (see, for example, Ellis 1965; Ewers 1987; Fleming and Luskey 1986; Jenkins 1993). At the same time, an air of authenticity was lent to the pottery, baskets, and textiles made by Indians, stimulating the market for native goods.

By 1889 newspapers and magazines were reporting the fascination of the American people with Indian baskets. People were encouraged to create an entire "Indian room" in their homes, full of Indian blankets, beadwork, pottery, and baskets (Starr 1889). A January 1891 article commented that the latest craze in California was to possess a collection of Indian baskets: "Who started the craze is not known, but someone discovered that the baskets possessed great artistic beauty, were rich in harmonious coloring, and formed attractive ornaments for library and parlor and the demand began" (Figure 4.1) (Holden 1891). Articles in a variety of magazines promoted the decoration of homes with baskets throughout the next few decades (*Craftsman* 1910; Guthrie 1901; James 1901b; Priestman 1908:137). Other publications emphasized the mythology embodied in baskets and profiled collectors and their collections (Brown 1898; Connor 1896; James 1901c; MacCurdy 1903; *Outlook* 1901; Shepard 1909). Interest in collecting baskets continued to grow in the early years of the twentieth century.

The first decade of the twentieth century has been referred to as the "golden decade" of basket collecting (Gogol 1985). Advertisers and interior decorators urged the creation of Indian corners or Indian dens, rooms that would be showplaces for Native American baskets and collectibles. Members of the prosperous American upper middle class had both time and money to emulate their European counterparts by designating large portions of their homes for the display of curios, which in the United States often meant a large collection of Indian baskets. Some wealthy collectors amassed collections that they subsequently loaned or donated to local museums.[5] Large department stores, such as John Wanamaker's in Philadelphia, displayed baskets in their windows and offered them for sale (Cohodas 1997: 78). The interest in Native American baskets was so intense that newspapers claimed basket making was one of the latest fads taken up by

Figure 4.1. Helen and Vivian MacQueen, Bishop, California, July 1906. This photo of Helen "Queenie" MacQueen and her daughter, Vivian, was taken at their family home in Bishop. Baskets collected by the MacQueens were part of the decor here and also at their summer cabin in Mammoth, California. Their collection grew as Dr. MacQueen was given baskets in return for his dental service. The basket cap at far left on the top shelf is pictured in Figure 4.19.

(non-Indian) women of fashion (*Star* 1901a; Winslow 1901).

Books and public lectures by basketry experts of the day also promoted the collecting of baskets and the use of basketry for home decoration. Perhaps the most well known of these advocates was George Wharton James (1858–1923), author of *Indian Basketry* (1901a, 1902, 1972). A defrocked Methodist minister escaping a scandalous divorce in California, James visited Arizona and the Havasupai Indians who lived in Cataract Canyon. While there he developed an admiration for the "tranquil" lives they led, away from the constraints of the modern world. In 1892 he moved to Pasadena, California, and began collecting Native American baskets. Like many others, James wrote articles in popular periodicals that promoted

Figure 4.2. Cover of *The Basket,* Volume II, Number 4, October 1904. Billed as a basket lovers' journal, this quarterly publication of the Basket Fraternity offered instruction in basket making, information about design patterns, and guidance for collectors.

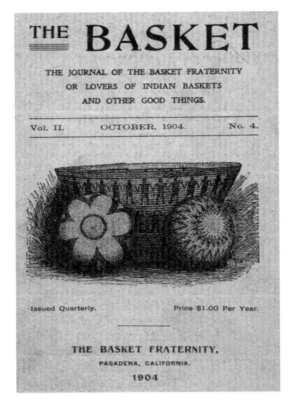

THE BASKET

THE JOURNAL OF THE BASKET FRATERNITY OR LOVERS OF INDIAN BASKETS AND OTHER GOOD THINGS.

Vol. II.   OCTOBER, 1904.   No. 4.

Issued Quarterly.   Price $1.00 Per Year.

THE BASKET FRATERNITY,
PASADENA, CALIFORNIA.
1904

the artistry of baskets and their use in decorating the home (James 1901b, c). He was especially interested in the interpretive and symbolic meaning of basketry designs, writing and lecturing extensively about this subject (James 1913, 1914). James founded the "Basket Fraternity," an organization for people interested in Indian basketry, and published the journal *The Basket* (Figure 4.2). This periodical offered basket-making instruction, purchasing information, authentication advice, and scholarly articles. One of the earliest issues described *The Basket* as "a special magazine written for a special purpose. It contains more lore on Indian baskets and their weavers than any other journal. It gives more information about how to make baskets than can be gained from any other source" (James 1903b:69).[6]

To serve the growing demand for Indian collectibles, professional collectors emerged in the form of curio dealers. W. L. Clark, D. M. Averill and Co., Mrs. Emma Rhodes, Grace Nicholson, and many others played an important economic role in encouraging the development of a market for Indian baskets.

They were also responsible, however, for influencing stylistic and functional changes in basketry. Helping supply prominent curio dealers were local traders who lived near the reservations. Mail-order businesses such as the Indian Arts Company of Gallup, New Mexico, and the Frohman Trading Company of Portland, Oregon, simplified buying even further (Gogol 1985:28). F. M. Gilham, from Highland Springs, Lake County, California, a wholesale dealer in Indian baskets, bought directly from the makers, claimed always to have some "old worn baskets" to sell, sent baskets on approval anywhere in the United States, and prepaid all postal charges (Gilham n.d., 1891). Abe Cohn, a Carson City businessman, promoted the sale of Washoe baskets, particularly those by Louisa "Datsolalee" Keyser, through his sales outlets at Lake Tahoe and Carson City, as well as in brochures and postcards (Figure 4.3).[7] The buying and selling of Indian baskets was a competitive business.

THE RISE OF ACADEMIC ANTHROPOLOGY

The discipline of cultural anthropology grew from a realization that societies around the world differed vastly from the "civilized" societies of Europe and North America. Nineteenth-century anthropologists used a unilineal evolutionary theory to explain this cultural diversity. They believed that all societies went through a single series of progressive stages but at different rates.[8] The inability to fit all societies into this schema, however, made anthropologists realize they had too little concrete information to explain the enormous variation in human customs. As a result, they stopped trying to propose general laws about the origin or role of culture and began gathering as much specific ethnographic data as possible through a process of firsthand, extended fieldwork known as "participant-observation."[9] Anthropologists spent years at a time living with the people whose way of life they were recording, in order to gain an intimate understanding of their culture. This method of field research became one of the hallmarks distinguishing professional anthropologists trained at universities from their amateur counterparts.[10]

Underlying anthropological interest in documenting cultures worldwide was the concern that indigenous societies were on the verge of disappearing. In the United States the belief in the imminent extinction of Native American cultures made anthropologists rush to study and document indigenous tribes "before it was too late." This sense of urgency was supported by two factors. First, the actual number of Indians had, in fact, decreased dramatically. European-introduced diseases and casualties from war had taken a large toll. The number of Native Americans living in California, for example, had fallen from about 300,000 in 1769 to approximately 16,000 in 1900 (Castillo 1978:-99, 118). Second, the traditional culture of those Indians still living had been severely disrupted. The U.S. military and non-Indian settlers had destroyed many of the Indians' food stores, ancestral lands, and possessions. Governmental policies had forced their relocation to reservations and imposed the written law of the non-Indian culture on them. Boarding schools interfered with their ability to transmit cultural traditions from one generation to another. In short, the concern of anthropologists to study and document Native American cultures before it was too late was well founded.

In the 1870s and 1880s a limited number of scholars had started recording valuable information about the western Native American tribes. John Wesley Powell, a geologist who later became the first director of the Bureau of American Ethnology, was the first person to study extensively the languages and ethnography of the Great Basin (D. Fowler 1986:23; Fowler and Fowler 1971:1–13; Fowler and Matley 1979:1–4). In the late 1880s Otis Tufton Mason, an expert on aboriginal basketry who later became curator of the Division of Ethnology of the Smithsonian Institution, had begun to study and write about baskets and other Indian artifacts. He proposed the "culture area" system of classification for organizing ethnographic data and material culture, a system that grouped various societies according

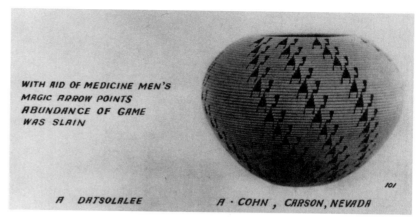

WITH AID OF MEDICINE MEN'S MAGIC ARROW POINTS ABUNDANCE OF GAME WAS SLAIN

A DATSOLALEE   A · COHN , CARSON, NEVADA

Figure 4.3. Postcard, ca. 1920. This postcard, promoting the basketry of Washoe weaver Louisa "Datsolalee" Keyser (ca. 1850–1925), was one of several cards issued by Indian basket and curio dealer Abe Cohn. The fanciful interpretation of the basket's design on the card was created not by the basket's maker but by Cohn. Such supposed interpretations of basket patterns were created to add to the allure and romance of Indian baskets, thus increasing sales to non-Indians.

to the similarity of their living patterns within particular ecological environments (D. Fowler 1986:15–16). During the first decade of the twentieth century Alfred Kroeber, who was to become a leading academic anthropologist, did extensive fieldwork in California, including the Great Basin. Based on dissimilar cultural patterns, he justified separating the study of Indian tribes living in the lush western Sierra Nevada from those residing in the arid, eastern parts of California (D. Fowler 1986:16, 24; Kroeber 1939:49–53).

Julian Steward (1902–72) is generally acknowledged as the principal ethnographer of the Owens Valley Paiutes. In 1933 his monograph *Ethnography of the Owens Valley Paiute* was published. This work was the result of three research visits to Owens Valley. When Steward was a graduate student at the University of California at Berkeley, he spent six weeks in Owens Valley during the summer of 1927 and another six weeks the following summer. He made a brief third visit in December 1931. While conducting fieldwork, Steward collected baskets for what would become the Phoebe Apperson Hearst Museum of Anthropology at the University of California at Berkeley (Figure 4.4).[11]

Steward's work with the Owens Valley Paiutes was the first of a series of studies he made in the Great Basin, which included important contributions in identifying protohistoric and prehistoric sites and mapping petroglyph locations. He also worked with the various Shoshonean tribes of Utah, Idaho, Nevada,

Figure 4.4. Owens Valley Paiute Winnowing Basket. Weaver, Mary Jim Harry, 1927. Julian Steward purchased several baskets from Mary Jim Harry during the course of his fieldwork in Owens Valley. Harry wove this winnowing tray in the distinctive Owens Valley style, which adds an additional strengthening rod for support across the center of the basket's back.

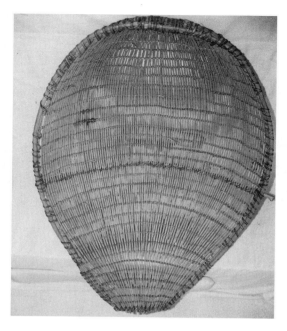

and eastern California and conducted surveys of Great Basin groups (Steward 1937, 1938a, 1941, 1943).

During the 1930s Kroeber, who had authorized Steward's field trips to Owens Valley, was the driving force behind a series of cultural element distribution surveys of western American Indian groups at the University of California, Berkeley. Omer Stewart, Harold Driver, and Julian Steward all did important work as part of this survey in the Great Basin (Driver 1937; Steward 1941; Stewart 1941). The goals of this project were to complete an ethnographic record of these peoples and verify the presence or absence of specific traits for each tribe or band. The accompanying explanatory notes in these publications were invaluable sources of supplemental information.

In the course of subsequent trips to the Great Basin while conducting work for the survey, Steward amassed a great deal of additional data. The 1938 publication of his *Basin-Plateau Aboriginal Sociopolitical Groups* offered specific cultural element data along with ethnohistoric information (1938a). In addition, his detailed accounts of family groups provided a foundation for the study of genealogy in the Great Basin. Steward also published brief biographies of Owens Valley Paiute people, a volume on Owens Valley Paiute mythology, and another

of Western Shoshone myths (Steward 1934, 1936a, 1938b, 1943).

Steward's 1935 trip to the Great Basin took him to Owens Valley and the surrounding region during April and May. Before his departure Steward had contacted Donald Scott, director of the Peabody Museum, and offered to collect items for the museum. Scott wired Steward one hundred dollars for his purchases. On this trip Steward purchased specimens of games made by John Hunter and his nephew Wilbur Patterson, Panamint Shoshone men from Saline Valley. He also obtained baskets made by a weaver he identified as "Sullivan Shaw's woman," the noted Panamint Shoshone weaver Laura Shaw (Sennett-Graham 1989:179). Steward also purchased baskets made by George Hanson's niece, Mabel.[12] The Shoshone field notes Steward compiled include a notebook containing drawings, precise measurements, design descriptions, and weaving details of a number of baskets, including those collected on this trip.

Steward worked at the Bureau of American Ethnology at the Smithsonian Institution from 1935 to 1946 and subsequently taught at Columbia University and the University of Illinois, Urbana. His later work focused on South America and Puerto Rico. His correspondence and the bulk of his research materials, including those dealing with the Owens Valley Paiutes and Panamint Shoshones, are in the archives of the University of Illinois at Urbana-Champaign.

The involvement of academic anthropologists in ethnographic fieldwork triggered a change in how and why cultural artifacts were collected. Anthropologists began to collect objects with the intent of preserving and studying them methodically rather than arbitrarily collecting them and displaying them in public museums detached from their cultural context. Although the amount of information recorded varied with the collector, information might include the native term for the object; the location from which it was acquired; its materials, function, and design elements; and in a few cases the name of the maker. The resulting catalog cards still serve today as the linchpins of serious study of the distribution and use of

Plate 1. Owens Lake Dry Bed. Owens Lake, looking like a lunar landscape, stretches between the Sierra Nevada and the town of Keeler. Its flaky salts and toxins made it the worst source of airborne pollution in the United States (Purdum 1998:1), until a rewatering program was implemented in 2001.

Plate 2. Owens Valley, California, in Autumn. Viewed from Highway 395, the bright colors of autumn foliage and the slick, black lava deposits near Big Pine contrast sharply with the rugged beauty of the Sierra Nevada.

Plate 3. Owens Valley Paiute Cap. Weaver unknown, ca. 1920. Made with a three-strand-twining start for reinforcement, this cap has two bands of vertical zigzag ("black water snake") patterns and a third band of simple design. A row of three-strand twining at the termination strengthens the rim. The design elements are made from painted, winter-peeled willow.

Plate 4. Owens Valley Paiute Water Jar. Weaver, unknown ca. 1900. Amphoric in shape with two handles and a narrow neck, this water jar has leather handles that could be attached to a strap for carrying. The pitch and red earth on the exterior, as well as the pitch on the interior, make it watertight. Rows of three-strand twining at the start add durability.

Plate 5. Owens Valley Paiute Coiled Basket. Weaver unknown, ca. 1900. This finely made basket is coiled in a leftward direction. It is an Owens Valley copy of a Panamint Shoshone basket in pattern and fineness of stitching. Most likely it was made for sale to a non-Indian in response to the demand for quality well-woven baskets. This basket was once part of Rose Black's collection (see the far right side of Figure 4.16, about one quarter of the way down).

Plate 6. Mono Lake Paiute Beaded Basket. Weaver, Sally Jackson Jim, ca. 1930. The impetus for beading baskets was a suggestion from the superintendent of the Mono Mills Lumber Company. He urged local Paiute women to cover their willow baskets with glass beads from Czechoslovakia, which he provided. Buyers liked the novel style, and the technique soon spread to neighboring Washoe and Paiute weavers. This basket uses more than ten different colors of beads in its geometric, floral, and realistic patterns. The collector, Frankie Beatty, often supplied glass beads to the Jackson sisters to use on their beaded baskets.

Plate 7. Panamint Shoshone Basket. Weaver, Addie Hanson, ca. 1950. This basket was woven by Isabel Hanson's niece, Addie; note how the pattern is similar to the basket made by Isabel in Figure 3.59, as well as the basket Isabel is weaving in Figure 3.60. This basket makes use of willow and devil's claw, both traditional Panamint Shoshone materials. In addition, it uses split redbud shoots for the red pattern, a new material for Panamint Shoshone weavers. The redbud, from west of the Sierra Nevada crest, was likely obtained by Addie from Owens Valley Paiute women who had acquired it in trade or by purchase.

Plate 8. Panamint Shoshone Baskets. Weaver, Sarah Hunter, Saline Valley, ca. 1930. These baskets are typical of the ones Panamint Shoshone women made for sale to non-Indians. Although the collector identified these baskets as those she had received from Sarah Hunter, it may be that some were made by Hunter's sister, Mamie Joaquin Button.

Plate 9. Mono Lake Paiute Globular Coiled Basket. Weaver, Susie Jackson Jim, ca. 1920. Redbud designs outlined in bracken fern root embolden the bird and pine tree designs that are evenly spaced around the basket.

Plate 10. Mono Lake Paiute Coiled Basket. Weaver, Daisy Young Charlie Cluette Mallory, ca. 1917. This basket is nearly identical to several sold by Daisy Mallory to Bridgeport collector Ella Cain in 1917. The negative image of a butterfly in a red-outlined, black diamond alternates with a bird design. Mallory, like her mother Nellie Charlie, was an innovative weaver who produced exceedingly fine baskets.

Plate 11. Mono Lake Paiute Bottleneck Basket. Weaver, Annie Poole McBride, ca. 1915. With a distinctive rim finish of alternating willow and bracken fern root stitches, this fancy basket exhibits fine coiling and an intricate polychrome pattern of vertical geometric designs.

Plate 12. Souvenir Playing Cards of the Great Southwest, 1911. Made and published exclusively for the Fred Harvey Company of Kansas City, Missouri, these cards depicted people, places, hotels, trains, and scenery of New Mexico, Arizona, California, and Colorado. The cards advertised the locations served by the Santa Fe Railroad, which transported tourists and cargo during the early twentieth century from the Great Lakes to the Pacific coast and the Gulf of Mexico.

Plate 13. Jessie Durant Winnowing Brine Fly Larvae at Mono Lake, 1995. Originally from the Mono Lake area, Jessie Durant demonstrates the use of the winnowing basket for harvesting brine fly larvae.

Plate 14. Miniature Baby Basket. Weaver, Gretchen Uhler Hess, 1999. This model cradle basket, made of willow in the traditional Paiute style, is covered in deerskin and the fringe decorated with glass beads. It is approximately half the size of those used in real life. The step design on the sunshade is made with embroidery floss.

different artifact types and the study of specific industries such as basketry.

THE COLLECTORS OF OWENS VALLEY BASKETS: FROM THE OUTSIDE LOOKING IN

With the rise of the Arts and Crafts movement, the curio trade, and academic anthropology, basket collecting in the United States flourished in the Southwest, on the Northwest Coast, and in California. Because of its geographic isolation, however, Owens Valley was not in the mainstream of these movements. As explained in Chapter 2, by the 1880s the cultural traditions of the indigenous people of Owens Valley were being disrupted. Their land and water were being usurped by miners, settlers, farmers, ranchers, cows, horses, and politicians. The local Paiutes adapted to a changing economy by becoming wage laborers and trading their crafts as commodities, bartering or selling their baskets for food and supplies. Non-Indians in the valley acquired baskets as gifts and were beginning to purchase them for souvenirs and home decoration. There were, however, a limited number of outsiders involved in this development.

Some collectors from other areas traveled to Owens Valley in search of Paiute and Panamint Shoshone basketry.[13] It was the Panamint Shoshone baskets that attracted the bulk of the interest. When a firsthand visit was impossible or when direct dealings with the Indians were unsuccessful, these outside collectors often enlisted the help of local residents and "traders" as intermediaries. One such go-between was Harry C. Floyd.

Harry C. Floyd (1866–?)

A native of England, Floyd suffered from tuberculosis and came to the dry, healthful climate of eastern California in the early 1900s. Father John J. Crowley (1891–1940), affectionately known as the Desert Padre, characterized Floyd as somewhat eccentric. According to Crowley, he was an "odd English remittance man[14] who . . . scorned a bed, slept in his blanket on the sand, lived on his remittance and the few vegetables he raised at the water's edge

between cloud bursts" (Brooks 1997:186). Floyd lived for a short time in Independence, where he began collecting Panamint Shoshone baskets. He moved to Darwin in 1905. In 1909 he met and courted Lucille Harman, a Darwin schoolteacher (Palazzo 1996:58). He would "come courting in the evenings — dirty 'longhandles' (union suits) — gray striped pants — prince Albert coat — no shirt — but a stiff — loose front from neck to top of pants and stiff cuffs around his wrists — the 'shirt front' looked like an oval piece of cardboard. How we used to laugh!" (Mecham 1978:2).

Floyd and Harman married in 1910. The bride apparently "objected not to his uncut hair and his filthy attire, and lived, as he did, beneath the stars" (Brooks 1997:187). Floyd was a farmer (William H. Michael, personal communication 1998), but he photographed plants and animals in the area as well. The photographs he sold to tourists illustrated "the torn banks of the wash and the timeless faces of the Indians" (Brooks 1997:186). Floyd's primary activity in Owens Valley, however, was supplying Indian baskets to important collectors and dealers. In this regard, Floyd was typical of this time and was of a genre found all over the West (Bruce Bernstein, personal communication 1998).

Little is known about the extent of Floyd's trading activities. Clearly, he tried to keep his dealings with the Indians quiet. Apparently unbeknown to local valley shopkeepers, Floyd purchased many of the supplies and staples that he traded for baskets from outside wholesale companies such as the Pacific Wholesale Company of San Francisco and Lyon Brothers in Chicago. Sometimes he had his clients advance money directly to the wholesale companies, and then he deducted that amount from the selling price of the baskets. This business practice caused some worry, as indicated by a letter he wrote to Grace Nicholson: "I cannot remit from here without store people catching on as they have the money order office & it might make unpleasantness" (Floyd 1912).

Floyd supplied baskets to collectors all across the country, including C. Hart Merriam and H. Shumway Lee.[15] He sold most of the baskets through the mail and specialized in those made by Panamint Shoshones. In a letter he wrote to Merriam in February 1903 he mentioned having obtained some Paiute baskets but described them as being "too rough" to send (Floyd 1903). Floyd's cautious behavior made it difficult to track all his clients. Catalog cards for Homer Sargent's Panamint Shoshone baskets at the Field Museum of Natural History in Chicago refer repeatedly to an "Old English Harry," who most probably was Harry Floyd (Figure 4.5).

Floyd and his wife left Darwin in 1914 and returned to England to fight in World War I (Mecham 1978:1).

Clinton Hart Merriam (1855–1942)

Most of the early collectors of Owens Valley Native American baskets visited the valley and tried to learn firsthand as much as possible about the Indian cultures of the region. One of the earliest collectors with an ethnographic interest was C. Hart Merriam. A preeminent naturalist, Merriam was perhaps most well known for helping found the National Geographic Society and what is now the U.S. Fish and Wildlife Service. He served as chief of the U.S. Biological Survey for twenty-five years and published extensively.

Merriam was the naturalist for the Hayden Survey of the Western Territories, starting in 1872. Eventually, he interacted with a variety of

Figure 4.5. Panamint Shoshone Coiled Basket. Weaver unknown, ca. 1909. This basket is typical of the finest Panamint Shoshone baskets made for sale before 1910. The combination of geometric patterns and human figures was popular with non-Indian buyers. Collector H. E. Sargent referred to dealer Harry Floyd, who sold him this basket, as "Old English Harry."

Native American groups, became interested in Indian cultures, and began to purchase Indian baskets. His first recorded basket purchase occurred in a Phoenix train station in 1894. Throughout the remainder of his life he continued to purchase baskets from native people as well as from dealers and curio shops.

In 1899 Merriam's interest in native peoples led him to organize a team of scientists, doctors, stenographers, and the photographer Edward Curtis for an Alaskan scientific study, funded by railroad financier E. H. Harriman. Soon afterward Merriam turned his attention to the various Indian tribes of California.

As he became more attuned to the important role of baskets in native culture, Merriam began to go to the Indians' seasonal camps to learn as much as possible about their way of life. While there he noticed that the Indians often had fancy or unusual baskets from other tribes among their personal belongings. Merriam suggested that they collected these "intrusive" baskets because "Indians [as well as non-Indians] love fine baskets" (1955:107). He was intrigued by the weavers' use of various natural materials, feeling an affinity with the Indian people because, like many others of his generation, he believed they were "born naturalists, familiar from earliest childhood with the animals and plants of the regions in which they live[d]" (Heizer 1966:3). He preferred utilitarian baskets over those that were made for sale and considered any basket whose design covered much of the surface to be "inauthentic" (Cohodas 1997:218).

The most active collecting years for Merriam were between 1900 and 1904, when he bought about 75 percent of his 1,050 documented pieces (Griset 1993:35). In 1902 he spent four months doing fieldwork on both sides of the Sierras, including a few days in Owens Valley during October.

Merriam purchased many of his baskets directly from the weavers and also did business, both in person and through the mail, with Harry Floyd, from whom he bought at least fourteen baskets between 1902 and 1903. During his time in Owens Valley, Merriam also purchased baskets from local residents Minnie C. Barrows Randolph (a teacher in Bishop) and Mrs. A. W. Eibeshutz (a collector from Independence) (Figure 4.6). In addition, he visited Bishop basket collectors Dr. Helen MacKnight Doyle (a physician) and Dr. John S. MacQueen (a dentist), whose collections both "contain[ed] a few jewels" (Merriam 1901:80).

Merriam was concerned with the proper identification of the Owens Valley Paiutes and other neighboring tribes, endeavoring to differentiate clearly among these groups on the basis of language. He visited various Indian settlements and compiled extensive vocabulary lists. He noted vocabulary differences among the Owens Valley Paiutes, the Panamint Shoshones, the Mono Lake Paiutes, and the Western Monos, and he felt that the vocabulary of the Mono Lake Paiutes was most closely allied to that of the Northern Paiutes. In fact, the Mono Lake Paiutes speak Northern Paiute, not Mono (Fowler and Liljeblad 1986:435, 437). And although the Owens Valley language was somewhat related to that of the Panamint Shoshones, it was most closely related to that of the Western Monos. Because the Owens Valley Paiute and Western Mono languages were so much alike, Merriam felt they should be classed as the same group and called Eastern and Western Monache (Merriam n.d.a:[a]).

Merriam's primary interest in basket collecting was preserving the culture of the Indian people he had come to admire. His ethnographic writings were the result of carefully organized study, thoughtful questioning, and a meticulous attention to detail, much of which was included on the catalog cards he made for his basket collection. His cards are so detailed compared with most others made during this time that he could be called the "father of the catalog card" (Figure 4.7). He began his documentation with the baskets he acquired in 1894 and persuaded major private collectors to retain such information themselves. Homer E. Sargent Jr. (a Chicago collector who amassed over five hundred baskets) and Henry K. Deisher (a mill owner from Kutztown, Pennsylvania,

Figure 4.6. Owens Valley Paiute Basket. Weaver, mother of "Sally," ca. 1900. This oval basket, identified as Owens Valley Paiute, is woven with a rightward coil direction, unlike most Owens Valley Paiute coiling, which is made with a leftward direction. The rightward coiled direction is more consistent with Panamint Shoshone weaving, although the patterns and relatively wide sewing strands on this basket are more like Owens Valley Paiute work.

whose Native American collection included more than four hundred baskets) sought out Merriam for assistance in recording appropriate documentation data (Deisher 1906; Sargent 1908a).

By the early 1900s Merriam's reputation as an authority on baskets and Native American culture was well established. Professional ethnographers consulted him about their collections and studies. Otis Mason asked him to review the manuscript of *American Indian Basketry* (Mason 1904). C. P. Wilcomb consulted him on basket designs (Wilcomb 1903). John Hudson requested his help in evaluating the merits of a particular basket he was unable to view himself (Hudson 1905).

Merriam's basket collection eventually numbered 1,050 pieces, 940 of which were from California and Nevada. Most of his baskets were acquired individually before 1910. After his death in 1942 it was more than twenty years before his family made a final disposition of his baskets and accompanying catalog cards, journals, field notes, and photographs; the baskets were kept in storage until 1962, when the family finally put the collection up for sale. Robert F. Heizer, an archaeologist at the University of California at Berkeley, who was aware of philosophical differences between his own institution's anthropology department and Merriam, contacted one of his former students, Martin Baumhoff.[16] Baumhoff, an archaeologist at the University of California at Davis, was instrumental in negotiating the sale of the collection to his own institution, with the stipulation that it be kept intact as a research

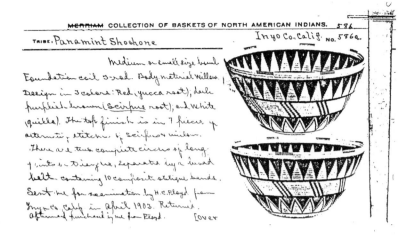

TRIBE: Panamint Shoshone   Inyo Co., Calif. No. 586a.

[handwritten catalog notes on the basket, including design description and dimensions]

Diam: 273mm (10¾in.)
Height: 148 " (5⅞").

Figure 4.7. Merriam Basket Catalog Card 586 and 586a, 1903. C. Hart Merriam was known for his exacting detail in documenting the baskets he collected. He included not only a picture of each basket but also the tribal affiliation of the weaver, the location where he acquired the basket, its size, descriptions of the materials and design elements used, and a reference number. This Panamint Shoshone basket was purchased from Harry C. Floyd in 1903.

ronments throughout the West, are located at the Smithsonian Institution's National Anthropological Archives.[17]

John W. N. Hudson (1857–1936)

Originally from Nashville, Tennessee, John W. N. Hudson arrived in Ukiah, California, in 1889, the same year that a railroad linked that town to San Francisco. Trained as a physician, he developed a great interest in the cultures of the indigenous people of the area. His wife, Grace Carpenter, grew up in Potter Valley, California, among the Pomo people. She and her mother had collected Pomo baskets long before she met Hudson.

After their marriage in 1890 the Hudsons' collecting fervor increased, and by 1893 they had amassed more than three hundred Pomo baskets. This collection, its associated documentation, and Hudson's subsequent publications helped establish John's reputation as an Indian basketry expert. Hudson successfully leveraged his expertise, creating a demand for Pomo baskets among private collectors and museums (McLendon 1993:51). In 1899 the Hudsons sold their collection to the Smithsonian Institution.

In January 1901 Hudson began work as an assistant ethnologist at the Field Museum of Chicago under George Dorsey, whom Hudson greatly admired. Following Dorsey's instructions, he traveled to California, where he collected artifacts, took photographs, and gathered ethnographic and linguistic information from many tribes (Sherrie Smith–Ferri, personal communication 1999). Hudson traveled to Owens Valley in the summer of 1904. Arriving from the south, he had already sent three boxes of collected material off to Chicago by the time he reached Lone Pine on July 24. Hudson expressed regret to Dorsey that his funds were limited, because he knew that "trips to Saline, Panamint, and Death valleys would reward me handsomely" (Hudson 1904b:2). However, he contemplated going there anyway. In another letter to Dorsey ten days later, he reported having questioned "everyone knowing anything

collection. Today the entire collection, along with the original catalog cards, resides at the University of California at Davis.

Merriam's papers and other documentary materials were divided among several institutions. The files and photographs about the California Indians first were sent to the University of California at Berkeley for publication under Merriam's name. Following their publication in the 1950s and 1960s, they were deposited at the Bancroft Library, at the University of California at Berkeley, where they remain today. The California journals were sent to the Smithsonian Institution and finally on to the Library of Congress. The original glass plate negatives for the photographs that appear on the basket catalog cards, as well as many other glass plate negatives of Indian people and envi-

of the country — all agree in one regard, that the roving bands living there during the coler [sic] season are now away on hunting and berry harvesting trips on the mts and would be very difficult to locate, in fact the search must be made by burro with a guide who knows absolutely the location of water along the trails or the expedition would fail" (Hudson 1904c:2). By this time Hudson was in Bishop with plans to continue northwest to Mammoth Hot Springs, leaving without seriously collecting from the Panamint Shoshones. His final comment to Dorsey in his last letter from Bishop voiced displeasure with dealers in the region who had "as usual ruined prices and ethnology" (Hudson 1904c:4).

He then spent several days in Long Valley attempting to "hunt . . . up legends and facts relative to the Indians" (*Inyo Register* 1904a). During much of his fieldwork in the region Hudson apparently had trouble locating Indians willing to talk to him. As he reported from Gardnerville, Nevada, about the Washoes, "The only sure way to find them is to follow up a stream, necessarily afoot, and search for the water trail in a camp, or to patiently follow the visiting Indian when in town to his lair. He will never direct you nor explain anything at any price" (Hudson n.d.:244).

In spite of these difficulties, Hudson managed to study Owens Valley baskets and to compile a vocabulary list relating to basket patterns and materials. He purchased water bottles, sifters, insect and sugar harvesters, winnowers, and raw materials directly from weavers (Figure 4.8). He became acquainted with Mr. and Mrs. A. W. Eibeshutz, who owned a general store in Independence and had a small collection of beadwork and baskets, most of which were acquired from local Indians in exchange for food and supplies.[18]

Hudson cut short his collecting career for the Field Museum when several issues created conflicts between himself and Dorsey (Sherrie Smith-Ferri, personal communication 1999). In 1903, in addition to his responsibilities at the Field Museum, Dorsey was hired by the Fred

Harvey Company to work in its Indian Department. He then hired Hudson to purchase for the Harvey Company at the same time he was doing his work for the museum. Because of potential conflicts of interest, Dorsey and Hudson kept their work for Harvey to themselves (Smith-Ferri 1996:125, 126). Hudson soon discovered that when Dorsey received the materials from Hudson's trips, he sometimes sifted through them and sold the better ones to the Harvey Company instead of placing them in the museum's collection (Smith-Ferri 1996: 129). Hudson questioned the ethics of such actions and apparently was quite "conflicted" over his dealings with Dorsey (Sherrie Smith-Ferri, personal communication 1999). In addition, in his 1903 *Indians of the Southwest,* Dorsey plagiarized from Hudson's writings and included, without attribution, several photographs taken by Hudson (Smith-Ferri 1996: 132). The two men finally parted ways after Hudson refused to accede to Dorsey's demand that he turn over all materials accumulated while in the museum's employ. Apparently, Dorsey planned on writing a basket book and, to make up for his lack of knowledge, wanted to use all of Hudson's materials (Sherrie Smith-Ferri, personal communication 1999). Hudson resigned his museum position in 1905.

Besides the extensive ethnographic records Hudson left in his journals, an equally important legacy was the public visibility he brought to California basketry as the curio trade was developing. His foresight in collecting not

Figure 4.8. Owens Valley Paiute Seed Beater. Weaver unknown, ca. 1900. This well-used seed beater is typical of the utilitarian baskets that J. W. Hudson collected for the Field Museum. Relatively few seed beaters made by Owens Valley Paiutes survive today. This basket is sturdily constructed and was woven with split willow shoots using plain twining. A sturdy rim stick is coiled to the edge of the basket, giving it shape and reinforcing it for use in beating seeds.

only fancy, highly decorated baskets but also utilitarian examples, tools, and unfinished materials enriched his contribution to the study of Native American basketry.

Charles P. Wilcomb (1865–1915)

Charles P. Wilcomb was another collector who focused on the lifeways and material culture of native California peoples, including the Panamint Shoshones. Wilcomb's interest in collecting, which began during his childhood and lasted throughout his lifetime, included artifacts of early New England settlers as well as those of California Indians. As a young man, Wilcomb showed a propensity for curating. He had one of his earliest exhibits of Indian artifacts in 1888 in the Visalia Museum of Curiosities, which formed a portion of the drugstore in Visalia, California, where he was employed at the time (Frye 1979:20).

By 1892 Wilcomb had accumulated nearly three thousand artifacts. Although documentation is scant, it is evident that Wilcomb purchased many of his Panamint Shoshone baskets from Floyd (Bernstein 1979a:76). He exhibited a large number of them at the Golden Gate Park Memorial Museum in San Francisco,[19] becoming the museum's first curator in 1894. His selection was fortuitous since the museum needed both objects for display and a knowledgeable professional. Wilcomb's tenure as curator was highlighted by his success in building the museum into an educational institution. For several years, he made semiannual trips to California to conduct interviews and collect baskets among various Indian tribes. He had the rare ability to identify raw materials in baskets and drew on this knowledge to differentiate between the baskets of the Inyo–Kern and Tulare–Fresno regions.

Wilcomb financed all his own collecting, both before and during his association with the Golden Gate Park Memorial Museum. In 1902 he protested to city civic leader M. H. de Young that he had "expended upward of one-half [his] earnings on the collection during the past twenty years" and that for reimbursement he would be "satisfied to get back merely cost price" (Frye 1979:31). In April 1905, when no financial agreement could be reached, Wilcomb sold all his anthropological Indian artifacts, including his Panamint Shoshone collection, to a private Pittsburgh collector, Robert C. Hall. The following month he resigned his curatorial position with the museum.

Wilcomb followed his collection to Pittsburgh, where Hall hired him to develop the Hall Museum of Anthropology, a private exhibit to be housed on the second floor of Hall's home. Wilcomb's interest in museums, however, lay primarily in their use as tools for public education. In 1908 he moved to Oakland, California, to help create the Oakland Public Museum. The city of Oakland funded several fieldwork trips, during which he collected extensively among the Maidu, Miwok, Pomo, Patwin, and other central California groups. During his fieldwork for the Oakland Museum, Wilcomb also created smaller collections that he sold to private collectors and institutions.[20]

When the Oakland Public Museum opened on October 21, 1910, it featured more than twelve thousand items displayed in fourteen exhibition rooms. Wilcomb devoted the rest of his life to developing the museum into an extraordinary learning center. He staffed it with docents whose job was to guide visitors through the exhibits. He provided ample space for reference materials in the galleries, as well as a reference library of scientific journals for use by the general public. The museum featured one of the first children's rooms in American museums, and schoolchildren were encouraged to visit regularly. In turn, museum staff members visited the children's classrooms, taking with them exhibits created especially for schools and public libraries.

In 1915 Wilcomb died suddenly at the age of fifty. His journals and notes were lost, and he left behind little in the way of published or written remarks about his collecting activities, save for those included in museum record keeping. His contributions to Otis T. Mason's 1904 book, *Aboriginal Indian Basketry,* are insightful commentaries that are still read by collectors and other aficionados of fine baskets today. The collection Wilcomb sold to Robert C. Hall of Pittsburgh eventually found a permanent home in the collection of the California State Indian Museum in Sacramento. Additional Panamint Shoshone and Owens Valley Paiute baskets that Wilcomb collected are at the Oakland Museum and at the Staatliche Museen zu Berlin, Ethnologisches Museum, Berlin (Figure 4.9).

Andrew William de la Cour Carroll (1845–1920)

Andrew "Willie" de la Cour Carroll was an Irish businessman who spent sixteen years (1883–99) in the United States, most likely because of his involvement in the timber industry. He lived in or near Lone Pine, California, in 1898–99 and probably did most of his basket collecting during that time. He focused on the Indian tribes of California and Oregon and included many baskets from the Owens Valley and Death Valley areas.[21]

Carroll collected both old and new basketry. He believed, "The old baskets are scarcely now to be had, but if of equally fine work I like the new as well, for time will bring the ripe desired tinge" (James 1972:251). Carroll was careful to document his acquisitions and attached small labels to each basket for recording pertinent information (Figures 4.10 and 4.11) (Winifred Glover, personal communication 1999). He corresponded with Otis T. Mason and George Wharton James and was given at least two baskets by Charles P. Wilcomb (Figure 4.12). In his list "Collectors and Collections" Mason (1904) described Carroll's baskets as "good California types," and James (1972:209) called Carroll "an enthusiastic basketry collector who . . . secured some choice specimens."

Eventually, de la Cour Carroll's collection numbered over one hundred baskets. After his death his entire collection was donated to the Ulster Museum in Belfast, Ireland. Many of his baskets were featured in *The Land of the Brave*, Winifred Glover's 1978 publication about the Ulster Museum's North American Indian collection. Although details of the collector's manner of acquisition are scant, his collection is important because it is a relatively early and

Figure 4.9. Panamint Coiled Basket. Weaver unknown, ca. 1900. Wilcomb, who collected a number of baskets in Inyo County, identified this one as Paiute. The basket exhibits all the characteristics of Panamint Shoshone basketry, however.

Figure 4.10. Panamint Shoshone Coiled Bottleneck Basket. Weaver unknown, ca. 1905. The shape of the basket, the band around its neck, and some of its designs are typical of Panamint Shoshone baskets, but the label indicated that Carroll purchased it from the wife of Popinake George, a Paiute from Keeler. The mixed provenance information is an example of the "border blur" that occurred when collectors identified baskets from the southern tip of Owens Lake.

Figure 4.11. Panamint Shoshone Coiled Basket. Weaver unknown, identified by collector only as "Popinase Lone Pine Squaw," ca. 1905. This is one of several small bowl-shaped baskets collected by de la Cour Carroll during his stay in California. It uses older-style patterns found on Panamint Shoshone baskets.

very well documented collection, allowing us to study the basketry of the Owens Valley Paiute and Panamint Shoshone people before 1899.

Grace Nicholson (1877–1948)

One of Harry Floyd's most prominent clients was Grace Nicholson, a leading dealer of Native American basketry who was based in Pasadena, California, during the heyday of the Arts and Crafts movement. Nicholson was born

Figure 4.12. Panamint
Shoshone Coiled Cap.
Weaver unknown, ca. 1900.
This coiled cap, given to Carroll by Charles Wilcomb, was
patterned with six stepped
elements. The cap may have
been made by a Kawaiisu
weaver because it has a
deer-grass bundle foundation.

in Philadelphia in 1877. Because her mother died shortly after her birth and her father died when she was a teenager, her grandparents reared her. Suffering from chronic bronchitis, she moved to Pasadena for her health in 1901, when she was not yet twenty-four (McLendon 1993:53, 1996:2).

To support herself, she began doing free-lance secretarial work. One of her first employers was the basket collector George Wharton James, who encouraged her to begin collecting (Cohodas 1997:171). By 1902 she was buying and selling baskets and had made a collection of more than eighty baskets from southern California. With the help of an old family friend, Carroll S. Hartman, she opened a curio shop. Pasadena was an ideal location for this venture in the early 1900s: it was an important center of the Arts and Crafts movement, a popular destination for health-conscious and wealthy travelers from all over the United States, and the home of a thriving community of intellectuals, many of whom were promoters and patrons of Indian arts (McLendon 1993:53, 1996:1–3).

In the summer of 1903 Nicholson made the first of many collecting trips among the California Indians, accompanied by her friend, Hartman. Despite adverse travel conditions, lack of dependable transportation, and unbearably hot weather, the two intrepid collectors gathered a plethora of material over the next twenty years. It is unclear if Nicholson ever collected in Owens Valley. Certainly Hartman did when he was there in 1908. He acquired very little, however, because Owens Valley materials

were hard to come by: "Even caps are scarce — only the older women have any . . . and, aside from meal trays, beaters, and large burdens, I only saw 8 or 10 baskets" (Hartman 1908:8).

Nicholson documented her acquisitions carefully in diaries, pencil drawings, and photographs. Otis T. Mason, with whom she corresponded, may well have influenced these collecting habits. From these records, we know that Nicholson sold to collectors all across the United States, including C. Hart Merriam, who was her first customer, in November 1902 (McLendon 1996:4). A variety of contacts supplied her with high-quality items to sell because she paid more than rival buyers. She sold baskets to such museums as the Smithsonian Institution; the Museum of the American Indian, Heye Foundation, New York;[22] and Harvard's Peabody Museum. Nicholson claimed to have placed "over 20,000 rare baskets and ceremonial objects in museums here and abroad" (Apostol 1976:23), although this figure may well include baskets donated at her suggestion by wealthy collectors (Figure 4.13).

In addition to her role as a dealer, Nicholson served as a patron for the notable Pomo weavers Mary and William Benson (McLendon 1990). She also contracted with Elizabeth Hickox, a renowned Wiyot weaver living on the Lower Klamath River. The exclusive agreements she negotiated with these weavers afforded her some control over their production, quality, style, and price and enabled her to establish strong markets for their works (Cohodas 1997: 177). In this regard, Nicholson was similar to Abe and Amy Cohn of Carson City, Nevada, who sponsored the work of Washoe weaver Louisa Keyser (better known as Datsolalee) (Cohodas 1997:172–173).

Nicholson had ties to collectors and traders in Owens Valley. Notations in her 1908 journal mention local collectors Rose Black, Dr. Doyle, and Dr. MacQueen. She purchased much of her Owens Valley material from Harry C. Floyd, with whom she apparently had a special business relationship (Figure 4.14). In a letter to her dated July 28, 1909, for example, he wrote: "I am selling you all my stuff & not

Figure 4.13. Baskets Offered for Sale by Grace Nicholson, ca. 1915. In this photograph are baskets from the Miwoks and Western Monos, as well as seven baskets from Inyo County, shown in the two lower rows. Nicholson's records include some information on five of these baskets; the two in the lower row, as well as the baskets second, fourth, and fifth in the next row up, were all considered "old" at the time Nicholson acquired them. She eventually sold the basket at lower left to a collector named Jones, and the basket second from the right on the next row up to collector Miss E. F. Hubby.

breaking it for anyone. I could dispose of some to some rich buyers but would rather they got them thru your hands if you can deal with them" (Floyd 1909). Floyd was cognizant of Nicholson's seasonal tourist business and gave her discounts, especially when she bought baskets in quantity (Floyd 1909). Sometimes he offered her "the right of first refusal" of a basket, sending it to her before offering it to anyone else (Floyd 1910).

In 1926 Nicholson built the Grace Nicholson Treasure House in Pasadena to accommodate her growing business of Oriental art and semiprecious stones, as well as Native American materials. When the market for collectibles declined in the aftermath of the 1929 stock market crash, her business faltered and never recovered (McLendon 1996:14). Nicholson gave the Treasure House to the city of Pasadena in 1943 to be used as a museum; she died five years later. In 1950 her two secretaries divided the remaining baskets. One of the secretaries sold her baskets to the Museum of the American Indian in 1968, and the other sold hers to a variety of collectors (Cohodas 1997:176).

The majority of her papers and photographs, which are a rich source of information on Indian people in Owens Valley and elsewhere, are at the Henry E. Huntington Library and Art Gallery in San Marino, California. Her ledger, in which she kept track of the baskets she sold, along with a few other albums and many photographs, are in the collections of the Phoebe Apperson Hearst Museum of Anthropology at the University of California, Berkeley.

THE COLLECTORS OF OWENS VALLEY BASKETS: FROM THE INSIDE LOOKING OUT

Even though many baskets found homes elsewhere, a cadre of Owens Valley residents, both Indians and non–Indians, had the foresight to maintain collections locally. The baskets of these collectors reflected family ties to the community, shared experiences, and interpersonal relationships based on mutual trust and respect. The early acquisitions of many of these collectors were gifts from local Indians. As collector Enid Ashworth explained, "They came to ranch doors with bags for food. If they liked

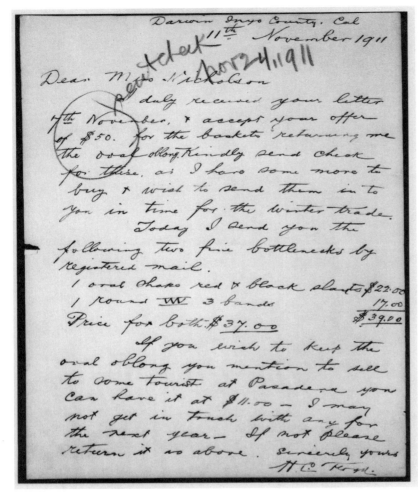

Figure 4.14. Letter from Harry C. Floyd to Grace Nicholson, November 11, 1911. Over the years, Nicholson and Floyd both benefited from their successful business relationship. Floyd supplied primarily Panamint Shoshone baskets, not only to Nicholson but also to many other prominent collectors and dealers of his time, including Merriam and Wilcomb.

you, they'd return with a gift basket" (personal communication 1997). Other baskets were bartered for food, medicine, or supplies as Indians began participating in the wage labor economy. Still others were acquired as people enriched their collections through outright purchase. In any case, local residents tended to form emotional attachments to their baskets and preferred to think of themselves as basket "protectors" or "caretakers" rather than collectors.

Rose Black (1861–1940)

One of the earliest Owens Valley collectors was Rose Black. She was born in Ventura, California, but she and her family later moved to Virginia City, Nevada, lured by the promise of gold and silver strikes. As a boom-and-bust town, Virginia City attracted such famous characters as Mark Twain, whom Black described as "a

street angel and a home devil" (Peggy Zimmerman, personal communication 1998).

In Virginia City, ironically, Rose both joined the Women's Christian Temperance Union and married a local saloonkeeper, Jack Black. In 1886 the couple moved to Bodie, California, and in 1888 to Bishop, where Jack opened the Red Front Saloon. In 1902 they moved to Big Pine, where Jack ran a saloon and financed mining ventures (Figure 4.15). According to his granddaughter, Peggy Zimmerman, he also was responsible for introducing fire hydrants to the town (personal communication 1998).

Rose became friends with many people in the valley, including Aurelia McLean, a noted basket collector from Lone Pine. Along with her husband, McLean operated a drugstore there in the 1920s. Her collection began when Indians brought in baskets to pay for medicine. It eventually grew to "between 400 and 500 baskets all from the Paiute and Panamint Shoshone tribes from Mono Lake to Death Valley" (Slater 1985a:60). Outgoing and gregarious, McLean was an accomplished painter, musician, and businesswoman (Peggy Zimmerman, personal communication 1998).

Black was well known for her sensitivity toward members of the local community. She "doctored everyone" (Peggy Zimmerman, personal communication 1998) and was especially caring toward Indian people. She had many opportunities to get to know the Indian population through the grocery and clothing businesses her children, Jack Jr. and Rosalind, operated. Often Indians patronized the Blacks' stores to replace the personal belongings they destroyed as part of their mourning tradition.[23] Sometimes they bartered baskets for goods. Other times they visited Rose at home, eager to give her baskets in exchange for food. Rose's reputation for kindness led the Indians to offer her their best work.

Rose accumulated a collection of Paiute and Panamint Shoshone baskets that eventually numbered over four hundred (Figure 4.16). In 1917 her entire collection was exhibited in San Diego at Ramona's Home, also known as Ramona's Marriage Place, which was Thomas

Figure 4.15. The Black Family, Big Pine, California, 1903. Rose Black, shown here with her husband, John H., daughter Rosalind, and son John D., obtained many of her baskets from the Indian people who shopped at the family's grocery store.

P. Getz's "picturesque repository of Spanish and Indian relics at Old Town." The collection, which was for sale, offered "perhaps the last opportunity to lovers of the bizarre and beautiful in Indian handicraft to obtain authentic, and sometimes historically interesting, specimens of the work of the northern tribes" (*San Diego Union* 1917).

Black had attempted to sell her collection before this time, at least as early as 1916. During a visit to Big Pine in 1916 Chicago collector Homer E. Sargent wrote to Carroll S. Hartman: "I do not see why you have neglected to buy this 'largest private collection' of baskets of Mrs. Black for the trifling sum of Twenty thousand. I had a look at it this afternoon and was unable to buy three baskets on which the first price quoted was right, but on making an offer for the three found that a mistake had been made" (Sargent 1916). Apparently, the value that Black placed on her collection precluded its ready sale.

Rose Black shared a special friendship with basket weaver Sarah Frank Hill (1881–1977), a Northern Paiute woman originally from Bodie (Figure 4.17 and 4.18). Hill's mother was a descendant of Wovoka (a.k.a. Jack Wilson), the Paiute man central to the Ghost Dance religion that spread among western Indian tribes during the late nineteenth century.[24] As a child, before her mother's death, Hill had attended Stewart Indian School near Carson City, Nevada. After her mother's death she and her brother moved to Keeler, California, to live with relatives. There she met a non-Indian miner named James Hill, with whom she moved to Tinnemaha (Fish Springs) in Owens Valley. In Tinnemaha, Hill pursued mining claims and worked as a farmer while Sarah worked as a housekeeper, kitchen assistant, and midwife. Together they reared seven children. The residents of Tinnemaha admired the Hills. Their daughter, Evelyn Hill Bacoch, described her parents as "dignified people . . . [who] reached out to Indian people as well as non-Indians [and] . . . had a great rapport with non-Indian business people and ranchers" (personal communication 1998). Sarah was said to be "a person who would help anybody . . . and would build a fire and put food on the stove [to welcome visitors]" (Dorothy Stewart, personal communication 1998).

The strong friendship between Rose Black and Sarah Hill began in Big Pine at the Blacks' grocery store, which was a shopping stop and social gathering place for Indians when they came to town. Their fellowship endured throughout their lives and was commemorated in death, when the graves of the two friends

Figure 4.16. Indian Baskets of Inyo County: The Rose Black Collection, Big Pine, California, ca. 1920. Mrs. Black collected more than four hundred Indian baskets, many of which are now at the Eastern California Museum in Independence. The unidentified woman in the picture is wearing a traditional Paiute twined cap.

were placed near each other in the Woodman's Cemetery in Big Pine.

Rose Black loved children. She had four granddaughters, all of whom worked in the family grocery store from an early age. On graduation from eighth grade, each one chose a basket from Rose's collection. One of her granddaughters described her selection, which remains her personal favorite: it was rectangular with tightly woven stitches and rim ticking and was decorated with ibex, bighorn sheep, men, and arrows (Peggy Zimmerman, personal communication 1998).

Basket collecting was an important part of Rose Black's life. Baskets lined the walls of her basement. She loved showing them off to friends. For her, they were tangible evidence of the many friendships and memories she had accrued over the years. When she died, her

family honored her request to keep the basket collection together. They sold it, en masse, to the county of Inyo in 1950. Her baskets are an important part of the collection of the Eastern California Museum of Inyo County.

John Simpson MacQueen (1864–1939) and Helen Squire MacQueen (1868–1962)

John and Helen "Queenie" MacQueen were longtime and much-loved residents of Bishop. They enthusiastically supported the arts and particularly admired Paiute culture. Born in Wisconsin, John MacQueen moved to Bishop in 1886. He went to work in a pharmacy owned by his sister's husband, Henry E. Wright. He later attended the Chicago School of Dental Surgery before returning to Bishop, where he practiced dentistry. He was known as the "Socialist of Owens Valley" (Donald Mac-Queen, personal communication 1998).

Helen Squire was born in Round Valley in 1868 and moved with her family to Independence several years later. When her mother died unexpectedly, she and her brother, George,[25] were sent to live with their aunt in Syracuse, New York. Her baby sister, Jessie, remained in Round Valley with family friends, the Parsons. Many of Jessie's childhood friends were Indians, and she "learned the Paiute language like a native. As she grew up, whenever there were court proceedings involving Indian people, she was usually called as interpreter" (MacQueen 1949:5). In 1887 Helen returned to Round Valley to visit her sister and stayed for good. She married John MacQueen in 1893.

The MacQueens made Bishop their permanent home and were deeply concerned with its welfare. They involved themselves actively in community functions and held numerous political get-togethers in their home. When the news of the impending Los Angeles aqueduct project broke in the summer of 1905, John MacQueen led the fight against it, calling a meeting that "set in motion steps for the protection of the interests of this [Owens] valley" (*Inyo Register* 1905). According to his grandson, John MacQueen, he considered the diversion of the Owens River to Los Angeles a "rape" of

Bishop, since most people there were eventually forced to sell their water rights and/or went bankrupt (personal communication 1998).

As a college-educated woman and the wife of the town dentist, Helen felt she had an ascribed role to play in the cultural and social life of her community. She helped found the Woman's Improvement Club, the Bishop library, and the Athena Club, which served as a social and intellectual focus for women of that time. In addition to their roles as community leaders, the MacQueens were committed to the health, education, and welfare of the local Indians. Dr. MacQueen believed in dental care for all and welcomed Indians as patients. Queenie, too, respected the Indian people. Like many white women in Owens Valley, she developed long-term relationships with the Paiute women, visiting their homes and encampments as well as employing them in her home (Donald MacQueen, personal communication 1998).

Their relationships with Indian people afforded the MacQueens opportunities to acquire baskets for their collection. John sometimes received baskets as payment for his dental services, and Queenie was sometimes given them as thanks for her friendship. In one case, she obtained a beautiful beaded basket from Nellie Charlie (the renowned Mono Lake Paiute weaver) because Daisy Mallory, Queenie's housekeeper, was the weaver's daughter (John MacQueen, personal communication 1998).

The MacQueens' collection numbered approximately sixty baskets, both utilitarian and made-for-sale types (Figure 4.19). The baskets were "objects to be admired, respected, and revered. They were items which were worthy things, not things to be trivialized." The MacQueens especially appreciated "those baskets of whatever size or shape, that exhibited the tightest, most uniform weaving," and their most prized baskets were "the narrow-necked, pitch-covered 'bottles' used to hold water" (Donald MacQueen, personal communication 1998).

The MacQueens had four children: Vivian, Bruce, Helen, and Donald (Figure 4.20). The

Figure 4.17. Sarah Frank Hill Outside Her Family Home, Fish Springs, California, Roasting Pine Nuts, ca. 1950. Sarah Frank Hill cooked pine nuts in the traditional way. Using a basket she made herself, she parched the nuts with hot coals, tossing them around with a flick of her wrists to roast them evenly and avoid burning the basket.

family spent summers at Mammoth Lake. Their cabin, built in 1913, was decorated with winnowing trays, baby cradles, burden baskets, and other, more ornamental baskets. Family members considered these objects "symbols of the solitude and the glory of the Mammoth region as well as the people who were there before them." Consequently, children and grandchildren learned to treat the baskets with respect. The MacQueens' grandson, Donald, recalled, "My cousins and I weren't allowed to

Figure 4.18. Owens Valley Paiute Coiled Basket. Weaver, Sarah Frank Hill, ca. 1930. There are two different designs on this basket, each of which repeats three times. One is a free-flowing geometric design of small rectangles. The other is a more common pattern, described in the Black collection inventory as "arrow follow."

Figure 4.19. Owens Valley Paiute Cap. Weaver unknown, ca. 1900. This fine example of a woman's cap was just one of the many elegant Paiute baskets acquired by the MacQueens. In Figure 4.1 this basket can be seen displayed on the top shelf of the bookcase in the MacQueen household in 1906.

Figure 4.20. Dr. John Mac-Queen and His Children, ca. 1903. The MacQueen family employed Daisy Young Charlie Cluette Mallory, a Mono Lake Paiute woman who wove fine baskets, as a house-keeper for their busy home. The MacQueens' collection of baskets included some made by Mallory's family.

play with the baskets, although there were one or two on chests of drawers that we could pick up and examine, carefully. . . . They were 'of the old days,' and so had to be treated with caution. Their beauty, of course, was obvious" (personal communication 1998).

The baskets collected by John and Helen MacQueen were "reminders of times and places they loved" (Donald MacQueen, personal communication 1998). They were remembrances also of the MacQueens' respect for the Paiute people and their cultural differences. Like their Paiute friends, the MacQueens had "a world view that transcended the here and now. . . . [They believed] that we are the custodians of things, but we don't really own them" (John MacQueen, personal communication 1998). This philosophy guided the family's disposi-

tion of the collection after the collectors' deaths. With the exception of three baskets the grandsons now treasure as memories of their grandparents (Figure 4.21), the entire collection was donated to the Los Angeles County Museum of Natural History, where the baskets could be preserved, studied, visited, and admired by interested people for generations to come.

Minnie C. Spear Barrows Randolph (1854–1933)

Mary (Minnie) C. Spear was born in Vermont in 1854 and moved to North Dakota with her family. Through a political appointment she became the matron of the Menominee Reservation Boarding School in Wisconsin, where she also taught. She married a Mr. Barrows and was widowed in 1878. She taught in public schools until she decided to take the civil service examination to be a teacher in an Indian school.

She began teaching Paiute children in Bishop in March 1894, working in an old barn that functioned as a classroom. She spearheaded a drive to build a schoolhouse for them, appealing to the Young People's Department of the Women's National Indian Association "for help in securing shelter for her little flock" (Ives 1900:3). Barrows finally secured land at the end of 1899 and then served as architect, general contractor, and financier of the project. The Indian people themselves, however, "did the work of quarrying and drawing the stone and sand for the foundation and did it willingly" (Ives 1900:6). The new school building opened on March 26, 1900 (Figure 4.22).

The 1900 annual report of the Young People's Department of the Women's National Indian Association recognized the work of Mrs. Barrows and her assistant, Miss Craig: "The ladies named are doing noble work for good among the Paiutes. The children of nature are learning many lessons not found in books. To be treated as really human beings, to feel that they are considered worthy of help, touches the Indian heart as no other plan has done" (Ives 1900:9). After teaching Paiute children for eleven years,

Barrows was ready for a change. She became a field matron and, functioning like a social worker, visited the Indians in their homes.

In 1906 Barrows married Richard L. Randolph. They made their home in Bishop, where Minnie, along with Helen MacQueen, was a charter member of the Athena Club.

In addition to her role as educator and social worker, Minnie Barrows Randolph was a knowledgeable and eager collector and broker of Indian baskets. Her collection numbered 126 baskets from about a dozen different tribes and included 50 Paiute baskets (Figure 4.23). In 1917 she claimed to have "sold over $1100 worth [of baskets] for the Indians" and to be "in touch with many collectors all the way from Florida to San Francisco" (Randolph 1917), including C. Hart Merriam and Homer Sargent. In 1916 Sargent, writing to Carroll S. Hartman, must have thought Randolph placed too high a price on her collection, for he commented, "Guess you will get Mrs. Randolph's baskets some day if you wait" (Sargent 1916). Apparently, Hartman and Nicholson never did secure baskets from Randolph.

Another of her customers was Horatio Shumway Lee (1867–1925), from Buffalo,

Figure 4.21. John Mac-Queen, Vista, California, 1998. The beaded basket John MacQueen holds is from his grandparents' collection. Inside is a handwritten note identifying the weaver as Nellie Charlie (Mono Lake Paiute). John's resemblance to his father can be seen from the photograph in the center. The photograph in the upper center is of his grandmother, Helen MacQueen.

New York. Business dealings between Lee and Randolph, who were likely introduced by Lee's cousin, Mrs. Frederick W. (Mary) Hess of Bishop, began in 1917. Randolph offered Lee

Figure 4.22. Paiute School in Bishop, California, ca. 1915. Minnie Barrows Randolph was the architect of and driving force behind this new school for Indian children in Bishop.

Figure 4.23. The Minnie Barrows Randolph Collection, Bishop, California, ca. 1911. A copy of this photograph appeared in the *Inyo Register*, June 29, 1911, identifying these baskets as part of the Randolph Collection. The collection included baskets from the Pimas and Navajos as well as the Owens Valley Paiutes and Panamint Shoshones. The bowl in the center with the beads around the rim is in the collections of the Phoebe Apperson Hearst Museum of Anthropology at the University of California, Berkeley (cat. no. 1–26845), as is the burden basket in the left center (cat. no. 1–26832), made by Hattie Jones. The small globular basket in the center with the six-point stars is an Annie Poole McBride basket that is in the Sargent Collection at the Field Museum, Chicago (Sargent n.d.a:catalog card 957).

guidance in amassing a collection of baskets that accurately reflected the Paiutes' traditional basketry (Randolph 1917). In February 1922 Randolph insured her baskets and turned the policy over to Lee. Lee then bought the collection for fifteen hundred dollars (Gifford 1927), but Minnie retained possession of it. For reasons unknown, she did not want anyone in Bishop, including her own husband, to know about this arrangement (Hess 1922). Randolph continued to offer Lee baskets for his collection until his death in 1925.

In May 1927 Lee's cousin, Florence Lee of Buffalo, New York, invited Alfred Kroeber to visit Bishop and look at her cousin's baskets in preparation for a possible donation. Kroeber was the director at what was then called the Museum of Anthropology at the University of California at Berkeley.[26] She also promised a meeting with Minnie Randolph. Unable to travel to Bishop himself, Kroeber sent E. W. Gifford, curator of the museum. Gifford visited with Randolph and documented the baskets

based on her recollections. He recognized that the collection would be particularly valuable to the university because its own holdings were rather weak in baskets from Inyo County (Gifford 1927).

The university accepted the donation, and the baskets were sent to the museum later in May. It took more than a year for them to be readied for display, but the task was completed in September 1928. For exhibit purposes, the materials were separated according to tribal attribution, and both Randolph and Lee were acknowledged.

Minnie C. Barrows Randolph died in 1933. She left behind a rich legacy of educational and financial support for the Indian people of Owens Valley and a fine collection of their baskets to be studied and admired.

Maude Hanna Dow (1886–1969)

Maude Hanna Dow was born in Nebraska. She met and married G. Walter Dow (1881–1967) in Denver in 1906 (*Inyo Register* 1967:11). They

lived in a tent near the nascent town of Parshall, Colorado,[27] where they ranched and ran
a general store. Several years later the Dows
relocated their business to Granby, Colorado,
where Walter also sold Ford automobiles. In
1918 they moved to Lone Pine, California, and
established the Lone Pine Lumber and Supply
Company.

The Dows loved to travel and visited 108
foreign countries in the fifty years they were
married (*Inyo Register* 1967:2). Probably the
most harrowing of their travel adventures
occurred on September 3, 1939, the day
England declared war on Germany, when they
survived the sinking of the SS *Athenia*.[28]

Walter Dow had a keen business sense. He
recognized the need for a hotel in Lone Pine to
service the movie industry, which was filming
numerous westerns on location in the nearby
Alabama Hills. Dow built the first wing of the
Dow Hotel in 1921 and later financed the construction of the Winnedumah Hotel in Independence and the Glacier Lodge in Big Pine
Canyon (Figure 4.24). Realizing that good
roads were necessary for the development of
local businesses in Owens Valley, he promoted
the Three Flags Highway, which ran from
Canada to Mexico through Idaho, Washington,
Oregon, Nevada, and California. Today part of
that highway is Interstate 395.

Dow was known for his philanthropy. As
a charter member of the Eastern California
Museum Association in Independence, he
funded the construction of its present building.[29] The museum now houses an outstanding
collection of baskets from the Owens Valley
and Great Basin area.

Maude Dow was involved with her husband's various business ventures as well as his
ranching. She had a reputation as a kind and
thoughtful woman who was interested in people and their various forms of artistic expres-
sion. She supported the local Indian people by
attending community events that featured their
dances and celebrations and by purchasing
their baskets.

Between 1920 and 1940 Dow amassed
approximately ninety Paiute and Panamint

Shoshone baskets. Most were obtained locally.
Some of the Paiute baskets had figures of birds,
animals, and trees. They were primarily coiled
baskets, "woven so well that light [did] not
show through and water [could] be carried in
them" (Morris 1967:2). By 2001 the Dow collection had been dispersed to a number of private collections.

Anna Theresa Gracey Kelley (1907–1994)

Anna Kelley was born in 1907 to Robert Gracey
and Kate Recker Gracey in Carson City, Nevada.
She was the eldest of eight children. In 1913
her father became the stationmaster of the
Kearsarge station, a depot for the Southern
Pacific narrow-gauge railroad that served Independence. Anna's childhood days were spent
among the Chinese, Japanese, Mexican, Italian, and Native American people who worked
for the railroad. This exposure to so many
different kinds of people instilled in her an
acceptance of cultural differences that lasted
throughout her life.

After graduating from high school in 1925,
Anna attended Oregon State Agricultural College (now Oregon State University) with plans
to become a research dietician. In 1929 she
returned to Independence, where she met
Orville Kenneth ("O.K.") Kelley, a filling station manager. They married in 1931 and had
one child, Jim.

While O.K. ran the gas station, Anna held
several jobs and became active in civic affairs.
She managed Jim's Café, a local restaurant,

Figure 4.24. The Winnedumah Hotel, Independence,
California, ca. 1927. Walter
Dow financed the construction of the Winnedumah
Hotel, which opened in April
1927, to serve the local needs
of the film and tourism industries. The hotel was later
sold to Bob Schaefer's family,
which owned it for sixty-five
years. Under new ownership,
it still exists as a historic bed
and breakfast.

Figure 4.25. Anna Kelley at Manzanar, 1942. Anna worked at the first-aid station at the Manzanar War Relocation Center near Lone Pine, California. Later she became welfare director for Inyo County, developing friendships with the Indians in the Owens Valley area which lasted long beyond the war years.

southern end of Inyo County and included Death Valley. As part of her duties she paid house calls on welfare recipients, putting more than ninety thousand miles on her "little 1937 Chevy" (Jim Kelley, personal communication 1998). Her travels enabled her to renew acquaintances with Indians and elderly people she had known during her childhood and also to make many new friends. She became well known and was well liked by local Indian people.

Jim, her son, told of a humorous encounter with some Indians during one of her welfare calls. Anna and Jim, who often accompanied his mother on such visits, stopped at the Furnace Creek gas station in Death Valley. A group of Indians dressed in traditional clothing was lined up on a bench, hoping to make money by posing for tourist photos. Anna explained to Jim, "They're working today." When a tourist asked, "How much?" the Indians grunted, pretended they did not understand, and passively accepted whatever money was offered. When the Kelleys got to the front of the gas line, however, the Indians rushed over and greeted them in perfect English, thoroughly embarrassing the stunned tourists (Jim Kelley, personal communication 1998).

Basket collecting was a natural outgrowth of the connections Anna had with the Indian community. She recognized that certain aspects of traditional Paiute and Panamint Shoshone culture would be lost as the Native Americans became assimilated. In an attempt to help preserve their material culture, Anna included utilitarian, ceremonial, and decorative baskets in her collection (Figures 4.26 and 4.27). She acquired winnowers, seed beaters, and water jugs, traditional utilitarian baskets, because she believed they were not going to be around much longer. To round out her collection, she commissioned examples of specific utility baskets that were no longer available and purchased a variety of fancy baskets made for sale. The strength of her collection was its representation of the past and the present, the old and the new, "the survival of a cultural form" (Jim Kelley, personal communication 1997).

and worked for the city of Los Angeles in its Independence office. Anna ran the first-aid station at Manzanar during the construction of the Japanese-American internment camp there (Figure 4.25). In 1942, after the camp was fully operational, she became the Inyo County Welfare director, a job she held through the duration of World War II. Although her early contact with a variety of ethnic groups made her well suited for this job, her son jokingly suggested that she was offered the position because "she was the only one left in Independence who wasn't drafted and had a Bachelor's degree" (Jim Kelley, personal communication 1998).

The territory for which Anna was responsible stretched from Independence to the

Anna's baskets symbolized her friendship with the Indians and were reminders of the role she often played as their advocate. One time during the war years Anna wanted Sarah Hunter to make her a water-carrying basket. When Mrs. Hunter refused to accept any money for it, Anna opened an account for her at the gas station and made sure the Hunters did not have to pay for gas for several years. When gasoline was rationed, she made certain that the Indian people in the community received their allocated amounts. On another occasion she arranged for a relative of Isabel Hanson, a well-known Panamint Shoshone weaver, to have corrective surgery for a birth defect.

In the 1950s Johnny Symmes, who had testified before the U.S. Senate twenty years earlier (see Chapter 3), spent countless hours with Anna answering her many questions. The son of weaver Emma Symmes, he was very knowledgeable about basket weaving. As a sign of their close relationship, he gave Anna a nineteenth-century water jar he had found on a pine-nut-gathering trip. He paid her the ultimate compliment when he told her, "You're getting it because I know you'll care for it" (Jim Kelley, personal communication 1998). Kelley was a good caretaker not only because the baskets held sentimental value for her but also because she appreciated their craftsmanship and beauty. Anna's granddaughter, Roseanne Kelley, recalled that "when she spoke about her baskets, there was a pride in her voice and a gleam in her eye" (personal communication 1998).

Enid Partridge Ashworth (1915–1998)

A close friend of Anna Kelley's, Enid Ashworth had deep roots in Owens Valley. Both sets of her grandparents, the Partridge family from Minnesota and the Gish family from San Jose, California, came to the valley in the nineteenth century. Enid was born and raised on the family ranch just south of Bishop. Her father sold the ranch to the Los Angeles Department of Water and Power in the late 1920s "for a good price" (Enid Ashworth, personal communication 1998). The Partridges had a reputation for

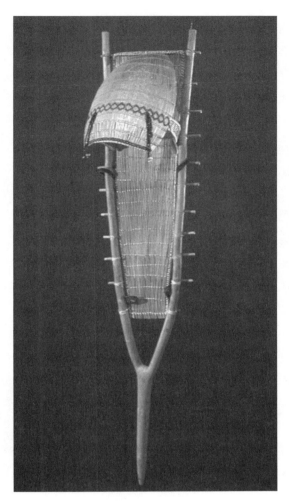

Figure 4.26. Panamint Shoshone Cradle Basket. Weaver, Mamie Joaquin Button, 1943. This type of cradle basket is an ancient Panamint Shoshone style, made with a forked sapling whose bottom is sharpened to anchor the cradle in the ground. Crosspieces are lashed to the sapling, and a twined basketry mattress is attached. The hood is a particularly ornate example; it not only uses diagonal twining in split willow but has rows of three-strand twining worked in split red-bud shoots.

giving, caring, and sharing. Groups of Indian people lived in a locust grove on their property and worked as ranch hands. As a child, Enid watched them at work and became friends with many of them.

After graduating from Claremont/Pomona University in southern California, Enid returned to Owens Valley and married Ben Ashworth, a civil engineer who later ran an automotive parts business. He also served on the Independence school board with Anna Kelley. Enid and Ben had three children.

Enid Ashworth had a large collection of baskets, most of which were Panamint Shoshone (Figure 4.28). Almost all these baskets were gifts to her grandmother, other family members, or herself from Indian friends. Because of the very personal way she obtained these baskets, she did not consider herself a collector. In a 1998 interview with the authors, she

Figure 4.27. Owens Valley Paiute Basket. Weaver, Emma Wright, ca. 1935. Coiled in a leftward direction with neat and even stitches, this basket has an exterior work surface and a self-tapering rim. It shows no signs of use and was probably made for sale. The designs, according to the collector, purportedly reveal family demographics: the vertical bands indicate how many children were born into the weaver's family; the number of zigzags in each band indicates the marital status and number of offspring; an attenuated zigzag designates the death of a spouse or child. This sort of explanation for a pattern was not reported by any native people to ethnographers; it appears to be an example of how non-Indians mythologized Indian baskets.

explained, "I don't call us 'collectors.' We just acquired 'em. Any old-timer has two or three, at least. If you were nice to Indians, you were given a basket."

Ashworth's baskets were a source of pleasure to her, evoking fond memories of interactions with her friends in the valley. One of her recollections concerned a small basket she purchased from a twelve-year-old Indian girl. It was beaded and was the child's first and only basket. The asking price was fifty cents, but Ashworth gave her a dollar. During the following winter the young weaver died from tuberculosis. Shortly thereafter, to thank Enid for her kindness, the child's mother, who also was a weaver, brought Enid a cradle basket. The

Figure 4.28. Enid Ashworth, Independence, California, 1998. Enid is holding her favorite basket, woven by her good friend Mary Wrinkle, sister of well-known Panamint Shoshone weaver Mamie Gregory. Wrinkle was a Panamint Shoshone weaver renowned for her small gift baskets decorated with realistic designs like the birds on this one. Ashworth's basket collection included newer made-for-sale baskets as well as older, traditional, twined baskets that had been given to her family over several generations.

mother then threw away her weaving materials and never made another basket. A couple of weeks later she was killed in an accident. Enid treasured the cradle basket and used it for all three of her own children.

Ashworth recalled the "work" baskets in her collection that came from Soda Tom, an older Mono Lake Paiute man who worked on her grandparents' ranch.[30] When she was a little girl, Soda Tom told her that the only bad thing about her grandmother's cooking was her failure to use grasshoppers in her soup. In response, Enid sneaked off to the haystacks to collect grasshoppers. When she brought some home, her grandmother rejected them and instead spanked her for running off without permission. As a young woman many years later, Enid ran into Soda Tom. She didn't recognize him at first, but when he asked how her grandmother's soup was, she realized who he was.

Ashworth's appreciation of her baskets was enhanced by her knowledge of how much time and effort went into making them. Occasionally, she gathered willow with her Indian friends and learned how to process it for baskets by splitting the willow shoots with her teeth. Because of the time it took to prepare the materials for weaving, Ashworth understood why so many of the younger generation of Indian women chose to enter the wage labor force rather than weave baskets.

Enid met Carrie Bethel, a famous Mono Lake Paiute weaver, in a restaurant near Conway Summit, California. The meeting may have occurred at Tioga Lodge, a resort and restaurant between Lee Vining and Conway Summit, where Bethel worked in the laundry (Bibby and Bates 1995:19). Enid accompanied her husband on weekly business trips to that area, and during that time she watched Bethel work on an oversized basket that took four years to complete. As an outgrowth of the friendship that developed between the two women, Bethel gave or sold Ashworth several baskets.

Like her friend Anna Kelley, Enid Ashworth kept her basket collection intact. In doing so, she helped preserve a portion of the history these baskets represented. Enid never commissioned baskets or kept records. Because the baskets were usually received as gifts or offered in trade, there was no receipt involved. Shortly before her untimely death in an automobile accident in 1998, Ashworth and one of her daughters began documenting her collection. She never collected as an investment and had only recently realized the monetary value of her baskets. But it did not matter. The baskets reflected her family's history, and each was a treasure to be preserved.

Vernon Johnson Miller (1927–2002)

Vernon J. Miller's heritage included a long list of Indian and non-Indian ancestors. In the mid-1850s Miller's great-grandfather, Albert H. Johnson, settled in Lone Pine, where he and his brother worked in the mines (Figure 4.29). In 1873 Johnson achieved a degree of local fame as a participant in the first ascent of Mount Whitney. Miller's maternal grandparents were Ora Charles Johnson and Nora Johannie, from Olancha. Their daughter, Leila Ida, married Harry Burke Miller, who was the son of Jennie Goodale, a Paiute Indian, and Jacob Charles Miller, a butcher from Switzerland. As Vernon put it, his bicultural background "provided the best of both the Indian and non-Indian worlds" (personal communication 1998).

Miller was one of seven children. As a child, he attended the Milton Public School in Fort Independence before going on to the Owens Valley Unified School District for grades nine through twelve. He served in the U.S. Army in Germany for two years, 1950–52. He worked for the county of Inyo for fifteen years in the capacity of chief deputy county recorder and treasurer.

In addition to active involvement in numerous civic organizations such as the Eastern Star and the Masons, Miller spent much of his adult life in ranching and politics. He was the Paiute tribal chairman of the Fort Independence Reservation for thirty-eight years. He was also actively involved with the Democratic Central Committee on both county and state levels. Miller did not enter politics for personal recognition but because, he explained, "we all have a

Figure 4.29. Albert H. Johnson. Great-grandfather of Vernon Miller, Johnson worked in the mines after arriving in Lone Pine in the mid-1850s. He was part of the first group to ascend the summit of Mount Whitney, in 1873.

responsibility to help out others. It's the simple, little things we do that may seem insignificant, but that make a difference" (personal communication 1998).

Miller always felt it was important to educate non-Indians about Paiute culture and history. He represented the interests of Indian people in Owens Valley water rights disputes but recognized both sides of the issue. He believed that ideally water "is like the air you breathe. It should be there for everyone to use freely." Since in real life water is not ubiquitous, however, he contended it is "worth fighting over" (personal communication 1998).

Vernon's interest in basket collecting began in the 1950s and stemmed from his belief that human beings have a close, almost reverent, relationship with nature. He recalled that the women learning to weave were told by the more experienced weavers, "Don't worry. As you're working, [the design] will come to you. In their minds, [the weavers] knew." He viewed weaving as a meaningful process through which Paiute women "challenged nature at its harshest to come up with something of beauty" (personal communication 1998). He appreciated both the artistry and work of basket weaving and marveled that, with nothing written down, the weavers could end up with something so special (Figure 4.30).

Like his friends Anna Kelley and Enid Ashworth, Miller felt he was a caretaker of his collection rather than an investor. He aligned himself with his Indian ancestors, who traditionally would burn baskets rather than see them neglected. In summing up his feelings about collecting baskets, Miller said, "All things come from the earth. You need to have respect for all these things" (personal communication 1998).

Over the years Miller's collection grew to seventy baskets and included cradle baskets, water jugs, seed-gathering baskets, winnowers, and made-for-sale baskets from Owens Valley, Death Valley, and both sides of the Sierra Nevada (Figure 4.31). Miller actively collected until the time of his death, always looking for the perfect basket. His baskets were important to him for the social and personal history they incorporated. He said, "They tell a story, a story of my heritage and my way of life. If we don't have a history, what are we? Who are we? And, where are we going?" (personal communication 1998).

Bob Schaefer (1942–)

Like Vernon Miller, Bob Schaefer treasured his basket collection as an important link to his ancestors. Bob's mother's family can be traced back many generations to Danuba, a legendary Northern Paiute woman whose descendants migrated from Nevada to Owens Valley. Rose Lochrie, his maternal grandmother, was born under a pine tree in Queen, Nevada, and was reared in Indian camps in the vicinity of Summit, Nevada. Her husband was a Scottish immigrant who worked in the gold mines near Aberdeen. When their marriage failed, Rose supported her four children by taking in laundry, ironing, and sewing, by selling homemade ice-cream, and by cooking in Bishop for the railroad workers. Sometimes, according to Schaefer, the children "dressed up like real Indians and sold arrowheads" by the train station in nearby Summit (personal communication 1998).

Although "Gram" Lochrie worked at odd jobs herself, she wanted something better for her children. She felt that education was the key to their success in a rapidly changing world and made sure that all four of them finished high school. Two even earned college degrees, a remarkable achievement for any Owens Valley resident during the 1920s. At the same time, she instilled in them a sense of their Indian heritage. She taught them the Paiute language and continued to use baskets from her mother's family for gathering pine nuts and cooking. She

Figure 4.30. Vernon Miller, Independence, California, 1998. Miller's basket collection included those that represented his family ties to the Owens Valley and others from tribes on both sides of the Sierra Nevada. Miller thought of himself as a caretaker of the baskets rather than a collector.

Figure 4.31. Baskets from the Vernon Miller Collection, 1999. The large bowl in the upper left is a Panamint Shoshone made-for-sale basket. The bowl in the upper right was made by Ida Bishop (Western Mono) of North Fork. The basket in the lower left was made by Carrie Bethel (Mono Lake Paiute), who was a friend of Vernon Miller. In the foreground is an old and worn soaproot brush, used for, among other purposes, cleaning baskets.

showed them how to make fry bread and how to use bacon grease for removing pine pitch from their hands.

Although farsighted in regard to her children's future, Lochrie herself was always a little suspicious of change. She did not trust automobiles. "There was no way," her grandson, Bob, recalled, that "she would get in a car that needed to move in reverse" (personal communication 1998). When her daughter, Lena, purchased a front-loading washing machine to make her mother's life easier, Rose sat and watched the clothes agitating through the front window, not quite trusting the machine to do the job.

Another of Rose's daughters, Hattie, was Bob Schaefer's mother. In 1927 Hattie married Fred Schaefer, who had come to Independence from Salem, Ohio. Together they managed the Winnedumah Hotel and eventually purchased it from the city of Los Angeles. Bob and his older brother, Fred, grew up in the hotel, which remained in the family for sixty-five years. Bob recalled that living at the Winnedumah was "like living with a different house full of company each night, meeting and visiting with people from all over the world, with friendships that continue to this day" (personal communication 1998).

Schaefer associated particular rooms with particular memories. Room 125, for example, was right above his parents' quarters. When the famous crooner, Bing Crosby, was a guest, they assigned him that room so his parents could find out whether or not Crosby sang in the shower.[31] Room 138 was "the ghost room." It squeaked so much for no apparent reason that Pearl A. Budke, daughter of Johnny Symmes, recalled refusing to go near it when she worked as a maid in the hotel (personal communication 1997).

Room 123 was "the basket room." There Hattie kept her collection of more than thirty Paiute, Panamint Shoshone, and Washoe baskets. She inherited some of these baskets from her mother. Others came from her sister, Lena, the first public health nurse in Inyo County during the 1950s, who often obtained baskets during house calls. Hattie also acquired baskets at the hotel, either in exchange for lodging or as direct purchases. Baskets sometimes decorated the mantel of the fireplace in the hotel's living room. Bob always found them interesting to look at and thought they fit in well with the rustic appearance of the place. He said, "We talked Indian once in a while and the baskets were always a part of our family" (personal communication 1998).

Figure 4.32. Baskets from the Bob Schaefer Collection, 1999. The figured Panamint Shoshone basket in the center, one of Schaefer's favorites, was the first basket he selected from his mother's collection.

Schaefer's interest in collecting became serious after his mother's death in 1990, when her baskets were put in his brother Fred's home for safekeeping. To decide who got first pick in dividing up the baskets, the brothers flipped a coin. Fred won the toss and selected a Panamint Shoshone basket with bird designs. Bob chose a Panamint Shoshone ceremonial basket whose "ancient feel" attracted him (Figure 4.32).

As a collector, Schaefer at first tried to acquire as many baskets as possible. As he learned more about the baskets in his collection, he began to narrow his focus and concentrate on precontact ones with traditional designs in pristine condition. He learned to document his baskets thoroughly, supplementing his recorded information with photographs.

Over time Schaefer formed a view of each basket as both an object of art and a piece of history (Figure 4.33). He said, "They are material objects that I can hold in my hand and feel the history of an earlier time come alive. I wonder and marvel at the exquisite beauty of each masterpiece, made under difficult hardships, no doubt, by the fingers of an Indian lady. What thoughts did the maker have in her mind as she laid out the symmetrical designs? Did it have any special meaning to the maker? What history can this basket tell me?" (personal com-

munication 1998). In truth, Schaefer believed that each of his baskets came home to be with him, safe and sound, for the rest of his life.

THE LEGACY OF OWENS VALLEY BASKET COLLECTORS

The collectors of Owens Valley baskets represented a rich diversity of character and intent. Those collectors who looked from the outside in brought the valley's baskets to others around the country and as far away as Europe. Although profit may have been a motive underlying the endeavors of some of these outsiders, their interest and curiosity about non-Western societies apparently was primary. Their efforts widely disseminated knowledge about Paiute and Panamint Shoshone culture and created an economic incentive for basket weaving. Ironically, however, their collecting practices also changed the kinds, sizes, designs, and functions of the very baskets they were trying to preserve.

The collectors who looked from the inside out considered themselves an integral part of the history of the baskets. In some cases, they were family or personal friends of the weavers. As valley residents, they shared a bond forged by the dramatic changes that occurred in the region during the last century and a half. The history they preserved was not of some distant,

Figure 4.33. Bob Schaefer, Bishop, California, 1999. Bob Schaefer was proud that he gave a local home to many Indian baskets from the Owens Valley area. Throughout his life he has endeavored to collect and protect these symbols of his heritage.

unfamiliar culture. Rather, it was an ongoing narrative of which they were a part.

Whether insiders or outsiders, the collectors of baskets in and from Owens Valley were patrons, historians, admirers, and protectors of a long-standing cultural tradition. Only by their collecting efforts was the tangible cultural legacy of the baskets of the Owens Valley Paiutes and Panamint Shoshones preserved and documented.

5. REPLANTING THE WILLOW

Contemporary Weavers of Owens Valley

At the end of the twentieth century in Owens Valley, few Indian people, if any, desired to live just as their ancestors did (Ruth Brown, personal communication 1998:1; Fisher 1983:3). Many of them nonetheless continued to incorporate remnants of their ancestors' traditions into their everyday lives. A few of the older women and their families, for example, still collected and prepared brine fly larvae, *piagui,* pine nuts, and acorn mush on special occasions (Plate 13). Although English supplanted Paiute as the primary language on Owens Valley reservations, the native language continued to be spoken by a few and taught by some parents and educators.[1] Widespread knowledge of myths and legends (and the ability to recount them in the native language) was largely a thing of the past, but the tradition of sharing such lore with the younger generation was still practiced by telling abbreviated forms in English. Respect for the land continued to permeate many people's belief systems, and time-honored healing practices were often still considered effective. Nettles, for example, helped ease arthritis pain, and ephedra tea was considered good for the kidneys (Phyllis Hunter, personal communication 1998). Some traditional religious rites also persisted, in spite of nearly a hundred years of missionary efforts during the twentieth century by the Presbyterian and Pentecostal churches. A modified form of the cry ceremony,[2] for instance, was still held by some Paiute people as a part of funeral observances.

Perhaps more than any other feature of traditional life, baskets became the primary symbol of continuity for the Owens Valley Paiutes. The physical survival of older baskets

was a tangible link to the ancestors and the traditional culture. Just as baskets were a connection to the past, the changes in size, materials, designs, and functions of the newer baskets signified adaptations to ongoing changes in the social and physical environment. As of 2004, the recognition of basketry as a marker of cultural identity and source of pride continues to be a thread that binds one generation to the next. Yet out of the approximately 1,800 Indians now living in Owens Valley (U.S. Census Bureau 2000), fewer than a dozen were actively making baskets.

THE DECLINE OF BASKET WEAVING IN OWENS VALLEY

Several factors have contributed to the decline of basket weaving in Owens Valley. One is the enormous amount of time and labor that basket weaving requires. As explained in Chapter 1, cutting enough willow shoots to provide the hundreds of warp rods and weft strands required for a basket requires hours of work. Cutting willow is only the beginning; next comes the time-consuming preparation of the willow into warp rods or sewing strands (Figure 5.1) (Richard Stewart, personal communication 1997).

The total time needed to make a basket varies according to the kind of basket (twined or coiled), its size, the type of materials, the intricacy of the designs, and the experience and skill of the weaver. Contemporary weavers have estimated between ten and seventy-five hours for small to average-size baskets, depending on technique, materials, and quality of weaving (Shirley Slee, personal communication 1999).[3] Because the process of basket weaving is so time-consuming and labor intensive, many people who express interest in learning to weave are quickly discouraged. When they are confronted with the reality of the tasks involved, their interest may "only last about four or five hours," weaver Richard Stewart estimated (personal communication 1997).[4]

Even aspiring weavers who possess the patience and inclination to learn sometimes cannot pursue their interests. Frequently, their work obligations outside the home leave them little free time or energy to weave. As explained in Chapter 3, the various changes in the economy of Owens Valley during the nineteenth and twentieth centuries led more and more Paiute women to enter the paid workforce to help support their families. For these women, time spent in extra-domestic labor was time not spent in activities related to basket weaving.

Another primary cause of the wane of basket weaving is the decreased need for woven baskets in everyday Paiute life. Traditionally, baskets were used in many aspects of daily life, particularly food-related activities. As the Paiutes' semi-nomadic way of life disappeared, however, their food habits changed. New, European-style foods such as flour, beans, and canned goods began to replace the seed grasses and tuber plants they originally ate, eliminating the need for gathering baskets of all kinds. Store-bought pots and pans began to replace both baskets and pottery in the late nineteenth century. Metal canteens, and eventually plastic jugs and modern plumbing, replaced water-carrying baskets. Twined caps, which once cushioned women's heads when they used tumplines, became unnecessary as the use of burden baskets disappeared and Indian women dressed more and more like non-Indians (Figure 5.2). In short, the overall demand for traditional utilitarian baskets steadily lessened. As Richard Stewart recently explained, "I guess Rubbermaid and other brand names have more or less supplanted the old ways" (personal communication 1997).

Concurrent with the reduction of basket use for practical purposes was the decreased

Figure 5.1. Richard Stewart Removing the Pith, 1997. Owens Valley weaver Richard Stewart demonstrates how to remove the pith from a split strand of willow he has just picked from a favorite site near his home in Big Pine.

availability of the natural resources used in their construction. Cattle and sheep, introduced to Owens Valley in the early 1860s, destroyed many native grasses and drastically changed local ecosystems. The purchase of land and water rights by the Los Angeles Department of Water and Power (LADWP) that began in 1904 restricted water availability and personal access to traditional locales for gathering willow.[5] In addition, the LADWP and the Inyo County Parks and Recreation Department began routinely clearing away stands of willow they deemed fire hazards (Michael Rogers, personal communication 1999). Preservation of traditional willow-gathering grounds became difficult to ensure (Richard Stewart, personal communication 1998). Although gathering became more problematic, there were fewer and fewer weavers gathering willow. By the 1920s not many young girls were learning to weave or were growing up to be competent weavers.

Finally, changes in the educational system that began in the 1870s and continued in the first half of the twentieth century also contributed heavily to the decline of weaving in Owens Valley. In the last half of the nineteenth

Figure 5.2. Twined Burden Basket with Cotton Repair. Weaver unknown, ca. 1900. Among other factors related to basketweaving's decline in the latter part of the nineteenth century, basket repairs began to be made with canvas or heavy cloth instead of hide.

century the prevailing attitude in the United States toward Indian people was that they were "savages" who needed to be "civilized" by replacing their traditional values with Western ones. Education was one of the primary means to achieve this goal (Adams 1995:1–21).

INDIAN EDUCATION POLICY IN OWENS VALLEY, 1890–1950

To accomplish the desired cultural transformation, in the 1870s the federal government established a system of segregated schools designed to sever Indian children's ties to their traditional cultural heritage and to train them for new roles in the quickly changing society. These educational institutions were of two types: reservation day schools and nonreservation boarding schools.

The day schools, located on the outskirts of Indian communities, offered English language instruction, provided some exposure to reading, writing, and math skills, and introduced the concept of industrial training. The theory behind the curriculum for the day schools was that "in the early morning hours, children would pour forth from the nearby Indian camp and at day's end return to their homes wiser in the ways of white civilization" (Adams 1995:

28). The boarding schools embraced the same philosophy as the day schools but were more effective because they removed Indian children completely from the influences of their tribal communities (Adams 1995:29).

In Owens Valley federal responsibility for Indian education was vested in what is now called the Carson Indian Agency of the Bureau of Indian Affairs (BIA).[6] Although some Indian students attended public schools with non-Indian students, special schools were established solely for Indian children (Bernasconi 1988:85). As early as March 1894, Minnie Barrows Randolph began teaching Paiute children in Bishop in an old barn that functioned as a classroom; as detailed in Chapter 4, Randolph spearheaded a drive to build a schoolhouse for her students, and it was completed in 1900 (Figure 5.3). By 1897 the federal government had also established an Indian public school in Big Pine, and Lone Pine acquired one a few years later (Jones 1897:12; Liljeblad and Fowler 1986:430).[7]

In 1890 the Carson Agency established a boarding school, the Stewart Indian School, in Carson, Nevada.[8] The school had an enrollment capacity of 525 (Wiley 1938), and in its early years the student population included not only Paiute and Panamint Shoshone children from Owens Valley but also students from the Bannock, Washoe, and Tenino tribes. At first, this school was only for primary education, but later it incorporated the upper grades. The school was billed as neither a college preparatory institution nor a correctional institution for problem cases but rather a vocational school whose aim was "to give to worthwhile young people practical training of a sort calculated to develop good citizenship and vocational efficiency" (Carson Agency 1935).

Students divided their time equally between academics and vocational training (Wiley 1938). The academic subjects, primarily English, social studies, mathematics, and practical science, all were taught as "incidents or necessary elements of some larger practical project or activity" (Carson Agency 1935). The vocational program for girls consisted largely of cooking, sewing, childcare, and other subjects pertaining to "efficient" home and family life.[9] The program for boys emphasized agriculture, animal husbandry, and various kinds of shop work, including both building and mechanical trades (Carson Agency 1936; Foster 1942:2).

In spite of the emphasis on vocational training, by the 1930s the Stewart School professed to "preserve and develop the best elements of the lives and culture of the Indian groups served" (Carson Agency 1935). Toward this end, the school's annual commencement exercises included a pageant consisting of Indian legends, customs, songs, dances, and tableaux, each episode of which was presented by a different tribal group (Figure 5.4) (Carson Agency 1935, 1938).

Indian students from Owens Valley attended Stewart Indian School early on.[10] Because the school's enrollment area grew too large in later years,[11] Indian children from Owens Valley also attended nonreservation boarding schools near Riverside, California (the Sherman Institute, opened in 1902), and in Greenville, California (the Greenville School, opened in 1895) (Adams 1995:57; Beatty 1941:1).

The Sherman Institute, with a capacity for one thousand pupils, was the largest nonreservation school of the Indian Service and was supported by an annual congressional appropriation of over $250,000 (Seymour 1928:1). Most of its students came from California and Arizona, from the Navajo, Hopi, Pima, Miwok, and Papago tribes, as well as Paiutes, including the Owens Valley Paiutes and other California Indian groups (Seymour 1928; Elmer Stanley, personal communication 1990).

The stated purpose of the Sherman Institute was "to create [for the Indian] a mode of living, to adapt him to alien ways, to furnish him with the means of making his livelihood and his home under conditions strange to his father" (Seymour 1928:3–4). To accomplish this goal, Sherman educators provided training "in regularity and industry," courses in various kinds of "practical work," and a paid, super-

Figure 5.3. Paiute School, Big Pine, California, 1909. As part of the federal government's plan to encourage the assimilation of Indian children into mainstream American society, this day school was built in 1899. It served the Owens Valley Paiutes until public schools were integrated in 1924.

vised work program called the "outing system," which was part of an apprentice system set up by the Office of Indian Affairs (Cheney 1938; Seymour 1928:4). Boys received training in farm duties and fruit growing, and girls learned to be seamstresses and domestic workers.

As at the Stewart school, administrators at the Sherman Institute had definite attitudes regarding the innate abilities and future lives of their students. In regard to one graduate who obtained employment in "mechanical work of an engineering nature," a member of the Board of Indian Commissioners commented:

> The aptitude of an Indian boy from a tribe where there has been absolutely no use of metals or machinery of any sort, for a work so completely foreign to anything in his tribal experience, is an astonishing thing. . . . Such training naturally means, if it is to be useful, that the boy cannot expect to return permanently to his people. He is definitely being prepared for life in a white community. It is worse than wasteful to train a boy to become a mechanic or engineer, even of a humble sort, and then send him back to a reservation where not even the simplest mechanical skill is in demand. (Seymour 1928:5–6)

Similarly, the Greenville School was dedicated to helping its students adapt to a Western way of life. Dictates about how to modify native

Figure 5.4. Dance exhibition, Carson Indian Agency, Stewart, Nevada, ca. 1935. During the 1930s educators softened their stance against banning all Indian traditions from the boarding schools. They encouraged Indians to demonstrate songs and dances during special events such as commencement. At the Stewart Indian School students dressed in often-stereotypical Indian attire in order to provide a dramatic scene that would increase the school's visibility.

customs often came directly from the commissioner of Indian Affairs. The school's superintendent, for example, was instructed to encourage his students to (1) wear "citizen's clothing, instead of the Indian costume and blanket," (2) cut their hair, (3) stop painting their faces, because perspiration made the paint melt, run into their eyes, and caused blindness, and (4) eliminate the dances and "so-called Indian feasts" that "in many cases" were "subterfuges to cover degrading acts and to disguise immoral purposes" (Jones 1902:2–3).

Many students from Owens Valley disliked their boarding school experiences (Winona Roach, personal communication 1999). They resented the efforts of white teachers to strip them of their cultural identity, they often felt they were being patronized, and they believed the institutions prepared them neither for life on the reservation nor for success in the outside world (anonymous personal communication 1999). Some students were so unhappy that they ran away and returned to their reservation homes, causing the Board of Indian Commissioners to investigate the "returned student problem" (Board of Indian Commissioners 1918; McDowell 1916). From the administrators' point of view, the boys and girls who left the Indian schools to go back to their reservations were short-sighted and unappreciative of the opportunities presented by the schools. As the secretary of the Board of Indian Commissioners put it:

Is there a flaw in the system? Do reservation life and environment kill ambition, initiative, the acquired discipline of regularity and industry? Do the boys and girls lose the desire to "get ahead" and the willingness to become self-respecting and self-supporting men and women? Are the influences and prejudices of the old, uneducated Indians still so strong that [the children] cannot break away from customs, traditions, and Indian conservatism and become independent? Is there something unchangeable in Indian blood which prevents white schooling and precept and example from getting under red skins? (McDowell 1916:1–2)

Other students felt they benefited from their years spent in boarding schools because they learned about the world outside the reservation. For example, one Owens Valley resident who attended the Sherman Institute during her high school years was amazed to discover how many different Indian tribes existed (Pearl A. Budke, personal communication 1997).

Between 1900 and 1920 the concept of segregated Indian schools lost popularity among educational policymakers. Responsibility for Indian education began to be transferred to the public schools, in exchange for financial remuneration (Adams 1995:318–319). During the 1930s and 1940s, increasing numbers of Indian students attended public schools in Owens Valley.[12]

The same attitudes toward the purpose of Indian education persisted when government Indian schools were integrated into local public schools. For example, in 1937 the Bishop Elementary School employed a special, full-time arts-and-crafts teacher. Her classes, which were open only to Indian students, focused on how to make things in brass and wood, to twist "strips of tissue paper into tight cords . . . to wind around jugs which were later shellaced [*sic*] and made into lamps" (Stewart 1937:10–11). Not only did these classes ignore traditional Paiute crafts and continue to segregate Indian students from their non-Indian counterparts, but they also represented a negative attitude about the innate abilities of Indian children. The Paiute children took these classes in lieu of social science because the white educators believed Indians were incapable of learning that subject. They also assumed the students could not read and placed them in special reading classes without any diagnostic or reading tests (Morgans 1937:1–2).

Indian education during the first half of the twentieth century affected the basket-weaving tradition in Owens Valley in two ways. First, it sometimes created among its students an ambivalence toward — or even a rejection of — their own cultural practices. These feelings reflected the more general attitude prevalent among Americans in the 1920s and 1930s that "being the same" was important whereas ethnicity and tradition largely were not. Consequently, some potential weavers chose not to learn the art of basket weaving. Second, the sustained absence from home of the children who attended boarding schools interfered with the total cultural immersion through which basket-making skills were traditionally acquired.

ECONOMIC OPPORTUNITY

Ongoing changes in economic opportunities during the twentieth century also played a role in the decline of basket weaving in Owens Valley. The early preeminence of agriculture, ranching, and mining as sources of work diminished as governmental and service jobs relating to tourism and recreation grew in importance (California State Employment Development Department [CSEDD] 1993, 1998, 1999a, 1999b, 2000, 2003; Barbara Goodman, personal communication 1999). As noted earlier, the land purchases begun in 1902 by the LADWP adversely affected the local agricultural economy. By 1927 a large portion of the non-Indian population present at the turn of the century had moved away from Owens Valley to find employment and raise their families elsewhere (Busby et al. 1979:83; Inyo County Planning Office 1988:4). These jobs never rebounded. In 1983 only 1.7 percent of the labor force in Inyo county was employed in agriculture (CSEDD 1993). That figure dropped to 1.1

percent in 1992, to 0.73 percent in 1998, and to 0.57 percent in 2002 (CSEDD 2003).

Ranching jobs also declined precipitously. By 1964 the number of ranches had dropped 80 percent, to approximately one hundred (Inyo County Board of Supervisors 1966:70, cited in Busby et al. 1979:94). Employment in ranching was so minimal in 2000 that the category was absent from labor statistics for Owens Valley.

Up to the 1960s mining was still somewhat important to the Owens Valley economy. During the 1960s profits fell below the level necessary to support the railways that carried ore or smelted materials out of the valley. In the first quarter of 1983 mining accounted for only 14 percent of wages paid in Inyo County (CSEDD 1993). This figure dropped to 3.5 percent by the last quarter of 1992 (CSEDD 2000), to 2.5 percent in 1998 (CSEDD 1998),[13] and to 1.7 percent in 2002 (CSEDD 2003).[14]

Government jobs (federal, state, and local combined) accounted for 29.2 percent of the labor force in Inyo County during 1983 (CSEDD 1993) and rose to 37.6 percent in 1992 (CSEDD 2003). Based on employment figures available for the hotel/lodging and food-related industries, tourism in 1983 accounted for 21.3 percent of the labor force (CSEDD 1993), peaked in 2000 at 24.5 percent, and fell slightly to 22.6 percent in 2002 (CSEDD 2003).

With the economic importance of tourism in Owens Valley today and the interest in Indian artistry burgeoning elsewhere, basket weaving should, by all rights, be a cottage industry with good growth potential. Several factors have raised obstacles to the formation of a strong market, however. First, there is a lack of older, knowledgeable weavers to train a younger generation. Second, people living a modern lifestyle have difficulty finding enough time to weave baskets. Finally, the workmanship of many of the baskets being made today does not equal that of the master weavers of the past.

Moreover, a widely held axiom among dealers of arts and crafts is that to generate an active market interest, there must be an ample supply in the marketplace (John Kania, personal communication 1999). A sufficient quantity of baskets for sale is currently unavailable in Owens Valley. Most of the present-day weavers in the valley produce baskets only sporadically based on their immediate financial needs. As one weaver explained, "When I need money for my kids' back-to-school clothes, I make a basket to sell" (personal communication 1998). Other weavers make baskets for friends and family only as specific occasions arise. The birth of a child, for example, is a common impetus for making a baby basket.

Those few Paiute weavers who work at it steadily and would like to earn a living from their efforts often make baskets on commission. The people who order their baskets, however, are rarely the same kind of wealthy clientele who sponsored weavers at the turn of the twentieth century. Some Owens Valley weavers put their work in shops and galleries on consignment and get paid only if their works sell. Others are able to sell their work outright, primarily to stores dealing in Indian materials located outside Owens Valley.

Although several contemporary Owens Valley weavers have their baskets in museums, their baskets are rarely exhibited in galleries. Owens Valley itself has few venues through which baskets can be sold. Gallery dealers outside the valley tend to be reluctant to handle new baskets, which lack the patina and the intrinsic historical value of older baskets. Moreover, as already noted, contemporary baskets made in Owens Valley during the 1990s and later were seldom if ever as well made as the older examples (John Kania, personal communication 1999). None of the practicing Owens Valley weavers have yet acquired the proficiency of such famous weavers of the first half

of the twentieth century as Sarah Hunter, Susie Jackson, and Nellie Charlie. This is especially true in the case of coiled baskets, which require more time, materials, and patience than twined ones.

The weavers at work at the beginning of the twenty-first century are, understandably, less experienced than weavers fifty or one hundred years before. Their proficiency and speed of weaving cannot match that of weavers who learned the craft as small children. Nonetheless, some of them price their baskets according to the number of hours invested in them, and consequently, new baskets sometimes cost much more than older ones. Given a choice between new, more expensive baskets that are not as well made as old ones, collectors generally prefer the old (John Kania, personal communication 1999).

Currently, Owens Valley weavers are apt to focus their efforts on twined baskets instead of coiled ones, which are harder to make. Within the Paiute community there is limited demand for new utilitarian baskets because, with the exception of baby baskets, their original functions are largely obsolete. For tourists and other buyers outside the community who want relatively inexpensive baskets, weavers fashion small replicas of traditional baskets (Figure 5.5). Miniatures are easier and quicker to make than their regular-sized counterparts and are priced lower. Although the relatively low price may attract buyers, it has been difficult for weavers to earn a sufficient income from them.

CONTEMPORARY WEAVERS OF OWENS VALLEY

As the twenty-first century began, a small coterie of weavers was present in Owens Valley, practicing the art in various ways. A few of these weavers, believing that Paiute traditions should remain only inside their native communities, declined to share their stories with non-Indian outsiders. Others generously agreed to talk about their lives and their baskets. The information below was obtained from face-to-face conversations and telephone interviews with the weavers, their family members, and

Figure 5.5. Miniature Yurok-Style Twined Baskets. Weaver, Alta Rogers, 1997. Although fine-quality baskets are often difficult to obtain today in Owens Valley, miniature replicas can sometimes be purchased directly from the weavers. These Yurok-style baskets are shown next to a penny to illustrate their small size. Alta Rogers, who is of Yurok and Paiute ancestry, lives on the Bishop Reservation.

their friends and from unpublished oral histories. Their stories weave together remembrances of the past with realities of the present.

Jessie Durant (1913–)

Jessie Durant is a soft-spoken nonagenarian with a wry sense of humor and a ready laugh (Figure 5.6). Representing the age group of Owens Valley weavers who grew up during the first third of the twentieth century, she links an older generation for whom basket weaving was an everyday activity with a younger one for whom the craft is almost anachronistic.

Durant's mother, Daisy Young Charlie Cluette Mallory, was widowed when Jessie was a baby. She worked as a cook at Mono Mills, a sawmill southeast of Lee Vining, California, before coming to Bishop in 1918 to work. Her first job was as a housekeeper for the Mac-Queen family and their next-door neighbors, the Doyles.[15] She later married Jack Mallory and moved with him to Round Valley, just north of Owens Valley. In 1938 she moved back to Bishop.

Jessie Durant spent her childhood in Mono County, California. She attended numerous primary schools, including the Carson Indian School in Carson City, Nevada. She finished eighth grade at Lee Vining School in 1929 and then attended high school in Bakersfield, California. Jessie has fond memories of the kindhearted Gilli family, with whom she lived while attending high school. They had three high-school-age children, and Mr. Gilli was an ambitious person who had a large cotton plantation, grew exotic fruits such as loquats,[16] and cured his own olives.

After high school Jessie returned to visit her family in Bishop. She was discontented and undecided about what to do with her life. She helped a woman in Bishop whose twelve-year-old son, Bobby, had hydrocephalus. She taught him to count in the Paiute language. Taking care of Bobby inspired Jessie to pursue a nursing career. She attended St. Vincent's School of Nursing in Santa Fe, New Mexico, graduating in 1939. She did private nursing in Santa Fe and worked in an Indian hospital on the Navajo

Figure 5.6. Jessie Durant, 1998. Pictured in her home in Bishop, California, Jessie displays a well-used winnowing basket made by her grandmother, the renowned Mono Lake Paiute weaver Nellie Charlie (ca. 1867–1965).

Reservation in Arizona, in a veterans' hospital in Los Angeles, and in a community hospital in Bishop, where she has resided since 1942.[17]

Jessie comes from a lineage of famous Mono Lake Paiute weavers that included her grandmother, Nellie Charlie; great-aunt, Tina Charlie; and great-grandmother, Patsy Jim. Jessie's mother, Daisy Mallory, was a remarkable weaver, but she never achieved a high degree of prominence. Daisy's three-rod baskets were beautifully made with complex and innovative patterning and are among the finest baskets produced by Mono Lake Paiute women. Her death in early adulthood, and the fact that many of her baskets were immediately purchased by a few private collectors and therefore were not widely marketed, may have led to her lack of wide recognition as an expert weaver.[18]

Jessie and her sister, Rosie Parsons, learned basket weaving at an early age, primarily from their grandmother, Nellie Charlie, with whom they spent much of their childhood. Their family members made seasonal trips to Yosemite, where they traded for acorns, bracken fern, and redbud. Both Jessie and her sister wove baskets sporadically as adults, in spite of pressures to the contrary. Jessie completed her last basketry object, a coaster, in 1960.

Throughout her life Jessie has included many of the ancient Paiute customs in her daily activities. Even today she prepares traditional meals, using her ancestors' grinding stones to crush and pulverize pine nuts and various kinds of nutritious seeds, and their baskets to cook pine nut mush, which she calls "Paiute poi." Jessie no longer actively makes baskets but she treasures the legacy of her family's baskets still in use or on display in nearby museums such as the Yosemite Museum.

Charlotte Bacoch (1938–)

Charlotte Bacoch was inspired to learn basket weaving by her mother, Lilly Baker.[19] Baker, a Paiute from Pyramid Lake, made baby baskets for each of Charlotte's children as they were born. When the *saquina* (hood) of one child's cradle basket needed to be replaced, Charlotte resolved to learn the basket-making process herself. Recalling memories of watching her mother work, at age twenty-eight Charlotte essentially taught herself how to weave. She began fashioning hoods for the Pyramid Lake–style buckskin baby baskets that her parents produced. Her father, a Paiute originally from Big Pine, made the frames and tanned the buckskin for the cradle baskets, and her mother sized, tanned, sewed, and folded the buckskin for the frame. Today Charlotte completes the whole process herself (Figure 5.7). In addition to the buckskin-covered cradle baskets, Charlotte makes the double-backed

Owens Valley Paiute style of cradle. She is also expert at beadwork designs, which she produces not only for leather-covered cradle baskets but also for dresses, gloves, and moccasins.

Like her contemporaries, Charlotte accepts commissions for cradle baskets from friends and relatives who want them for their personal use and from tourists and collectors. She has consigned beadwork to the Paiute-Shoshone Cultural Center in Bishop, but more often she sells her baby baskets directly from home. She contributes to the perpetuation of Paiute ancestral traditions by teaching basket-weaving classes at the Paiute-Shoshone Cultural Center, in spite of a high student dropout rate.[20]

Sandra Jefferson Yonge (1947–)

Sandra's father was a Mono Lake Paiute, and her mother was a Panamint Shoshone. Her mixed heritage is indicative of the interaction that took place among the Indian communities of eastern California. It also illustrates why some of the baskets woven and collected in Owens Valley today present combinations of previously distinct weaving techniques, designs, and styles. Sandra was born and raised in Lone Pine and still lives in the house her grandmother willed to her.

Yonge learned her basket-weaving skills in stages. Her grandmother, Susan Johnson (who lived to be 106 years old), was the primary influence on her weaving education. When Sandra was a young child, her grandmother taught her where, how, and when to pick willow, as well as how to "clean 'em straight" using a very sharp knife. Sandra remembers cutting every finger and breaking every nail, especially when taking the nibs off the shoots. These early lessons were sometimes a source of conflict between Yonge's mother and grandmother, since Grandmother Johnson's taking Sandra out of school for willow gathering and processing ran counter to Sandra's mother's belief in the importance of education.[21]

Yonge often watched her grandmother weave outside in a simple homemade shelter. She wanted to learn about weaving while she was in grade school. Her grandmother, however, said, "This is not for you to know now." Only when Sandra was a teenager did her grandmother teach her how to split willow, sharpen awls, and size the peeled strands through holes punched in tin-can lids. Later on, her friend Mamie Boland, a Panamint Shoshone weaver from Death Valley, taught the aspiring weaver how to grow, prepare, and use devil's claw for black designs in her baskets.

As an adult, Sandra wove baby baskets for her children and others (Figure 5.8). She fondly remembers the one she improvised for her first child. Since her baby's arrival was imminent, there was insufficient time to gather and prepare willows properly. Instead, Sandra cut an inset for the baby in a piece of plywood, covered it with leather, and then padded and quilted it. The baby loved it.

During the late 1990s Yonge's position as chairperson of the Lone Pine Paiute-Shoshone Reservation left her little time to weave. She simply found "politics and art too hard to do at the same time." Today she devotes her limited free time to beadwork, sewing, and gardening.

Alta Rogers (1933–)

A descendant of both the northern California Yuroks and Owens Valley Paiutes, Alta Rogers specializes in Yurok-style miniature baskets, beadwork, and Paiute baby carriers, hats, and seed beaters that she sells to tourists and collectors (Figure 5.9). She learned basket weaving from her maternal Yurok grandmother, Lucinda Minard. Her grandmother showed her how to gather willow roots in early spring after the Klamath River runoff receded. She taught Rogers to use the black maidenhair fern stem and shiny white-yellow bear grass and to dye woodwardia fern stem a beautiful orange-rust color with alder bark.[22]

Before the 1970s, when Owens Valley still had some swampy areas, Alta was able to gather the willow shoots she needed locally. She recalled: "I used to start out early, around six o'clock in the morning, with a packed lunch of jerky, salmon, and Indian bread. I'd go about ten miles to gather willow and didn't come home until nine or ten o'clock at night." Today,

Figure 5.7. Charlotte Bacoch, Big Pine, California, 1999. Charlotte is standing in front of two of her cradle baskets that are now on permanent display at the Paiute-Shoshone Cultural Center in Bishop, California.

however, the reduced availability of water has forced her to go to Bridgeport to gather materials and sometimes to trespass on private land.

Alta periodically teaches private weaving classes for children and adults, and she sometimes gives demonstrations at the Paiute-Shoshone Cultural Center. She and her husband, Michael Rogers, a Paiute jewelry maker who has assumed responsibility for gathering and preparing Alta's willow, sell to a shop in Lone Pine but primarily market their

Figure 5.8. Sandra Jefferson Yonge, 1999. Seated outside her home in Lone Pine, California, Sandra poses with a willow cradle basket she is just beginning, along with bundles of scraped willow rods.

Figure 5.9. Alta Rogers, Bishop, California, ca. 1988. Alta wears a traditional Owens Valley Paiute cap. The willow cradle basket she holds has a plain twined back. Deer hide is used to cover the bottom of the cradle basket and also for the thongs that secure the baby. The zigzag design on the sunshade, indicating a male baby, is made with yarn. The padding is made of rabbit skin.

wares outside Owens Valley. They have chosen to do this for economic reasons, as Michael explained:

> You put too much labor and too much time and work into a basket, and people here [in Owens Valley] offer you too little money. They offer you fifty or a hundred bucks. Either you turn it out and go to market to get enough money for the month, or you dribble along and get another job. This is a government, tourist-oriented town. The demand for crafts is seasonal and not enough to make a living from. You can't make enough money if you just do it locally. (Personal communication 1999)

In order to earn a sufficient income, Alta and Michael have gone to Indian Market in Santa Fe, New Mexico, since 1987 and have traveled to craft shows in Denver, Pasadena, Yosemite, and San Diego. Starting in the 1990s they placed their work on consignment with the Eastern California Museum in Independence and with the Inyo County Arts Council. They also took commissions from their home on the Sunland Reservation in Bishop. As of 2004, Michael was still actively making jewelry, but because of illness, Alta was no longer weaving.

Lillian I. Andreas (1961–)

Born in Bishop, Lillian Andreas comes from a family of Paiute basket makers that includes her great-grandmothers, Minnie Shephard and Nanny Collins, and her grandmothers, Esther Andreas and Effie Hackett (Figure

5.10). She credits these women for giving her "the feeling for wanting to do it" (Andreas 1992:2), but she learned the basics of weaving from her father, Dan Andreas. Like many other weavers, Lillian became interested in learning to weave because of the pending arrival of her first child, Little Bear. Since she could not afford to pay for weaving lessons at the time, her father, who as a child had watched his mother weave, offered to show her what he knew.[23]

Lillian made her first baby basket out of willow with a birch sapling frame, because "the birch keeps it sturdy and strong and the willow makes it light."[24] She tried to incorporate the traditional ways of doing things, such as using obsidian to clean the willows, but could not find a piece that would fit her hand. Instead, she used a small, two-inch knife, which she still uses today.

Once Andreas began making baskets, her interest in basket weaving grew. Accompanied by her sister, Janet Stone, she spent many hours in museums studying the various kinds of baskets on display. Under the tutelage of weavers Minnie Williams and Norma Brown, she learned to make some of them. Today she and Janet gather willows together and are rather competitive about their weaving. They race to see who finishes her basket first but then cooperate to sell their baskets.

Lillian has been weaving for about twenty years. She says, "I weave whenever I can find the right willows and when my arthritis permits. It's fun to do and it takes a lot of stress off you. If you make a basket when you are mad, it comes through. You have to have a positive attitude." She is a versatile weaver whose repertoire includes winnowing baskets, Shoshone-style and Paiute-style cradleboards, and traditional-style burden baskets both full-size and miniature (Figure 5.11). Her baskets often include stylized feather, butterfly, and eagle designs.

Although her grandmother, Effie Hackett, taught her to make coiled baskets, Andreas avoids making them because she believes her recompense would not justify her time investment. Instead, she gears her efforts toward special-order baskets to sell to Indian art buyers. She explained, "I have . . . people that called in and they want a certain type of basket. Now I have one person from Winnemucca that wants a Washoe basket. I don't even know what a Washoe basket looks like. I would like to see a Washoe basket so I can make it for these people" (Andreas 1992:4).

Lillian has four children, all of whom grew up watching her weave and helping her gather, split, and clean willows. Her daughter, who in 1999 was in high school, draws but does not weave. Her sons, however, have helped Lillian teach basket weaving at the Paiute–Shoshone Cultural Center. Andreas is proud of their skills and hopes they will pass their knowledge on to their own children. She is also optimistic that her daughter will become interested when she has children of her own.

Janet Andreas Stone (1954–)

Janet Stone was born and reared in Bishop by her Paiute parents, Dan and Jane Andreas. Like her sister, Lillian, Janet did not participate in weaving activities as a child. Only in the late 1970s, when she became pregnant, was her interest in the process aroused. At that time, Gretchen Hess, a friend who attended the same church as Janet, taught her to weave using raffia. Later Lillian helped her switch to willow. Janet's first willow basket, a cradle basket, was covered with tanned buckskin. It was very plain — no design, no beading — but very special. She recalled, "I remember how small my baby looked in the basket. She weighed only five pounds."[25]

In the 1990s Janet made baby baskets for home use by friends and relatives (Figure 5.12). She also made them for sale, marketing them through word of mouth. She explained, "When I need money, I make a basket and sell it. I count on certain buyers to buy a lot. One lady bought five baskets from me, and that helped pay the bills." Janet has learned about sedge root and other materials but chooses to use only willows in her baskets and yarn for the hood design on her cradle baskets. She would like to learn to weave other kinds of

Figure 5.10. Lillian Andreas, ca. 1990. Lillian Andreas accepts commissions to make various kinds of twined baskets. She is pictured here standing in front of a *havatoni,* an Owens Valley Paiute–style home, outside the Paiute-Shoshone Cultural Center in Bishop, California.

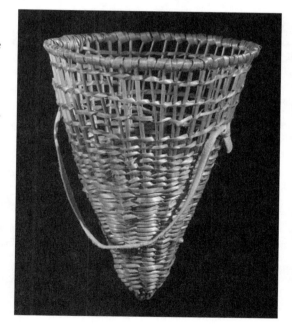

Figure 5.11. Miniature Twined Burden Basket. Weaver, Lillian Andreas, 1997. This miniature basket illustrates several forms of plain twining. The number of enclosed warps varies from one to three.

baskets but has not yet found the time or a good teacher.

Stone would also like to pass the basket-weaving tradition along to the next generation. Her two grown children used to help clean the willows, but neither has shown any interest in weaving as adults. Nonetheless, Janet has made cradle baskets for her son's three babies, and

Figure 5.12. Janet Stone, Bishop, California, 1999. Janet's cradle basket is done in the Paiute style and has a flat back woven in open twining. It is covered with deerskin. The sunshade design, made with yarn, indicates a boy.

she hopes her daughter will "take it up when she has her own babies, since that's usually the way."

Bernardine M. Summers (1960–)

Bernardine started weaving at age nineteen while pregnant with her daughter, Amity, who coincidentally was a nineteen-year-old college student in 1999 when we interviewed Summers for this book (Figure 5.13). Although her sister's great-grandmother, Ida Warlie, was a weaver, Bernardine's opportunities for learning as a child were limited. Her mother reared six children by herself and thus did not have time to weave. As a young adult, Summers began with weaving a cradle basket with raffia. Her first willow basket was intended for a doll but was used instead as a bassinet for Amity, who was born prematurely. Bernardine also learned many techniques about basket making from her neighbor, Gretchen Hess.[26]

Over the years Summers made baby baskets for friends when they were needed, but she never sold them for profit or tried to make a living from her efforts. Eventually, she became

so skilled that in 1992 the Los Angeles County Museum of Natural History commissioned her to weave a replica of one of the summer cradle baskets in its collection that had been irreparably broken. Bernardine's full-time employment at the local Indian casino currently leaves her little time to pursue her weaving interests.

Ellen Pueblo (1951–)

Ellen Pueblo is a Paugvik Aleut from Nak Nek, Alaska. With the help of the BIA, she left Alaska in the early 1970s to attend school in San Jose, California. She attended nursing school, then secretarial school, and eventually became an administrative assistant in the American Indian Studies Program at the University of California at Berkeley. There she first saw baskets woven out of willow, which reminded her of the ryegrass ones made in her native community.[27]

Between 1976 and 1980 Pueblo lived on the Walker Indian Reservation in Schurz, Nevada. She became friends with Wuzzie George, a famous Northern Paiute weaver then in her nineties. Wuzzie helped Ellen learn how to prepare willow, carry out the basic techniques of twined basketry, and make hoods for cradle baskets. Although the two women spoke different languages, they communicated readily with gestures and eyes. Wuzzie showed her how to make baskets that were taut enough to "make the willow sing." Ellen also received advice from basket makers who lived on other reservations, including Lena Wright of Pyramid Lake and the late Frances Sam of the Walker River Reservation, both in Nevada.

Ellen moved to Bishop in 1980 and married Leonard Pueblo three years later. During Ellen's first pregnancy, Leonard's mother, Thelma Pueblo, loaned Ellen one of her old summer cradle baskets and said, "Here, you know how to weave baskets. Make this!" The time they spent together over the next few months, while Thelma taught Ellen the finer points of weaving, helped the two women bond.

In the late 1990s Pueblo continued to weave when time allowed (Figure 5.14). Her full-time job helping kidney-dialysis patients, however, left her little free time. Ellen believed the fast pace of modern society, the effects of women's entrance into the workforce, and the results of mass production have all diffused the interest of young Paiutes in basket weaving. Other factors, such as the 1983 seat–belt law that negates the use of cradle baskets, played a part as well. Nevertheless, she was hopeful about the future. In this regard, she believed in giving back the culture she, as an outsider, learned. She said, "In my life, the kids would go play, my husband would go hunting. I would go gather willow."

Gretchen Uhler Hess (1956–)

Gretchen Hess was born in Lakewood, Ohio, and spent her childhood in nearby Richfield. Her mother was Ukrainian; her father, western European. In the late 1970s her father moved the family to California, hoping that a milder climate would ease his wife's arthritis. They first lived in southern California, where her father worked for the Mattel Toy Company. He did not like city life, however, so they moved to Bishop. While in high school there, Gretchen met James (Jim) Vernon Hess, whom she eventually married.[28]

Jim came from a long line of notable Northern Paiute basket weavers, including his great-grandmothers, Nellie Charlie and Leanna Tom. Gretchen's inspiration to weave came partially from her husband's family legacy and partially from her own desire to participate as fully as possible in her husband's culture. When she learned that traditionally "young Paiute ladies expecting babies learned to make cradle-boards," she decided that her own children should have them. While pregnant with her first child, Hess asked Thelma Pueblo, her landlady and neighbor at the time, to make her a traditional Paiute summer baby basket. Thelma said, "No, but I'll teach you how to do it." As a result, the two women spent many afternoons together.

Gretchen became quite proficient and began teaching basket-making classes in Big Pine in 1980 (Figure 5.15). She taught again in 1985 and 1986 at the Indian Education Center

Figure 5.13. Bernardine M. Summers, 1998. Pictured in her home on the Sunland Reservation in Bishop, California, Bernie holds a Paiute-style cradle basket. Its open-weave willow frame is covered with deerskin, and it is decorated with beaded geometric designs and fringe. The hood design indicates a male child.

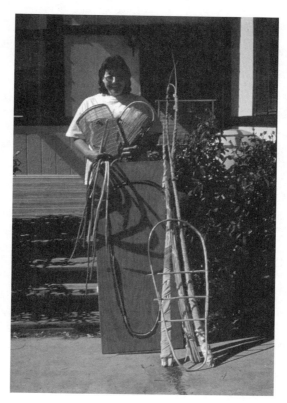

Figure 5.14. Ellen Pueblo with Works in Progress, 1998. Ellen stands outside her home in Bishop, California, showing four cradle baskets in various stages of completeness. Bundles of peeled willow are wrapped with cloth to keep the willows straight and to protect them until they are used.

through Cerro Coso Community College (Figure 5.16). Participation in these classes evoked childhood memories in many of her students. She recalled, "When they started, they had flashbacks of seeing their grandmothers' hands at work weaving. Weaving seemed natural and easy for them to pick up, but it needed to be developed."

Figure 5.15. Gretchen Uhler Hess, 1999. Pictured in front of a stand of willows at the Paiute-Shoshone Indian Cultural Center in Bishop, California, Gretchen holds two winnowing trays she recently completed. The Paiute-style shallow one on the left has a horizontal design done in redbud with a support at the bottom made of red birch. It was made for cleaning pine nuts whereas the deeper one on the right was made for gathering and knocking nuts out of cones. Both are open-twined weave on vertical willow rods.

Figure 5.16. Gretchen Uhler Hess and Basket-Weaving Students, 1986. Students display the weaving projects they completed during the basket-weaving class taught by Gretchen Uhler Hess at the Indian Education Center in Bishop, California. Alta Rogers, holding a completed winnower, stands in front. Behind her *(left to right)* are Lorraine Cash, Helen Platsohon, Edna Piper, unknown, and Gretchen Uhler Hess.

In addition to weaving, Hess enjoys writing songs and singing for her church. She weaves cradle baskets and repairs many of the old, damaged Paiute baskets that are still in use by older Paiute women or owned by collectors (Plate 14). She made a concerted effort to pass down the basket-weaving tradition to her three daughters and was especially successful with one, Shirley Hess Slee.

Shirley Hess Slee (1980–)

Shirley Slee, the youngest daughter of Gretchen Hess, hopes that her own basket weaving will encourage a new generation of Paiute artisans in Owens Valley (Figure 5.17). Like many of the other weavers, Shirley learned how to gather willow as a child, accompanying her mother on day trips. Later she traveled with her to Yosemite to obtain sedge root and other materials. Under her mother's direction, Shirley made her first basket at age twelve. Unlike her weaving contemporaries, who initially honed their skills on baby baskets, Shirley's first project was a single-rod coiled basket.[29]

From that time on, Shirley continued to concentrate on coiled baskets. She used redbud and bracken fern root for her designs, just as her father's Mono Lake Paiute ancestors did. Slee sometimes got inspiration from photographs she saw of the beautiful baskets made long ago by Paiute masters, including her great-great-grandmother, Nellie Charlie. Just as her ancestors, Leanna Tom and Nellie Charlie, used sedge root from west of the Sierras for their fine coiled baskets, Shirley used this most prized sewing strand in her baskets when she could obtain it.

Shirley is married to John Slee, whom she has known since fifth grade. They have two children. By age twenty, Shirley had already gained recognition for her baskets and was hoping to earn a living from her weaving skills (Figures 5.18, 5.19). In 2002 she moved with her family to Santa Barbara, California, where she currently works as a cosmetologist. Despite her busy schedule, Shirley still makes a little time to weave.

Richard Stewart (1944–)

Richard Stewart's heritage is a mixture of Paiute, Pima, Irish, and Italian (Figure 5.20). Along with being a basket maker, he has been a successful painter, photographer, potter, writer, and teacher.[30] Richard became interested in the basket-making process in 1989.

His grandmother had woven during his childhood, and when he realized that basket weaving was disappearing as a cultural tradition in Owens Valley, he decided to help resurrect the process. He studied the basket collections of various museums and concluded that although some small decorative baskets were still being produced for the tourist market, no one was making the older-style utilitarian baskets. Richard therefore decided to teach himself how to make the utilitarian ones. He soon realized he needed instruction.

At a craft fair in 1993 Richard met Julia Parker, an accomplished Kashaya Pomo–Coast Miwok basket weaver who wove in the styles of both her husband's Paiute-Miwok family and her Pomo ancestors and who demonstrated at the Yosemite Museum. Julia offered to teach Richard the Pomo method of weaving twined, unpeeled-willow workbaskets and acorn-gathering baskets. At first, Richard was uncomfortable with the offer because he thought weaving was women's work. Julia reminded him that Pomo men made baskets too, citing the fish traps and burden baskets they traditionally wove.

As word of Richard's interest in making baskets spread in the valley, an older weaver from Big Pine, Edna Piper, offered to teach him everything she knew. Edna showed him where to find willow, how to tend it, the best time to pick it, how to preserve it, and how to split it.[31] The learning process was long and tedious, but after three years of practice, patience, and commitment Richard mastered the basic steps of gathering and preparing the willow for basket weaving.

Over the years Richard has produced a number of baskets, but his primary interest in the weaving process remains tied to his passion for preserving the local history and cultural traditions of Owens Valley. This interest has left him little time to continue weaving, however. He works at the Environmental Office of the Fort Independence Reservation doing historical research and global positioning system (GPS) survey work. He also is deeply involved in developing "soft" tourism on a year-round

Figure 5.17. Shirley Hess Slee Gathering Willow, 1998. In preparation for weaving, Shirley gathers willow on a September day from a favorite site near her former home in Bishop, California. Of all the current weavers in the valley, only she makes coiled baskets.

Figure 5.18. Paiute Coiled Basket. Weaver, Shirley Hess Slee, 1999. This three-rod basket, one of the first ten that Shirley made, required 55 hours of work. The flame design, which repeats four times, is borrowed from a basket made ca. 1924 by her great-great-grandmother, Nellie Charlie.

Figure 5.19. Paiute Coiled Basket. Weaver, Shirley Hess Slee, 1999. The flame design on the outside is done with dyed sedge root because Shirley ran out of bracken fern root. On the bottom is a sunburst design.

Figure 5.20. Richard Stewart at Manzanar, 1999. As part of an effort to promote tourism in Owens Valley, Richard Stewart obtained a federal grant to give tours of the Manzanar National Historic Site near Lone Pine, California. He uses the tours as an opportunity to draw comparisons between the internment experiences of the Japanese and the Paiutes and Shoshones.

basis in the valley. Toward this end he directs walking and bicycle tours of the Manzanar Historical Site and has consulted on the sensitive issue of promoting educational tours of selected petroglyph sites. Although Richard has put his weaving on hold, at least temporarily, he supports community efforts to continue the basket-weaving tradition.

THE PRESENT AND THE FUTURE

Today in Owens Valley, women are the standard bearers of the basket-weaving tradition, although some men help in the preparation process and at least one man is a basket maker in his own right. As a result of geographic mobility and intermarriage, the weavers' ancestral roots have spread far beyond Owens Valley.

Despite their diverse cultural backgrounds, these weavers have similar patterns of involvement in the basket-making process. Some were initially exposed to weaving as children, when they watched and/or aided family elders gather and prepare willow. Imminent parenthood commonly spurred serious interest. Most began by weaving cradle baskets, usually due

to the pending arrival of a child. They usually made their initial baby baskets for home use and sometimes went on to make additional baskets for sale. A few were able to turn their efforts into sustainable ventures.

Those who make their weaving publicly known in Owens Valley today have adopted identifiable features from the Paiute tradition, although most have freely incorporated features from other Indian groups as well. Like their ancestors, they continue to use willow as their main basket material, though some augment their efforts with nonlocal materials. They persist in making older kinds of baskets but usually in altered or miniature form. For the most part, they tailor their made-for-sale baskets to the tastes of collectors, tourists seeking relatively inexpensive souvenirs, and other buyers of Indian art. In short, the current generation of Owens Valley weavers, like many before them, has adapted a time-honored tradition to the exigencies of modern life.

As a response to the many recent social and physical changes in the Paiutes' ancestral lands, resources, and customs, today's Paiute weavers have developed multiple strategies and rationales for continuing their craft. Their efforts cannot exist in a vacuum, however. In order to sustain the basket-weaving tradition, several levels of community support are needed. In recent years, this support has been forthcoming. As part of a wider effort to preserve local and regional history and culture, the Owens Valley community is trying to sustain those portions of traditional Paiute culture that still persist.

The Paiute-Shoshone Indian Cultural Center, located in Bishop and staffed by local Indian people, plays a central role in the effort to preserve the Paiute cultural heritage. Its impressive displays of traditional willow and tule dwellings, clothing, foods, jewelry, and baskets allow residents and visitors alike to appreciate Paiute and Shoshone traditions, heritage, and art. Various basket weavers offer classes there on a periodic basis,[32] as well as at the Indian Education Center. The Cultural

Center has a small gift shop where beadwork and other Indian artisan goods are sold. Only rarely does the shop's inventory include a few baskets. The center is currently reassessing its operating procedures in an attempt to regulate its hours and raise money for hiring a permanent, professional staff.

The Indian community has also helped educate the public about ancient traditions by participating in such community festivals as Mule Days, fandangos, and pow wows. Mule Days provides an opportunity for Indians and non-Indians to come together and celebrate the history of the region. At fandangos and pow wows non-Indians can observe the dances, music, food, and games that are part of the local Paiute Indians' culture.

Non-Indians have helped the Paiute and Shoshone communities preserve the heritage and history of Owens Valley in other ways. The Eastern California Museum of Inyo County, located in Independence, has long housed a significant collection of eastern Sierra Indian basketry, beadwork, pottery, and other artifacts. Its photo archive, which includes hundreds of photographs of local Paiute and Panamint Shoshone people, is available for public study. In addition, the museum has a selection of oral histories gathered by volunteers from long-time local residents. It also offers a fine selection of books on the history, geology, and anthropology of Owens Valley and the surrounding area. A small selection of Indian crafts, along with books and other local memorabilia, are for sale.

The Laws Railroad Museum and Historical Site, located just north of Bishop, comprises a number of restored nineteenth-century buildings. It has an outstanding aggregation of historical documents, books, and photographs, as well as a small Paiute basketry collection. Its library is open to the public, and its gift shop carries a good selection of books about local and regional history.

As city planners have directed the region's economic development toward year-round recreation and tourism, efforts have been made to incorporate the preservation of Indian culture as a marketing strategy. Toward this end, both Indians and the National Park Service have assumed responsibility for protecting the valley's prehistoric petroglyphs, which have attracted both visitors and vandals in the past. Controversial discussions are under way among the Indian community, concerned non-Indians, and local politicians regarding potential tours of certain petroglyph sites that are already well known. Visitors may take walking tours and bicycle tours of nearby Manzanar, site of the World War II internment camp for Japanese Americans. The excavation of an archaeological site at Manzanar is also being considered to further knowledge of prehistoric Indian lifeways. In addition, the Indian community is working with the National Park Service to support the care and maintenance of willow-gathering sites.

With the support of all these community efforts to highlight local history, basket weaving persists as a cultural tradition in Owens Valley, albeit in a somewhat altered form. In former times making baskets was a part of everyday life. It was an immersion process that evolved over the course of a lifetime. Today the art is disconnected from its original social context. Young weavers are continuing the tradition, but it is not a fundamental part of their upbringing as it was for their grandmothers. Today's weavers are learning basket weaving as just one of many crafts available, as a leisure activity to pursue in fragments of time and space.

At the beginning of the twenty-first century, Paiute baskets are a tangible link with the past and the people who made them. To many, the baskets are evidence of a relationship between the Indians and non-Indians of Owens Valley, who have negotiated their way through multiple social and economic changes. Through the legacy of their baskets the Paiute and Panamint Shoshone people have maintained a material connection to their past. Their story will be told and retold in the future, as the people continue to intertwine old traditions with new ways.

APPENDIX I.
Selected Flora and Fauna of Owens Valley

FLORA

Baltic rush (*Juncus balticus*)
Bitterbrush (*Sarcobatus vermiculatus*)
Blazing star (*Mentzelia laevicaulis*)
Blue dick (see Wild hyacinth)
Bracken fern (*Pteridium aquilinum*)
Buckberry (*Shepherdia argentea*)
Bulrush (*Scirpus nevadensis, S. maritimus*)
Bunch grass, deer grass (*Muhlenbergis rigens*)
Camas (*Camassia leichtlinii*)
Cane (*Phragmites communis* Trin.)
Cattail (*Typha latifolia*)
Chia (*Salvia columbariae*)
Coffeeberry (*Rhamnus californica*)
Cottontop cactus (*Echinocactus polycephalus*)
Cottonwood (*Populus fremontii*)
Currant (*Ribes aureum*)
Desert mallow (*Sphaeralcea ambigua*)
Devil's claw (*Proboscidea parviflora* var. *hohokamiana*)
Elderberry (*Sambucus melanocarpa*)
False Solomon's seal (*Smilacina stellata*)
Jeffrey pine (*Pinus jeffreyi*)
Juncus (*Juncus balticus*)
Juniper (*Juniperus* spp.)
Love grass (*Eragrostis secundflora* Presl.)
Manzanita (*Arctostaphylos patula*)
Mormon tea (*Ephedra viridis, E. nevadensis*)
Mountain mahogany (*Cercocarpus ledifolius*)
Oak (*Quercus kelloggii, Q. palmeri*)
Piñon pine (*Pinus monophylla*)
Prickly pear cactus (*Opuntia basilaris*)
Rabbitbrush (*Chrysothamnus nauseosus*)
Redbud (*Cercis occidentalis*)
Rice grass (*Oryzopsis hymenoides, O. miliacea*)

Sagebrush (*Artemesia tridentata*)
Sedge (*Carex* spp.)
Sego lily (*Calochortus nuttallii*)
Shadscale (*Atriplex confertifolia*)
Sumac (*Rhus trilobata*)
Spike rush (*Eleocharis* sp.)
Sunflower (*Helianthus annuus, H. balnaderi*)
Tobacco (*Nicotiana attenuata*)
Tule (*Scirpus acutus*)
Tüpüsi (*Brodiaea capitata* Benth.)
Water birch (*Betula occidentalis* Hook.)
Watercress (*Nasturtium officinale*)
Wild hyacinth (*Dichelostemma pulchella*)
Wild rose (*Rosa californica*)
Wild rye (*Elymus cinereus*)
Willow (*Salix lasiandra*)
Yellow bee plant (*Cleome lutea*)
Yellow nutgrass (*Cyperus esculantus* L.)
Yucca (*Yucca schidigera, Y. brevifolia*)

FAUNA

Bear, black (*Ursus americanus*)
Bear, grizzly (*Ursus horribilis*)
Brine fly (*Ephydra hians*)
Chuckwalla (*Sauromalus obesus*)
Cicada (*Okanagodes* spp.)
Common flicker (*Colaptes auratus*)
Ground squirrel (*Spermophilus beecheyi, Ammospermophilus leucurus*)
Mountain sheep (*Ovis canadensis*)
Mule deer (*Odocoileus hemionus*)
Mussel (*Anodonta* sp.)
Pandora moth (*Coloradia pandora*)
Pronghorn (*Antilocapra americana*)
Rabbit (*Sylvilagus auduboni, Lepus californicus*)

Sources: Busby et al. 1979:163–165; C. Fowler 1986, 1990; Smith 1995:161–204.

APPENDIX II.
Known Owens Valley Weavers During the Heyday Period

Many talented weavers spent at least part of their lives in Owens Valley and made baskets there. Incomplete recordkeeping by early collectors and loss of information over time, however, make a definitive list of weavers impossible. Documentation for most weavers is minimal; often only a name and tribal affiliation exist. Despite the paucity of information, the following people are referred to in a sufficient number of sources to merit their inclusion in a list of basket weavers known to have been associated with Owens Valley. All locations are in California.

OWENS VALLEY PAIUTE WEAVERS

Maggie Bell (Big Pine)
Emma Berges (cousin of Joe Eugley)
Anna Best
Big Min
Jennie Burcham (Long Valley)
Suzie Butcher
Minnie Chiatovich (Bishop)
Emma Crawford
Sallie Davis (Big Pine)
Joe Eugley
Mary Gorman (Fort Independence)
Emma Westerville Harry
Mary Jim Harry (Fish Springs)
Sarah Frank Hill (Tinnemeha)
Jennie Horton (Bishop)
Mary Horton (Big Pine)
Martha Horton (Big Pine)
Mattie Horton (Bishop)
Hattie Jones
Susie Kimbel
Emma Leete
Ivy Lent
Rosie Lent (Bishop)
Emma Muller (Big Pine)
Old Maggie
Old Sally (Big Pine)
Edna Piper

Juda Piper
Minnie Piper (Big Pine)
Thelma Pueblo
Mattie (Minnie?) Sullivan (Big Pine)
Emma Earl Symmes (Fort Independence)
Teha
Susie Watterson
Mary Westerville (Tinnemeha)
Sally Wing
Emma Wright (Round Valley)
Mary Harkness Yandell (Bishop)

PANAMINT SHOSHONE WEAVERS

Maggie Bellas (Darwin)
Big Maggie
Mable Billson
Dolly Doc Boland
Jenny Bowers
Mamie Joaquin Button
Mary Button Charlie (Lone Pine)
Dina or Tina "Grandma" Doc
Mamie Gregory (Darwin)
Addie Hanson
Isabel Hanson
Mable (listed as George Hanson's niece)
Sarah Hunter (Saline Valley)
Ella Lockery
Annie G. Milton (Saline Valley)

Rosie Nobles Ness
Sally Boland Patterson
Jennie Price
Jennie Ramshaw
Laura Button Shaw (a.k.a. Lola or Sullivan
    Shaw's wife) (Keeler)
Rosie Shaw
Susie Shepherd
Minnie Patterson Thompson
Sarah Wilson
Susie Wilson
Mary Wrinkle (Darwin)

MONO LAKE PAIUTE/ YOSEMITE MIWOK WEAVERS

Carrie Bethel
Nellie Charlie

Tina Charlie
Lula Charlie Hess
Patsie Jim
Sally Jackson Jim
Susie Jackson Jim
Mary Lowe
Daisy Young Charlie Cluette Mallory
Annie Poole McBride
Mattie Jackson McBride
Lena Phoenix
Emma Pine
Jennie Poole
Mary Poole
Lucy Telles
Louisa Tom
Minnie Betoit Williams

APPENDIX III.
Selected Museum Collections Associated with Owens Valley Baskets

MUSEUM ABBREVIATIONS

ECM   Eastern California Museum of Inyo County, Independence

FM   Field Museum, Chicago

LACMNH   Natural History Museum of Los Angeles County, Los Angeles

PAHMA   Phoebe Apperson Hearst Museum of Anthropology, University of California, Berkeley

PSCC   Paiute–Shoshone Cultural Center, Bishop, California

SMRC   State Museum Resource Center, California Department of Parks and Recreation, Sacramento

SWM   Southwest Museum of the American Indian, Autry National Center, Pasadena

UCD   University of California, Davis

UM   Ulster Museum, Belfast, Ireland

YM   Yosemite Museum, Yosemite National Park

PROVENANCE ABBREVIATIONS

MLP   Mono Lake Paiute

OVP   Owens Valley Paiute

PS   Panamint Shoshone

TWINED BASKETS

Basket Type	Weave	Provenance	Weaver	Museum	Catalog No.
Seed beater	Plain	OVP		SWM	811.G.1036
Seed beater	Plain	OVP		UCD	516
Seed beater	Plain	Paiute		YM	6
Seed beater	Plain	OVP		FM	59021
Seed beater	Plain	OVP		PAHMA	1-26841
Seed beater	Plain	OVP	Mary Westerville	PAHMA	1-26983
Seed beater	Plain	OVP		LACMNH	FA.1127.71-38
Cradle	Buckskin-covered	Paiute		YM	28640
Cradle (boy's)	Bound	OVP		PAHMA	1-26917
Cradle (girl's)	Bound	OVP		PAHMA	1-26914
Cradle	Bound	OVP		PAHMA	1-2327-
Cradle	Bound	OVP		PAHMA	1-2328-
Cradle	Bound	OVP		YM	29014
Cradle	Bound	OVP	Mary Jim Harry	PAHMA	1-26987
Cradle	Flat-back	OVP		PSCC	
Cradle	Bound	PS or OVP		YM	38413
Cradle	Bound	MLP		YM	69
Cradle	Bound	Paiute		YM	1054
Water jar	Diagonal	OVP		YM	26985
Water jar	Diagonal	OVP		FM	59002
Water jar	Diagonal	Paiute		PAHMA	216541
Water jar	Diagonal	Paiute		PAHMA	216548
Water jar	Diagonal	Paiute		PAHMA	1-71571
Water jar	Diagonal	OVP		LACMNH	FA.2570.85-8
Water jar	Diagonal	Paiute		UM	LCC 33

Basket Type	Weave	Provenance	Weaver	Museum	Catalog No.
Water jar	Diagonal	OVP		PAHMA	1-26918
Water jar	Diagonal	OVP		PSCC	
Winnower	Plain	OVP		PAHMA	1-19673
Winnower	Plain	OVP		FM	59025
Winnower	Plain	OVP		UCD	511
Winnower	Plain	OVP		PAHMA	1-19679
Winnower	Plain	OVP	Minnie (Pete Yandell's wife)	PAHMA	1-26830
Winnower	Diagonal	Paiute		FM	59042
Winnower	Diagonal	OVP		PAHMA	1-19681
Winnower	Diagonal	OVP		PAHMA	1-26984
Winnower	Diagonal	OVP		FM	59023
Winnower	Diagonal	PS (materials)		FM	58990
Winnower	Diagonal	OVP		UCD	514
Winnower	Plain	OVP	Mary Jim Harry	PAHMA	1-26986
Winnower	Diagonal	OVP		PAHMA	1-26828
Winnower	Diagonal	OVP		SMRC	082-190-189
Winnower	Plain	PS		UCD	606
Winnower	Plain	PS		UCD	605
Winnower	Diagonal	OVP		UCD	512
Winnower	Diagonal	OVP		UCD	513
Winnower	Plain	OVP		PAHMA	1-19678
Winnower	Plain	OVP		PAHMA	1-26985
Winnower	Diagonal	MLP	Tina Charlie	YM	21746
Winnower	Diagonal	OVP?		UM	53:1946
Winnower	Plain	MLP	Nellie Charlie	YM	37871
Winnower	Diagonal	MLP	Nellie Charlie	UCD	670
Winnower	Diagonal	MLP	Tina Charlie	YM	85476
Winnower	Plain	MLP?		SWM	811.G.1045
Winnower	Diagonal	MLP?		SWM	811.G.1046
Winnower	Diagonal	MLP?		SWM	811.G.1047
Burden	Diagonal	OVP		LACMNH	FA. 1127.71-3
Burden		OVP		YM	26984
Burden	Diagonal	Shoshone	I. Hanson's maternal grandmother	ECM	A1018.1
Burden	Diagonal	OVP		PAHMA	1-26829
Burden	Diagonal	OVP? PS?		UCD	515
Burden	Diagonal	OVP		FM	58995
Burden	Diagonal	OVP		UCD	517
Burden	Diagonal	OVP		PAHMA	1-19675
Burden	Diagonal	OVP		FM	59019
Burden	Plain	OVP		FM	59009
Burden	Plain	Paiute		PAHMA	1-19680
Burden	Diagonal	OVP?	Hattie Jones	PAHMA	1-26832
Burden	Diagonal	OVP		FM	59022
Burden	Diagonal	MLP?		SWM	811.G.1409
Burden		OVP?		SMRC	8710
Burden		OVP?		SMRC	6344
Burden	Diagonal	OVP		FM	59010
Burden	Diagonal	MLP	Tina Charlie	YM	21761
Burden	Diagonal	OVP	Mary Jim Harry	PAHMA	1-26990
Burden	Plain	OVP	Mary Jim Harry	PAHMA	1-26989
Burden	Plain	OVP	Mary Jim Harry	PAHMA	1-26988
Burden	Diagonal	MLP	Nellie Charlie	UCD	653
Cap	Diagonal	OVP		PAHMA	1-26919
Cap	Diagonal	OVP		PAHMA	1-70601
Cap	Diagonal	OVP		UCD	507
Cap	Diagonal	PS		UCD	592A
Cap	Diagonal	OVP		UCD	508

Basket Type	Weave	Provenance	Weaver	Museum	Catalog No.
Cap	Diagonal	OVP	Mary Harkness Yandell	ECM	B 278
Cap	Diagonal	OVP	Mattie Sullivan	ECM	B 294
Cap	Diagonal	OVP	Mary Horton	ECM	B 298
Cap	Diagonal	OVP		ECM	B 243?
Cap	Diagonal	OVP		ECM	B 295
Cap	Diagonal	OVP		ECM	B 283
Cap	Diagonal	OVP	Mattie Horton	ECM	B 273
Cap	Diagonal	OVP	Mary Horton	ECM	B 286
Cap	Diagonal	OVP		ECM	B 317
Cap	Diagonal	OVP	Sallie Davis	ECM	B 292
Cap	Diagonal	OVP	Old Sally	ECM	B 297
Cap	Diagonal	OVP	Peggie	ECM	B 296
Cap	Diagonal	Washo	Emma Payne	ECM	B 288
Cap	Diagonal	OVP		ECM	B 214
Cap	Diagonal	OVP	Martha Farrington	ECM	B 293
Cap	Diagonal	OVP		UCD	506
Cap	Diagonal	OVP	"Mother of Jerry Bowers' woman"	FM	452 (102975)
Cap	Diagonal	OVP		YM	25231
Cap	Diagonal	OVP		YM	27815
Cap	Diagonal	OVP		FM	59004
Cap	Diagonal	OVP		FM	59005
Cap	Diagonal	OVP		FM	59020
Cap	Diagonal	OVP		SWM	611.G.713
Cap	Diagonal	OVP		PAHMA	1-20964
Cap	Diagonal	PS		UCD	603
Cap	Diagonal	PS		UCD	591
Cap	Diagonal	PS		UCD	592B
Cap	Diagonal	OVP		SMRC	6574W
Cap	Diagonal	OVP		SMRC	2089H
Cap	Diagonal	Washo		SMRC	L12714
Cap	Diagonal	OVP		SMRC	082-190-200
Cap	Diagonal	OVP		SMRC	AJF
Cap	Diagonal	OVP		FM	102964 (420)
Cap	Diagonal	OVP		SWM	1163.G.27
Cap	Diagonal	OVP	Mary Jim Harry	PAHMA	1-26991
Cap	Diagonal	OVP	Mary Jim Harry	PAHMA	1-26992
Cap	Diagonal	OVP		LACMNH	A.2562.58-148
Cap	Diagonal	OVP		LACMNH	A.2562.58-149
Cap	Diagonal	OVP		LACMNH	FA.1127.71-22
Cap	Diagonal	OVP		LACMNH	FA.1127.71-26
Cap	Diagonal	OVP		LACMNH	A.1820.25-5212
Cap	Diagonal	OVP		SMRC	BWH-13-BT-1-SL
Piagui	Diagonal	OVP		YM	9635
Piagui	Plain	MLP		UCD	664
Piagui	Plain	OVP	Hattie Jones	PAHMA	1-26834
Piagui	Plain	OVP?		FM	59006
Sugar and berry harvester	Plain	OVP		FM	59007
Mush boiler	Diagonal	MLP	Nellie Charlie	YM	25475
Mush boiler	Diagonal	MLP		YM	37868
Urn	Diagonal	PS		UCD	577
Bowl w/neck	Diagonal	PS		UCD	601
Bowl	Diagonal	OVP?		SMRC	082-190-194
Bowl/cup	Diagonal	OVP?		SMRC	3958W
Small bowl	Diagonal	OVP		UCD	651
Basket pot	Diagonal	OVP? MLP?		FM	59000
Basket pot	Diagonal	OVP? MLP?		FM	58999
Basket pot	Diagonal	OVP? MLP?		PAHMA	70600

COILED BASKETS

Basket Type	Weave	Provenance	Weaver	Museum	Catalog No.
Meal sifter		OVP?		FM	59003
Meal sifter		OVP?		FM	58989
Circular winnower		PS		UCD	604
Circular winnower		PS		SMRC	3653W
Circular winnower		Monache?		UCD	510
Gambling tray		PS		UM	CLCC 31
Gambling tray		PS		UM	C83.1946
Basket	Gap-stitched	OVP		UCD	509
Basket	Gap-stitched	MLP	Nellie Charlie	UCD	636
Basket	Gap-stitched	OVP	Nellie? Long Valley John's wife	PAHMA	1-26866
Basket	Gap-stitched	MLP	Sally Jackson Jim	PAHMA	1-26884
Basket	Gap-stitched	MLP	Sally Jackson Jim	PAHMA	1-26875
Basket	Gap-stitched	OVP		SWM	424.G.28
Basket	Gap-stitched	OVP		UCD	501
Basket	Gap-stitched	MLP	Nellie Charlie	YM	37859
Basket	Gap-stitched	MLP	Nellie Charlie	YM	3877
Basket	Gap-stitched	MLP	Nellie Charlie?	YM	Acc.# 5907
Flared		OVP		SWM	421.G.1426
Elliptical		OVP		SWM	1296.G.1
Basket		OVP		SWM	813.G.6
Basket	Tight-stitched	MLP	Sally Jackson Jim	PAHMA	1-26878
Basket	Tight-stitched	MLP	Sally Jackson Jim	PAHMA	1-26877
Basket	Tight-stitched	MLP	Sally Jackson Jim	PAHMA	1-26899
Basket	Tight-stitched	MLP	Sally Jackson Jim	PAHMA	1-26888
Basket	Tight-stitched	MLP	Susie Jackson Jim	PAHMA	1-26900
Basket	Tight-stitched	MLP	Susie Jackson Jim	PAHMA	1-26881
Basket	Tight-stitched	MLP	Susie Jackson Jim	PAHMA	1-26858
Basket	Tight-stitched	MLP	Susie Jackson Jim	PAHMA	1-26898
Basket	Tight-stitched	MLP	Susie Jackson Jim	PAHMA	1-26890
Basket	Tight-stitched	MLP	Sally/Susie Jackson Jim	YM	38436
Bottleneck		MLP	Annie Poole McBride	PAHMA	1-26885
Bottleneck		MLP	Annie Poole McBride	PAHMA	1-26857
Flared		MLP	Annie Poole McBride	PAHMA	1-26865
Flared		MLP	Annie Poole McBride	PAHMA	1-26887
Basket		Paiute	Mattie Jackson McBride	PAHMA	1-26882
Basket	Tight-stitched	Paiute/Miwok	Leanna Sam Tom	PAHMA	1-26906
Basket	Tight-stitched	Paiute/Miwok	Lucy Telles	PAHMA	1-26905
Basket		MLP	Daisy Young Charlie Cluette Mallory	PAHMA	1-70563
Basket		MLP		PAHMA	1-26845
Basket		MLP		PAHMA	1-70559
Basket		MLP		PAHMA	1-70565
Basket		MLP		PAHMA	1-144980
Basket		MLP		PAHMA	1-144981
Basket		MLP		PAHMA	1-144982
Basket	Tight-stitched	MLP	Nellie Charlie	UCD	608
Basket		MLP?		SWM	1935.G.124
Basket		MLP	Mary Poole	LACMNH	F.A.2570.85-14
Basket		Paiute	Emma Crawford	ECM	B 75
Basket		OVP	Minnie Chiatovich	ECM	B 189
Basket		OVP	Minnie Chiatovich?	ECM	B 72
Basket		OVP	Big Min	ECM	B 60
Basket		OVP		ECM	B 97
Basket		OVP		ECM	76.78.17
Basket		OVP		ECM	76.78.16
Basket		OVP		ECM	B 61
Basket		Paiute	Florence Butler	ECM	B 217

Basket Type	Weave	Provenance	Weaver	Museum	Catalog No.
Basket		OVP	Topsy	ECM	B 98
Basket		Paiute	Emma Leete	ECM	B 90
Basket		MLP	Emma Pine	ECM	B 96
Basket		Paiute	Mattie Goan	ECM	B 55
Basket		OVP		ECM	B 82
Basket		OVP		ECM	B 154
Basket		OVP		ECM	B 43
Basket		Paiute	Mary Shelton	ECM	B 79
Basket		OVP		ECM	B 25
Basket		Shoshone	Big Maggie	ECM	B 100
Basket		OVP	Mary Harkness Yandell	ECM	B 156
Basket		OVP	Mary Gorman	ECM	B 206
Basket		OVP	Sarah Frank Hill	ECM	B 41
Basket		OVP	Joe Eugley	ECM	B 226
Basket		OVP		ECM	76.4.6
Basket		OVP	Mary Harkness Yandell	ECM	B 155
Basket		OVP	Joe Eugley	ECM	B 71
Basket		OVP	Sarah Frank Hill	ECM	B 53
Basket		OVP	Mary Harkness Yandell	ECM	B185
Basket	Beaded	MLP	Sally Jackson Jim	YM	25501
Basket	Beaded	Paiute	Elsie Watterson	PAHMA	1-26920
Basket	Beaded	Washoe type		PAHMA	1-70664
Basket		PS		UCD	578 & 578a
Basket		PS		UCD	596
Basket		PS		UCD	584 & 584a
Basket		PS		FM	58984
Basket		Monache		UCD	505
Basket		Monache		UCD	504
Basket		PS		UM	CLCC16
Basket		OVP?		SMRC	2191W
Basket		OVP		FM	59024
Basket		Western Mono		UCD	540
Basket		OVP		PAHMA	1-26926
Basket		PS		SMRC	1868W
Bottleneck		PS		UM	CLCC9
Basket		PS?		FM	58983
Bottleneck		PS		PAHMA	1-26838
Bottleneck		PS		FM	102914 (231)
Basket		PS		FM	102997 (479)
Basket		PS		FM	102996 (478)
Mortuary		Monache		UCD	497
Mortuary		OVP	Sala (or Salla)	UCD	498
Bottleneck		Monache		UCD	499
Bottleneck		Monache		UCD	500
Mortuary		PS		UCD	568
Basket		OVP	Sally's mother	UCD	502
Flared		Yokuts		UCD	902
Flared		Yokuts		UCD	903
Basket		Chuckchancy		UCD	841
Basket		PS		UM	C29.1946
Basket		PS?		SWM	1849.G.1
Cap		PS		UM	C7.1946
Cap		PS		UM	C9.1946 or LCC36
Cap		PS		UM	C11.1946 or LCC21
Cap		PS		UM	C1.1946
Cap		PS		UM	CLCC22
Cap		PS		UM	CLCC23
Cap		PS		UM	C3.1946

Basket Type	Weave	Provenance	Weaver	Museum	Catalog No.
Cap		PS		UM	C8.1946
Cap		PS		UM	C2.1946
Cap		PS		UM	C6.1946
Cap		PS		UM	C12.1946
Cap		PS		UM	C4.1946
Cap		PS		UM	CLCC37
Cap		PS		UM	C5.1946
Cap		PS		FM	58986
Basket		PS		SWM	1563.G.93
Basket		OVP?		SWM	116.L.200
Basket		PS		SWM	1499.G.121
Basket		PS	Susie Wilson	SWM	491.P.3134

Note: Attributions are according to museum catalogs or cards unless otherwise noted.

APPENDIX IV.
Owens Valley Baskets, by Figure or Plate Number

LOCATION ABBREVIATIONS

ASM Arizona State Museum, University of Arizona, Tucson

CMNH Cleveland Museum of Natural History, Cleveland

ECM Eastern California Museum of Inyo County, Independence

FM Field Museum, Chicago

LACMNH Natural History Museum of Los Angeles County, Los Angeles

PAHMA Phoebe Apperson Hearst Museum of Anthropology, University of California, Berkeley

PC Private collection

SMBEM Staatliche Museen zu Berlin, Ethnologisches Museum, Berlin

UCD C. Hart Merriam Basket Collection, Department of Anthropology Museum, University of California, Davis

UM Ethnographical Collections, Ulster Museum, Belfast, Ireland

YM Donna Burgner and Elma Blaver Collections, Yosemite Museum, Yosemite National Park

FIGURES

Figure/Plate No.	Description	Maker/Year	Collector/Year	Current Location
Figure 1.8	Owens Valley Paiute basket cap	unknown, ca. 1900	Anna Kelley, ca. 1950	PC
Figure 1.10	Panamint Shoshone burden basket	Mamie Joaquin Button(?)	Anna Kelley, ca. 1950	PC
Figure 1.12	Owens Valley Paiute *piagui* gathering basket	unknown, ca. 1900	J. W. Hudson, 1904	FM 59006
Figure 1.13	Owens Valley Paiute seed beater	unknown, ca. 1940	Anna Kelley	PC
Figure 1.14	Panamint Shoshone winnowing basket	Mamie Joaquin Button, ca. 1930	Anna Kelley	PC
Figure 1.18	Panamint Shoshone water jar	unknown, ca. 1910	Anna Kelley	PC
Figure 2.8	Owens Valley Paiute burden basket	unknown, ca. 1900	Anna Kelley	PC
Figure 3.5	Owens Valley Paiute cap	unknown	Rose Black, ca. 1910	ECM B243
Figure 3.7	Owens Valley Paiute cap	Mattie Sullivan	Rose Black, ca. 1910	ECM B294
Figure 3.8	Owens Valley Paiute cap	unknown, ca. 1900	C. Hart Merriam, 1902	UCD 507
Figure 3.9	Owens Valley Paiute cap	Mary Horton	Rose Black, ca. 1910	ECM B298
Figure 3.10	Owens Valley Paiute cap	unknown, ca. 1910	unknown	PAHMA 1-70601
Figure 3.11	Owens Valley Paiute cap	unknown	Rose Black, ca. 1910	ECM B295
Figure 3.12a	Panamint Shoshone cap	unknown	C. Hart Merriam, 1902	UCD 592A
Figure 3.12b	Owens Valley Paiute cap	unknown	C. Hart Merriam, 1909	UCD 508
Figure 3.13	Northern Paiute cap, Pyramid Lake (?)	unknown, ca. 1910	Grace Geyer, ca. 1910; gift to Anna Kelley	PC

Figure/Plate No.	Description	Maker/Year	Collector/Year	Current Location
Figure 3.14	Owens Valley Paiute conical burden basket	Mary Jim Harry	Julian H. Steward, 1927	PAHMA 1-26988
Figure 3.15	Owens Valley Paiute conical seed gathering basket	Mary Jim Harry	Julian H. Steward, 1927	PAHMA I-26990
Figures 3.16 and 3.17	Owens Valley Paiute parching/winnowing tray	unknown	E. W. Gifford, 1915	PAHMA 1-19673
Figure 3.18	Owens Valley Paiute sifter or scoop	unknown	C. Hart Merriam, 1901	UCD 512
Figures 3.19 and 3.20	Owens Valley Paiute winnowing/sifting tray	unknown	C. Hart Merriam, 1901	UCD 513
Figure 3.21	Owens Valley Paiute seed beater	unknown	Horatio Shumway Lee, ca. 1910	PAHMA 1-26841
Figure 3.22	Owens Valley Paiute seed beater	Mary Westerville	Julian H. Steward, 1927	PAHMA 1-26983
Figure 3.24	Owens Valley Paiute model cradle basket	Mary Jim Harry	Julian H. Steward, 1927	PAHMA 1-26987
Figure 3.26	Owens Valley Paiute *piagui* gathering basket	Hattie Jones	Horatio Shumway Lee, ca. 1910	PAHMA 1-26834
Figure 3.27	Owens Valley Paiute berry and sugar harvesting basket	unknown	J. W. Hudson, 1904	FM 59007
Figure 3.29	Western Mono cooking basket	unknown	C. Hart Merriam, 1901	UCD 540
Figure 3.30	Owens Valley Paiute coiled basket	unknown, ca. 1920	Mrs. Hugh Patrick (Frankie) Beatty	YM 25511
Figure 3.31	Owens Valley Paiute (?) circular sifting tray	unknown	C. Hart Merriam, 1909	UCD 510
Figure 3.32	Owens Valley Paiute (?) bottleneck basket	unknown	J. W. Hudson, 1904	FM 58983
Figure 3.33	Owens Valley Paiute unfinished (?) bowl	unknown	C. Hart Merriam, 1902	UCD 504
Figure 3.34	Owens Valley Paiute spaced-stitched basket	unknown	C. Hart Merriam, ca. 1900	UCD 501
Figure 3.35	Owens Valley Paiute spaced-stitched three-rod basket	Emma Westerville Harry, ca. 1930	PC	PC
Figure 3.36	Mono Lake Paiute space-stitched three-rod basket	Nellie Charlie, ca. 1950	PC	PC
Figure 3.37	Mono Lake Paiute flared bowl	Annie Poole McBride, ca. 1915	Horatio Shumway Lee	PAHMA 1-26887
Figure 3.38	Owens Valley Paiute lidded basket	Mary Gorman, ca. 1910	Rose Black, ca. 1910	ECM B206
Figure 3.39	Mono Lake Paiute coiled basket	Susie Jackson Jim, ca. 1915	Horatio Shumway Lee	PAHMA 1-26890
Figure 3.40	Mono Lake Paiute coiled basket	Sally Jackson Jim, ca. 1915	Horatio Shumway Lee	PAHMA 1-26888
Figure 3.46	Panamint Shoshone winnowing or sifting tray	Mamie Joaquin Button, 1943	Anna Kelley	PC
Figure 3.47	Panamint Shoshone basket	Mamie Joaquin Button, ca. 1940	Anna Kelley	PC
Figure 3.49	Panamint Shoshone lidded basket	Mary Button Charlie, ca. 1938	Anna Kelley, 1943	PC
Figure 3.51	Mono Lake Paiute basket	Nellie Charlie, ca. 1940	Elma Blaver, ca. 1940	YM 37859
Figure 3.55	Mono Lake Paiute basket	Tina Charlie, ca. 1950	PC	PC
Figure 3.56	Owens Valley Paiute oval basket	Joe Eugley, ca. 1910	Rose Black, ca. 1910	ECM B71

Figure/Plate No.	Description	Maker/Year	Collector/Year	Current Location
Figure 3.58 (right)	Panamint Shoshone fancy basket	Mamie Gregory(?), ca. 1930	Anna Kelley	PC
Figure 3.58 (left)	Panamint Shoshone fancy basket	Mamie Gregory, ca. 1930	Anna Kelley	PC
Figure 3.59	Panamint Shoshone basket	Isabel Hanson, 1939	Anna Kelley	PC
Figure 3.61	Owens Valley Paiute cap	Mary Jim Harry, ca. 1927	Julian Steward, 1927	PAHMA 1-26992
Figure 3.64	Panamint Shoshone basket	Sarah Hunter, 1943	Dale Inkley, 1943	CMNH 2001-.19aL
Figure 3.66	Mono Lake Paiute gap-stitched basket	Sally Jackson Jim	Horatio Shumway Lee, ca. 1920	PAHMA 1-26875
Figure 3.67	Mono Lake Paiute beaded basket	Sally or Susie Jackson Jim, or Mattie Jackson McBride, ca. 1930	Mrs. Hugh Patrick (Frankie) Beatty	YM 25504
Figure 3.68	Mono Lake Paiute beaded basket	Sally or Susie Jackson Jim, or Mattie Jackson McBride, ca. 1930	Mrs. Hugh Patrick (Frankie) Beatty	YM 25505
Figure 3.72	Mono Lake Paiute bottleneck basket	Annie Poole McBride	Horatio Shumway Lee, ca. 1906	PAHMA 1-26857
Figure 3.75	Owens Valley Paiute open-twined winnowing basket	Emma Earl Symmes, ca. 1934	Anna Kelley, ca. 1935	PC
Figure 3.77	Mono Lake Paiute winnowing basket	Minnie Betoit Williams, ca. 1962	Unknown	ASM E-5768
Figure 3.78	Owens Valley Paiute cap	Mary Harkness Yandell, ca. 1905	Rose Black, ca. 1910	ECM B278
Figure 3.79	Owens Valley Paiute flared bowl	Mary Harkness Yandell, ca. 1905	Rose Black, ca. 1910	ECM B155
Figure 4.4	Owens Valley Paiute winnowing basket	Mary Jim Harry, 1927	Julian Steward, 1927	PAHMA 1-26986
Figure 4.5	Panamint Shoshone coiled basket	unknown, ca. 1909	Harry Floyd sold to H. E. Sargent, March 30, 1909	FM 102996
Figure 4.6	Owens Valley Paiute basket	mother of "Sally," ca. 1900	Mrs. Minnie C. Barrows (Randolph) purchased in March 1902 for C. Hart Merriam	UCD 502
Figure 4.8	Owens Valley Paiute seed beater	unknown, ca. 1900	J. W. Hudson, 1904	FM 59021
Figure 4.9	Panamint Shoshone coiled basket	unknown	C. P. Wilcomb, ca. 1900	SMBEM IV.B. 12063
Figure 4.10	Panamint Shoshone coiled bottleneck basket	unknown, ca. 1905	Andrew W. de la Cour Carroll, ca. 1905	UM CLCC9
Figure 4.11	Panamint Shoshone coiled basket	"Popinase," ca. 1905	Andrew W. de la Cour Carroll, ca. 1905	UM CLCC16
Figure 4.12	Panamint Shoshone-style coiled cap (likely Kawaiisu)	unknown	Andrew W. de la Cour Carroll, ca. 1900	UM 7.1946
Figure 4.18	Owens Valley Paiute coiled basket	Sarah Frank Hill	Rose Black, ca. 1930	ECM B41
Figure 4.19	Owens Valley Paiute cap	unknown, c. 1900	John S. and Helen S. MacQueen	LACMNH F.A.1127.71-22
Figure 4.26	Panamint Shoshone cradle basket	Mamie Joaquin Button, 1943	Anna Kelley, 1943	PC
Figure 4.27	Owens Valley Paiute basket	Emma Wright, ca. 1935	Anna Kelley, ca. 1935	PC
Figure 5.2	Paiute or Panamint Shoshone twined burden basket with cotton repair	unknown, ca. 1900	Anna Kelley	PC
Figure 5.5	Miniature Yurok-style twined baskets	Alta Rogers, 1997	PC	PC

Figure/Plate No.	Description	Maker/Year	Collector/Year	Current Location
Figure 5.11	Miniature twined burden basket	Lillian Andreas, 1997	PC	PC
Figure 5.18	Paiute coiled basket	Shirley Hess Slee, 1999	PC	PC
Figure 5.19	Paiute coiled basket	Shirley Hess Slee, 1999	PC	PC
PLATES				
Plate 3	Owens Valley Paiute cap	unknown, ca. 1920	Horatio Shumway Lee, ca. 1920	PAHMA 1-26919
Plate 4	Owens Valley Paiute water jar	unknown, ca. 1900	Helen S. and John S. MacQueen, ca. 1900	LACMNH F.A.2570.85-7
Plate 5	Owens Valley Paiute coiled basket	unknown, ca. 1900	PC	PC
Plate 6	Mono Lake Paiute beaded basket	Sally Jackson Jim, ca. 1930	Mrs. Hugh Patrick (Frankie) Beatty	YM 25501
Plate 7	Panamint Shoshone basket	Addie Hanson, ca. 1950	PC	PC
Plate 8	Panamint Shoshone baskets	Sarah Hunter, ca. 1930	Anna Kelley, ca. 1940	PC
Plate 9	Mono Lake Paiute globular coiled basket	Susie Jackson Jim	Horatio Shumway Lee, ca. 1920	PAHMA 1-26898
Plate 10	Mono Lake Paiute coiled basket	Daisy Young Charlie Cluette Mallory, ca. 1917	PC	PC
Plate 11	Mono Lake Paiute bottleneck basket	Annie Poole McBride	Horatio Shumway Lee, ca. 1915	PAHMA 1-26885
Plate 14	Miniature baby basket	Gretchen Uhler Hess, 1999	PC	PC

NOTES

1. Gathering the Willow

1. This estimated time frame is based on radiocarbon and obsidian-hydration dating methods, climatic studies, and the presence of such artifact forms as projectile points, marine shell beads, obsidian tools, and structural remains (Bettinger 1977:3, 1991:476–479).

2. Archaeological materials from nearby regions also shed light on the ancient past of Owens Valley. For example, the arid climate of the Great Basin has helped preserve fragments of basketry materials for centuries. Dating back ten thousand years, these materials allow scientists to codify the longest basketry sequence in the world (Adovasio 1986:194). Although such ancient baskets have not been found in Owens Valley, many are similar to those produced in historic times by the Owens Valley Paiutes. Certainly the basketry of the Paiute people of Owens Valley is a part of this sequence.

3. Photographs of early-twentieth-century Owens Valley Paiute villages can be found in Bosak 1975:51–55.

4. Native linguistic terms are taken from several sources, as there is no published, standardized reference guide for the Owens Valley Paiute language. Many of the words were compiled by researchers at different times and from speakers with varying levels of familiarity with the language. Sources used in this book are Merriam 1979, Steward 1933, and personal communications with contemporary speakers who speak a combination of Northern Paiute, Owens Valley Paiute, and Panamint Shoshone languages.

5. An anonymous writer reported in 1857 of the Owens Valley, "It is thickly inhabited by Indians, who are cultivating the land to a considerable extent, raising many kinds of vegetables and grain" (*Mariposa Gazette* 1857).

6. Connections between these other groups and the Owens Valley Paiutes went beyond trading and intermarriage. For example, in some Kawaiisu myths specific locations in Owens Valley territory figure prominently (Zigmond 1980:45, 55, 139). Trading with groups across the Sierra Nevada continued a practice that was thousands of years old in the Great Basin (Hughes and Bennyhoff 1986).

7. This game survived into the early twentieth century. For a 1920s photograph of women playing it near Big Pine, see Liljeblad and Fowler 1986:Figure 11.

8. For photographs of men playing this game near Big Pine in the 1920s, see Liljeblad and Fowler 1986: Figure 10.

9. By the end of the twentieth century Paiute hand-game players observed at events in California generally guessed the marked bone. The time when this change took place is unknown. Information on the handgame as it was played in the early 1970s can be found in Schultheis 1975.

10. See Steward 1936a for examples of these legends, one of which, the story of Hai'nanu (397–498), especially describes the importance and value of well-made and beautiful baskets.

11. These time estimates are by Craig Bates, who has gathered and processed willow basket material and replicated numerous Paiute-, Miwok-, and Maidu-style baskets of these types.

12. The excavation of an archaeological site south of Lone Pine, thought to be a Paiute winter village abandoned before 1850, recovered more than nine hundred shards of pottery (Burton and Farrell 1996:159).

13. Similarly, the skill of pottery making survived among the neighboring Western Monos into the early twentieth century (Gayton 1929).

14. The following reconstruction of the seasonal life of the Owens Valley Paiutes, unless otherwise noted, is based primarily on Bettinger 1991; Fowler and Liljeblad 1986; and Steward 1933 and 1934.

15. The Owens Valley Paiutes differentiated between the brine fly larvae from Mono Lake, which they called *cutsavi,* and those from Owens Lake (Steward 1933:256).

16. These trenches were commented on as early as 1858, when one non-Indian traveler (identified only as "L.A.B.") noted them in the Jeffrey pine forests but had no idea as to their purpose (B. 1858). In August 1864 another observer mistook the trenches as an attempt by Indians to protect the trees from fire, supposing that these pines were the ones that supplied pine nuts for food (Farquhar 1930:540).

17. Since neighboring groups cooked mush by stone-boiling it in baskets (see, for example, Parcher 1937:7), it is probable that the Owens Valley Paiutes also used this cooking method before the introduction of pottery (Driver and Massey 1957:229, 235; Fowler and Dawson 1986:712; Liljeblad and Fowler 1986:421). Although there are no extant archaeological specimens of cooking baskets from the pre-pottery era, cooking baskets were occasionally collected from the Owens Valley Paiutes (see, for example, Field Museum, cat. no. 59000, collected by J. W. Hudson in 1904), suggesting that such baskets were occasionally made locally. This particular

extant example is much like Mono Lake Paiute twined cooking baskets except that it uses winter-peeled willow in its design band instead of the usual Mono Lake Paiute design band of bracken fern root or other material.

18. For photographs of pine nut gathering, see C. Fowler 1986:66; Wheat 1967:30.

2. Splitting the Willow

1. The situation was very different for other Paiute groups, such as the Surprise Valley Paiutes far to the north (Layton 1981). The lack of horses among the Paiutes in Owens Valley can be documented, for example, in the reports of U.S. cavalry officers during the Owens Valley War (see especially O'Neill 1862, where the capture of one horse is worthy of note). Similarly, oral histories of Paiute people and ethnographies regarding the Owens Valley Paiutes do not mention horses in the early nineteenth century but often document their use in the last quarter of the nineteenth century. See especially Steward 1933, 1934, 1941.

2. Recent epidemiological studies suggest that native-to-native transmission of such Old World pathogens as chickenpox, smallpox, tuberculosis, and cholera occurred even before intensive face-to-face contact with whites, perhaps as far back as the sixteenth, seventeenth, and eighteenth centuries (Cook 1976; Preston 1996). The spread of such diseases reached crisis proportions at least by the mid-nineteenth century, as evidenced by a cholera epidemic that moved westward from Nevada and killed several hundred Northern Paiutes in 1850 (Nissen 1982:66–69, 115–116; Scott 1966:26–27). Although there is no evidence that diseases predated the arrival of whites in Owens Valley, the possibility exists.

3. It has been suggested that Spanish soldiers in the eighteenth century could have been among the earliest non-Indian visitors. According to an account cited in Father Pedro Munoz's diary of Lt. Gabriel Moraga's 1806 exploratory expedition along the western slope of the Sierra Nevada foothills of California, the leader Sujoycomu, at the Yokuts village of Pitcachi, knew of a previous visit of Spanish soldiers: "From this chief the following information was obtained, the testimony being from eyewitnesses. Other soldiers from the other side of the mountains—who we presume were from New Mexico—appeared about twenty years ago, according to the communication of the Indian. The heathen Indians having acted in a hostile manner, the soldiers began to fight and killed many of the Indians" (Cook 1960: 251). The "other side of the mountains" would have been Owens Valley. Thus it is possible that Spanish soldiers passed through Owens Valley in the late eighteenth century. Perhaps further archaeological work, along with study of archives in Madrid and Mexico City, will eventually shed light on this possibility (Michael Morratto, personal communication 1980:1).

4. For more on Walker, see Gilbert 1983.

5. Apparently, Walker kept no diaries (Lawton et al. 1976:21), and sources for these subsequent trips are limited. Kern (1976) describes the 1845 trip but says little about Owens Valley.

6. Davidson reports finding no horses (Wilke and Lawton 1976), although a newspaper account of Davidson's trip reports that "very few horses" were seen and that those on the upper Owens River had been obtained from "Walker River Indians" (Wilke and Lawton 1976: 34; Chalfant 1922:78). Davidson's report is clear that the party found no horses, and thus the source for the newspaper account is unknown.

7. Davidson's guide judged them "much more numerous" (Wilke and Lawton 1976:29), as did mountaineer David McKenzie, who gave a figure of two thousand for the Paiute population of Owens Valley during his visit there a year earlier (Walker and Lawton 1976:46).

8. Chalfant (1922:90–112) gives a detailed description of these events.

9. Whitney (1865:460), for example, mentions that the California State Geological Survey was unable to complete its work in Owens Valley because of this fighting.

10. It is interesting that there was no proposal to establish a reservation in the Owens Valley area. In 1859 Special Agent J. Ross Browne had suggested to the commissioner of Indian Affairs that Indian people on the Kings River, west of the Sierra crest, be moved to Owens Valley and a reservation be established there (Browne 1859, in Heizer 1974:153). This idea was never acted on.

11. Other portions of Cashbaugh's account are reproduced in Ewan 2000:105–107.

12. In autumn Paiute labor for the harvest became scarce as the Indians left the farms for their annual piñon harvest in the mountains. At these times the Paiutes who remained in the valley to work raised their wage requirements (Michael 1993:133).

13. Although no Owens Valley Paiutes were moved to the Tule River Reservation, in 1875 Stephan Powers listed "Manaches (Monáchees) as one-time residents at the Tule River Reservation." Powers defines "the Piutes [sic] of Inyo County" as "locally called Monos, (or by the California Indians Monáchees)" (quoted in Heizer 1975:30, 29). It may be that he was referring to the earlier residence of Owens Valley Paiute people on the Tule River Farm in 1864. The listing of this group as one of three tribes who lived or had lived on the reservation suggests that some Owens Valley Paiutes resided on the reservation after 1864. Alternately, it may be that these "Monáchees" were Western Mono people from farther north in the western Sierra Nevada foothills.

14. For a photograph of the Big Pine School, see Bosak 1975:51.

15. President Theodore Roosevelt, who favored massive public works and the urbanization of California as a means of promoting his progressive agenda, supported a bill introduced in 1906 by California senator Frank Flint that gave Los Angeles title to public lands for the aqueduct right-of-way (Walton 1992:151). A year later, when the original Owens Valley Agricultural Irrigation Project was officially annulled, Roosevelt failed to return thousands of acres of the watershed to the public domain for homesteading (Reisner 1987:86). In that

same year Gifford Pinchot, chief of the U.S. Forest Service, proposed placing 275,000 acres of treeless valley land in a newly established reserve, the Inyo National Forest, in order to prevent settlement on land that Los Angeles needed to complete the aqueduct's right-of-way (Kahrl 1976:98). Despite objections by Owens Valley civic leaders and Congressman Sylvester Smith, the reserve was extended. Pinchot's action ran counter to the provisions of the Organic Act that created the Forest Service, which expressly prohibited including lands in the reserve that were more valuable for agricultural use than for forest purposes (Reisner 1987:86).

16. Research has yielded no evidence of direct Paiute participation in these episodes.

17. Because the area was less densely settled and developed than in Owens Valley itself, there were fewer citizens to object. In addition, people in the Mono Basin had already become accustomed to Los Angeles as a presence on the eastern side of the Sierras. Moreover, Mono Basin was not as heavily used for agriculture as Owens Valley so there was not as great a demand for water. Finally, in the 1930s the unique geological features of the Mono Basin were beginning to be recognized as potential sites for attracting tourism, recreation, and related revenues to the area.

18. In spite of continued resistance, an additional 50 percent allowance of water from the Owens Valley was granted to Los Angeles as late as 1970 (Busby et al. 1979:96). This supplementary water came from increased underground pumping and both old and new wells and prompted a series of lawsuits between the residents of eastern California and the LADWP. In 1972 Inyo County sued to halt the extended groundwater pumping of the underground basin on the grounds that such pumping dried up local springs, presented irreparable ecological damage or extinction of local plants and wildlife, and increased the frequency and severity of dust storms around the dry Owens Lake bed. Los Angeles countered Inyo County's claims, but subsequent legal rulings mostly favored the county. A 1983 state law required Los Angeles to "take reasonable measures" to control the "clay particles, salts, arsenic, and other substances deposited over geologic time" that blew off the lake bed, polluted the air, and threatened the well-being of area residents (Purdum 1998:A1, A14). Implementing a practical solution to the problem remained difficult, however, because of high costs.

In June 1997 the LADWP and the Inyo County Water Department (ICWD) finalized a long-term agreement for joint management of the Owens Valley water supply that called for monitoring of vegetation, water quality and flows in the Owens River channel, and groundwater and soil water in the valley (ICWD 1997). Based on the outcome of these measurements, maximum limits for groundwater pumping were set annually. In addition, the Great Basin Unified Air Pollution Control District (APCD) ordered the LADWP to control dust on Owens Lake by dampening the lake bed (ICWD 1998: 1–2). The order did not specify the source of the water to be used for dust abatement on the lake bed surface,

however, so the LADWP proposed using groundwater from under Owens Lake.

A 1998 state-approved plan called for the rewatering process to be accomplished by pumping groundwater and/or by using water from the Los Angeles Aqueduct (Gansberg et al. 1998; Lukins 1998a:A1; ICWD 1998: 1–2). This remedy was scheduled to begin by 2001. If it was not implemented as agreed, the federal Environmental Protection Agency threatened to impose its own plan for curbing pollution (Purdum 1998:A14). The urgency to locate water for dust control increased in October 1998, when the Inyo County Board of Supervisors (ICBS) passed an ordinance prohibiting the transfer of any water within Inyo County without the county's approval (Lukins 1998b). This law was intended to prevent increased water pumping or diversion that might cause desiccation elsewhere.

As of 2004, twenty square miles of Owens Lake are under various methods of dust control. There are four and a half square miles of managed vegetation (primarily salt grass) and one square mile of pond area; the rest of the lake is under shallow flood irrigation. All the water for this project is coming from the Los Angeles Aqueduct; there is no groundwater pumping. The yearly amount of water is forty thousand acre-feet, enough for forty thousand families. The cost to date for this project (design and construction) is over $400 million, and additional improvements are being implemented. The rewatering project has aided the local economy through jobs and has resulted in improved air quality and the return of some waterfowl species to the lake area (Chris J. Plakos, LADWP, personal communication 2003).

19. The 1930 LADWP survey of Paiute and Shoshone living conditions in Owens Valley classified the Indians, according to their living conditions, as independents, state wards, or government wards. These designations were used in reallocating land to the Indians through the Land Exchange Act of 1937, which moved Indians onto home sites that were designated either reservations or rancherias. A reservation was defined as land owned by the federal government whereas a rancheria allowed Indians to own land and maintain water rights. See *Land Exchange Act of 1937,* 75th Cong., 1st sess. (April 20, 1937).

20. Under previous federal land grants the water rights on the original land parcels belonged to the U.S. Indian Service but could be transferred to an Indian allottee when a permanent home was established on the tract (Ford et al. 1932:16). The only tracts where such transfers actually occurred were at the Fort Independence home site. Since the Paiutes at Camp Independence in effect owned their land, they were unwilling to relinquish it.

21. An example of this problem was provided by Vernon Miller (personal communication 1998), two-time chairman of the Independence Band of Owens Valley Paiutes. Miller recounted how the electricity for the tribal office was turned off because of lack of payment, due to the failure of Paiute council members to decide who should be responsible for writing the check.

22. *Tule* refers to the leaves and stalks of the bulrush plant, used for building shelters, making duck decoys, and weaving one type of basket. When referring to a design material for basket weaving, *tule* means the root of the plant and is called *bulrush*.

3. Weaving the Willow

1. Similarly, prestige was gauged among the nearby Yosemite Miwoks by the number of large feasting baskets displayed at ceremonies, the ownership of baskets made by neighboring tribes, and the burning or burying of baskets at funerals and mourning ceremonies (Bates and Lee 1990:39).

2. There are a few documented instances of men weaving baskets (see, for example, Joe Eugley's biography later in this chapter). Even though in other tribal groups men made fish traps, the Owens Valley Paiutes used old baskets, dragging open-twined baskets through the water or catching fish coming over dams with conical carrying baskets (Steward 1933:251, 272, 274).

3. Irwin (1980:70) mentions Panamint Shoshones burning the willow.

4. Paiute terms for baskets in the following section are drawn from Hudson n.d., 1904a; Merriam n.d.a, n.d.b; and Steward 1933.

5. Although Hudson (1904a) recorded the word *turup* and noted that the Spanish name for this root is *cañota*, he provided no further explanation. Merriam (1979:65) recorded *turup* as the Paiute word for ephedra, which definition we have used here.

6. Numic refers to an extensive language family that is a branch of the Uto-Aztecan stock. The family of Numic speakers extends over most of the Great Basin culture area but also includes the Western Monos from the western slope of the Sierras.

7. In the use of coiled caps the Panamint Shoshones were much like the Kawaiisus, whose women's caps were very similar (Fowler and Dawson 1986:723–724; Zigmond 1978).

8. Similar twined woman's caps were also made by the Northern Paiutes and Chemehuevis (Fowler and Dawson 1986:707, 710, 725).

9. One such eating bowl, collected from the Northern Paiutes at Stillwater, Nevada, has the design band enclosed. See C. Fowler 1992:Figure 92 for an illustration of this basket, cat. no. 13/4177, National Museum of the American Indian, Smithsonian Institution.

10. Although caps were reportedly scarce in the early twentieth century, some Paiute women still had them and wore them on special occasions, especially when demonstrating Paiute culture to non-Indians, into the 1930s and later; see, for example, Harrington 1932.

11. Lee donated the twined cap shown in Plate 3 to the Phoebe Apperson Hearst Museum of Anthropology, University of California, Berkeley. It was later featured as Plate 10h in Steward's *Ethnography of the Owens Valley Paiute* (1933).

12. Closely twined burden baskets from the Panamint Shoshones are so similar to those of the Owens Valley Paiutes that it seems as though the Owens Valley Paiutes could have made them. This possibility is further suggested by the fact that the rim bundle on the Panamint Shoshone–collected burden baskets always coils to the left, just as such baskets coil to the left among the Paiutes. The Panamint Shoshones' baskets coil to the right, and on one openwork burden basket made by a Panamint Shoshone weaver in the Anna Kelley collection, the rim bundle and rim stick both coil to the right. It seems quite likely that those burden baskets with a rim bundle that coils leftward were indeed made by Owens Valley Paiutes.

13. Steward (1941:340) noted this form among the Owens Valley Paiutes. The same shape was also produced by their northern neighbors, the Mono Lake Paiutes (Bates and Lee 1990:66).

14. For an excellent demonstration of the technique of pitch coating such a basket among the Northern Paiutes, see Wheat 1976.

15. Although a seed beater is mentioned in ethnographic accounts, it would seem that seed beaters were too small to serve this purpose. More likely a winnower or sifting tray was used.

16. This type of cradle was occasionally used without a sunshade. For a 1959 photograph of Elsie Kinney, at the Paiute Reservation near Bishop, holding such a cradle back with a child bound onto it, see Pietroforte 1965:31.

17. The only cradle basket we located that was made with dyed sinew is Yosemite Museum cat. no. YM 29014. Every other example we examined was bound with non-native, postcontact materials such as yarn, string, or strips of cloth.

18. See Wheat 1967:100–101 for the production of a Northern Paiute example identical to those once made in Owens Valley.

19. For a basket of this type hanging on a tree near the home of a Mono Lake Paiute woman in Yosemite Valley, see Bates and Lee 1990:Figure 14.

20. Hudson (1904a:35) relates, "Basket pots are obsolete—they were usually of coil weave, tho I saw fragments of a *chusĕt* of *Ni'ūm* type." Hudson's *chusĕt* refers to diagonal twining, *Ni'ūm* to the Western Monos.

21. See, for example, the Field Museum cat. no. 59000, collected near Big Pine.

22. See Steward 1933:245–246 for discussion of how sugar was made.

23. The small spots on the tules in the basket in Figure 3.27 look like those that appear on dead tule stalks gathered during the winter months.

24. The ending of the warps on the tule basket in Figure 3.27 is nearly identical to a technique used by the Klamath and Modoc peoples as a warp ending on one style of tule basket. An example of this basket is in the Phoebe Apperson Hearst Museum of Anthropology, University of California, Berkeley, cat. no. 1–14125. An illustration of this basket can be found in Barrett 1910: Plate 13, Figure 5.

25. See Wheat 1967:84–86 for the construction of another type of tule basket among the Northern Paiutes.

26. This species of devil's claw is apparently *Proboscidea parviflora* var. *hohokamiana,* the white-seeded variety, although one of the black-seeded varieties, probably *Proboscidea parviflora* subsp. *parviflora,* may also have been used (Armstrong 1992:23).

27. For an example of a lost shipment of basket materials in the U.S. mail, see Telles 1919.

28. Weavers who eventually lived temporarily or permanently in Owens Valley include Nellie and Tina Charlie, Lucy Telles, and Louisa Tom (see Bates and Lee 1990).

29. Hudson (1904a:36) gives *säkŭ.*

30. Examples include two collected by John Hudson (the Field Museum cat. nos. 59003 and 58989) and another collected by Charles P. Wilcomb (State of California Department of Parks and Recreation, Museum Resource Center, cat. no. 3653W).

31. These baskets are cat. nos. 487, 497, 498, 499, 500, 504, C. Hart Merriam Basket Collection, Department of Anthropology Museum, University of California, Davis; 16–683, Oakland Museum; and 58984, 58983, the Field Museum.

32. For Owens Valley examples, see cat. nos. 501 and 509, C. Hart Merriam Basket Collection, Department of Anthropology Museum, University of California, Davis.

33. Cat. nos. 636, 637, 693, 640, C. Hart Merriam Basket Collection, Department of Anthropology Museum, University of California, Davis.

34. Two such baskets by Sally Jackson are cat. nos. 1–26875 and 1–26884, Phoebe Apperson Hearst Museum of Anthropology, University of California, Berkeley.

35. The information about Owens Valley weavers copying materials they saw in print is from Jim Kelley, son of the collector Anna Kelley (personal communication 1998).

36. Indian people living on the Columbia River Plateau probably taught the craft to Northern Paiute people, who subsequently introduced it to the Mono Lake Paiutes.

37. Other Mono Lake Paiute weavers who participated in the Yosemite Indian Field Days and who later lived in Owens Valley include the sisters Nellie and Tina Charlie. Nellie spent the last quarter of her life with her daughter, Daisy Mallory, and her granddaughter, Jessie Durant, in Bishop. Tina joined them in the early 1950s.

38. Some baskets identified as the work of Hattie Jones are a part of the MacQueen collection, Los Angeles County Museum of Natural History.

39. This image by Andrew Forbes of the Bishop Harvest Days was previously published in Bates and Lee 1990:88 and Bosak 1975:57. Another previously published image purportedly of the Bishop Harvest Days (Fowler and Dawson 1986:733) was actually taken at the June Lake Indian Field Days ca. 1929.

40. Fannie Stewart, Emma's mother, was born in Big Pine. Doctor Jim, her father, was born in Fish Springs. Her sister was Minnie Sport.

41. Much of the information in this biography is from Mamie Button's daughter, Dorothy Button (personal communication 2001). Our use of the spelling *Joaquin* is based on several sources: in the records of the Indian Arts and Crafts Board she is listed as Mamie Joaquin, and her husband's enrollment record is Tom Joaquin (application no. 10720, Application for Enrollment with the Indians of the State of California under the Act of May 15, 1928, U.S. Department of the Interior, Office of Indian Affairs, on file, National Archives, Washington, D.C.). Collector Aurelia McLean referred to Mamie as Maggie Juaquin, a spelling and first name selection followed by Slater (2000:51–52). Dorothy Button asserted that her mother was known only as Mamie. Thus we use *Mamie,* not *Maggie,* and *Joaquin,* not *Juaquin.* It may be that McLean was unfamiliar with Spanish and misspelled the last name and confused the first. Other data for this biography are drawn from Davenport 1999; Blair Davenport, personal communication 2001; A. Kelley n.d.; Beth Sennett Porter, personal communication 2001; Sennett-Graham 1989; Slater 1985a:62–63, 1985b: 20, 1986:19, 2000:58; and Smith and Simpson n.d.:35, 45–46.

42. Tom Joaquin was also married to the well-known Panamint Shoshone weaver Mary Wrinkle, by whom he had one daughter, Annie Brown. See application no. 5476, Annie Brown, Application for Enrollment with the Indians of the State of California under the Act of May 15, 1928, U.S. Department of the Interior, Office of Indian Affairs, on file, National Archives, Washington, D.C.

43. Bill Button had been previously married to Sarah Holmes. See applications no. 8876, Sarah Button, and no. 8877, Bill Button, Application for Enrollment with the Indians of the State of California under the Act of May 15, 1928, U.S. Department of the Interior, Office of Indian Affairs, on file, National Archives, Washington, D.C.

44. For an example of the frontal-view sheep as produced by Button, see Slater 2000:51, where the weaver is identified as Maggie Juaquin (see note 41).

45. The appendix to the pictorial record of the Golden Gate Exhibition (Indian Arts and Crafts Board 1939) also listed as "Indian participants and demonstrators of tribal arts and crafts" Paiute and Shoshone weavers Carrie Bethel, Mary Lowe, Lena Phoenix, Lucy Telles, and Mary Wrinkle.

46. Unless otherwise noted, information for Charlie's biography was drawn from Irene Button (personal communication 2001) and applications nos. 5494, Mary Button Charlie; 8900, Margaret Boland Patterson; 8896, Johnnie Boland; 8898, Sally Boland; 8897, Nellie Kennedy Boland; 5348, Emma Wright; and 8877, Bill Button, Applications for Enrollment with the Indians of the State of California under the Act of May 15, 1928, U.S. Department of the Interior, Office of Indian Affairs, on file, National Archives, Washington, D.C.

47. Patterson's mother was Minnie, born in Pilgrim Springs, Nevada. Hank never knew his father. Bill "Grapevine" Doc (b. 1862, from Grapevine Canyon), son of Old Man Doc, raised Hank. Doc was later the second husband of Paiwunga, Dina, or Tina, the weaver affectionately known in her later years as Grandma Doc.

Bill, the son of Tina and Old Man Doc, was interviewed by Julian Steward and is identified as informant "BD" in Steward's works. Doc's daughter, Dolly (1902–1987), married Johnnie Boland and was a well-known weaver of Panamint Shoshone baskets. Johnnie Boland was the brother of Hank Patterson's wife, Margaret, and Dolly was the daughter of Hank Patterson's stepfather and his second wife. A story of the role of Bill "Grapevine" Doc and Tina Doc in the rescue of a miner in the desert can be found in Wortley 1959.

48. Scotty's Castle (officially called Death Valley Ranch) was a Mediterranean-style mansion built for Chicago financier Albert M. Johnson.

49. Patterson's cousin, Wilbur Patterson, was born in 1900 in Saline Valley, California. Along with his uncle, Johnny Hunter, Wilbur made specimens of traditional games for Julian Steward, who collected them for the Peabody Museum, including a toy bullroarer and gambling bone cylinders. Wilbur was the second husband of weaver Sally Boland.

50. Laura married Sullivan Shaw, who worked at Scotty's Castle from 1926 through 1931. They had five children: Raymond, Esther, Dave, Catherine, and Florence. Anthropologist Julian Steward's field notes include information on several of Laura's baskets, and he purchased one, for four dollars, for the Peabody Museum (cat. no. 35–78–1–/5003). In 1948 Anna Kelley purchased a basket made by Laura Shaw; it is a coiled basket in bottleneck form, with a short neck and a typical Panamint Shoshone stepped zigzag pattern worked in juncus, outlined in dyed bulrush root. Further information on Laura Shaw can be found in Slater 2000:62–66.

51. Minnie Patterson later married Robert Thompson (b. 1881), whose parents were Panamint Tom and Maggie Tom. Robert's siblings were Sarah (Hunter), Mamie (Joaquin Button), Sue (wife of Long Hair Johnny), and Harry (Rollin) Panamint. Minnie made baskets, including a lidded one purchased by Albert Johnson, likely in 1929, while Thompson was working at Scotty's Castle. Margaret (Boland) Patterson, Hank's second wife, may have given some of her mother-in-law Minnie's baskets to Wilma Ely, who served as postmaster of Dyer, Nevada, a small town in the Fish Lake Valley. Ely collected about twenty-four baskets between 1925 and 1942.

52. Relationships among other Western Shoshone groups sometimes included polyandry, the practice of one woman having two husbands (Steward 1936b). Although this custom was documented for other Western Shoshones, no obvious evidence of it was found in research either on the weavers described in this book or by Steward in his work in southern Nevada (1936b: 563).

53. Mary Charlie's brother, Bill Button, married Mamie Joaquin, an extremely talented weaver. Mamie was the sister of Robert Thompson, the second husband of Minnie Patterson, who was the mother of Mary's first husband, Hank Patterson. Bill Button and Mamie Joaquin did not marry until after 1939, and it may be that Mary was not very familiar with Mamie's basketry until after that time.

54. Unless otherwise noted, the information in Nellie Charlie's biography is drawn from Bates and Lee 1990: 87, 98–99, 146–151; Elma Blaver, personal communication 1978, 2001; Richard Blaver, personal communication 2000–2001; Jessie Durant, personal communication 1996, 1998; Mary Josephine Einerson, personal communication 2001; Patsy Hall, personal communication 2001; Merriam n.d.a:608, 621, 636, 638, 653, 670, 1955:108–109; and Application for Enrollment with the Indians of the State of California under the Act of May 15, 1928, application nos. 4973, 4975, 4976, 4977, 4984, U.S. Department of the Interior, Office of Indian Affairs, on file, National Archives, Washington, D.C.

55. Patsy Jim was the daughter of We-do-si and his wife, To-ne-va, according to Application for Enrollment with the Indians of the State of California under the Act of May 15, 1928, application no. 5146, of Daisy Mallory, Nellie Charlie's daughter, U.S. Department of the Interior, Office of Indian Affairs, on file, National Archives, Washington, D.C.

56. Although Young Charlie's contemporary descendants and other Indian people in the Yosemite–Mono Lake region refer to Charlie as a Miwok, Charlie, his two wives, and his children identified him as a full-blood Paiute from Mono County in the applications listed in note 54.

57. *Berdachism* is a term anthropologists use to denote a recognized "third gender" alternative to "male" and "female" social status. It is interpreted as representing either a distinct gender (Jacobs 1983; Williams 1986) or an intermediate, mixed-gender status (Callender and Kochems 1983; Whitehead 1981). Male berdaches have been documented in more than 155 North American Indian tribal groups and are present cross-culturally in almost all societies (Roscoe 1998:7). Female berdaches are sometimes covered by this third-gender term, but other times they constitute a "fourth gender" called a variety of names, including "cross-gender female" (Blackwood 1984) and "amazon" (Williams 1986:234).

58. As for the origin of *Mahala,* see Foster n.d.:270n: "The common name for Indian woman in California among such as know Indians. I believe the credit identifying its etymology—inevitable when once thought of (a corruption of the Spanish mujer)—belongs to Eve Lummis."

59. Austin's story was that when Joe was but a few days old, his Paiute mother agreed to be a wet nurse for a white baby, Walter Baker, whose own mother had died during childbirth. Walter and Joe grew up together, splitting their early childhood years between the Paiute camp and the cabin where Joe's father lived. The two boys were inseparable and swore allegiance to each other as "brothers." They agreed never to take up arms against each other, even if the growing conflict between Indians and whites escalated. According to legend, when fighting eventually broke out between the Paiutes and whites in Owens Valley, Walter was sent away permanently by his father, unbeknown to Joe. Not realizing that Walter was gone, Joe upheld his oath and refused to fight. For this refusal, the Paiute community allegedly

sentenced Joe to take on the role of a woman for the rest of his life (Austin 1999:93–113).

60. These are cat. nos. B-71 and B-226 in the Eastern California Museum. Another basket in the museum, B-163, although identified as Eugley's work, is likely not. It is made in a rightward coil direction and is identical to Panamint Shoshone baskets in every way.

61. A basket in this style by Gorman is cat. no. B-206 in the Eastern California Museum; see Fowler and Dawson 1986:733 for an illustration. Examination of this basket, along with other baskets in the Eastern California Museum identified as the work of Joe Eugley (B-71) and Anna Best (B-69), leads one to ponder if all three baskets were by the same hand. With such a small sample of documented baskets, it is unclear if these three weavers all wove in near-identical style or if all the baskets were woven by one weaver and were somehow misattributed.

62. Much of this biographical information is from Mamie Gregory's death certificate, County of Inyo, no. 1450–52; Davenport 1999; Mecham 1979:1; Vernon Miller, personal communication 1998; and application nos. 5467 and 5468 of George and Mamie Gregory, Application for Enrollment with the Indians of the State of California under the Act of May 15, 1928, U.S. Department of the Interior, Office of Indian Affairs, on file, National Archives, Washington, D.C. There are some discrepancies in these documents; for example, her birth date is shown as 1867 on her death certificate but as 1870 on her enrollment record.

63. George and Mamie Gregory's daughter, Annie, married Mike Hanson, the brother of well-known weaver Isabel Hanson. See application nos. 5470 and 5469 of Annie and Mike Hanson, Application for Enrollment with the Indians of the State of California under the Act of May 15, 1928, U.S. Department of the Interior, Office of Indian Affairs, on file, National Archives, Washington, D.C.

64. See Bernstein 1979b:68 (Figures 1, 3) and 70 (Figure 4) for photographs of three Panamint Shoshone baskets that use this pattern.

65. For example, compare with the basket held by Gregory in Slater 2000:38 and with other baskets in Bernstein 1979b.

66. One such basket is Eastern California Museum cat. no. 70.250.10.

67. A small basket with a band of flicker quill diamonds and with black (devil's claw) and yellow (Juncus sp.) ornamentation is in the Eastern California Museum, cat. no. 70.2540.11.

68. Much of the following is based on Mecham 1978:4; application no. 5472 of George Hanson, Application for Enrollment with the Indians of the State of California under the Act of May 15, 1928, U.S. Department of the Interior, Office of Indian Affairs, on file, National Archives, Washington, D.C.; and Potashin 1997. Indian Ranch is in what is known today as Panamint Valley. It was a rancheria (originally an Indian homestead granted to Hanson) until the 1950s. Hanson's death certificate (County of Inyo, no. 1400–75–64) lists her birthplace as California.

69. Although Slater (1985a:62) states that Hanson's weaving was influenced by Kawaiisu and Tubatulabal weaving traditions, Hanson's baskets actually are traditional Panamint Shoshone baskets in style and pattern (as defined in Bernstein 1979b).

70. See especially the death certificate for Isabel Hanson, County of Inyo, no. 1400–75–64, and the application for Molly Hanson, no. 5473, Application for Enrollment with the Indians of the State of California under the Act of May 15, 1928, U.S. Department of the Interior, Office of Indian Affairs, on file, National Archives, Washington, D.C.

71. This biographical information is drawn from Steward 1938a:314–15; Mary Harry's enrollment application, no. 5362, Application for Enrollment with the Indians of the State of California under the Act of May 15, 1928, U.S. Department of the Interior, Office of Indian Affairs, on file, National Archives, Washington, D.C.; and her death certificate, County of Inyo, no. 1450–27.

72. Information here is largely drawn from Sarah Hunter's death certificate, County of Inyo, no. 1400–37–67; Esteves 1983; A. Kelley n.d.; Moyer 1996; Slater 2000; Smith and Simpson n.d.:33, 35, 45–46; and group application no. 10,720 and application nos. 491–493, Applications for Enrollment with the Indians of the State of California under the Act of May 15, 1928, U.S. Department of the Interior, Office of Indian Affairs, on file, National Archives, Washington, D.C. Additional information was provided by Hunter's niece, Dorothy Button (personal communication 2001), and by Dale Inkley, who visited with the Hunters in 1943 (Inkley 1991; personal communication 2001).

73. John Hunter is Steward's informant "JH" (Steward 1941:213). William Lyle Hunter employed a large group of Indian people at the Hunter Mountain Ranch in the Panamint Range (Burton and Wehrey 1996:132).

74. Phillip Hunter, born September 18, 1936, the son of John Kennedy, died at the Kern General Hospital in Bakersfield, California, on August 13, 1966 (State of California Certificate of Death, Kern County, no. 1585). Phillip Kennedy's mother, Annie Shoshone (1913–?), and his father, John Kennedy, were distant relatives of Bill Button, the husband of Sarah Hunter's sister, Mamie Joaquin Button. See Sennett-Graham 1989:177,178; also application no. 8868 of Joe, Herbert, Johnny, Alice, and Harry Kennedy, Application for Enrollment with the Indians of the State of California under the Act of May 15, 1928, U.S. Department of the Interior, Office of Indian Affairs, on file, National Archives, Washington, D.C.

75. Steward's consultant "JH" is identified as Johnny Hunter in accession file 35–78, Peabody Museum Collections Department, Harvard University. Both he and Wilbur Patterson are mentioned by name as making specimens on page 2 of a list of specimens collected by Julian H. Steward.

76. A fine example of one of Hunter's baskets in this style is in the Eastern California Museum, cat. no. A357, collected in 1939 (see Slater 2000:61). Another, larger basket, 23 inches in diameter, is in the Philbrook Mu-

seum of Art, Tulsa, Oklahoma (cat. no. 1949.4.5); see Tisdale 2001:89, Plate 38; Wyckoff 2001:208.

77. Unless otherwise noted, this discussion of Susie and Sally Jackson is drawn from their Applications for Enrollment with the Indians of the State of California under the Act of May 15, 1928, U.S. Department of the Interior, Office of Indian Affairs, nos. 5172 (Sally Jackson) and 5175 (Susie Jackson), on file, National Archives, Washington, D.C.; County of Inyo Certificate of Death for Sally Jackson, no. 10272; discussions with Susie's granddaughter, Eleanor Bethel, in 2001; data in accession file 3879 of the Yosemite Museum; and Ford 1930.

78. The years 1865–77 have been characterized as "the quiet period" in Mono County, when most mining operations shut down (Fletcher 1987:37–42).

79. For an example of multiple wives of Paiute men (the marriage of Bridgeport Tom to sisters Louisa and Leanna Tom), see Bates and Lee 1990:178–183.

80. On beaded basket techniques, see Bates 1979; Bates and Lee 1990:80–83, 1993.

81. The beaded baskets referred to here, which were collected by Frankie Beatty, who lived in Bishop during 1920–40, were part of the Burgner collection from Bishop, formerly on loan to the Yosemite Museum, accession 3879. The collection was returned to the owner in the 1980s, and as of 2001, the location of these baskets is unknown.

82. Accession 625.

83. Unless otherwise noted, this discussion of Daisy Mallory is drawn from conversations with her daughter, Jessie Durant, in 1999 and 2001, and conversations in 2001 with three of her nieces: Elma Blaver, Mary Josephine Einerson, and Patsy Hall. Additional sources include a study of baskets by Mallory in the Ella Cain collection and application nos. 5146 and 5147 (Daisy and Jack Mallory), Application for Enrollment with the Indians of the State of California under the Act of May 18, 1928, U.S. Department of the Interior, Office of Indian Affairs, on file, National Archives, Washington, D.C.

84. There is some confusion as to when Ed Cluette died; Daisy Mallory's Application for Enrollment (cited in note 83) states that he died in 1917; their daughter, Jessie Durant (b. 1913), says that he died when she was a baby and that she never knew him.

85. Doyle's autobiography (Doyle 1934, republished as Doyle 1983) tells of the challenges she faced during medical training. It briefly discusses some of her contact with Indian people but does not mention Daisy Mallory by name.

86. Art Hess came to Owens Valley in 1907 (Ewan 2000:205). He is not to be confused with the Hess brothers, August (Gus) and William Hess, who came from Switzerland and settled in Mono County. The Hess brothers married Daisy Mallory's two sisters, Lula and Mildred, respectively.

87. For example, a collection of baskets deposited in 1951 at the Phoebe Apperson Hearst Museum of Anthropology, University of California, Berkeley, by Hamilton Hess included one basket identified as by "Daisy Young Charlie" (cat. no. 1–70563). Daisy was some-

times identified with her father's full name as her surname. Hamilton Hess may be a descendant of the Art Hess family, for whom Daisy worked.

88. This date is according to notes affixed to the baskets themselves by collector Ella Cain. As of 2001, the baskets are still in the possession of Cain's heirs.

89. Unless otherwise noted, this discussion of Annie Poole McBride is drawn from her death certificate, County of Inyo, no. 1450–140, and her Application for Enrollment with the Indians of the State of California under the Act of May 18, 1928, U.S. Department of the Interior, Office of Indian Affairs, on file, National Archives, Washington, D.C. (application no. 5042), which also lists her son, Jim.

90. This Jim McBride should not be confused with Jim McBride who was the father of Joe McBride, who was, in turn, the father of the Joe McBride born in 1886. Information on these McBrides can be found in application nos. 5026 and 5027, Application for Enrollment with the Indians of the State of California under the Act of May 18, 1928, U.S. Department of the Interior, Office of Indian Affairs, on file, National Archives, Washington, D.C. The various Paiute men with the last name McBride may have taken the name from the non-Indian family of that name which settled in Benton, Mono County (Jenner 1994).

91. Curiously, this colorful rim embellishment was not popular with other Paiute weavers; only Mono Lake Paiute weaver Nellie Charlie is known to have used it on baskets produced later in her life. For an illustration of one basket by Charlie using this rim finish, see Bates and Lee 1990:Figure 278.

92. A basket in this style, attributed to McBride, can be seen in Mercer 1997:54.

93. See Fowler and Dawson 1986:Figure 6-b for an example of this style of twined basket.

94. Nicholson acquired at least three baskets made by Annie Poole McBride (Nicholson n.d.b:161, nos. 4305, 5406, and 2522). Their current location is unknown.

95. At least two baskets made by Mary Pool(e), identified as living at "Hot Creek" or "Hot Springs," were acquired by collector-dealer Grace Nicholson (Nicholson n.d.b:160, nos. 205, 206). Unfortunately, their current location is unknown. No further information has been located regarding Mary Pool.

96. Information on Symmes is drawn from application no. 5429, Application for Enrollment with the Indians of the State of California under the Act of May 18, 1928, U.S. Department of the Interior, Office of Indian Affairs, on file, National Archives, Washington, D.C.

97. Symmes likely acquired his surname from Manzanar rancher and Inyo County supervisor John W. Symmes. This connection is suggested in an account in which John Symmes, Emma's son, received the name from the Manzanar rancher (Bernasconi 1988:102). However, that is likely not the case since John's father, George, also used the surname Symmes.

98. This biographical information is based on information supplied by Williams's daughter, Eleanor Bethel (personal communication 2001) and application no.

5174, Application for Enrollment with the Indians of the State of California under the Act of May 18, 1928, U.S. Department of the Interior, Office of Indian Affairs, on file, National Archives, Washington, D.C.

99. In the Eastern California Museum the cap by Yandell, B-278, appears to have been made by the same woman who made caps B-288, B-243, and B-214.

100. Cat. nos. B-185 and B-6, respectively, in the collection of the Eastern California Museum.

101. The basket not pictured here is Eastern California Museum cat. no. B-156.

4. Treasuring the Willow

1. Charles Augustus Keeler (1871–1937), poet, scientist, architect, and religious innovator, was apparently in no way connected with the town of Keeler on Owens Lake. The town was named in 1882 after J. M. Keeler, manager of the Inyo County Marble Quarry (Gudde 1998:191). The authors were unable to ascertain if J. M. was in some way related to Charles Augustus. "To an Indian Basket" appeared in 1894 in *Overland Monthly* 24(143):528.

2. Beginning in the mid-nineteenth century and continuing into the twentieth, the United States and principal European countries periodically held world fairs, "large-scale happenings that combined features of trade and industrial fairs, carnivals, music festivals, political manifestations, museums, and art galleries" (Corbey 1993: 339). They showcased the latest industrial and technological advancements of the Western world and displayed, as living exhibits, members of non-Western societies and their cultural traditions and materials. Thus these fairs helped bring public attention to the discipline of anthropology.

3. Although not directly relevant to geographically isolated Owens Valley, the railroad was largely responsible for bringing tourism to the Southwest and western California. Only the short-lived narrow-gauge railroad serviced the Owens Valley region.

4. The Fred Harvey Company provided tourists with food and accommodations and offered a variety of Indian pottery, textiles, and baskets at its stores in Arizona and New Mexico along the route of the Santa Fe Railroad.

5. Examples of these collections include those of Pittsburgh collectors G. A. Steiner and Robert Hall, described in Bernstein 1979a, Frye 1979, and Zigmond 1979.

6. On James, see Maurer 1986 and Arreola 1986.

7. On Cohn's role in the history of Washoe basketry, see Cohodas 1979.

8. In his 1877 book *Ancient Society*, Lewis Henry Morgan, for example, posited three stages of human development: savagery, barbarism, and civilization.

9. A concept developed by Bronislaw Malinowski (1961:4–24), referring to the act of participating in the everyday life of a society while making systematic observations of it. The object of this approach was to see cultures from the inside: to understand people's own interpretations of how and why they acted in particular ways.

10. The first academic anthropology department was started at Columbia University in 1900 by Franz Boas, whose first Ph.D. student was Alfred Kroeber. Kroeber organized numerous research projects in California, including Julian Steward's research in Owens Valley (1927–43).

11. Discussion of Steward is drawn from D. Fowler 1986:25–26; Manners 1996; and Steward n.d., 1941: 209–214.

12. Mabel was therefore cousin of the Panamint Shoshone weaver Isabel Hanson.

13. Although the Owens Valley Paiutes and Panamint Shoshones were culturally distinct, they were both associated with Owens Valley because their territorial boundaries were ill defined (Grosscup 1977:113) and because the Panamint Shoshones migrated seasonally through the valley. This geographic overlap of the two groups meant that baskets were available from both.

14. The term refers to a person living abroad on funds sent from home.

15. Evidence for these associations comes from catalog cards at the Phoebe Apperson Hearst Museum; University of California, Davis; and journal entries and personal correspondence.

16. Merriam often found himself at odds with Alfred Kroeber and other members of the Department of Anthropology at the University of California at Berkeley. In the early 1900s many "professionals" weren't interested in the work of "avocationals" (such as Merriam), whose work, they felt, didn't have the same validity as their own (Griset 1993:33, 37). Therefore, Heizer surmised that Merriam and his family would not have liked Berkeley to be the recipient of Merriam's baskets.

17. Suzanne Griset provided all information regarding the disposition of Merriam's materials in a personal communication to Judith Finger in June 1999.

18. The Eibeshutzes' collection of beadwork was eventually donated to the Eastern California Museum, but their baskets were inadvertently sold by a friend without the family's knowledge or consent (William H. Michael, personal communication 1998).

19. In 1894 San Francisco hosted a national exposition, the San Francisco Mid-Winter Fair. At its close the city commissioners decided to turn one of its buildings into a permanent museum; the Golden Gate Park Memorial Museum opened in 1895.

20. See Blackburn and Hudson 1990:98–102 for an inventory of one of these collections at the Staatliche Museen zu Berlin, Ethnologisches Museum, Berlin.

21. Carroll, referred to as Alfred de la Cour Carroll, is mentioned by Mary Austin in her book *Earth Horizon: Autobiography* (Austin 1932:252–254, 280). He may have received an annual payment from his family and was thus described as a "remittance man" by Austin (Ringler 1963:57).

22. When taken over by the Smithsonian Institution in 1990, the museum's name changed to the National Museum of the American Indian, Smithsonian Institution.

23. Among Paiutes and Shoshones, when people died, their relatives often burned their houses and belongings (Liljeblad and Fowler 1986:428).

24. See Mooney 1896 for a discussion of the Ghost Dance.

25. George was thought to be the first white child born in Round Valley.

26. The Museum of Anthropology later became the Robert H. Lowie Museum of Anthropology. It was renamed the Phoebe Apperson Hearst Museum of Anthropology in 1992.

27. Dow named this town Parshall after the rancher who then owned the land.

28. The SS *Athenia* was en route from Belfast to Liverpool when it was torpedoed by a German warship two hundred miles off the coast of Ireland. The Dows spent nearly nine hours in the water before being rescued (*Inyo Register* 1967:1).

29. A new addition to the museum was completed in 1999.

30. Soda Tom was born at Mono Lake in 1867 but as an adult lived in Bishop, where he worked as a ranch hand. He was married to Katie Tom, who had also been born at Mono Lake. See application nos. 5050 and 5051, Application for Enrollment with the Indians of the State of California under the Act of May 18, 1928, U.S. Department of the Interior, Office of Indian Affairs, on file, National Archives, Washington, D.C.

31. He did.

5. Replanting the Willow

1. For example, in the 1990s, Paiute language classes were taught to children at the Even Start preschool in Bishop.

2. In the past the cry was an annual ritual held in autumn to mark the end of the obligatory year of mourning that followed the death of a spouse. During the ceremony the mourner's sorrow was publicly and symbolically ended with a face-washing ritual performed by a designated person (Liljeblad and Fowler 1986:428). Today the ceremony is performed immediately following the death of a spouse or child and is no longer seasonal (Ruth Brown, personal communication 1998).

3. Craig Bates, who has made more than a hundred baskets, corroborates these approximations of the amount of time it takes to complete a basket.

4. Making a large basket took an incredible amount of labor. For example, one of the largest coiled baskets made in the region (40 inches in diameter and 20 inches high) took Mono Lake weaver Lucy Telles four years to produce (Bates and Lee 1990:116).

5. In the 1990s the small number of Paiute weavers were able to secure enough willow locally, at no cost, for their baskets. They often trespassed on what is now federal, state, county, city, or private land to do so.

6. In the late 1880s, when the federal Department of the Interior first established a system for governing Indian people across the United States, Owens Valley was placed under the auspices of the Bishop Agency. This agency was consolidated in 1926 with the Walker River Agency, which in 1935 was consolidated with the Carson Indian Agency in Nevada, putting Inyo and Mono counties in California under the jurisdiction of the latter.

7. Photographs of students at the Big Pine School can be found in Bosak 1975:50–51.

8. It was the plan of the Carson Indian Agency that only children who were unable to attend a public school, who were orphans, or who otherwise needed special care should go to the nonreservation boarding schools. If, however, they were unable to secure "the proper" vocational training at home or in public school, they could go to a boarding school no matter where they lived. Prospective students needed to meet certain other criteria: they had to be at least one-fourth Indian, in good health, and between the ages of six and twenty-one (Bowler 1938:1).

9. Other aspects of housekeeping that "good" Indian wives and mothers were expected to do included keeping or managing a house, learning to buy and market with little expense, giving first aid in case of accidents, nursing in case of sickness, growing a garden, raising chickens and possibly turkeys, doing simple mechanical jobs around the home such as repairing a broken chair or making one from orange crates, mending leaking drainpipes, painting woodwork, making butter and cheese from the milk of the family cow, and solving the difficult problem of living happily with family, friends, and neighbors (Wiley 1936:1).

10. For example, Lucy Sepsey, a Paiute woman of Owens Valley, attended public school in Aberdeen and later attended Stewart Indian School (Bernasconi 1988:85).

11. The Carson Agency also acquired jurisdiction over Alpine County in 1938.

12. For examples, see Bernasconi 1988:68, 85, 102.

13. The March 2002 Benchmark, from which this statistic came, combines the categories of mining and natural resources.

14. The 2000 U.S census lumped agriculture, forestry, fishing, hunting, and mining in one category.

15. On the Doyles and MacQueens, see Chapter 4.

16. Loquats are the yellow, pear-shaped fruit of the loquat tree, *Eriobotrya japonica*, which is native to eastern Asia and has fragrant white flowers.

17. Unless otherwise noted, information regarding Jessie Durant was obtained in interviews with her in 1997, 1998, 1999, and 2000.

18. The largest number of documented Daisy Mallory baskets were located in the collection of the late Ella Cain of Bridgeport, California. Cain purchased most of them directly from the weaver. The baskets, along with many others from Cain's collection, are thought to be in private storage in Los Angeles and never exhibited.

19. Lily Baker is also the grandmother of another weaver, Robert Baker of Pyramid Lake (Fulkerson 1995: 77–80).

20. Unless otherwise noted, information about Bacoch was obtained in interviews with her in 1998 and 1999.

21. Unless otherwise noted, information about Yonge was obtained in interviews with her in 1998.

22. Unless otherwise noted, information about Rogers was obtained in interviews with her in 1997 and from Bernasconi 1988:79–80.

23. Unless otherwise noted, information about and quotations from Andreas were obtained in interviews with her in 1999.

24. Birch is the common name used in Owens Valley to identify creek dogwood, *Cornus stolinifera*.

25. Unless otherwise noted, information about and quotations from Stone were obtained in interviews with her in 1999.

26. Unless otherwise noted, information about Summers was obtained in interviews with her in 1999.

27. Unless otherwise noted, information about and quotations from Pueblo were obtained in interviews with her in 1998.

28. Unless otherwise noted, information about and quotations from Hess were obtained in interviews with her in 1998.

29. Unless otherwise noted, information about Slee was obtained from interviews with her in 1998–2002.

30. Unless otherwise noted, information about Stewart was obtained in mulitple interviews in 1996–2003.

31. The Paiutes usually picked willow between late fall and early spring (Wheat 1967:92), even though the bark on fall willows was more difficult to remove than that on spring willows.

32. These classes often have a high dropout rate as students learn how much work is involved. In one class of twenty students, for example, only two people finished the class and completed baskets, and in another class only one out of forty students finished (Charlotte Bacoch, personal communication 1998).

BIBLIOGRAPHY

Adams, David W.

1995 *Education for Extinction: American Indians and the Boarding School Experience, 1875–1928.* Lawrence: University of Kansas Press.

Adovasio, James M.

1974 *Prehistoric North American Basketry.* Nevada State Museum Anthropological Papers 16: Collected Papers on Aboriginal Basketry. Carson City: Nevada State Museum.

1986 Prehistoric Basketry. In *Great Basin,* edited by Warren L. d'Azevedo, pp. 194–205. Handbook of North American Indians, vol. 11, William C. Sturtevant, general editor. Washington, D.C.: Smithsonian Institution.

Aldrich, J. M.

1921 *Coloradia pandora blake,* a Moth of Which the Caterpillar Is Used as Food by Mono Lake Indians. *Annals of the Entomological Society of America* 16:36–38.

Andreas (Bowman), Lillian I.

1992 Interview with William H. Michael. Ms. on file, Eastern California Museum, Independence.

Apostol, Jane

1976 Saving Grace. *Westways* 68(10):22–24, 71, 73.

Arkush, Brooke S.

1993 Yokuts Trade Networks and Native Culture Change in Central and Eastern California. *Ethnohistory* 40(4):619–640.

1995 *The Archaeology of CA–Mno–2122: A Study of Pre-Contact and Post-Contact Lifeways Among the Mono Basin Paiute.* Anthropological Records 31. Berkeley: University of California Press.

Armstrong, Wayne P.

1992 Devil's Claws. *Pacific Horticulture* 53(4):19–23.

Arreola, Paul R.

1986 George Wharton James and the Indians. *The Masterkey* 60(1):11–18.

Austin, Mary

1903 The Basket Maker. *Atlantic Monthly* 91:235–238.

1932 *Earth Horizon: Autobiography.* Cambridge, Massachusetts: Riverside Press.

1999 *The Basket Woman: A Book of Indian Tales.* Reprint. Reno: University of Nevada Press. Originally published 1904.

B., L. A.

1858 A Trip to Walker's River. *Mariposa Gazette,* September 21.

Baldwin, Gordon C.

1950 The Pottery of the Southern Paiute. *American Antiquity* 16(1):50–56.

Barrett, S. A.

1910 The Material Culture of the Klamath Lake and Modoc Indians of Northeastern California and Southern Oregon. *University of California Publications in American Archaeology and Ethnology* 5(4):239–292. Berkeley.

Barrett, S. A., and E. W. Gifford

1933 Miwok Material Culture. *Bulletin of the Public Museum of the City of Milwaukee* 2(4).

Bates, Craig D.

1979 Beaded Baskets of the Paiute, Washoe, and Western Shoshoni. *Moccasin Tracks* 5(1):4–7.

1982 *Coiled Basketry of the Sierra Miwok.* San Diego Museum Papers 15. San Diego: San Diego Museum.

Bates, Craig D., and Martha J. Lee

1988 Yosemite: A Melting Pot for Indian People and Their Baskets. In *Strands of Time: Yokuts, Mono, and Miwok Basketmakers,* by Linda Dick, Lorrie Planas, Judy Polanich, Craig D. Bates, and Martha J. Lee, pp. 23–30. Fresno: Fresno Metropolitan Museum.

1990 *Tradition and Innovation: A Basket History of the Indians of the Yosemite–Mono Lake Area.* Yosemite National Park, California: Yosemite Association.

1993 New Materials and Old Traditions: The Beadwork and Basketry of the Yosemite–Mono Lake Indians. *Art in California* 6(5):64–65.

Beatty, Willard W.

1941 Memorandum to Reservation and School Superintendents, Principals, and Field Agents in Oregon, California, and Nevada. October 31. Record Group 75, Carson Agency, Decimal Subject Files, 1912–1950, Box 56. National Archives Federal Records Center, San Bruno, California.

Bernasconi, Mel

1988 *Inyo County Pioneers.* Self-published. N.p.

Bernstein, Bruce

1979a A Native Heritage Returns: The Wilcomb–Hall–Sheedy Collection. In *Natives and Settlers: Indian and Yankee Culture in Early California,* edited by M. Frye, pp. 69–86. Oakland, California: Oakland Museum.

1979b Panamint–Shoshone Basketry: A Definition of Style. *American Indian Art Magazine* 4(4):68–74.

1985 Panamint–Shoshone Basketry, 1890–1960: The Role of Basket Materials in the Development of a New Style. *American Indian Basketry* 5:4–11.

Bettinger, Robert L.

1976 The Development of Pinyon Exploitation in Central Eastern California. *Journal of California Anthropology* 3(1):81–95.

1977 Aboriginal Human Ecology in Owens Valley: Prehistoric Change in the Great Basin. *American Antiquity* 42(1):3–17.

1982 Aboriginal Exchange and Territoriality in Owens Valley, California. In *Contexts for Prehistoric Exchange,* edited by

Jonathon E. Ericson and Timothy K. Earle, pp. 103–127. New York: Academic Press.

1991 Native Land Use: Archaeology and Anthropology. In *Natural History of the White-Inyo Range, Eastern California*, edited by Clarence A. Hall Jr., pp. 463–486. Berkeley: University of California Press.

Bibby, Brian
1996 *The Fine Art of California Basketry.* Sacramento: Crocker Art Museum; Berkeley: Heyday Books.

Bibby, Brian, and Craig Bates
1995 A Native American Oral History of the Yosemite National Park Region: Interview with Elma (Hess) Blaver and Harry Blaver, November 8, 1995, Lee Vining, California. On file at the Eastern California Museum, Independence.

Bishop Harvest Festival
1916 *Harvest Festival Premium List.* Pamphlet. Original at Laws Museum, Laws, California.

Blackburn, Thomas C., and Travis Hudson
1990 *Time's Flotsam: Overseas Collections of California Indian Material Culture.* Ballena Press Anthropological Papers 35. Menlo Park, California: Ballena Press; Santa Barbara: Santa Barbara Museum of Natural History.

Blackwood, Evelyn
1984 Sexuality and Gender in Certain Native American Tribes: The Case of Cross-Gender Females. *Signs: Journal of Women in Culture and Society* 10(1):27–42.

Blunt, N. B.
1906 Topographic Map Showing the Owens River Region and Route of the Proposed Los Angeles Aqueduct. Unpublished. Bancroft Library, University of California, Berkeley.

Board of Indian Commissioners
1918 Letter to Ray R. Parrett, Superintendent, Bishop Indian Agency, July 4. Record Group 75, Sacramento Area Office, Bureau of Indian Affairs, Coded Records of Programs and Administration, 1910–1958, Box 7. National Archives Federal Records Center, San Bruno, California.

Bosak, Jon
1975 Andrew A. Forbes — Photographs of the Owens Valley Paiute. *Journal of California Anthropology* 2(1):38–59.

Bowler, Alida C.
1936 Memorandum to All Carson Indian Agency Personnel, February 14. Record Group 75, Carson Agency, Decimal Subject Files, 1912–1950, Box 262. National Archives Federal Records Center, San Bruno, California.
1938 Letter to Thomas Gutierrez, November 8. Record Group 75, Carson Agency, Decimal Subject Files, 1912–1950, Box 60. National Archives Federal Records Center, San Bruno, California.
1939 Letters to Rene d'Harnoncourt, April 27, June 1, July 8. Record Group 75, Decimal Subject Files, 1912–1950, Box 64. National Archives Federal Records Center, San Bruno, California.

Brooks, Joan
1997 *Desert Padre: The Life and Writings of Father John J. Crowley, 1891–1940.* Desert Hot Springs, California: Mesquite Press.

Brown, Clara Spalding
1898 The Art of Indian Basketry. *Catholic World* 68:52–59.

Buckmelter, Jerome
1998 The Owens Gorge: Recovery Continues. *California Flyfisher* May/June: 42–45, 83.

Burton, Jeffery F., and Mary M. Farrell
1996 Ethnography and Pre-History. In *Three Farewells to Manzanar: The Archaeology of Manzanar National Historic Site, California*, by Jeffery F. Burton, pp. 151–176. Publications in Anthropology 67. Tucson: Western Archaeological and Conservation Center, National Park Service.

Burton, Jeffery F., and Jane C. Wehrey
1996 History Background. In *Three Farewells to Manzanar: The Archaeology of Manzanar National Historic Site, California*, by Jeffery F. Burton, pp. 123–150. Publications in Anthropology 67. Tucson: Western Archaeological and Conservation Center, National Park Service.

Busby, Colin I., John M. Findlay, and James C. Bard
1979 *A Culture Resource Overview of the Bureau of Land Management: Coleville, Bodie, Benton, and Owens Valley Planning Units, California, for the United States Department of the Interior, Bureau of Land Management, Bakersfield District Office.* Contract YA512CT8181. Oakland, California: Basin Research Associates.

Cain, Ella M. Cody
1961 *The Story of Early Mono County: Its Settlers, Gold Rushes, Indians, Ghost Towns.* San Francisco: Fearon.

California State Employment Development Department (CSEDD), Labor Market Information Division
1993 Inyo County Wages Paid by Quarter, 1983–1992. http://www.calmis.ca.gov.
1996 Inyo County Labor Force and Industry Employment, December 1997–December 1998. http://www.calmis.cahwnet.gov.
1999a Inyo and Mono Counties — Occupations with Greatest Growth, 1995–2002. http://www.calmis.cahwnet.gov.
1999b Monthly Historical Industry Employment of Inyo County, 1983–1999. http://www.calmis.cahwnet.gov.
2000 Wage and Salary Employment by Industry: Annual Averages, 1992–1999. http://www.calmis.cahwnet.gov.
2003 Inyo County Industry Employment and Labor Force by Annual Average, March 2002 Benchmark. http://www.calmis.ca.gov/file/indhist/inyohaw.xls.

Callender, Charles, and Lee M. Kochems
1983 The North American Berdache. *Current Anthropology* 24(4): 443–470.

Campbell, Charles W.
1974 Origins and Ethnography of Prehistoric Man in Owens Valley. *Eastern California Museum Anthropological Papers* 1:1–14.

Carson Agency
1935 Knumi Knuga Tumue Aligne Loss [Carson Indian School Commencement Week Program], May 30–31. Record Group 75, Carson Agency, Decimal Subject Files, 1912–1950, Box 60. National Archives Federal Records Center, San Bruno, California.
1938 Carson Indian School Commencement Week Program, May 22–28. Record Group 75, Carson Agency, Decimal Subject Files, 1912–1950, Box 60. National Archives Federal Records Center, San Bruno, California.

1942   Letter to Paul Fickinger, September 23. Record Group 75, Carson Agency, Decimal Subject Files, 1912–1950, Box 64. National Archives Federal Records Center, San Bruno, California.

Castillo, Edward D.
1978   The Impact of Euro-American Exploration and Settlement. In *California,* edited by Robert F. Heizer, pp. 99–127. Handbook of North American Indians, vol. 8, William C. Sturtevant, general editor. Washington, D.C.: Smithsonian Institution.

Chalfant, William A.
1922   *The Story of Inyo.* Chicago: Hammond Press, W. B. Conkey Co.
1928   *Outposts of Civilization.* Boston: Christopher Publishing House.
1933   *The Story of Inyo.* Rev. ed. Bishop, California: Chalfant Press.

Chappell, Maxine
1947   Early History of Mono County. *California Historical Society Quarterly* 26(3):233–248.

Cheney, Lela M.
1938   Letter from the Supervisor of Social Work, Office of Indian Affairs, Washington, D.C., to Lucille Hamner, Carson (Stewart) Indian School, January 28. Record Group 75, Carson Agency, Decimal Subject Files, 1912–1950, Box 60. National Archives Federal Records Center, San Bruno, California.

Cline, Gloria
1963   *Exploring the Great Basin.* Norman: University of Oklahoma Press.

Cohodas, Marvin
1979   *Degikup: Washoe Fancy Basketry, 1895–1935.* Vancouver: University of British Columbia, Fine Arts Gallery.
1997   *Basket Weavers for the California Curio Trade: Elizabeth and Louise Hickox.* Tucson: University of Arizona Press.

Connor, J. Torrey
1896   Confessions of a Basket Collector. *Land of Sunshine* 5(1): 3–10.

Cook, Sherburne F.
1960   Colonial Expeditions to the Interior of California, Central Valley, 1800–1820. *University of California Anthropological Records* 16(6):239–292. Berkeley.
1976   *The Conflict Between the California Indian and White Civilization.* Berkeley: University of California Press.

Corbey, Raymond
1993   Ethnographic Showcases, 1870–1930. *Cultural Anthropology* 8(3):338–369.

Coville, Frederick Vernon
1892   The Panamint Indians of California. *American Anthropologist* 5(4):351–361.

Craftsman
1910   Indian Blankets, Baskets, and Bowls: The Product of the Original Craftworkers of This Continent. *Craftsman* 17 (February): 588–90.

Cragen, Dorothy C.
1975   *The Boys in the Sky-Blue Pants: The Men and Events at Camp Independence and Forts of Eastern California, Nevada, and Utah, 1862–1877.* Fresno: Pioneer Publishing.

Crum, Steven
2001   Deeply Attached to the Land: The Owens Valley Paiutes and Their Rejection of Indian Removal, 1863–1937. *News from Native California* 14(4):18–20.

Curry, R. R.
1969   Holocene Climatic and Glacial History of the Central Sierra Nevada, California. In *United States Contributions to Quaternary Research,* edited by S. A. Schumm and W. C. Bradley, pp. 1–47. Geological Society of America Special Paper 123. Washington, D.C.

Curtis, Edward S.
1907–30   *The North American Indian: Being a Series of Volumes Picturing and Describing the Indians of the United States and Alaska, Volume 1.* Edited by Frederick Hodge. Norwood, Massachusetts: Plimpton Press. Reprint. Johnson Reprint, New York, 1970.

Dale, Edward E.
1949   *The Indians of the Southwest: A Century of Development Under the United States.* Norman: University of Oklahoma Press.

Davenport, Blair
1999   Timbisha Family Information. Typescript, 30 September. File for cat. no. 28,151, Museum Collections, National Park Service, Death Valley National Park, California.

Davis, George B., Leslie J. Perry, and Joseph W. Kirkley
1897   *The War of the Rebellion: A Compilation of the Official Records of the Union and Confederate Armies,* part 2. Washington, D.C.: Government Printing Office.

Davis, James T.
1974   *Trade Routes and Economic Exchange Among the Indians of California.* Ramona, California: Ballena Press.

Dawson, Lawrence E.
1974   Letter to Craig Bates, January. On file, Yosemite Museum, Yosemite National Park, California.
1975   Letter to Craig Bates, January. On file, Yosemite Museum, Yosemite National Park, California.

DeDecker, Mary
1988   Owens Valley, Then and Now. In *Mountains to Desert: Selected Inyo Readings,* pp. 7–15. Independence: Friends of the Eastern California Museum.
1993   *Mines of the Eastern Sierra.* Glendale, California: La Siesta Press.

Deisher, Henry K.
1906   Letters to C. Hart Merriam, November 16, December 26. C. Hart Merriam Collection, Bancroft Library, University of California, Berkeley.

Doyle, Helen MacKnight
1934   *A Child Went Forth.* New York: Gotham House.
1983   *Doctor Nellie: The Autobiography of Dr. Helen MacKnight Doyle.* Mammoth Lakes, California: Genny Smith Books.

Driver, Harold E.
1937   Culture Element Distributions: VI, Southern Sierra Nevada. *University of California Anthropological Records* 1(2):53–154. Berkeley.

Driver, Harold E., and William C. Massey
1957   Studies of North American Indians. *Transactions of the American Philosophical Society* 47(2):167–439. Philadelphia.

Dykstra, C. A.

1929 Owens Valley — A Problem in Regional Planning. *Community Builder* 1:9–12.

Earl, Guy Chaffee

1976 *The Enchanted Valley and Other Sketches.* Glendale, California: Arthur H. Clark Co.

1980 *Indian Legends and Songs.* Glendale, California: Arthur H. Clark Co.

Eastern California Museum

1962 Inventory of the Rose Black Collection. Ms. on file, Eastern California Museum of Inyo County, Independence.

Eerkins, Jelmer, Hector Neff, and Michael D. Glasscock

1999 Early Pottery from Sunga'Va and Implications for the Development of Ceramic Technology in Owens Valley, California. *Journal of California and Great Basin Anthropology* 21(2):275–285.

Ellis, E. S.

1978 *Seth Jones; Or, The Captives of the Frontier.* Reprint. New York: Garland. Originally published 1860.

Elston, Robert G.

1986 Prehistory of the Western Area. In *Great Basin,* edited by Warren L. d'Azevedo, pp. 135–148. Handbook of North American Indians vol. 11, William C. Sturtevant, general editor. Washington, D.C.: Smithsonian Institution.

Esteves, Madeline

1983 Interview notes, March 12, 1983. On file, Cleveland Museum of Natural History, Department of Anthropology and Visual Arts, Cleveland.

Etcharren, Bernice

1977 The Aqueduct. In *Saga of Inyo County,* pp. 65–66. Covina, California: Taylor.

Ewan, Rebecca Fish

2000 *A Land Between: Owens Valley, California.* Baltimore: Johns Hopkins University Press.

Ewers, John C.

1959 *Adventures of Zenas Leonard, Fur Trader.* Norman: University of Oklahoma Press.

1987 Charlie Russell's Indians. *Montana: The Magazine of Western History* 37 (Summer 1987): 36–53.

Farquhar, Francis P., editor

1930 *Up and Down California in 1860–1864: The Journal of William H. Brewer.* New Haven: Yale University Press.

1965 *History of the Sierra Nevada.* Berkeley: University of California Press.

Finger, Judith

2003a Twined Basketry Caps of Eastern California and the Great Basin. *American Indian Art Magazine* 28 (Spring): 64–73.

2003b Fancy Coiled Caps of Central California. *American Indian Art Magazine* 28 (Summer): 56–63, 93.

Fisher, Jane

1983 Owens Valley Indians Keep Heritage Alive. *Sierra Weekender,* July 22–28, 1(4):3, 11.

Fleming, Paula R., and Luskey, Judith

1986 *The North American Indians.* Washington, D.C.: Smithsonian Institution Press.

Fletcher, Thomas C.

1987 *Paiute, Prospector, Pioneer: The Bodie–Mono Lake Area in the Nineteenth Century.* Lee Vining, California: Artemisia Press.

Floyd, Harry C.

1903 Letter to C. Hart Merriam, February 19. C. Hart Merriam Collection, Bancroft Library, University of California, Berkeley.

1909 Letter to Grace Nicholson, July 28. Grace Nicholson Collection, Huntington Library, San Marino, California.

1910 Letter to Grace Nicholson, September 5. Grace Nicholson Collection, Huntington Library, San Marino, California.

1912 Letter to Grace Nicholson, January 11. Grace Nicholson Collection, Huntington Library, San Marino, California.

Ford, A. J.

1930 *Owens River Valley, California Indian Problem.* Los Angeles: Department of Water and Power.

Ford, A. J., E. A. Porter, and C. D. Carll

1932 *Report on the Conditions of the Indians in Owens Valley, California.* Los Angeles: Department of Water and Power.

Foster, Don C.

1942 Letter to Mildred Bray, Superintendent, Department of Public Instruction, Carson City, Nevada, November 10. Record Group 75, Carson Agency, Decimal Subject Files, 1912–1950, Box 56. National Archives Federal Records Center, San Bruno, California.

Foster, Julia B.

n.d. A Little Curio. *Land of Sunshine.* [From a partial copy of an issue of the magazine in possession of Craig D. Bates; date and volume number unavailable.]

Fowler, Catherine S.

1986 Subsistence. In *Great Basin,* edited by Warren L. d'Azevedo, pp. 64–97. Handbook of North American Indians, vol. 11, William C. Sturtevant, general editor. Washington, D.C.: Smithsonian Institution.

1990 *Tule Technology: Northern Paiute Uses of Marsh Resources in Western Nevada.* Smithsonian Folklife Studies 6. Washington, D.C.: Smithsonian Institution Press.

1992 *In the Shadow of Fox Peak: An Ethnography of the Cattail Eater Northern Paiute People of Stillwater Marsh.* Cultural Resource Series 5, U.S. Department of the Interior, Fish and Wildlife Service, Region 1, Stillwater National Wildlife Refuge. Washington, D.C.: Government Printing Office.

Fowler, Catherine S., and Lawrence E. Dawson

1986 Ethnographic Basketry. In *Great Basin,* edited by Warren L. d'Azevedo, pp. 705–737. Handbook of North American Indians, vol. 11, William C. Sturtevant, general editor. Washington, D.C.: Smithsonian Institution.

Fowler, Catherine S., and Sven Liljeblad

1986 Northern Paiute. In *Great Basin,* edited by Warren L. d'Azevedo, pp. 435–465. Handbook of North American Indians, vol. 11, William C. Sturtevant, general editor. Washington, D.C.: Smithsonian Institution.

Fowler, Catherine S., and Nancy Peterson Walter

1985 Harvesting Pandora Moth Larvae with the Owens Valley Paiute. *Journal of California and Great Basin Anthropology* 7(2): 155–165.

Fowler, Don D.

1986   History of Research. In *Great Basin,* edited by Warren L. d'Azevedo, pp. 15–30. Handbook of North American Indians, vol. 11, William C. Sturtevant, general editor. Washington, D.C.: Smithsonian Institution.

Fowler, Don D., and Catherine S. Fowler

1971   *Anthropology of the Numa: John Wesley Powell's Manuscripts on the Numic Peoples of Western North America, 1868–1880.* Smithsonian Contributions to Anthropology 14. Washington, D.C.

Fowler, Don D., and John F. Matley

1979   *Material Culture of the Numa: The John Wesley Powell Collection, 1867–1880.* Smithsonian Contributions to Anthropology 26. Washington, D.C.

Frye, Melinda Young

1979   Charles P. Wilcomb, Cultural Historian (1865–1915). In *Natives and Settlers: Indian and Yankee Culture in Early California: The Collections of Charles P. Wilcomb,* edited by Melinda Young Frye, pp. 15–39. Oakland, California: Oakland Museum.

Fulkerson, Mary L.

1995   *Weavers of Tradition and Beauty: Basketmakers of the Great Basin.* Reno: University of Nevada Press.

Gansberg, Chris, Linda Arcularius, Brian J. Lamb, Richard Riordan, John Ferraro, Ruth Galanter, and S. David Freeman

1998   Memorandum Agreement Between the City of Los Angeles and the Great Basin Unified Air Pollution Control District. On file, Department of Water and Power, City of Los Angeles, Bishop, California.

Gayton, Anna H.

1929   Yokuts and Western Mono Pottery-Making. *University of California Publications in American Archaeology and Ethnology* 24(3):239–251.

1948   *Yokuts and Western Mono Ethnography.* University of California Anthropological Records 10. Berkeley.

Gelvin, Ralph M.

1947   Letter to E. Morgan Pryse, District Director, U.S. Indian Service in Portland, Oregon, December 12. Record Group 75, Sacramento Area Office, Coded Records of Programs and Administration, 1910–1958, Box 8. National Archives Federal Records Center, San Bruno, California.

Gifford, E. W.

1927   Letter to W. W. Campbell, May 17. Accession file no. 625. Phoebe Apperson Hearst Museum of Anthropology, University of California, Berkeley.

Gilbert, Bil

1983   *Westering Man: The Life of Joseph Walker.* New York: Atheneum.

Gilham, F. M

n.d.   [Catalog of baskets and other Indian artifacts.] Highland Springs, Lake County, California. On file at the Yosemite Museum, Yosemite National Park.

1891   [Advertisement.] *The Herald.* January 10. On file at the Yosemite Museum, Yosemite National Park, and the Bancroft Library, University of California, Berkeley.

Glover, Winifred

1978   *The Land of the Brave: The North American Indian Collection in the Ulster Museum, Belfast.* Belfast: Blackstaff Press.

Gogol, James

1985   The Golden Decade of Collecting Indian Basketry. *American Indian Basketry* 5(1):12–29.

Graulich, Melody, editor

1987   *Western Trails: A Collection of Short Stories by Mary Austin.* Reno: University of Nevada Press.

Griset, Suzanne

1986   Notes on Ceramic Analysis. In *Pottery of the Great Basin and Adjacent Areas,* edited by Suzanne Griset, pp. 119–124. University of Utah Anthropological Papers 111. Salt Lake City: University of Utah Press.

1993   C. Hart Merriam: The Naturalist as Ethnographer. *Museum Anthropology* 17(2):33–40.

Grosscup, Gordon L.

1977   Notes on Boundaries and Culture of the Panamint Shoshone and Owens Valley Paiute. *University of California Archaeological Research Papers* 35:109–150. Berkeley.

Gudde, Erwin G.

1998   *California Place Names: The Origin and Etymology of Current Geographical Names.* Berkeley: University of California Press.

Guthrie, Jane W.

1901   Indian Baskets as Decoration. *Harper's Bazaar* 35:468–471.

Hall, Gilbert L.

1979   *The Federal-Indian Trust Relationship.* Washington, D.C.: Institute for the Development of Indian Law.

Hall, Parker L.

1936   Letter to Alida C. Bowler, February 29. Record Group 75, Carson Agency, Decimal Subject Files, 1912–1950, Box 66. National Archives Federal Records Center, San Bruno, California.

Harrington, Mark R.

1932   Museums and Fiestas. *The Masterkey* 6(3):72–83.

Hartman, C. S.

n.d.   [Notes regarding Paiutes of Owens Valley region.] Grace Nicholson Collection, Huntington Library, San Marino, California.

1908   Letter to Grace Nicholson, June 17. Grace Nicholson Collection, Huntington Library, San Marino, California.

Heizer, Robert F.

1966   *Languages, Territories, and Names of California Indian Tribes.* Berkeley: University of California Press.

1974   *The Destruction of the California Indians.* Santa Barbara and Salt Lake City: Peregrine Smith.

Heizer, Robert F., editor

1975   *California Indian Characteristics and Centennial Mission to the Indians of Western Nevada and California by Stephen Powers.* Berkeley: Friends of the Bancroft Library.

Hess, Mary Lee

1922   Letter to Horatio Shumway Lee, February 28. Accession no. 625, Phoebe Apperson Hearst Museum of Anthropology, University of California, Berkeley.

Hill, Mary

1975   *Geology of the Sierra Nevada.* Berkeley: University of California Press.

Holden, C. F.

1891   A California Craze: The Latest Fad Among Artistic People: Collections of Indian Baskets. *Placer Herald,* January 10.

Hudson, John W.

n.d. Typescript of California Field Notes. Field Museum, Chicago.

1904a Journal of John Hudson. Manuscript. Grace Hudson Museum and Sun House, Ukiah, California.

1904b Letter of July 24, from Lone Pine, to Dr. George Dorsey. Field Museum, Chicago.

1904c Letter of August 4, from Bishop, to Dr. George Dorsey. Field Museum, Chicago.

1905 Letter to C. Hart Merriam, January 25. C. Hart Merriam Collection, Bancroft Library, University of California, Berkeley.

Hughes, Richard, and James A. Bennyhoff

1986 Early Trade. In *Great Basin,* edited by Warren L. d'Azevedo, pp. 238–255. Handbook of North American Indians, vol. 11, William C. Sturtevant, general editor. Washington, D.C.: Smithsonian Institution.

Hulse, Frederick S.

1935 Ethnological Documents: Fort Independence Paiute Ethnographic Notes. Manuscript. Bancroft Library, University of California, Berkeley.

Hurtado, Albert L.

1982 Hardly a Farmhouse, a Kitchen Without Them: Indians in White Households on the California Borderland Frontier in 1860. *Western Historical Quarterly* 13:245–270.

Indian Arts and Crafts Board

1939 *Indian Art in the United States and Alaska: A Pictorial Record of the Indian Exhibition at the Golden Gate International Exhibition.* Washington, D.C.: Indian Arts and Crafts Board of the Department of the Interior. University Microfilms, Ann Arbor, Michigan.

Inkley, Dale

1991 Three Corner Round: A Western Adventure. *[Cleveland Museum of Natural History] Explorer* 33(2):12–14.

Inter-University Consortium for Political and Social Research (ICPSR)

1996 Historical, Demographic, Economic, and Social Data: The United States. Ann Arbor: University of Michigan. http://fisher.lib.virginia.edu/census.

Inyo County Board of Supervisors (ICBS)

1966 *Inyo, 1866–1966.* Inyo County Board of Supervisors. Independence, California.

Inyo County Planning Office (ICPO)

1988 *Population, Income, and Land Characteristics, Inyo County, California; and County of Inyo 1988 Population Report.* Independence: Inyo County Planning Department.

Inyo County Water Department (ICWD)

1997 *The Owens Valley Monitor: Inyo County Water Department's Report on Activities and Conditions in the Owens Valley.* Bishop.

1998 *The Owens Valley Water Reporter* 11(1):1–4. Bishop.

Inyo Register

1904a Items of Interest. April 1, p. 1.

1904b The Aboriginal Inhabitants — Beginning of Trouble — A Treaty, Soon Violated. February 18, p. 1.

1905 Los Angeles Plots Destruction. August 3, pp. 1–2.

1967 Final Rites Held for G. W. Dow. May, issue 20.

Irwin, Charles N.

1980 *The Shoshone Indians of Inyo County, California: The Kerr Manuscript.* Ballena Press Publications in Archaeology, Ethnology, and History 11. Socorro, New Mexico: Ballena Press; Independence, California: Eastern California Museum.

Ives, Marie E.

1900 Report of the Young People's Department of the Women's National Indian Association for 1900. Women's National Indian Association, December.

Jacobs, Sue-Ellen

1983 Comment on "The North American Berdache." *Current Anthropology* 24(4):459–460.

James, George Wharton

1901a *Indian Basketry.* Pasadena: privately printed.

1901b Indian Basketry in House Decoration. *The Chautauquan* 33(6):619–624.

1901c Indian Basketry. *Outing* 38:177–186.

1902 *Indian Basketry.* New York: Henry Malkan.

1903a Indian Handicrafts. *The Basket* 1(3):19–27, inside back cover.

1903b Improvements for 1904. *The Basket* 1(4):69.

1903c Basketmakers of California at Work. *The Basket* 1(3):2–18.

1913 Poetry and Symbolism of Indian Basketry. *Out West* (November/December): 207–223.

1914 Poetry and Symbolism of Indian Basketry. *Out West* (January): 26–35.

1972 *Indian Basketry.* 4th ed. Reprint. New York: Dover. Originally published 1909.

Jenkins, David

1993 The Visual Domination of the American Indian. *Museum Anthropology* 17(1):9–21.

Jenner, Demila

1994 Benton's Mormon McBrides. *The Album: Times and Tales of Inyo-Mono* (Summer 1994):40–45. Bishop, California: Chalfant Press.

Jones, John E.

1992 I Had No Can't in My Book. *Newsletter for the Friends of the Eastern California Museum* 8(3):1, 5–7.

Jones, T. E.

1977 Owens Lake in 1885. In *Saga of Inyo County,* p. 10. Covina, California: Taylor.

Jones, William Arthur

1897 *Annual Report of the Commissioner of Indian Affairs to the Secretary of the Interior.* Washington, D.C.: Government Printing Office.

Jones, W. F.

1902 Letter to the Superintendent, Greenville School, California, January 13. Record Group 75C, California Agency, Box 3. National Archives Federal Records Center, San Bruno, California.

Kahrl, William L.

1976 The Politics of California Water: Owens Valley and the Los Angeles Aqueduct, 1900–1927. *California Historical Quarterly* 55(1):2–25, (2):98–120.

Kelley, Anna

n.d. Personal Notes on the Anna Kelley Basket Collection. Private collection, Independence, California. Copies on file, Cleveland Museum of Natural History, Department of Cultural Anthropology and Visual Arts, Cleveland.

1955 Personal Notes on the Anna Kelley Basket Collection. Private collection, Independence, California. Copies on file, Cleveland Museum of Natural History, Department of Cultural Anthropology and Visual Arts, Cleveland.

1956 Personal notes, February 19. Private collection, Independence, California. Copies on file, Cleveland Museum of Natural History, Department of Cultural Anthropology and Visual Arts, Cleveland.

1957 Personal Notes on the Anna Kelley Basket Collection. Cleveland Museum of Natural History, Department of Cultural Anthropology and Visual Arts, Cleveland.

Kern, Edward M.

1876 Journal of Mr. Edward Kern of an Exploration of Mary's or Humboldt River, Carson Lake and Owens River and Lake. Appendix Q in *Report of Explorations Across the Great Basin of the Territory of Utah for a Direct Wagon Route from Camp Floyd to Genoa, in Carson Valley, in 1859,* by Captain J. H. Simpson. Washington, D.C.: Government Printing Office.

Kerr, Mark, collector

1936 Biography of an Old Woman. Kerr Manuscript [unedited papers collected by Mark Kerr], Book 56, pp. 1–2. Independence: Eastern California Museum.

King, Clarence

1872 *Mountaineering in the Sierra Nevada.* Boston: James R. Osgood.

Kirk, Ruth E.

1952 Panamint Basketry — A Dying Art. *The Masterkey* 26:76–86.

Kroeber, Alfred

1925 *Handbook of the Indians of California.* Bureau of American Ethnology 78. Washington, D.C.

1939 Cultural and Natural Areas of Native North America. *University of California Publications in American Archaeology and Ethnology* 38(1):1–242. Berkeley.

Latta, Frank F.

1949 *Handbook of Yokuts Indians.* Bakersfield, California: Kern County Museum.

Lawton, Harry W., Philip J. Wilke, Mary DeDecker, and William M. Mason

1976 Agriculture Among the Paiute of Owens Valley. *Journal of California Anthropology* 3(1):13–50.

Layton, Thomas N.

1981 Traders and Raiders: Aspects of Trans–Basin and California–Plateau Commerce, 1800–1830. *Journal of California and Great Basin Anthropology* 3(1):127–137.

Liljeblad, Sven, and Catherine S. Fowler

1986 Owens Valley Paiute. In *Great Basin,* edited by Warren L. d'Azevedo, pp. 412–425. Handbook of North American Indians, vol. 11, William C. Sturtevant, general editor. Washington, D.C.: Smithsonian Institution.

Los Angeles Department of Water and Power (LADWP)

1988 *Sharing the Vision: The Story of the Los Angeles Aqueduct.* Los Angeles: Department of Water and Power.

1993 *The Los Angeles Aqueduct System: Points of Interest.* Los Angeles: Department of Water and Power.

1998 New Approach to Stream Restoration. Owens River Gorge Rewatering Project Information Sheet. April 24.

Lukins, Julian

1998a Locals Voice Concerns over Pump Plan. *Inyo Register,* October 8, pp. A1, A3.

1998b Pumping Ordinance OK'd. *Inyo Register,* October 8, pp. A1, A3.

MacCurdy, George Grant

1903 A Basketry Collection: The Valuable Moseley Specimens of Indian Basketry on Exhibition in Peabody Museum. *The Papoose* 1(3):12–15.

MacQueen, Helen S.

1949 Letter to Bishop Athena Club. Personal correspondence in possession of John MacQueen, Vista, California.

Madsen, David B.

1986 Prehistoric Ceramics. In *Great Basin,* edited by Warren L. d'Azevedo, pp. 206–214. Handbook of North American Indians, vol. 11, William C. Sturtevant, general editor. Washington, D.C.: Smithsonian Institution.

Malinowski, Bronislaw

1961 *Argonauts of the Western Pacific: An Account of Native Enterprise and Adventure in the Archipelagoes of Melanesian New Guinea.* Reprint. New York: E. P. Dutton. Originally published 1922.

Manners, Robert A.

1996 Julian Haynes Steward. *National Academy of Sciences of the United States of America Biographical Memoirs* 69:325–334. Washington, D.C.

Mariposa Gazette

1857. Local. August 24.

Mason, Otis T.

1904 Letter to C. Hart Merriam, March 29. C. Hart Merriam Collection, Bancroft Library, University of California, Berkeley.

Maule, William M.

1938 A Contribution to the Geographic and Economic History of the Carson, Walker, and Mono Basins in Nevada and California. Manuscript, Bancroft Library, University of California, Berkeley.

Maurer, Stephan G.

1985 In the Heart of the Great Freedom: George Wharton James and the Desert Southwest. *The Masterkey* 60(1):4–10.

McLuhan, T. C.

1972 Curtis: His Life. In *Portraits from North American Indian Life,* pp. viii–xii. New York: Promontory Press.

McDowell, Malcolm

1915 Letter from the Secretary of the Board of Indian Commissioners, Department of the Interior, to Edgar K. Miller, Superintendent, Greenville Indian Agency, January 8. Record Group 75, Sacramento Area Office, Coded Records, 1910–1958, Box 24. National Archives Federal Records Center, San Bruno, California.

McLendon, Sally

1990 Pomo Baskets: The Legacy of William and Mary Benson. *Native Peoples* 4(1):26–37.

1993 Collecting Pomoan Baskets, 1889–1939. *Museum Anthropology* 17(2):49–60.

1996   Grace Nicholson and the California Indian Basket Market. Paper presented at the 95th meeting of the American Anthropological Association, November, San Francisco.

McWilliams, C.

1973   *Southern California: An Island on the Land.* Santa Barbara: Peregrine Smith.

Mecham, Elizabeth

1978   Letter to Mr. Charles Irwin, Director, Eastern California Museum, July 14. Mecham Collection, Eastern California Museum of Inyo County, Independence.

1979   Letter of April 17. Mecham Collection, Eastern California Museum of Inyo County, Independence.

Mercer, Bill

1997   *Lená Taku Wasté: These Good Things; Selections from the Elizabeth Cole Butler Collection of Native American Art.* Portland, Oregon: Portland Art Museum.

Merriam, C. Hart

n.d.a   Catalog cards of C. Hart Merriam Basket Collection. Department of Anthropology, University of California, Davis.

n.d.b   Miscellaneous Notes on Owens Valley Paiute. Manuscript. C. Hart Merriam Collection, Bancroft Library, University of California, Berkeley.

1901   Basketry Among the Mono Paiutes, unpublished notes, August. C. Hart Merriam Collection, Bancroft Library, University of California, Berkeley.

1902   Personal journal. Manuscript. Library of Congress, Washington, D.C.

1955   *Studies of California Indians.* Berkeley: University of California Press.

1966–67   *Ethnographic Notes on California Indian Tribes.* Edited by Robert F. Heizer. University of California Archaeological Survey Reports 68. Berkeley: University of California.

1979   *Indian Names for Plants and Animals Among Californian and Other Western North American Tribes.* Assembled and annotated by Robert F. Heizer. Ballena Press Publications in Archaeology, Ethnology, and History 14. Socorro, New Mexico: Ballena Press.

Michael, William H.

1985   Eastern California Museum. *American Indian Basketry and Other Native Arts* 5(3):21.

1993   At the Plow and in the Harvest Field: Indian Conflict and Accommodation in the Owens Valley, 1860–1889. Master's thesis, Department of Anthropology, University of Oklahoma, Norman.

Mooney, James

1896   The Ghost Dance Religion and the Sioux Outbreak of 1890. In *Fourteenth Annual Report of the Bureau of American Ethnology for the Years 1892–1893,* pt. 2, pp. 641–1136. Washington, D.C.

Morgan, Judith, and Neil Morgan

1976   California's Parched Oasis. *National Geographic* 149 (January): 98–127.

Morgans, Otis J.

1936   Letter to Mary Stewart, Superintendent of Indian Education, July 20. Record Group 75, Carson Agency, Decimal Subject Files, 1912–1950, Box 58. National Archives Federal Records Center, San Bruno, California.

Morris, Loverne

1967   Dows Live Traditional Pioneer Success Story. *Whittier (California) Daily News* 58(3):1–2.

Moser, Christopher L., editor

1986   *Native American Basketry of Central California.* Riverside, California: Riverside Museum Press.

Moyer, Wendell W.

1996   Saline Valley Indian Ranch: Its Rise and Fall. In *The Album 1996:* 30–44. Bishop: Chalfant Press.

Muir, John

1894   *The Mountains of California.* New York: Century.

Nabhan, Gary Paul

1987   *Gathering the Desert.* Tucson: University of Arizona Press.

Nadeau, Remi

1997   *The Water Seekers.* Santa Barbara: Crest.

Nelson, E. W.

1893   The Panamint and Saline Valley (Cal.) Indians. *American Anthropologist* 4(4):371–372.

Nicholson, Grace

n.d.a.   Notes of Paiutes/Owens Valley area. Manuscript. Grace Nicholson Collection, Huntington Library, San Marino, California.

n.d.b   [Basket notebook.] Accession. no. 2881, Phoebe Apperson Hearst Museum of Anthropology, University of California, Berkeley.

Nissen, Karen M.

1982   Images from the Past: An Analysis of Six Western Great Basin Petroglyph Sites. Ph.D. dissertation, University of California, Berkeley. Ann Arbor: University Microfilms.

Northern California Historical Records Survey Project

1940   *Inventory of the County Archives of California, 27: Mono County, Bridgeport.* San Francisco.

O'Barr, William M.

1994   *Culture and the Ad: Exploring Otherness in the World of Advertising.* Boulder: Westview Press.

O'Neill, John M.

1862   Letter of August 28. In *The War of the Rebellion: A Compilation of the Official Records of the Union and Confederate Armies,* by George B. Davis, Leslie J. Perry, and Joseph W. Kirkley, pt. 2, p. 92, 1897. Washington, D.C.: Government Printing Office.

Osborne, Carolyn M., and Harry S. Riddell Jr.

1978   A Cache of Deer Snares from Owens Valley, California. *Journal of California and Great Basin Anthropology* 5(1):101–109.

Ostrom, Vincent

1953   *Water and Politics: A Study of Water Policies and Administration in the Development of Los Angeles.* Monograph Series, 35. Los Angeles: Hayes Foundation.

Outlook

1901   Indian Industrial Development. *The Outlook* 67(2):101–102.

Packard, Walter E.

1925   Report on the Agricultural Situation in Owens Valley, as It Relates to the Agricultural Development of Lands Belonging to the City of Los Angeles. Report to Mr. R. F. Del Valle, President of the Board of Public Service of the City of Los Angeles, California, July 25. Manuscript. Henry E. Huntington Library and Art Gallery, San Marino, California.

Palazzo, Robert P.
1996 *Darwin, California.* Lake Grove, Oregon: Western Places.

Parcher, Genevive C.
1937 Wa-Pai-Shone Basketry. Manuscript. Record Group 75, Native Arts, Music Project, 1936–1943, Box 121. National Archives, Washington, D.C.

Phillips, Fred M.
1977 *Desert People and Mountain Men: Exploration of the Great Basin, 1824–1865.* Bishop, California: Chalfant Press.

Pietroforte, Alfred
1965 *Songs of the Yokuts and Paiutes.* Healdsburg, California: Naturegraph.

Pippin, Lonnie C.
1986 Intermountain Brown Wares: An Assessment. In *Pottery of the Great Basin and Adjacent Areas,* edited by Suzanne Griset, pp. 9–21. University of Utah Anthropological Papers 111. Salt Lake City: University of Utah Press.

Plakos, Chris J.
1999 *Fact Sheet: Los Angeles/Inyo County Long-Term Groundwater Management Plan and Agreement.* Bishop, California: Department of Water and Power, City of Los Angeles.

Polanich, Judith K.
1994 Mono Basketry: Migration and Change. Ph.D. dissertation, University of California, Davis.
1995 The Origins of Western Mono Coiled Basketry: A Reconstruction of Prehistoric Change in Material Culture. *Museum Anthropology* 19(3):58–68.

Potashin, Richard
1992 Manuscript on file. Eastern California Museum, Independence, California.
1997 Oral history interview with Dugan Hanson, February 19. On file at the Eastern California Museum, Independence.

Preston, William
1996 The Serpent in Eden: Dispersal of Foreign Diseases into Pre-Mission California. *Journal of California and Great Basin Anthropology* 18(1):2–97.

Priestman, Mabel Tuke
1908 *Art and Economy in Home Decoration.* New York: John Lane.

Prince, Eugene R.
1986 Shoshonean Pottery of the Western Great Basin. In *Pottery of the Great Basin and Adjacent Areas,* edited by Suzanne Griset, pp. 3–8. University of Utah Anthropological Papers 111. Salt Lake City: University of Utah Press.

Purdum, Todd S.
1997 This Time, Los Angeles May Lose Water War. *New York Times,* June 15, A1, A14.

Randolph, Minnie C.
1902 Letter to C. Hart Merriam, June 5. C. Hart Merriam Collection, Bancroft Library, University of California, Berkeley.

1917 Letter to Horatio Shumway Lee, September 28. Accession file no. 625. Phoebe Apperson Hearst Museum of Anthropology, University of California, Berkeley.
1918 Letter to Horatio Shumway Lee, February 8. Accession file no. 625. Phoebe Apperson Hearst Museum of Anthropology, University of California, Berkeley.

Reed, Adele
1982 *Old Mammoth.* Palo Alto, California: Genny Smith Books.

Reisner, Marc
1987 *Cadillac Desert: The American West and Its Disappearing Water.* New York: Penguin Books.

Ringler, Donald P.
1963 Mary Austin: Kern County Days. *Southern California Quarterly* 45(1):25–64.

Roscoe, Will
1987 Bibliography of Berdach and Alternative Gender Roles Among North American Indians. *Journal of Homosexuality* 14(3–4):81–171.
1998 *Changing Ones: Third and Fourth Genders in Native North America.* New York: St. Martin's Griffin.

San Diego Union
1917 Indian Baskets Are Displayed. March 4.

Sargent, Homer E.
n.d. Catalog cards, nos. 660 and 957. Field Museum, Department of Anthropology, Chicago.
1908a Letter to C. Hart Merriam, May 21. C. Hart Merriam Collection, Bancroft Library, University of California, Berkeley.
1908b Catalog card no. 452 (102975, Field Museum), August 12. Field Museum, Department of Anthropology, Chicago.
1916 Letter to Mr. H., April 29, Big Pine, California. Grace Nicholson Collection, Huntington Library, San Marino, California.

Sauder, Robert A.
1993 *The Lost Frontier: Water Diversion in the Growth and Destruction of Owens Valley Agriculture.* Tucson: University of Arizona Press.

Schultheis, Robert
1975 Hand Game. *Mountain Gazette* 9(75):15–19.

Scott, Lala
1966 *Karnee: A Paiute Narrative.* Reno: University of Nevada Press.

Sennett-Graham, Beth
1989 Basketry: A Clue to Panamint-Shoshone Culture in the Early Twentieth Century. Master's thesis, University of Nevada, Reno.

Seymour, Flora W.
1928 Letter to Hon. Samuel A. Eliot, Chairman, Board of Indian Commissioners, Washington D.C., August 15. Record Group 75, Sacramento Area Office, Box 24. National Archives Federal Records Center, San Bruno, California.

Shepard, Clarence E.
1909 Collecting Indian Baskets. *Home and Garden* 15(12):199.

Simon, Ted
1994 *The River Stops Here.* New York: Random House.

Slater, Eva

1985a Panamint Shoshone Basketry, 1920–1940, at the Bowers Museum. *American Indian Art* 11(1):58–63, 75.

1985b Panamint Shoshone Basketry, 1920–1940. *American Indian Basketry and Other Native Arts* 5(3):18–20.

1986 Panamint-Shoshone Basketry, A Change of Style. In *Native American Basketry of Central California,* by Christopher L. Moser, pp. 19–20. Riverside, California: Riverside Museum Press.

2000 *Panamint Shoshone Basketry: An American Art Form.* Morongo Valley, California: Sagebrush Press.

Smith, Genny S., editor

1978 *Deepest Valley: A Guide to Owens Valley, Its Roadsides and Mountain Trails.* Palo Alto: Genny Smith Books.

1995 *Deepest Valley: A Guide to Owens Valley, Its Roadsides and Mountain Trails.* 2nd ed. Palo Alto: Live Oak Press.

Smith, Gerald A., and Ruth Dee Simpson

n.d. *Indian Basket Makers of San Bernardino County.* Bloomington, California: San Bernardino County Museum.

Smith-Ferri, Sherrie

1996 Hidden at the Heard: The Harvey Company Pomo Collection. In *The Great Southwest of the Fred Harvey Company and the Santa Fe Railway,* edited by Marta Weigle and Barbara Babcock, pp. 125–140. Phoenix: Heard Museum.

Spier, Robert F. G.

1978 Monache. In *California,* edited by Robert F. Heizer, pp. 426–436. *Handbook of North American Indians, vol. 8, William C. Sturtevant, general editor.* Washington, D.C.: Smithsonian Institution.

Star

1901 Basketmaking Now a Fad. *The Star,* March 12. On file at the Bancroft Library, University of California, Berkeley.

Starr, Laura B.

1889 An Indian Room. *Decorator and Furnisher* 14(2):38.

Steward, Julian H.

n.d. Manuscript and typescript of "Some Western Shoshone Myths." University of Illinois Archives, Julian H. Steward Papers, Box 10. University of Illinois, Urbana-Champaign.

1933 Ethnography of Owens Valley Paiute. *University of California Publications in American Archaeology and Ethnology* 33(3):233–350. Berkeley.

1934 Two Paiute Autobiographies. *University of California Publications in American Archaeology and Ethnology* 33(5):423–438. Berkeley.

1936a Myths of the Owens Valley Paiute. *University of California Publications in American Archaeology and Ethnology* 34(5):355–440. Berkeley.

1936b Shoshoni Polyandry. *American Anthropologist,* 38(4):561–564.

1937 Linguistic Distributions and Political Groups of the Great Basin Shoshoneans. *American Anthropologist* 39(4):625–634.

1938a *Basin-Plateau Aboriginal Socio-Political Groups.* Bureau of American Ethnology Bulletin 120. Washington, D.C.

1938b Panatübiji', an Owens Valley Paiute. Anthropological Papers 6. *Bureau of American Ethnology Bulletin* 119:183–195. Washington, D.C.

1941 Cultural Element Distributions, XIII: Nevada Shoshone. *University of California Anthropological Records* 4(2):209–360. Berkeley.

1943 Some Western Shoshone Myths. Anthropological Papers 31. *Bureau of American Ethnology Bulletin* 136:249–299. Washington, D.C.

Stewart, Mary

1936 Report to Superintendent Alida C. Bowler on Indian Schools in Mono and Inyo Counties, June 9. Record Group 75, Carson Agency, Decimal Subject Files, 1912–1950, Box 58. National Archives Federal Records Center, San Bruno, California.

Stewart, Omer

1941 Cultural Element Distributions, XIV: Northern Paiute. *University of California Anthropological Records* 4(3):361–446. Berkeley.

Sutton, Mark Q.

1988 *Insects as Food: Aboriginal Entomophagy in the Great Basin.* Ballena Press Anthropological Papers 33. Menlo Park, California: Ballena Press.

Taber, Cornelia

1911 *California and Her Indian Children.* San Jose: Northern California Indian Association.

Telles, Lucy

1915 Letter to Miss Estella Falla, November 10. Accession no. 2959, Yosemite Museum, Yosemite National Park, California.

1919 Letter to Joe Ammis [*sic*], October 31. Accession no. 1766-G, Southwest Museum, Los Angeles.

Thomas, David Hurst, Lorann S. A. Putnam, and Stephen C. Cappanari

1986 Western Shoshoni. In *Great Basin,* edited by Warren d'Azevedo, pp. 262–283. Handbook of North American Indians, vol. 11, William C. Sturtevant, general editor. Washington, D.C.: Smithsonian Institution.

Tisdale, Shelby J.

2001 Intermontane West. In *Woven Worlds: Basketry from the Clark Field Collection at the Philbrook Museum of Art,* edited by Lydia L. Wyckoff, pp. 79–105. Tulsa: Philbrook Museum of Art.

Twain, Mark

1993 *Roughing It.* Reprint. Los Angeles: University of California Press. Originally published 1872.

Uhlmeyer, Clarice Tate

1991a Maggie Deep Springs Jim. *The Album* 4(1):20–22.

1991b Mahala Joe. *The Album* 4(2):44–47.

U.S. Department of Commerce, Bureau of the Census

2000 http://www.census.gov/gfd/states/06/06027/html.

1915 *Indian Population in the United States and Canada, 1910.* Washington, D.C.: Government Printing Office.

U.S. Department of the Interior

1860 *Report of the Secretary of the Interior Communicating the Correspondence Between the Indian Office and the Present Superintendents and Agents in California, and J. Ross Browne, Esq., Together with the Report of the Commissioner of Indian Affairs.* Washington, D.C.

U.S. Senate, Committee on Indian Affairs

1934 *Survey of the Conditions of the Indians in the United States. Part 29, California.* Hearings before a Subcommittee of the Committee on Indian Affairs, September 20, 1932. 72d Congress, 1st session. Washington, D.C.: Government Printing Office.

Walter, Nancy Peterson

1986   The Land Exchange Act of 1937: Creation of the Indian Reservations at Bishop, Big Pine, and Lone Pine, California, Through a Land Trade Between the United States of America and the City of Los Angeles. Ph.D. dissertation, Department of Anthropology, Union Graduate School.

Walton, John

1992   *Western Times and Water Wars: State, Culture, and Rebellion in California.* Berkeley: University of California Press.

Wheat, Margaret M.

1967   *Survival Arts of the Primitive Paiutes.* Reno: University of Nevada Press.

1976   Pitch n' Willows. *International Native Arts and Crafts* 1:22–23.

Whitehead, Harriet

1981   The Bow and the Burden Strap: A New Look at Institutionalized Homosexuality in Native North America. In *Sexual Meanings: The Cultural Construction of Gender and Sexuality,* edited by Sherry B. Ortner and Harriet Whitehead, pp. 80–115. Cambridge: Cambridge University Press.

Whitney, J. D.

1865   *Report of Progress and Synopsis of the Field-Work from 1860–1864, Vol. 1, Geology.* Geological Survey of California. Philadelphia: Caxton Press of Sherman and Co.

Wilcomb, C. P.

1903   Letter to C. Hart Merriam, October 6. C. Hart Merriam Collection, Bancroft Library, University of California, Berkeley.

Wiley, Ross B.

1936   Letter to Parents of Carson Indian School Students, April 28. Record Group 75, Carson Agency, Decimal Subject Files, 1912–1950, Box 60. National Archives Federal Records Center, San Bruno, California.

1938   Letter to Ellsworth E. R. Wallace, Director of Counsel Guidance and Research, Providence, Rhode Island, March 23. Record Group 75, Carson Agency, Decimal Subject Files, 1912–1950, Box 60. National Archives Federal Records Center, San Bruno, California.

Wilke, Philip J., and Harry W. Lawton

1976   *The Expedition of Capt. J. W. Davidson from Fort Tejon to the Owens Valley in 1859.* Ballena Press Publications in Archaeology, Ethnology, and History 8. Socorro, New Mexico: Ballena Press.

Williams, Walter L.

1986   *The Spirit and the Flesh: Sexual Diversity in American Indian Culture.* Boston: Beacon.

Winslow, Isabel Bates

1901   Modern Basket Makers. *Los Angeles Times,* December 29.

Wortley, Ken

1959   Alec Ramy's Lost Bonanza. *Desert Magazine* (May): 24–26.

Wyckoff, Lydia L., editor

2001   *Woven Worlds: Basketry from the Clark Field Collection at the Philbrook Museum of Art.* Tulsa, Oklahoma: Philbrook Museum of Art.

Zigmond, Maurice L.

1978   Kawaiisu Basketry. *Journal of California Anthropology* 5(2): 199–215.

1979   Gottlieb Adam Steiner and the G. A. Steiner Museum. *Journal of California and Great Basin Anthropology* 1(2):199–215.

1980   *Kawaiisu Mythology: An Oral Tradition of South-Central California.* Ballena Press Anthropological Papers 18. Socorro, New Mexico: Ballena Press.

FIGURE CREDITS

Frontis
Photograph by Sharon Dean, 1996

Figure 1.1
L. approx. 75 cm
Photograph by Sharon E. Dean, 1998

Figure 1.2
Prepared by Gwen Jensen

Figure 1.3
Prepared by Peggy S. Ratcheson

Figure 1.4
Photograph by Andrew A. Forbes
Courtesy, County of Inyo, Eastern California
    Museum, neg. no. FOR 63

Figure 1.5.
Photograph by A. E. Holt, ca. 1920
Courtesy, National Park Service, Death Valley
    National Park, neg. no. DEVA 38627

Figure 1.6.
Photograph by Mark Harrington
Courtesy, The Southwest Museum, neg. no.
    P2297

Figure 1.7
Photograph by Andrew A. Forbes
Courtesy, Seaver Center for Western History
    Research, Los Angeles County Museum
    of Natural History, neg. no. F63

Figure 1.8
Collected by Anna Kelley
Willow rods, split willow, sunburned willow,
    paint
H. 14 cm, D. 23 cm
Photograph by Bruce Frumker and Greg
    Petusky
Courtesy, The Cleveland Museum of Natural
    History

Figure 1.9
H. 21.5 cm, D. 23.5 cm
Courtesy, County of Inyo, Eastern California
    Museum, cat. no. 81.64

Figure 1.10
Collected by Anna Kelley

Willow rods, split willow, split redbud shoots
H. 54 cm, D. 49.6 cm
Photograph by Bruce Frumker and Greg
    Petusky
Courtesy, The Cleveland Museum of Natural
    History

Figure 1.11
Photograph by Andrew A. Forbes
Courtesy, County of Inyo, Eastern California
    Museum, neg. no. FOR 65

Figure 1.12
Collected by J. W. Hudson near Indepen-
    dence, California, 1904
Willow rods, split willow shoots
H. 14", D. 10"
Courtesy, The Field Museum, cat. no. 59006

Figure 1.13
Collected by Anna Kelley
Willow rods, split willow shoots
H. 9 cm, L. 54 cm, W. 26 cm
Photograph by Bruce Frumker and Greg
    Petusky
Courtesy, The Cleveland Museum of Natural
    History

Figure 1.14
Collected by Anna Kelley
Willow rods, split willow shoots
H. 12.0 cm, L. 29.5 cm
Photograph by Bruce Frumker and Greg
    Petusky
Courtesy, The Cleveland Museum of Natural
    History

Figure 1.15
Photograph by Andrew A. Forbes
Courtesy, Seaver Center for Western History
    Research, Los Angeles County Museum
    of Natural History, neg. no. F2401

Figure 1.16
Photograph by Andrew A. Forbes
Courtesy, Seaver Center for Western History
    Research, Los Angeles County Museum
    of Natural History, neg. no. F5918

Figure 1.17
Photograph by Andrew A. Forbes
Courtesy, County of Inyo, Eastern California
    Museum, neg. no. FOR 62

Figure 1.18
Collected by Anna Kelley
Willow rods, split willow shoots, piñon pine
    pitch, red earth, commercial cotton
    cordage
H. 35 cm, circum. 84.5 cm, D. 26.9 cm
Photograph by Bruce Frumker and Greg
    Petusky
Courtesy, The Cleveland Museum of Natural
    History

Figure 1.19
Photograph by Bruce Frumker and Greg
    Petusky
Courtesy, The Cleveland Museum of Natural
    History

Figure 1.20
Photograph by Burton Frasher Sr.
Courtesy, The Marie Rozier Collection, The
    Yosemite Museum, Yosemite National
    Park, neg. no. RL-15,298

Figure 2.1
Prepared by Peggy S. Ratcheson

Figure 2.2
Photograph by Andrew A. Forbes
Courtesy, Seaver Center for Western History
    Research, Los Angeles County Museum
    of Natural History, neg. no. F1038.

Figure 2.3
Photograph by Sharon E. Dean, 1998

Figure 2.4
Photographer unknown
Courtesy, County of Inyo, Eastern California
    Museum, neg. no. UNK 826

Figure 2.5
Photograph by Andrew A. Forbes
Courtesy, Seaver Center for Western History
    Research, Los Angeles County Museum
    of Natural History, neg. no. F161

Figure 2.6
Photograph by Andrew A. Forbes
Courtesy, Seaver Center for Western History
 Research, Los Angeles County Museum
 of Natural History, neg. no. F 2405.

Figure 2.7
Photograph by Andrew A. Forbes
Courtesy, Seaver Center for Western History
 Research, Los Angeles County Museum
 of Natural History, neg. no. 6868 C.

Figure 2.8
Collected by Anna Kelley, ca. 1940
Willow rods, split willow, canvas, commercial
 leather, cotton string
H. 67.0 cm, D. 70 cm
Photograph by Bruce Frumker and Greg
 Petusky
Courtesy, The Cleveland Museum of Natural
 History

Figure 2.9
Ninth, Tenth, Eleventh, Twelfth, Thirteenth,
 Fourteenth, and Fifteenth U.S. Census
 of Population and U.S. Census of
 Agriculture.

Figure 2.10
Photographer unknown
Courtesy, County of Inyo, Eastern California
 Museum, LAWP no. 16

Figure 2.11
Photographer unknown
Courtesy, County of Inyo, Eastern California
 Museum, LAWP no. 14

Figure 2.12
Photographer unknown
Courtesy, County of Inyo, Eastern California
 Museum, cat. no. UNK 1049

Figure 2.13
Photograph by Andrew A. Forbes
Courtesy, Seaver Center for Western History
 Research, Los Angeles County Museum
 of Natural History, neg. no. F133

Figure 2.14
Photographer unknown
Courtesy, The Los Angeles Department of
 Water and Power

Figure 2.15
Photographer unknown
Courtesy, County of Inyo, Eastern California
 Museum, no. Forbes 46

Figure 2.16
Photograph by Sharon Dean, 1998

Figure 3.1
Prepared by Gwen Jensen

Figure 3.2
Prepared by Gwen Jensen

Figure 3.3
Prepared by Gwen Jensen

Figure 3.4
Photograph by Andrew A. Forbes
Courtesy, Seaver Center for Western History
 Research, Los Angeles County Museum
 of Natural History, neg. no. 5912

Figure 3.5
Collected by Rose Black, Big Pine, California,
 ca. 1910
Willow rods, split willow, split willow with
 inner bark, dye, buckskin
H. 15 cm, D. 22.5 cm
Photograph by Andrew D. Finger
Courtesy, County of Inyo, Eastern California
 Museum, cat. no. B243

Figure 3.6
Interior of Plate 3

Figure 3.7
Collected by Rose Black, Big Pine, California,
 ca. 1910
Willow rods, split willow, split willow with
 inner bark, dye, brain-tanned deerskin
H. 15 cm, D. 23.125 cm
Photograph by Andrew D. Finger
Courtesy, County of Inyo, Eastern California
 Museum, cat. no. B294

Figure 3.8
Purchased by C. Hart Merriam, Indepen-
 dence, California, 1902
Willow rods, split willow, split willow with
 inner bark, dye
H. 14.5 cm, D. 23 cm
Photograph by Andrew D. Finger
Courtesy, C. Hart Merriam Basket Collection,
 Department of Anthropology Museum,
 University of California, Davis, cat. no. 507

Figure 3.9
Collected by Rose Black, Big Pine, California,
 ca. 1910
Willow rods, split willow, split willow with
 inner bark, dye
H. 12.5 cm, D. 22.5 cm
Photograph by Andrew D. Finger
Courtesy, County of Inyo, Eastern California
 Museum, cat. no. B298

Figure 3.10
Willow rods, split willow, split willow with
 inner bark, dye
H. 16 cm, D. 21.5 cm
Photograph by Judith W. Finger
Courtesy, The Phoebe Apperson Hearst
 Museum of Anthropology and the

Regents of the University of California,
 cat. no. 1–70601

Figure 3.11
Collected by Rose Black, Big Pine, California,
 ca. 1910
Willow rods, split willow, split willow with
 inner bark, dye, brain-tanned deerskin
H. 12.5 cm, D. 22.5 cm
Photograph by Andrew D. Finger
Courtesy, County of Inyo, Eastern California
 Museum, cat. no. B295

Figure 3.12a
Collected by C. Hart Merriam, Keeler, Califor-
 nia, 1902
Willow rods, split willow, split willow with
 inner bark, dye
H. 13.5 cm, D. 22 cm
Photograph by Andrew D. Finger
Courtesy, C. Hart Merriam Basket Collection,
 Department of Anthropology Museum,
 University of California, Davis, cat. no. 592A

Figure 3.12b
Collected by C. Hart Merriam, Lone Pine,
 California, 1909
Willow rods, split willow, split willow with
 inner bark, dye, commercial yarn
H. 13 cm, D. 21 cm
Photograph by Andrew D. Finger
Courtesy, C. Hart Merriam Basket Collection,
 Department of Anthropology Museum,
 University of California, Davis, cat. no. 508

Figure 3.13
Collected by Grace Geyer, ca. 1910, gift to
 Anna Kelley
Willow rods, split willow, split willow with
 inner bark, dye
H. 13 cm, D. 20.5 cm
Photograph by Bruce Frumker and Greg
 Petusky
Courtesy, The Cleveland Museum of Natural
 History

Figure 3.14
Collected by Julian H. Steward, Big Pine,
 California, 1927
Willow rods, split willow, canvas, brain-
 tanned deerskin
H. 62.5 cm, D. 55.5 cm
Photograph by Judith W. Finger
Courtesy, The Phoebe Apperson Hearst
 Museum of Anthropology and the
 Regents of the University of California,
 cat. no. 1–26988

Figure 3.15
Collected by Julian H. Steward, Big Pine,
 California, 1927
Willow rods, split willow, split willow with
 inner bark, dye, canvas

H. 42 cm, D. 42 cm
Photograph by Judith W. Finger
Courtesy, The Phoebe Apperson Hearst
    Museum of Anthropology and the
    Regents of the University of California,
    cat. no. 1–26990

Figure 3.16
Collected by E. W. Gifford, Bishop, California,
    1915
Willow rods, split willow, split willow with
    inner bark
L. 73 cm, W. 41 cm
Photograph by Judith W. Finger
Courtesy, The Phoebe Apperson Hearst
    Museum of Anthropology and the
    Regents of the University of California,
    cat. no. 1–19673

Figure 3.17
Collected by E. W. Gifford, Bishop, California,
    1915
Willow rods, split willow, split willow with
    inner bark
L. 73 cm, W. 41 cm
Photograph by Judith W. Finger
Courtesy, The Phoebe Apperson Hearst
    Museum of Anthropology and the
    Regents of the University of California,
    cat. no. 1–19673

Figure 3.18
Collected by C. Hart Merriam, Bishop, Califor-
    nia, 1901
Willow rods, split willow
L. 36.5 cm, W. 29 cm
Photograph by Andrew D. Finger
Courtesy, C. Hart Merriam Basket Collection,
    Department of Anthropology Museum,
    University of California, Davis, cat. no. 512

Figure 3.19
Collected by C. Hart Merriam, Bishop, Califor-
    nia, 1901
Willow rods, split willow, split willow with
    inner bark, dye
L. 53 cm, W. 44 cm
Photograph by Andrew D. Finger
Courtesy, C. Hart Merriam Basket Collection,
    Department of Anthropology Museum,
    University of California, Davis, cat. no. 513

Figure 3.20
Collected by C. Hart Merriam, Bishop, Califor-
    nia, 1901
Willow rods, split willow, split willow with
    inner bark, dye
L. 53 cm, W. 44 cm
Photograph by Andrew D. Finger
Courtesy, C. Hart Merriam Basket Collection,
    Department of Anthropology Museum,
    University of California, Davis, cat. no. 513

Figure 3.21
Collected by Horatio Shumway Lee, possibly
    purchased from Minnie Randolph in
    Round Valley, California, ca. 1910
Willow rods, split willow
L. 26.5 cm
Photograph by Judith W. Finger
Courtesy, The Phoebe Apperson Hearst
    Museum of Anthropology and the
    Regents of the University of California,
    cat. no. 1–26841

Figure 3.22
Collected by Julian H. Steward, Fish Springs,
    California, 1927
Willow rods, split willow
L. 56 cm, W. 21 cm
Photograph by Judith W. Finger
Courtesy, The Phoebe Apperson Hearst
    Museum of Anthropology and the
    Regents of the University of California,
    cat. no. 1–26983

Figure 3.23
Photograph by Andrew A. Forbes
Courtesy, Seaver Center for Western History
    Research, Los Angeles County Museum
    of Natural History, neg. no. 64

Figure 3.24
Collected by Julian H. Steward, Big Pine, Cal-
    ifornia, 1927
Willow rods, split willow, cloth
L. 67 cm, W. 25 cm
Photograph by Judith W. Finger
Courtesy, The Phoebe Apperson Hearst
    Museum of Anthropology and the
    Regents of the University of California,
    cat. no. 1–26987

Figure 3.25
Photograph by Andrew A. Forbes
Courtesy, Seaver Center for Western History
    Research, Los Angeles County Museum
    of Natural History, neg. no. 2340

Figure 3.26
Collected by Horatio Shumway Lee, possibly
    from Minnie Randolph, Round Valley, Cali-
    fornia, ca. 1910
Willow rods, split willow, commercial
    cordage
H. 49 cm, D. 25 cm
Photograph by Judith W. Finger
Courtesy, The Phoebe Apperson Hearst
    Museum of Anthropology and the
    Regents of the University of California,
    cat. no. 1–26834

Figure 3.27
Collected by J. W. Hudson near Indepen-
    dence, California, 1904

Tule
L. 30 cm, W. 27.5 cm
Photograph by Andrew D. Finger
Courtesy, The Field Museum, cat. no. 59007

Figure 3.28
Prepared by Gwen Jensen

Figure 3.29
Collected by C. Hart Merriam, Bishop, Califor-
    nia, 1901
Sedge root, bracken fern root, deer grass
H. 18.5 cm, D. 42.5 cm
Photograph by Andrew D. Finger
Courtesy, C. Hart Merriam Basket Collection,
    Department of Anthropology Museum,
    University of California, Davis, cat. no. 540

Figure 3.30
Collected by Mrs. Hugh Patrick (Frankie)
    Beatty
Willow rods, split willow, devil's claw
H. 14.3 cm, D. 30.0 cm
Photograph by Michael Dixon
Courtesy, Donna Burgner Collection, The
    Yosemite Museum, Yosemite National
    Park, cat. no. YM 25511

Figure 3.31
Collected by C. Hart Merriam, Lone Pine, Cal-
    ifornia, 1909
Willow rods, split willow, bulrush root
H. 4 cm, D. 43.5 cm
Photograph by Andrew D. Finger
Courtesy, C. Hart Merriam Basket Collection,
    Department of Anthropology Museum,
    University of California, Davis, cat. no. 510

Figure 3.32
Collected by John Hudson, Owens Lake, Inyo
    County, California, 1904
Willow rods, split willow, bulrush root
H. 21.25 cm
Photograph by Judith W. Finger
Courtesy, The Field Museum, cat. no. 58983

Figure 3.33
Collected by C. Hart Merriam, Independence,
    California, 1902
Willow rods, split willow, devil's claw, bulrush
    root, common flicker quills
H. 12 cm, D. 24 cm
Photograph by Andrew D. Finger
Courtesy, C. Hart Merriam Basket Collection,
    Department of Anthropology Museum,
    University of California, Davis, cat. no. 504

Figure 3.34
Collected by C. Hart Merriam from Mrs. J. J.
    McLean, Independence, California, ca.
    1900
Willow rods, split willow, bracken fern root

H. 8 cm, D. 9 cm
Photograph by Andrew D. Finger
Courtesy, C. Hart Merriam Basket Collection,
    Department of Anthropology Museum,
    University of California, Davis, cat. no. 501

Figure 3.35
Willow rods, split willow, devil's claw
H. 53 cm, D. 37.5 cm
Photograph by Andrew D. Finger
Courtesy, private collection

Figure 3.36
Willow rods, split willow, bracken fern root,
    redbud
H. 21.5 cm, D. 43.5 cm
Photograph by Bruce Frumker and Greg
    Petusky
Courtesy, The Cleveland Museum of Natural
    History

Figure 3.37
Collected by Horatio Shumway Lee, possibly
    from Minnie Randolph, Bishop, California
Willow rods, split willow, bracken fern root
H. 18.75 cm, D. 35 cm
Photograph by Judith W. Finger
Courtesy, The Phoebe Apperson Hearst
    Museum of Anthropology and the
    Regents of the University of California,
    cat. no. 1–26887

Figure 3.38
Collected by Rose Black, Big Pine, ca. 1910
Willow rods, split willow, bulrush root
H. 15 cm, W. 15 cm
Photograph by Andrew D. Finger
Courtesy, County of Inyo, Eastern California
    Museum, cat. no. B206

Figure 3.39
Collected by Horatio Shumway Lee, possibly
    from Minnie Randolph, Bishop, California
Willow rods, split willow, bracken fern root,
    redbud
H. 13 cm, D. 25.5 cm
Photograph by Judith W. Finger
Courtesy, The Phoebe Apperson Hearst
    Museum of Anthropology and the
    Regents of the University of California,
    cat. no. 1–26890

Figure 3.40
Collected by Horatio Shumway Lee, possibly
    from Minnie Randolph, Bishop, California
Willow rods, split willow, bracken fern root,
    redbud
H. 11.25 cm, D. 11.5 cm
Photograph by Judith W. Finger
Courtesy, The Phoebe Apperson Hearst
    Museum of Anthropology and the
    Regents of the University of California,
    cat. no. 1–26888

Figure 3.41
Photograph by Andrew A. Forbes
Courtesy, Seaver Center for Western History
    Research, Los Angeles County Museum
    of Natural History, neg. no. 1762

Figure 3.42
Collection of the Laws Railroad Museum and
    Historical Site

Figure 3.43
Photograph by Andrew A. Forbes
Courtesy, Seaver Center for Western History
    Research, Los Angeles County Museum
    of Natural History, neg. no. 2355

Figure 3.44
Photograph by Andrew A. Forbes
Courtesy, Seaver Center for Western History
    Research, Los Angeles County Museum
    of Natural History, neg. no. 2317

Figure 3.45
Photographer unknown
Courtesy, Dorothy Stanley Collection, The
    Yosemite Museum, Yosemite National
    Park, neg. no. RL-14238

Figure 3.46
Purchased from the maker by Anna Kelley,
    Independence, California, 1943
Willow rods, split willow, redbud
L. 29 cm, W. 29 cm, D. 17 cm
Photograph by Bruce Frumker and Greg
    Petusky
Courtesy, The Cleveland Museum of Natural
    History

Figure 3.47
Collected by Anna Kelley
Willow rods, split willow, bulrush root, yucca
    root
H. 11 cm, D. 13.5 cm
Photograph by Bruce Frumker and Greg
    Petusky
Courtesy, The Cleveland Museum of Natural
    History

Figure 3.48
Photographer unknown
Courtesy, National Archives, Washington,
    D.C.

Figure 3.49
Collected by Anna Kelley, Independence, Cali-
    fornia, 1943
Willow rods, split willow, bulrush root, juncus
H. 9 cm, D. 10 cm
Photograph by Bruce Frumker and Greg
    Petusky
Courtesy, The Cleveland Museum of Natural
    History

Figure 3.50
Photograph by C. Hart Merriam
Courtesy, The Bancroft Library, University of
    California, Berkeley

Figure 3.51
Made by Nellie Charlie for her granddaughter,
    Elma Blaver
Willow, split willow, redbud, bracken fern
    root
H. 21.0 cm, D. 61.0 cm
Photograph by Michael Dixon
Courtesy, Elma Blaver Collection, The
    Yosemite Museum, Yosemite National
    Park, cat. no. YM 37859

Figure 3.52
Photographer unknown
Courtesy, Elma Blaver

Figure 3.53
Photographer unknown
Courtesy, Elma Blaver

Figure 3.54
Photograph by Sharon E. Dean, 1998

Figure 3.55
Willow, sedge root, redbud, bracken fern
H. 8.0 cm, D. 14.9 cm
Photograph by Craig D. Bates
Courtesy, private collection

Figure 3.56
Collected by Rose Black, Big Pine, California,
    ca. 1910
Willow rods, split willow, bulrush root (?)
L. 25 cm, W. 17.5 cm, H. 10 cm
Photograph by Andrew D. Finger
Courtesy, County of Inyo, Eastern California
    Museum, cat. no. B71

Figure 3.57
Photograph by C. Hart Merriam
Courtesy, C. Hart Merriam Collection, The
    Bancroft Library, University of California,
    Berkeley, neg. no. 7 P2 35 3

Figure 3.58 (right)
Collected by Anna Kelley, Independence,
    California
Willow rods, split willow, dyed bulrush root,
    devil's claw, juncus
H. 11 cm, L. 28 cm, W. 22 cm
Photograph by Bruce Frumker and Greg
    Petusky
Courtesy, The Cleveland Museum of Natural
    History

Figure 3.58 (left)
Collected by Anna Kelley, Independence,
    California
Willow rods, split willow, bulrush root, juncus

H. 10.5 cm, D. 16.5 cm
Photograph by Bruce Frumker and Greg
Petusky
Courtesy, The Cleveland Museum of Natural
History

Figure 3.59
Collected by Anna Kelley
Willow rods, split willow, bulrush root, yucca
root
H. 10 cm, D. 25.5 cm
Photograph by Bruce Frumker and Greg
Petusky
Courtesy, The Cleveland Museum of Natural
History

Figure 3.60
Photographer unknown
Courtesy, County of Inyo, Eastern California
Museum, neg. no. MECH 86

Figure 3.61
Collected by Julian Steward, 1927
Willow rods, split willow, split willow with
inner bark, dye
H. 18.5 cm, D. 23 cm
Photograph by Judith W. Finger
Courtesy, The Phoebe Apperson Hearst
Museum of Anthropology and the
Regents of the University of California,
cat. no. 1–26992

Figure 3.62
Photograph by Dane Coolidge
Courtesy, The Bancroft Library, University of
California, Berkeley

Figure 3.63
Photographer unknown
Courtesy, County of Inyo, Eastern California
Museum, neg. no. KERR 5a

Figure 3.64
Purchased by Dale Inkley from Sarah Hunter,
1943
Willow rods, split willow, dyed bulrush root,
juncus
L. 23.5 cm, W. 16.5 cm, H. 7.0 cm
Photograph by Bruce Frumker and Greg
Petusky
Courtesy, The Cleveland Museum of Natural
History, cat. no. 2001-.19aL

Figure 3.65
Photograph by Andrew A. Forbes
Courtesy, County of Inyo, Eastern California
Museum, neg. no. UNK 1521

Figure 3.66
Collected by Horatio Shumway Lee, possibly
from Minnie Randolph, Bishop, California,
ca. 1920
Willow rods, split willow, bracken fern root

H. 10.8 cm, D. 16.4 cm
Photograph by Judith W. Finger
Courtesy, The Phoebe Apperson Hearst
Museum of Anthropology and the
Regents of the University of California,
cat. no. 1–26875

Figure 3.67
Collected by Mrs. Hugh Patrick (Frankie)
Beatty
Willow, willow rods, glass beads 11/0 size
H. 12.5 cm, D. 12 cm
Photograph by Michael Dixon
Courtesy, Donna Burgner collection, The
Yosemite Museum, Yosemite National
Park, cat. no. YM 25504

Figure 3.68
Collected by Mrs. Hugh Patrick (Frankie)
Beatty
Willow, willow rods, glass beads 11/0 size
H. approx. 12.5 cm, D. approx. 12 cm
Photograph by Michael Dixon
Courtesy, Donna Burgner collection, The
Yosemite Museum, Yosemite National
Park, cat. no. YM 25505

Figure 3.69
Photographer unknown
Courtesy, County of Inyo, Eastern California
Museum, neg. no. McM 13

Figure 3.70
Photographer unknown
Courtesy, Jessie Durant

Figure 3.71
Photographer unknown
Courtesy, Jessie Durant

Figure 3.72
Collected by Horatio Shumway Lee, possibly
from Minnie Randolph at Bishop, Califor-
nia, ca. 1906
Willow rods, sedge root, bracken fern root
H. 14.5 cm
Photograph by Judith W. Finger
Courtesy, The Phoebe Apperson Hearst
Museum of Anthropology and the
Regents of the University of California,
cat. no. 1–26857

Figure 3.73
Photographer unknown
Courtesy, County of Inyo, Eastern California
Museum, no. JEW 26

Figure 3.74
Photographer unknown
Courtesy, County of Inyo, Eastern California
Museum, neg. no. UNK 1401

Figure 3.75
Collected by Anna Kelley, Independence,
California, ca. 1935
Willow rods, split willow
L. 62 cm, W. 50.5 cm, D. 14 cm
Photograph by Bruce Frumker and Greg
Petusky
Courtesy, The Cleveland Museum of Natural
History

Figure 3.76
Photographer unknown
Courtesy, Eleanor Bethel

Figure 3.77
Willow rods, split willow
L. approx. 72 cm
Photographer unknown
Courtesy, Arizona State Museum, cat.
no. E-5768

Figure 3.78
Collected by Rose Black in Big Pine,
California, ca. 1910
Willow rods, split willow, split willow with
inner bark, dye
H. 13.75 cm, D. 21.875 cm
Photograph by Andrew D. Finger
Courtesy, County of Inyo, Eastern California
Museum, cat. no. B278

Figure 3.79
Collected by Rose Black, Big Pine, California,
ca. 1910
Willow rods, split willow, devil's claw
H. 11.25 cm, D. 25 cm
Photograph by Andrew D. Finger
Courtesy, County of Inyo, Eastern California
Museum, cat. no. B155

Figure 4.1
Photographer unknown
Photograph from Grace Nicholson's Album A
This item is reproduced by permission of The
Huntington Library, San Marino, California

Figure 4.2
Photograph by Bruce Frumker and Greg
Petusky
Courtesy, The Cleveland Museum of Natural
History

Figure 4.3
Courtesy, private collection

Figure 4.4
Purchased from Mary Jim Harry by Julian
Steward, Big Pine, California, July 1927
Willow rods, split willow
L. 68.5 cm, W. 40.0 cm
Photograph by Judith W. Finger
Courtesy, The Phoebe Apperson Hearst
Museum of Anthropology and the

Regents of the University of California, cat. no. 1–26986

Figure 4.5
Collected by Harry Floyd, sold to H. E. Sargent, March 30, 1909
Willow rods, deer grass, sumac, devil's claw, Joshua tree root
H. 12.5 cm, Dia. at top 22.5 cm
Photograph by Judith W. Finger
Courtesy, The Field Museum, cat. no. 102996

Figure 4.6
Purchased by Mrs. Minnie C. Barrows (Randolph) from Sally at Independence in March 1902 for C. Hart Merriam
Willow rods, split willow, split winter-peeled willow with stain
D. 16.5 cm, H. 14.0 cm
Photograph by Judith W. Finger
Courtesy, C. Hart Merriam Basket Collection, Department of Anthropology Museum, University of California, Davis, cat. no. 502

Figure 4.7
Courtesy, C. Hart Merriam Basket Collection, Department of Anthropology Museum, University of California, Davis

Figure 4.8
Collected by J. W. Hudson near Big Pine, California, 1904
Willow rods, split willow
L. 45.6 cm
Photograph by Judith W. Finger
Courtesy, The Field Museum, cat. no. 59021

Figure 4.9
Collected by C. P. Wilcomb, ca. 1900
Willow rods (?), deer grass (?), split willow, Joshua tree root, bulrush root
H. 9.5 cm, D. 23.0 cm
Photograph by Martha J. Lee
Courtesy, Staatliche Museen zu Berlin, Ethnologisches Museum, Berlin, cat. no. IV.B. 12063

Figure 4.10
Collected by Andrew W. de la Cour Carroll in Keeler, California, ca. 1905
Willow rods, split willow, split devil's claw (?)
H. 11.5 cm, D. 13 cm
Photograph reproduced with the kind permission of the Trustees of the Museums & Galleries of Northern Ireland, cat. no. CLCC9, Ethnographical Collections, Ulster Museum, Belfast, photograph © Ulster Museum 2004

Figure 4.11
Collected by Andrew W. de la Cour Carroll, ca. 1905

Willow rods, split willow, Joshua tree root (?)
H. 5.0 cm, D. 20.0 cm
Photograph reproduced with the kind permission of the Trustees of the Museums & Galleries of Northern Ireland, cat. no. CLCC16, Ethnographical Collections, Ulster Museum, Belfast, photograph © Ulster Museum 2004

Figure 4.12
Acquired from C. P. Wilcomb by Andrew W. de la Cour Carroll, ca. 1900
Willow, yucca root, devil's claw, deer grass
H. 11 cm, D. 19 cm
Photograph reproduced with the kind permission of the Trustees of the Museums & Galleries of Northern Ireland, cat. no. 7.1946, Ethnographical Collections, Ulster Museum, Belfast, photograph © Ulster Museum 2004

Figure 4.13
Photographer unknown
Courtesy, Grace Nicholson Collection, The Phoebe Apperson Hearst Museum of Anthropology and the Regents of the University of California, ACC 2881, No. 5

Figure 4.14
This item is reproduced by permission of The Huntington Library, San Marino, California

Figure 4.15
Photographer unknown
Courtesy, Peggy Zimmerman

Figure 4.16
Photograph by H. W. Mendenhall
Courtesy, County of Inyo, Eastern California Museum, cat. no. H.W.M. 9A

Figure 4.17
Photographer unknown
Courtesy, Evelyn Hill Bacoch

Figure 4.18
Collected by Rose Black, Big Pine, California, ca. 1930
H. 10.5 cm, D. 27.5 cm
Willow rods, split willow, bulrush root
Courtesy, County of Inyo, Eastern California Museum, cat. no. B41

Figure 4.19
Collected by John S. and Helen S. MacQueen
Willow rods, split willow, split willow with inner bark, dye
H. 13.75 cm, D. 21.25 cm
Photograph by Dick Meier
Courtesy, Natural History Museum of Los Angeles County, Anthropology Section, MacQueen Collection, cat. no. F.A.1127.71–22

Figure 4.20
Photographer unknown, possibly Helen S. MacQueen
Courtesy, John MacQueen

Figure 4.21
Photograph by Andrew D. Finger

Figure 4.22
Photograph by Andrew A. Forbes
Courtesy, Seaver Center for Western History Research, Los Angeles County Museum of Natural History, neg. no. 5713

Figure 4.23
Photograph by Andrew A. Forbes
Courtesy, County of Inyo, Eastern California Museum, cat. no. 5978

Figure 4.24
Photographer unknown
Courtesy, The Dow Family

Figure 4.25
Photographer unknown
Courtesy, County of Inyo, Eastern California Museum, cat. no. Kel 12

Figure 4.26
Commissioned by Anna Kelley, 1943
Unidentified wooden fork, split willow, split redbud, willow rods, leather, sinew, wool yarn, imported seed and glass beads, commercial threads, cotton cloth
H. 127 cm, W. 23.0 cm
Photograph by Bruce Frumker and Greg Petusky
Courtesy, The Cleveland Museum of Natural History

Figure 4.27
Collected by Anna Kelley, Independence, California, ca. 1935
Willow rods, split willow, bulrush root
H. 19.5 cm, D. 41 cm
Photograph by Bruce Frumker and Greg Petusky
Courtesy, The Cleveland Museum of Natural History

Figure 4.28
Photograph by Judith W. Finger

Figure 4.29
Photographer unknown
Courtesy, County of Inyo, Eastern California Museum, cat. no. UNK 486

Figure 4.30
Photograph by Sharon E. Dean

Figure 4.31
Photograph by Andrew D. Finger

Figure 4.32
Photograph by Andrew D. Finger

Figure 4.33
Photograph by Andrew D. Finger

Figure 5.1
Photograph by Sharon E. Dean

Figure 5.2
Willow rods, split willow, canvas, cotton
   string
Collected by Anna Kelley
Photograph by Bruce Frumker and Greg
   Petusky
Courtesy, The Cleveland Museum of Natural
   History

Figure 5.3
Photograph by Andrew A. Forbes
Courtesy, Seaver Center for Western History
   Research, Los Angeles County Museum
   of Natural History, neg. no. 5906

Figure 5.4
Photographer unknown
Courtesy, The Yosemite Museum, Yosemite
   National Park, neg. no. RL-19468

Figure 5.5
Willow rods, conifer roots, maidenhair fern
   stem, woodwardia fern stem, raffia
H. 1–1.5 cm, D. 1–1.5 cm
Photograph by Bruce Frumker and Greg
   Petusky

Courtesy, The Cleveland Museum of Natural
   History

Figure 5.6
Photograph by Sharon E. Dean

Figure 5.7
Photograph by Ellen F. Daus

Figure 5.8
Photograph by Ellen F. Daus

Figure 5.9
Photograph by Michael Rogers
Courtesy, Alta Rogers

Figure 5.10
Photographer unknown
Courtesy, Lillian Andreas

Figure 5.11
Willow rods, split willow, deerskin
H. 20 cm, D. 14.5 cm
Photograph by Bruce Frumker and Greg
   Petusky
Courtesy, The Cleveland Museum of Natural
   History

Figure 5.12
Photograph by Ellen F. Daus

Figure 5.13
Photograph by Stan Summers
Courtesy, Bernadine Summers

Figure 5.14
Photograph by Peggy S. Ratcheson

Figure 5.15
Photograph by Ellen F. Daus

Figure 5.16
Photographer unknown
Courtesy, Gretchen Uhler Hess

Figure 5.17
Photograph by Sharon E. Dean

Figure 5.18
Sedge root, redbud, bracken fern root, willow
   rods
H. 5.0 cm, D. 5.5 cm
Photograph by Bruce Frumker and Greg
   Petusky
Courtesy, The Cleveland Museum of Natural
   History

Figure 5.19
Willow, dyed sedge root, redbud, willow rods
H. 17.6 cm, D. 25.7 cm
Photograph by Bruce Frumker and Greg
   Petusky
Courtesy, The Cleveland Museum of Natural
   History

Figure 5.20
Photograph by Sharon E. Dean

PLATE CREDITS

Plate 1
Photograph by Sharon E. Dean, 1994

Plate 2
Photograph by Sharon E. Dean, 1998

Plate 3
Collected by Horatio Shumway Lee, possibly
    from Minnie Randolph in Bishop, Califor-
    nia, ca. 1920
Willow rods, split willow, split willow with
    inner bark, dye
H. 15.5 cm, D. 23.5 cm
Photograph by Judith W. Finger
Courtesy, The Phoebe Apperson Hearst
    Museum of Anthropology and the
    Regents of the University of California,
    cat. no. 1-26919

Plate 4
Collected by Helen S. and John S. MacQueen,
    ca. 1900
Willow rods, split willow, pine pitch, red
    earth, unidentified cordage
L. 39 cm, W. 23.1 cm
Photograph by Dick Meier
Courtesy, Natural History Museum of Los
    Angeles County, Anthropology Section,
    MacQueen Collection, cat. no.
    F.A.2570.85-7

Plate 5
Willow rods, split willow, devil's claw, Joshua
    tree root
H. 9.0 cm, D. 13.3 cm
Photograph by Geoffrey Mendelsohn
Courtesy, private collection

Plate 6
Collected by Mrs. Hugh Patrick (Frankie)
    Beatty
Willow, willow rods, glass beads 11/0 size
H. 12.5 cm, D. 12 cm
Photograph by Michael Dixon
Courtesy, Donna Burgner collection, The
    Yosemite Museum, Yosemite National
    Park, cat. no. YM 25501

Plate 7
Willow rods, split willow, devil's claw, redbud
H. 9.0 cm, D. 19.0 cm
Photograph by Geoffrey Mendelsohn
Courtesy, private collection

Plate 8
Collected by Anna Kelley, Independence,
    California, ca. 1940
Willow, bulrush root, yucca root, common
    flicker quill, willow rods
Max. H. 9.5 cm, max. D. 18.5 cm
Photograph by Bruce Frumker and Greg
    Petusky
Courtesy, The Cleveland Museum of Natural
    History

Plate 9
Collected by Horatio Shumway Lee, possibly
    from Minnie Randolph, Bishop, California,
    ca. 1920
Willow rods, split willow, bracken fern root,
    redbud
H. 13 cm, D. 16.7 cm
Photograph by Judith W. Finger
Courtesy, The Phoebe Apperson Hearst
    Museum of Anthropology and the

Regents of the University of California,
    cat. no. 1-26898

Plate 10
Willow rods, sedge root, bracken fern root,
    redbud
H. 7.0 cm, D. 10.5 cm
Photograph by Geoffrey Mendelsohn
Courtesy, private collection

Plate 11
Collected by Horatio Shumway Lee, possibly
    from Minnie Randolph at Bishop, ca. 1915
Willow rods, split willow, bracken fern root,
    redbud
H. 21.25 cm, W. 25 cm
Photograph by Judith W. Finger
Courtesy, The Phoebe Apperson Hearst
    Museum of Anthropology and the
    Regents of the University of California,
    cat. no. 1-26885

Plate 12
Photograph by Bruce Frumker and Greg
    Petusky
Courtesy, Sharon E. Dean

Plate 13
Photograph by Steven Fisher, 1995
Courtesy, Jessie Durant

Plate 14
Willow rods, split willow, buckskin, embroi-
    dery floss, glass beads
L. 50.5 cm, W. 20.0 cm
Photograph by Bruce Frumker and Greg
    Petusky
Courtesy, private collection

INDEX

Kearsarge Station, 4, 105
Keeler (California), 99
Kelley, Anna Theresa Gracey, 64, 69, 80, 105, 107, 110
Kelley, Jim, 105
Kelley, O.K., 105
Kelley, Roseanne, 107
King, Clarence, 24
Kroeber, Alfred, 87, 88, 104

labor force, 120
language, 91, 110; Mono, 1; Numic, 2; Uto-Aztecan, 1, 2
laundry basket, 54, 65
Lee, Horatio Shumway, 40, 76, 90, 103, 104
Lee Vining (California), 54, 64, 77, 121
Leonard, Zenus, 16
Lochrie, Lena, 111
Lochrie, Rose, 110, 111
Lone Pine (California), 18, 24, 26, 27, 52, 74, 105, 109, 122
Long Valley, 123
Los Angeles, 27, 28, 30, 31, 32
Los Angeles Aqueduct, 27, 28, 80, 100
Los Angeles Basin, 28
Los Angeles Department of Water and Power, 29, 30, 31, 32, 115
Los Angeles Water Commission, 28

Mabel, niece of George Hanson, 70, 88
MacQueen, Helen Squire, 100, 101, 102
MacQueen, John Simpson, 77, 78, 91, 96, 100, 101, 102, 121
Mallory, Daisy, 65, 77, 78, 79, 101, 121
Mallory, Jack, 78, 121
Mammoth (California), 4, 75, 101
mano, 12
Manzanar (California), 25, 32, 106, 130, 131
marriage, 7
Mason, Otis Tufton, 87, 91, 94, 95, 96
material culture items: collection of, 83, 106; artifacts as souvenirs, 83, 84; expositions, 83, 84; museum activities, 83
McBride, Annie Poole, 79
McBride, Mattie Jackson, 75, 76
McLaughlin, Captain Moses A., 12
McLean, Aurelia, 98
Meacham, Elizabeth, 70
Merriam, Clinton Hart, 37, 89, 90, 91, 96, 103
metate, 12, 43
Middle Archaic period, 16
migration, 12
Mike, Minnie, 54
Miller, Joe, 74

Miller, Vernon Johnson, 109, 110
Minard, Lucinda, 123
miniature baskets, 120
mining, 18, 119
Mojave Desert, 1, 2, 50
Mono, 1
Mono Basin, 28
Mono County, 18, 19, 75, 77, 79, 121
Mono Gulch, 18
Mono Lake, 17, 18, 28, 64, 98
Mono Lake Paiute, 1, 35, 46, 48, 51, 52, 75, 79, 121
Mono Mills, 64, 77, 121
Monoville, 18
Montieth, Colonel A. E., 74
mourning ceremony, 6, 35, 98, 114
Mule Days, 131
museum activities, 83
museums: California State Indian Museum, 95; Eastern California Museum, 37, 81, 100, 105; Field Museum, 92, 93; Golden Gate Park Museum, 94; Hall Museum of Anthropology, 94; Laws Railroad Museum and Historical Site, 131; Los Angeles County Museum of Natural History, 102, 126; Museum of the American Indian, Heye Foundation, 96; Oakland Museum, 94; Peabody Museum of Archaeology and Ethnology, 70, 72, 88, 96; Phoebe Apperson Hearst Museum of Anthropology, 76, 87, 97, 104; role of in collecting, 83; Smithsonian Institution, 96; Staatliche Museen zu Berlin, Ethnologistes Museum, 95; Ulster Museum, 95; University of California, Davis, 91, 92; Yosemite Museum, 122, 129
myths, 6

Nak Nek (Alaska), 126
National Forest Service, 26
National Indian Association, 26
Navajo Johnson's Trading Post, 60
Nicholson, Grace, 67, 89, 95, 96
Noble, W. B., 27
Northern California Indian Association, 26
Numic, 2

obsidian, 2, 4, 10, 36, 49, 125
Office of Indian Affairs, 117
Olancha (California), 52, 69
Old Man Doc, 63
on-reservation day schools, 116
outing system, 117
Owens Lake, 1, 2, 4, 17, 22
Owens River, 1

Owens Valley, 1, 17, 23, 24, 28, 31, 118
Owens Valley Paiute, 1, 2, 3, 4, 7, 25, 26, 28, 31, 33–35, 53, 80
Owens, Richard, 1

paints, 10
Paiute Shoshone Cultural Center, 33, 122, 133
Pan-Indian, 34
Panamint Shoshone, 1, 2, 7, 8, 41, 50, 68, 70, 72, 98, 112, 122, 131; coiled baskets, 35, 53, 69, 70, 73, 89, 90
Panamint Tom, 70, 72
Panamint Valley, 70
Pandora moth larvae/*piagui*, 2, 4, 11, 20, 33, 35, 37, 47, 48, 114
Parker, Julia, 129
Parrett, Ray, 30
Parsons, Rosie, 122
Patterson, Hank, 63
Patterson, Josephine, 63
Patterson, Wilbur, 88
petroglyphs, 131
Pine Creek, 17
piñon pine nuts, 2, 4, 6, 16, 33, 37, 114; mush, 14; pitch, 37, 45
Piper, Edna, 18, 129
pipes, 10
polygyny, 7
Pool, Mary, 79
Poole, Jennie, 79
post cards, picture, 84
pottery, 8, 12, 48, 51, 52
pow-wow, 34, 131
Powell, John Wesley, 87
Pre-Archaic period, 16
Presbyterian Board of Missions, 26
Price, W. N., 26
puberty ceremony, 7
Pueblo, Ellen, 126
Pueblo, Leonard, 126
Pueblo, Thelma, 126, 127
Putnam's Store, 20
Pyramid Lake, 122

Queen Dick, 67

rabbits, 6, 10, 13
raffia, 125
ranchero, 24
ranchers and ranching, 19, 26, 27, 115, 119
Randolph, Minnie C. Spear Barrows, 40, 76, 91, 102, 104, 116
Rawson Creek, 50, 62, 74
recreation, 120
recreational opportunities, 30
redbud, 43, 50, 52, 76